Fundraiser's Phrase Book

Deluxe Edition

Gail Hamilton

Hamilton House

Hamilton House, 630 County Rd. 14
RR3 Demorestville, Canada ON K0K 1W0
www.hamilhouse.com

Library and Archives Canada Cataloguing in Publication

2. Hamilton, Gail (Margaret Gail)
Fundraiser's phrase book / Gail Hamilton. -- Deluxe ed.

ISBN 978-0-9811689-0-6 (bound).--ISBN 978-0-9680853-6-3 (spiral bound)

1. Nonprofit organizations--Finance--Terminology.
2. Fund raising--Terminology. I. Title.

HV41.2.H34 2009 361.7068'1 C2008-908046-7

Contents

Section Six

Section Seven

Section Eight

Introduction

Do you find yourself struggling time and again, knowing what you want to say – but you just can't put your finger on the words?

Well, now the words you need – the right words – are here at your fingertips. The ***Fundraiser's Phrase Book*** contains a huge, infinitely versatile collection of phrases designed for the nonprofit professional. An easy-to-use resource that practically does your writing for you.

How does it work?

Just look up your key words and you'll find a lavish smorgasbord of ways to use them. Ways you probably haven't thought of before. Use the phrases as construction blocks. Delve into the vast store of material for creative new ways to state your ideas. Use the book as a springboard for your imagination.

Today, the nonprofit field is exploding. As need and competition for charitable dollars increases, it's more important than ever to write fundraising appeals that work. Here's where the ***Fundraiser's Phrase Book*** can really help with tested and proven phrases that have already raised millions of dollars successfully.

Find all the "trigger" words that send donors rushing for their checkbooks. Choose from hundreds of ways to ask for help. Watch the effectiveness of your fundraising packages shoot skyward as you get your message across with powerful emotional impact.

The ***Fundraiser's Phrase Book*** has dozens of other uses too. It provides building elements you can combine in endlessly new ways to turn out terrific business letters and reports, strong grant applications, impressive proposals, dynamite speeches, chatty newsletters and anything else you need to write. And it functions as a giant idea bank. The phrases naturally contain hordes of concepts you can adapt to your own projects.

How To Use The Phrases

Step One

Decide on your purpose. For instance, you wish to ask donors to give in order to help children.

Step Two

The phrases are arranged alphabetically by key word. Look up **"CHILDREN"** and choose a phrase, such as: **"the greatest gift of all – children."**

Look up **"SATISFACTION"** and choose a phrase such as: **"you feel a deep personal joy and satisfaction"**.

Look up **"GIFT"** and choose a phrase such as: **"no matter how large or small your gift may be, it is deeply valued"**.

Look up **"FINANCIAL"** and choose a phrase such as: **"your financial encouragement means so much"**.

Step Three

Combine the phrases into a warm, moving appeal that brings dollars rolling in to help youngsters in need:

"In reaching out to others, I know **you feel a deep personal joy and satisfaction. No matter how large or small your gift may be, it is deeply valued. Your financial encouragement means so much** as we work together to make tomorrow brighter for **the greatest gift of all – children."**

Step Four

Consult subsequent sections for lapsed donor/member urgings, smart beginnings, handy transition phrases, lively exclamations, warm salutations and signatures, envelope teasers, reply device wordings and much more.

Sample Entry

BENEFIT
- You'll enjoy a number of very special benefits and privileges
- Our activities are designed to benefit all those who
- The benefits provided by even a small donation are enormous
- Find out how you will benefit from generous action now
- Everyone would benefit from
- Increasing access to our services could bring more benefits to more people at less cost than any other single method now available
- You can benefit from the following
- And the benefits don't stop there
- Reap immeasurable benefit

Benefit: advantage, well-being, welfare, betterment, improvement, furtherance, advancement, promotion, help, aid, gain, profit, service, use, improve, do good to, be of service to, avail oneself
See also: ADVANTAGE, BLESSING, GOODNESS, HELP

"BENEFIT" is the key word present in every phrase.

Where appropriate, a number of alternatives to "**benefit**" are suggested below the bulleted list of phrases.

"See also: ADVANTAGE, BLESSING, GOODNESS, HELP" indicates that under the entries with the above headings, you will find even more phrases closely related to the meaning you are looking for.

Section One

Fundraising Phrases

ABANDON

- We must not abandon such a priceless heritage
- How can we abandon so many who need our help
- We must not abandon our roots
- Feeling abandoned by friends who didn't understand,
- Abused, abandoned, they have nowhere else to turn but to you and me
- Seeking out those whom society has callously abandoned
- Seemingly abandoned by everybody
- Prevent the heartbreak of abandoning such a promising project so soon
- The abandonment of the weakest is a shame to us all
- The worst abandonments take place out of the public eye
- Making sure there will be no more of these shocking abandonments in our city

ABET

- We are abetting the very best
- By our very inaction, we will be abetting the worst sort of neglect and indifference
- Never be caught aiding and abetting the forces of social destruction

See also: AID, ASSIST, HELP

ABILITY

- Give according your heart and your ability
- Give us the ability to keep on helping
- Our ability depends on your support

See also: CAPACITY, TALENT

ABLE

- Sadly, I'm not able to do that
- To make sure the most able get the chance to
- No one is more able than our dedicated field workers
- Those least able need our help the most
- Only because of your generous help are we able to
- We not only have to be able, we have to be willing
- I know you are able to give just a little more toward

ABUNDANCE

- Wanting health and wealth in abundance
- Sharing the rich abundance of our nation with others
- Blessed with an abundance of so many things
- Love produces the greatest abundance of all
- Come share in the abundance
- Such overflowing abundance fills hearts with joy
- Helping everyone partake of this abundance
- Now is the time to reap the abundance of
- Who could have imagined the efforts of people like you could produce such abundance

Abundance: bounty, plentitude, plenty, richness, luxuriousness, lavishness, heaps, lots, overflowingness, wealth, prosperity, resources, wherewithal

ABUSE
- Victims of abuse are imprisoned, suffering unspeakable physical and mental agonies
- We vehemently oppose arbitrary abuses committed by
- Abuse isn't always visible to the eye
- Being physically abused can quickly wreck a life
- Triumphantly breaking out of an endless cycle of abuse
- To end the abuses sanctioned by heartless policies
- Opposes abuses committed by far too many
- Afraid to call it what it really is – outright abuse
- The very worst abuses are those that destroy the soul
- Only with your help can we stop such blatant abuse
- Whatever the abuse, we can't let it continue
- Above all, we work to prevent abuse before it starts
- Abuse makes growing up hard
- Nearly a quarter of all women will be abused by a partner or former partner at some point in their lives
- Abuse and neglect can now be viewed as a national health crisis
- Chronic unemployment and oppressive living conditions foster abusiveness

See also: AGONY, ATROCITY, EXPLOITATION, INJUSTICE, PAIN, SADISM, SUFFERING, TORTURE

ABUSER
- The primary targets of abusers are women and children
- Determined to find out who these abusers really are
- Put the abusers where they belong – in jail
- If we pass by without helping, we become abusers too
- Able to look an abuser in the eye and say
- Drug and alcohol abusers sinking toward oblivion

ACADEMIC
- Please consider supporting your area of academic interest
- This outstanding academic performance must not be wasted because of lack of funds
- With the funds to really help, the problem remains academic
- Because the academic basics are stressed, a solid foundation is laid
- The idea will be merely academic unless we make reality of our vision
- Let's face it, academic excellence costs money
- Pay for the academic now so we're not paying for the unemployed later
- More than any other time in history, our country needs academic development

See also: EDUCATION, SCHOOL, UNIVERSITY

ACCESS
- Much-needed access to crucial services
- This battle is all about access to a decent life

- Means that young people, adults and seniors may be denied access to some of our programs because we can't afford them
- I encourage you to consider this opportunity to increase access for
- Accessing the funds we require for our next venture in the most timely, cost-effective manner possible
- So that everyone in need has access
- Managing to improve access all round
- Access to government support is all important
- Could you see those in such need denied access to help

ACCESSIBLE
- Struggling to make this service accessible to all
- Your dollars make this process accessible and friendly
- So proud of the universal accessibility of
- Accessibility is our main concern here

See also: AVAILABLE

ACCIDENT
- It's no accident that this crisis happened now
- If accident or illness strikes, the costs can be devastating
- We can't leave such a crucial matter to mere accident
- Such a bizarre accident of fate happens only once in a lifetime
- If we can't shield people from the accidents of life, we can help them
- Those laid low by accidents that were no fault of their own need help

See also: CHANCE, CHANGE, DISASTER

ACCOMMODATE
- In order to accommodate everyone, we really have to scramble
- Please try to accommodate this urgent request
- If you can't accommodate us now, won't you please remember us in the future
- The most accommodating solution would be to

ACCOMPLISH
- It's simple – the more you can assist us, the more we can accomplish
- To show you what has been accomplished
- With your help, we've already accomplished a great deal
- Help people who have already accomplished so much with so little
- It's hard to imagine how anyone could possibly accomplish more
- So determined to accomplish beneficial changes that
- We can only accomplish it through help from people like you who have already supported us so generously in the past
- Helping to finish faster and accomplish more
- Helping accomplish more in less time
- Here's something you can help accomplish right now
- Just imagine what can be accomplished if we work together immediately to
- We've accomplished a great deal because of your past support
- Exactly what we work so hard to accomplish

Accomplish: perform, do, execute, discharge, bring off, carry out, engineer, bring about, finish, complete, attain, achieve, effect, make happen, arrive at, negotiate, consummate

ACCOMPLISHMENT
- We are extremely proud of this accomplishment
- A teary-eyed family shared her accomplishments
- Thanks to your support, thousands will have experienced these splendid accomplishments
- I've enclosed a few pictures and examples of our recent accomplishments
- In recognition of the breathtaking accomplishments since the organization began
- When you support us, our accomplishments are also your accomplishments

See also: ACHIEVEMENT, BREAKTHROUGH

ACCOUNT
- A gripping account of their heroic struggle
- The accounts of their suffering are almost impossible to read
- Unless we take these factors into account, our plan will not
- Make sure all of them are called to account for their actions
- Taking care of others, not just our bank account

See also: CONSIDER, RESPONSIBILITY, STORY

ACHIEVE
- With your help, there's no limit on what we can achieve
- Striving to achieve the very minimum this is acceptable for
- Helping each to achieve the fullest, most satisfying life imaginable
- The joy of showing them how they can achieve the things they want
- Achieving the optimum effects with the resources we have
- We have seen what can be achieved

See also: ACCOMPLISH, WIN

ACHIEVEMENT
- The achievement we are most proud of
- I feel confident that our achievements during the past years justify the faith you've placed in us
- An outstanding roster of achievements
- Our achievements this season were only possible with your support
- Even with these splendid achievements, we can't meet our costs
- While extremely proud of last year's achievements
- We won't rest on the laurels of our past achievements
- These achievements would not have been possible without research
- So very pleased with these achievements
- What great years, filled with achievement, they've been

Achievement: realization, success, attainment, fulfilment, exploit, performance, accomplishment, fruition, stroke of genius, consummation, deed, feat, tour de force, coup

See also: ACCOMPLISHMENT, BREAKTHROUGH

ACKNOWLEDGE
- A unique opportunity to acknowledge and accept a need in their lives
- Gratefully acknowledging your past support
- In warm acknowledgment, please accept this recognition
- So happy to acknowledge your very kind generosity

ACT
- Must act immediately for optimum results
- Please post this notice in any place where concerned people might read it and feel compelled to act
- We'll show you how to act now to ensure
- The more people who act, the sooner we can solve
- If we don't act at once, a rich opportunity will be lost
- Unless you and I act without delay
- Now is the time to act
- Not the only reason to act now
- I urge you to act at once
- They act as if we can do nothing
- Each act of kindness lights the world and soothes an aching heart
- With this one simple act, you help so many
- Act in concert
- Acting for nearly half a century, they're still going strong

See also: ACCOMPLISH, DEED, DO

ACTION
- You and I must take action right now to see it doesn't happen.
- Your actions in support have already had a tremendous effect on
- Quick and determined action on all our parts
- Your actions in supporting us have already had a tremendous effect on making the government think twice about continued neglect of
- We must turn this support into genuine action
- You can – and you should – take action today
- Your action, along with thousands of others, can be life-saving
- Totally comfortable with their actions
- Have promised swift action again and again
- Taking appropriate action should these symptoms occur
- Your dollars have rushed straight into action
- In the real world, action is what really counts
- Once a need has been identified, we swing into action
- This requires a desire to take action

Action: act, exploit, doings, deed, transaction, adventure, effort, endeavor, enterprise, enactment, dispatch, handiwork

See also: ACTIVITY

ACTIVITY
- Today, I want to emphasize that our major activity is
- A nurturing, sharing activity that contributes so much to improving quality of life

- This is an area of intense activity requiring our close involvement
- Making sure you're up to date on the activities of
- Support, as well, a number of volunteer activities unique to this organization
- Substituting healthy activity and guidance for the dangerous savagery of the streets
- You'll hear about activities and educational meetings in your area – news and stories from other members.
- We refuse to countenance such unwholesome activities

ADAPT
- Adapt to meet a fresh attack
- To quickly adapt to meet changing conditions
- Determined to be there for those who need help to adapt
- Those who refuse to adapt go the way of the dinosaurs
- Thank you for adapting with us
- Thanks to our built-in flexibility, our organization was able to adapt quickly and effectively

ADDITION
- In addition to your generous gift of
- Your donation will make a wonderful addition to the fund we are building up
- You are a very welcome addition to our family of loyal supporters
- Every addition counts, no matter how modest
- Each small addition brings us closer to our goal
- In addition to the benefits you have already made possible
- Any addition to your regular donation is greatly appreciated

ADDRESS
- We've already taken several steps to address this issue
- We hope to address some of your concerns immediately
- A problem crying out to be addressed
- I'm addressing you directly because of the sudden crisis on our hands

See also: SOLVE

ADMINISTRATION
- It saves on administration costs at our end
- No administrative costs will be deducted
- The administration falls to one of our best teams
- Administration is lean and efficient
- Always working towards a more effective administration

ADMIRATION
- Awe and admiration at the courage and tenacity these individuals must display each day in order to survive
- Our admiration was unbounded at
- Earned an immense amount of admiration by

ADOPT
- Adopt the cause of
- We hope you'll adopt us by giving
- Help us adopt even more unwanted orphans
- If you can adopt even one, you'll make such a difference

ADVANCE
- Every new advance is another success for
- Can have the labs and the people to keep making these ground-breaking advances
- Advancing methodically, step by step
- Advances won through hard work and a very substantial financial investment
- Have already made advances of awesome proportions
- With your help, our team has already made such incredibly exciting advances that
- If we're to remain on the very cutting edge of advances, we must have your support
- Recently, I've seen so many advances in treating
- Yes, there have been tremendous advances in medical care with the development of new drugs and better emergency services
- Great advances have already been made – new drugs, new treatments, new insights
- Already made many exciting advances in easing the struggle
- So much progress has been made that major advances are likely in the near future
- To stay on top of the latest advances we must
- Such an advance is worth almost any cost

Advance: progress, headway, forward movement, improvement, enhancement, innovation, creation, invention, finding, breakthrough, production

See also: BREAKTHROUGH, CURE, INNOVATION, LEAP, PROGRESS, RESEARCH, STRIDE

ADVANTAGE
- Need to take advantage of services that have passed the test of time and use
- Unfair advantage can put an end to
- The smallest of advantages can still be the deciding factor
- Poised to take swift advantage of
- The advantages are real and very exciting
- You give so many advantages when you
- This program has several major advantages
- Without the advantage of immediate help, many will fall by the wayside
- The advantage is immeasurable
- Take of advantage of the rewards and benefits of
- Now have the ultimate advantage in

See also: ASSET, BENEFIT, EDGE

ADVENTURE
- A new adventure that draws the hopes for the future closer

- Join us on a great adventure
- Adventuring into a new world of caring and sharing
- Help these young people share the adventure of learning

See also: **CHALLENGE, RISK**

ADVERTISE

- We must advertise more widely to promote the benefits of the institution of
- We're advertising our success in order to assure you
- Trying so hard not to advertise how much in need they remain

See also: **BROCHURE, INFORM**

ADVICE

- Given invaluable advice and assistance in many other aspects of
- Must seek and heed the very best advice
- Naturally, we pay closest attention to any advice you might like to share
- Often a little advice is all they need to steer them straight
- Provide advice and guidance on the following
- My advice to friends and family is
- The very best advice we can give to them is

Advice: guidance, counsel, wisdom, instruction, teaching

See also: **COUNSELLING, GUIDANCE, INFORMATION, WISDOM**

ADVOCACY

- Advocacy activities to demand better health care
- Unlike so many other advocacy groups, we are
- Please become part of a powerful advocacy movement
- Always working to improve our advocacy for
- The most important advocacy is your advocacy

ADVOCATE

- A leading advocate and trouble shooter for
- Among other things we are advocating
- An advocate of the common sense solution
- An advocate of the people deserves the greatest respect
- You can become one of our best advocates

See also: **CHAMPION, FIGHTER, HERO, LOBBY, PARTNER, TORCHBEARER**

AFFECT

- Something that will eventually affect us all
- Affects their lives in so many ways
- Millions are now affected by
- Many groups simply fail to understand how deeply this affects them
- You can help affect so many changes just by writing a letter and giving a small sum
- Without your help, the number affected will continue to climb
- This affecting scene left me choked with emotion

- Trying to gain some control over the things that will vitally affect their lives

AFFILIATION
- Through their affiliation with
- Your affiliation with our cause is one of the best indications of its profound worth
- To show how very much we value affiliation with you
- So we can extend our affiliations with like-minded organizations dedicated to helping those in need

See also: ASSOCIATION, COLLABORATION, GROUP, PARTNERSHIP

AFFINITY
- You feel a great affinity with
- The affinity between those who have suffered this tragedy can form a very powerful bond for good
- We've cultivated this precious affinity through years of careful effort
- Their affinity for this endangered land is evident in their every move
- The powerful affinity between our two groups
- The strong affinity built up over the years is paying off

AFFIRMATIVE
- Affirmative action is necessary
- Please answer in the affirmative
- Voices lifted, strong and affirmative
- The most affirmative thing to do in this situation is to

See also: AGREE, POSITIVE, YES

AFFORD
- We can't afford to go that route
- Much as they need it, they just can't afford it
- Those who cannot afford food and shelter, the very basics of life
- No longer can we afford to ignore such emphatic warning signs
- Please give as much as you can afford so that others can enjoy
- Please think carefully about how much you can affort
- We can't afford not to help
- Who otherwise simply could not afford to
- Affording a new way to increase results

See also: BUDGET, COST, MANAGE, PROVIDE

AGAINST
- When you consider what we're up against – governments and powerful industrial interests
- Going bravely into battle against dark forces
- I know you stand with us against such abuses

AGENCY
- Overwhelmingly cited as the most credible agency to speak and act on the issue

- Along with so many other aid agencies, we had to rush in to deal with this catastrophe
- No other agency has been able to offer as much as ours
- Taking over the agency to help has been a very serious responsibility

See also: FOUNDATION, GOVERNMENT, GROUP, ORGANIZATION

AGENDA

- We want to present a real people's agenda
- It's time we ripped the disguises from these deceptive hidden agendas
- Your support will help us adopt an expanded agenda that includes
- Our agenda is to help, plain and simple
- The first thing on the agenda should be the most important
- Take a few moments to review this outstanding agenda
- This unique and information-packed agenda
- Hidden agendas and conflicting value systems could bring it all to grief

See also: CAMPAIGN, PLAN, PROGRAM

AGONY

- No one should have to suffer the unpredictable agony of
- The agony of having to watch a loved one suffer
- It's sheer agony to look on and not be able to help
- Could you bear this kind of agony
- Dragging out the agony doesn't accomplish anything

See also: ABUSE, CRUELTY, HURT, PAIN, SUFFERING, TORTURE

AGREE

- What's more, I think you'll agree that
- Thousands now agree because they've tried it
- I'm sure you will agree with me when you know the hard facts
- How can anyone fail to agree after they've witnessed
- Both your head and your heart will agree on this one
- We all agree that the most prudent course to follow is

See also: AFFIRMATION, YES

AGRICULTURAL

- Members working to improve agricultural yields as well as
- A strengthened agricultural base is essential
- Agricultural peoples are by no means simple
- Agricultural assistance is what will be of the most use to these famine-stricken thousands

AHEAD

- We've already forged boldly ahead
- Now it's time to look ahead to the new year
- We believe that during the eventful months ahead, we must
- A little boost from you helps a hardworking person to get ahead
- I'm so eager to tell you this tender story that I'm getting ahead of myself already

- The best way to stay ahead of the pack is to

See also: FUTURE

AID

- Our aid is given as an outright gift
- Another aid to understanding this problem is
- Aid needy children in
- They need all the aid you can give
- Comes to their aid rapidly with a wide range of medical, professional and other resources
- Dealing out compassion and active, practical aid for every kind of human suffering
- We provide comfort and practical aid to victims and their families
- Aid can come in so many different forms
- Won't you contribute just a little aid to
- To quickly and compassionately come to the aid of
- The simplest kind of aid is often the most effective

See also: ABET, ASSIST, BOOST, CONTRIBUTION, DONATE, GIFT, HELP, SUPPORT

AIM

- Aimed at supporting the needs of
- Our aim is to work closely with and educate
- Aim higher, try harder
- Worthwhile aims deserve worthwhile support
- Aiming at the highest target of all
- Taking aim at poverty and misery
- Aiming to please
- When your aims are our aims, we can work in harmony

See also: GOAL, MANDATE, MISSION, PURPOSE, TARGET

ALARM

- Many people try to alarm us with statistics
- We must raise the alarm immediately
- Who wouldn't be alarmed at such statistics
- If you could see what we see every day, you would be thoroughly alarmed
- Though the alarm has been sounding for some time, people are only now beginning to pay heed
- I don't want to alarm you, but
- Can we respond quickly enough to this silent alarm

See also: FRIGHTEN, WARNING

ALIVE

- My mother wouldn't be alive today if it weren't for the people at this compassionate facility
- For those of us who have come through this alive
- Alive to a thousand possibilities

- When just to be alive is a triumph
- It takes so little to keep one of these people alive
- Celebrating the immense joy of just being alive
- Their first goal is staying alive
- So wonderful just to watch their faces come alive when help arrives

See also: **AWARE, LIVE, SURVIVE**

ALL

- No longer possible to be all things to all people
- All in all, it's been a very productive year
- I think you'll want to help them all
- And it all depends on you
- I'm afraid it's an all or nothing situation here
- Going all out just to stay even with the demand

See also: **EVERYBODY**

ALLOW

- Deliberately allowed to come to such conclusions
- Please don't allow this to happen
- The more neglect we allow, the more trouble we'll have
- Because we allowed this take place we now have a giant problem on our hands
- Nobody should be allowed to fall into such a state

Allow: permit, authorize, approve of, tolerate, bear, suffer, brook, abide, sanction, admit, agree to, acquiesce in, consent to, assent to, concede

ALONE

- They make you believe you are completely alone
- But they can't do it alone
- No one should be alone when this tragedy strikes
- Feeling alone as the last person on earth
- Without you they'd be more alone than ever

ALTERNATIVE

- Give them a viable alternative
- Often the alternative is starvation or death
- We provide a high quality alternative to
- You're holding one alternative in your hand right now
- Without your help, their only alternative is
- By far the best alternative would be the one you would choose anyway
- Now we urgently have to find alternative sources of support
- A precious gift when you consider the alternatives for them
- Alternatives must be developed at once
- Doing our best to avoid the worst of all these alternatives

See also: **CHANGE, CHOICE, CROSSROADS, OPTION**

ALUMNI

- Ideals which we, as alumni, expect our college to live up to and must help it

achieve
- Love for the alma mater always lives in the hearts of the alumni
- We are turning to our alumni now, asking them to give back something of what they have received
- In appreciation for a superb education and a fine start in life, the alumni contribute generously

AMAZE
- Find ourselves standing amazed at
- You would be truly amazed to see how much progress has been made
- It's amazing that so little is said about
- Just how amazing is this
- Help comes from the most amazing places
- Amazing improvements have resulted from
- Even more amazing is the fact that

See also: SURPRISE, WONDER

AMBUSH
- Too many young people are being ambushed by these diseases in the primes of their lives
- Surprised to find ourselves so suddenly ambushed by love
- This cruel ambush awaits the unprepared and the unsuspecting
- Ambushed by the unthinkable scale of this disaster
- To make certain we're not unexpectedly ambushed by

See also: ATTACK, SHOCK, SURPRISE

AMOUNT
- Even a small amount will become greater
- Whatever amount you can possibly afford
- The thought matters as much as the amount you give
- Sometimes I get discouraged thinking about the amount we really need
- I'm not asking you for a large amount
- Any amount is deeply appreciated
- You choose the amount – just please give
- Some people feel they can only give a small amount and that's all right too
- No matter what the amount, it is sorely needed
- An even larger amount can do even more to improve conditions
- The suggested amount will help put us ahead
- No matter what amount you think appropriate
- Yes, the amount really matters
- Thank you for increasing the amount you give this year
- Even if you can only manage a modest amount, please help

Amount: sum, measure, total, quantity, number, portion
See also: CONTRIBUTION, DONATION, GIFT, MONEY

ANGEL
- You are our guardian angel

- Be an angel and help out now
- Calling all angels

See also: **BENEFACTOR, CHAMPION, SPONSOR**

ANGER

- Put your anger to good use
- Triggered angry and emotional calls for
- Must rise up in anger at such injustice
- What are we to do with all this anger
- Find constructive use for otherwise dangerous, smoldering anger
- Anger, anxiety and depression management must come first
- I can't tell you the anger I feel just at seeing this

See also: **OUTRAGE**

ANIMAL

- Without your help, more animals will be forced to suffer in silence
- Though the animals cannot speak, their eyes tell everything
- And the animals are dying
- As more and more animals disappear, perhaps we should remember that we are animals too
- Looking to you to prevent cruelty to animals

See also: **EARTH, ENVIRONMENT, NATURE**

ANNOUNCE

- We are pleased to announce that
- The first to announce a reduction in
- Announcing that some changes are in the offing
- You see, I'm about to announce
- With your backing, we can announce a great success

See also: **ADVERTISE, INFORM, TELL, SPEAK, VOICE**

ANSWER

- I think your answer will be no to this travesty
- If your answer is no, there's something you can do
- Our program may be the lasting answer to
- The long answer would take several pages; the short answer is they need help
- Not an answer we like to contemplate
- We anxiously await your answer
- There can be only one answer to such a question
- This has been the perfect answer for us
- Here's the answer to
- Nobody knows the answer like we do
- We answer to you
- Helping us find a better answer to a very tough question
- We're making it a lot easier to get straight answers
- When you need answers that work, look to us
- We're making it a lot easier to get straight answers

- Your answers will help us find out what people really hope
- Sometimes we may have been slow getting answers to your questions or sending out tax receipts
- We must find answers soon or else
- They need answers and they need them soon
- Please take a moment to give your personal answers to the questions
- We must spend the time necessary to find all the right answers
- Helping to find the right answers to build success
- To find out the answers, I spoke with our new director
- We're all dedicated to finding the answers
- Clearly, these are not all the answers – but they're a start
- People pursuing answers to today's most challenging puzzles
- I don't pretend to have the answers
- We have some answers already

Answer: response, acknowledgement, rejoinder, comeback, reply, confirmation, key, clue, solution, reason, justification, explanation, atone for, recompense, repay, redress, serve, measure up, satisfy, fulfill, solve

See also: ACKNOWLEDGE, CURE, KEY, REPLY, RESPOND, SOLUTION, SOLVE

ANXIETY

- A cause of great anxiety on their part
- In order to reduce this anxiety, we must
- Everyday anxieties can loom large enough to obscure the whole picture
- When someone is peaking in a state of high anxiety
- As funding drops, anxiety rises, causing disruption and uncertainty all round
- There is no worse anxiety than that caused by lack of
- You wouldn't want them to suffer any more anxiety than absolutely necessary
- What a mighty load of anxiety you will be helping to lift off their fragile shoulders

See also: EMBARRASSED, FEAR, SUFFERING, WORRY

APATHY

- Apathy is our greatest enemy
- Apathy is just what it says – lack of feeling
- To rouse them from their apathy and get them to take vigorous action on the issue
- A population sinking into the quicksand of apathy and hopelessness
- Battling apathy every step of the way

See also: DEAF, INDIFFERENCE, LIP SERVICE, NEGLECT, SILENCE

APOLOGY

- Make apology for such incompetence
- They make no apology for their needs
- On a note of apology
- Will we have to apologize in the future for our indifference today

See also: REGRET, SORRY

APPEAL
- This is a personal appeal from one deeply concerned person to another
- In urging you to respond to this appeal, I now want to write in a personal way
- An urgent appeal from
- Among the many appeals you constantly receive, please consider this one carefully
- I am making this appeal on behalf of those who cannot speak for themselves
- Could you resist the silent appeal in their eyes
- Must respond to this timeless appeal
- Every year it's the same eloquent appeal, the same enduring need
- Concluded with a desperate appeal for help
- This letter would have absolutely no appeal to some people, those people with hearts of stone
- In case you are wondering why you receive different appeals at different times of the year
- This appeal is straight from our hearts
- I'm appealing to you now, help us make up this deficit
- An appeal that simply cannot be ignored
- They appeal to us without even saying a word
- Please stand with us again, as you have throughout the years through vigorous and generous support of our appeal
- I know you receive appeals from many worthy causes

Appeal: entreaty, request, supplication, plea, petition, suit, address
See also: ASK, BEG, CAMPAIGN, PETITION, PLEA, REQUEST

APPRECIATE
- You are appreciated for the difference you make
- We appreciate your support over the last many years
- Your generous support is deeply appreciated
- We not only deeply appreciate your help, we surely depend upon it
- We appreciate your kind interest
- Appreciate the tremendous difference a few more dollars can make
- We couldn't appreciate your concern more
- It's about appreciating all the little things in life
- We can't tell you how much we appreciate
- We will truly appreciate whatever you can give

See also: CELEBRATE

APPRECIATION
- Given to you in appreciation of your support of our ideals and all our worthwhile efforts
- To raise awareness and appreciation for
- Well-deserved appreciation of their efforts is steadily growing
- I welcome this opportunity to say a few words to you, in appreciation of your past support
- Please accept this certificate of appreciation for your continued loyal support
- I am writing to you to express our appreciation for your effort

- Promoting understanding and appreciation of the fine arts
- I wish to express my sincere appreciation for
- A token of our appreciation for your strong personal commitment to
- Develop an extraordinary appreciation for the wonders of

Appreciation: recognition, comprehension, cognizance, gratitude, gratefulness, thanks, thankfulness, thanksgiving, acknowledgement, praise, tribute, applause
See also: SECTION FIVE

APPROACH
- A new and innovative approach to
- Approaching the issue from a different angle, everything changes drastically
- Clearly, our current approach doesn't work
- The more we vary our approach, the more success we have
- I approach you on this matter only because of the most pressing need
- This year we're changing our approach
- The tremendous value of this kind of approach
- This fresh approach has proved invaluable
- Switching to the gentle approach
- For those searching for an alternative approach
- A nonthreatening, interactive approach
- Our approach is tough, seasoned and pragmatic
- Once again, we must approach you with an urgent request

See also: AGENDA, CONCEPT, IDEA, PLAN

APTITUDE
- You've demonstrated a marked aptitude for caring
- Students displaying such outstanding aptitude cannot be ignored due to short funding
- Developing their every aptitude is our pride and joy
- So that such tremendous aptitude can now be recognized

See also: ABILITY, CAPACITY, TALENT

ARMOR
- The courage to finally drop the armor
- Wearing the armor of a righteous cause, we cannot fail
- Able to penetrate the thick, defensive armor and get to the hurting, lonely heart inside
- Wearing such tough armor is the only way they can survive

See also: DEFENCE, GUARD, PROTECTION

ART
- Discovering the magic of art
- Making art come alive for them
- A true test of how much we value the arts
- Without the joys of art, our city life would be barren
- Enhance the arts at all levels
- Successful in our efforts to build support for the arts

- Continue to work for a healthy arts environment
See also: COLLECTION, CULTURE, EDUCATION

ASK
- You may well ask why somebody doesn't do something about it
- I'm taking the liberty of writing to you to ask for your help
- Thankfully, we can turn directly to you and ask for your financial support
- Surely not too much to ask
- I'm asking you to do two things
- Here's why I'm asking for your help more urgently than ever
- Ask yourself do you really need that extra luxury when
- That's why I'm asking caring people like you to help make it happen
- We ask you personally to help
- But now you are probably asking yourself what does it all mean
- Please understand that I am not writing to ask you for anything frivolous
- I'm asking for the kinds of serious, practical help these people need every day
- I'm writing to ask you to do a wonderful thing for the kids today
- Asking you to help us stay alive and vibrant
- I'm writing to ask you to sign the enclosed
- I'm asking you to consider increasing your involvement
- We're asking you not to ignore our plea
- Asking caring citizens like you
- Today, I'm writing to ask that you help us to give even more kids that same chance
- Then ask yourself, do you really need
- Friends sometimes ask us why we send you so many letters
- We asked you how we're doing

Ask: inquire, query, question, request, petition, plead, apply to, turn to, solicit, clamour for, beg, beseech, supplicate, pray to, entreat, implore, cry to, demand, call for, invite, beckon, importune
See also: APPEAL, BEG, PLEA, PETITION, REQUEST

ASPECT
- One of the most significant aspects has always been
- Sometimes it's hard to keep so many diverse aspects in perspective all at the same time
- Let me show you just one aspect that changes everything
- You can appreciate the problem from this unusual aspect
- Every day a different aspect provides us with a bright new challenge

See also: CHARACTER, FEATURE, LOOK

ASSAULT
- Our very foundation is under assault
- Poised for another vicious assault upon
- Your dollars have rushed straight into action, staving off this latest assault on
- Help stop the unconscionable assaults on
- The funding cuts amount to assault and battery

- These new assaults come in the wake of
- People who are under assault every day because

See also: **ABUSE, AMBUSH, ATTACK, BATTLE, FIGHT, WAR**

ASSET
- To help people retain their most valuable asset, their good health
- Never lose sight of the many fine assets already at our disposal
- You continuing support is by far our most precious asset
- Need your help in increasing our assets in order to extend the capability of our organization to
- Their biggest asset is your understanding heart
- Watching our assets being eaten away by spiralling costs

See also: **ADVANTAGE, BENEFIT**

ASSIST
- The more you can assist us, the more we can accomplish
- Doing everything we can to assist
- Very happy to assist with the implementation of this new program
- Joyfully assist at the birth of a bright new vision

See also: **ABET, AID, BOOST, HELP, SUPPORT**

ASSISTANCE
- We provide hands-on support and financial assistance
- This has put us in a position where we turn to you for assistance
- Support this important work by giving financial assistance
- Added so much by their generosity and assistance down the years
- Able to call on back-up assistance the instant it's needed
- With assistance like yours, the work can forge ahead
- With your assistance, she has grown up to be an independent, confident young woman
- Always there to help people in urgent need of assistance
- Help many more who would otherwise not receive assistance
- Now, I am asking your special assistance for our unique program
- Provided direct assistance to local projects all across the
- Service and assistance the moment it is needed
- Provides direct assistance where it is most required
- Desperately need your assistance

Assistance: help, aid, boost, relief, service, benefit, succor, lift, consolation, protection, friendship, backing, care, helping hand, sustenance, advocacy, sponsorship, advancement

See also: **AID, DONATION, FRIENDSHIP, GIFT, HELP, SUPPORT**

ASSOCIATION
- We look forward to many years of happy association with you
- Welcoming you to our association of friends
- This has always been a very prudent association to maintain
- In order to continue our association with you

- Helping our association to grow and prosper
- As we develop a fruitful association with you

See also: **AGENCY, AFFILIATION, COLLABORATION, GROUP, ORGANIZATION, PARTNERSHIP**

ASSUME
- Never can we just assume that
- I'm just assuming that help is on the way
- So many people assume that all is well
- It's so easy to assume that someone else will take care of the problem
- Everything you've always assumed is now thrown into question

ASSUMPTION
- The assumption that we'll always be there
- Unfortunately, we can no longer afford the luxury of these assumptions
- Forcing us to rethink so many comfortable assumptions
- Based upon the erroneous assumption that

ATMOSPHERE
- In an atmosphere of helpful understanding
- A loving, joyful atmosphere is so important to
- The atmosphere has been improved so much
- An atmosphere of kindly encouragement works wonders
- Clearing away a thick atmosphere of doubt and distrust
- A much better atmosphere now that all these concerns have been dragged out into the open

See also: **AURA, FEELING**

ATROCITY
- This atrocity must be obliterated
- That such atrocities still continue is hardly to be believed
- Please help put an end to such atrocities
- Unfortunately, similar atrocities take place every day
- That this has happened is nothing short of an atrocity
- Found ourselves gasping at the atrocities
- Without your help, these ghastly atrocities will continue
- This atrocity occurred because no one acted promptly

See also: **ABUSE, PAIN, OUTRAGE, SUFFERING, TORMENT, TORTURE**

ATTACK
- Mounting an vigorous attack on the proposals
- An attack the likes of which we have never seen before
- The target of frightening attacks
- A stubborn problem that must be attacked head on
- About to launch an all-out attack on our charitable foundation
- Grapple with mindless, groundless, misinformed attacks
- Such attacks and their implications would have repercussions in

- Vigorously attacking this complex riddle from all possible directions
- Help our dedicated scientists lead the attack on

See also: **ABUSE, ASSAULT, BATTLE, FIGHT**

ATTENTION
- Ongoing attention is required
- Particular attention has been devoted to
- I wish to call your attention to
- Conveniently on hand to draw attention to
- We're paying attention to critically neglected areas such as
- Naturally we are concentrating most attention upon the primary goal
- It's only fitting that we dedicate significant attention to
- In order to draw attention to our work we must
- Making sure they get the attention they truly deserve
- Paying attention to the details is the key to success
- May I direct your attention to

See also: **AWARENESS, EYE, FOCUS**

ATTITUDE
- That attitude is one reason we have been able to forge ahead
- This very generous attitude is also a great source of encouragement as we care for and nurture
- Her attitude was so positive she is often asked to speak to
- Foster a take-charge attitude for everyone
- These kinds of negative societal attitudes are very destructive to the families of people with
- Happy to generate a whole new attitude to
- Now, as a result, reporting changes in attitude we wouldn't have believed possible a short time ago
- Gaining in the struggle to change the attitudes of society to this unfortunate condition
- So gratifying to see this change for the better in attitude
- A healthy attitude is the first, essential requirement
- A complete and wonderful change in mental attitude

AUTHORITY
- By authority of a compassionate heart
- Internally respected authority on
- Your voice gives us the authority to speak up
- There is no greater authority than the people's demand
- To speak, at all times, with authority
- To glean these facts from an impeccable authority

See also: **AGENCY, GOVERNMENT**

AUDIENCE
- Audiences have been steadily going up
- Methods to present this information to a target audience

- Building an audience for this kind of work
- Audience support has been overwhelming
- You are our most important audience
- A rapidly developing audience must be involved in our

AURA
- So wonderful seeing them project an new aura of self-confidence
- Producing an aura of health and well being that radiates out to affect the entire family
- Nothing is more touching than the aura of happiness that surrounds these people after they receive even the simplest of help and recognition

See also: ATMOSPHERE, FEELING

AUTHOR
- Finally becoming the author of their lives
- You become the author of their good fortune
- In short, the author of a great many radical changes

AUTHORIZED PAYMENT PLAN
See: SECTION FIVE, SECTION SEVEN

AUTONOMY
- A service to help provide individuals with independence and autonomy
- Fighting to keep a very hard-won autonomy
- Give us the means to act with disinterested autonomy
- Preserving the vital autonomy of our organization

See also: ALONE, FREEDOM, INDEPENDENCE

AVAIL
- Without your help it will be all to no avail
- So that people can avail themselves of this service
- Hope you will avail yourself of this opportunity to help out

See also: HELP, USE

AVAILABLE
- We simply don't have the money available
- Please become one of those available to help
- Please help us make more critical services available
- Every available resource is strained to the limit
- Increasing the availability of this service has to be our first priority

See also: ACCESSIBLE

AWARE
- I wanted to make everyone as aware as I am of
- Certainly you must be aware that
- I know that as soon as you become aware of this appalling problem you'll want to help

- More people have to be aware of this
- I want you to aware of something of grave and immediate concern

AWARENESS
- Wanted to boost awareness about the quality of
- Saw the potential to raise awareness of what's at stake
- Once public awareness has increased, concerned individuals can take meaningful action to
- Education and public awareness activities to create a better understanding of the
- This keen awareness made her plight all the more difficult to bear
- Determined to raise awareness of this appalling situation

See also: **ATTENTION, FOCUS**

AWAY
- Take this away and you have a disaster
- Never want to turn any child away for lack of money
- Please don't take their dignity away
- This problem isn't going to just go away
- Without your help, they'll take even more services away

AXE
- The axe is poised to crash down upon
- To save our funding from the axe
- So many projects have already been axed that
- The terrible tension of waiting for the axe to fall
- Few believe the axe will only fell deadwood

See also: **CUT, CUTBACK, SETBACK, SLASH**

BACK
- Back a winner all the way
- Refuse to back down on this matter
- Your support will back us up
- Back up this argument with irrefutable facts
- With your backing, we can make it all the faster
- Resist the urge to back away
- We can't coldly turn our backs on people in need

See also: **BOOST, INDIFFERENCE, HELP, SUPPORT**

BACKBONE
- The very backbone of our national campaign
- It's time to develop some backbone and stand up to these bullies
- Imperative to strengthen the backbone of the program
- Search out those with true backbone
- Help force the government to develop a backbone

See also: **COURAGE, SUPPORT**

BALANCE
- We need to restore the balance between the needs of
- Working hard to achieve a sensible balance
- In order to evolve as physically and emotionally balanced
- How much longer can we keep up this balancing act
- In order to balance the downside, we must work fast
- Strike a balance between our use and the protection of
- Quickly putting a system of checks and balances in place

BARGAIN
- Cannot accept this Faustian bargain
- In order not to make a bad bargain worse
- Suddenly, we're getting a lot more than we bargained for
- Shouldn't have to bargain for survival
- Where could you find a better bargain for your charitable dollar
- A bargain we can't refuse
- Weren't counting on this as part of the bargain
- End up bargaining all our rights away
- It's no bargain if we have to lose these precious creatures as the price
- I've never seen a better bargain

See also: BUSINESS, DEAL

BARRIER
- Smashing down the many barriers that hinder
- Avoiding the barriers, assumptions and biases that hamper
- Sweeping away artificial barriers and boundaries
- We work hard to break down barriers
- The only barrier is lack of adequate funds

See also: BLOCK, CHALLENGE, OBSTACLE, WALL

BASIC
- The basic things we take for granted in our daily lives are denied to so many people in the world
- First, take care of the basics
- Absolutely basic to a decent quality of service
- Making sure life's basic needs are met
- Providing at least the bare basics of existence
- Even the most basic improvements cost more money that we are currently able to raise
- Nothing could be more basic than these needs

Basic: primary, fundamental, basal, meat-and-potatoes, elementary, underlying, essential, supporting, nitty-gritty, indispensable, necessary, vital, substantive

BATTER
- Every few seconds a woman is battered in this country
- Battering is the greatest single cause of injury to women
- Determinedly battering down the doors of opportunity

- Help and comfort for battered women and children with nowhere else to turn
- Battering is a problem society has swept under the rug for far too long
- If you've ever seen a battered woman cowering in terror, you won't hesitate one moment to give

See also: ABUSE, PAIN

BATTLE
- In the endless battle against social ills
- Battle against the disabling effects of
- Her determination to win her emotional battles against the frustration and despair brought on by the crippling effects of this condition
- If we can't convince you that what we're doing is crucial, then we may as well consider the battle lost
- Silently losing her battle with the disease that has killed so many
- March into battle beside us today
- It's a classic battle between two ever-warring visions
- We face a very difficult battle to
- Respond to a ringing battle cry
- No matter how many skirmishes we lose, we will win this battle one day – with your help
- It was a battle just to make it through the week
- Winning the battles that helped institute the first
- The battle is not just for us
- An uphill battle you must help us win
- We are determined to win this battle
- Find ourselves losing the battle to indifference and cost-cutting

See also: CONFLICT, FIGHT, STRUGGLE, WAR

BEAT
- With your support, this devastating disease can be beaten
- We can't let this problem beat us
- Help us beat up on nasty threat
- With your support, nothing can beat them down

See also: DEFEAT, FIGHT, OVERCOME, SOLVE

BEG
- I can still hear her begging me piteously to
- Begging for help day after day
- When you hurt the most, begging is the hardest
- I beg you to please, please do what you can to help relieve this unspeakable suffering
- Too proud to beg for what they need so badly
- The wrenching sight of women and children reduced to begging by the roadside just to stay alive
- No one should have to beg for what they have a basic human right to enjoy

See also: APPEAL, ASK, PETITION, PLEA, REQUEST

BEGINNING

- Welcome to a wonderful beginning
- And this is just the beginning
- I just know this is the beginning of a long and productive relationship between us
- This is merely the beginning of a glorious future
- Those who are just beginning their lives deserve a fair start
- Remember that endings can also mean new beginnings
- The beginnings of hope, the beginnings of healing, comfort and joy
- Here's how you can be part of this exciting new beginning

See also: INCEPTION, INNOVATION, INITIATIVE, SEED, SPARK, START

BEHIND

- Stuck behind the proverbial eight ball
- Will be left behind in the dust
- Finding out what's really behind it all
- We must all get behind this effort
- I'd love to know that you're behind us all the way
- To find and help those who have been left behind in life's race
- With you behind us, we can achieve anything
- Tenderly gathering up all the little ones who have fallen behind through no fault of their own
- As more and more of you get behind us in this effort, those closer we come to winning

See also: BACK, LATE, PAST

BELIEF

- It is my firm belief that we can succeed
- Once again we must all rise to the defence of these cherished beliefs that have sustained us time and again
- We must change these outdated attitudes and beliefs in order to make speedy progress toward
- Marching staunchly forward, imbued with the firm belief that our cause is just
- The sheer power of belief can turn everything around
- So wonderful to watch this belief deepen and grow
- Feel so strongly because its in tune with our values and beliefs
- We hope your beliefs will be supported by decisive action

See also: CONFIDENCE, CREDIBILITY, FAITH, UNDERSTANDING

BELIEVE

- We do not believe, as some do, that this problem can't be solved
- When you believe that no one can help you, despair begins to creep up into your heart
- I can't tell you how sincerely I believe that
- Fervently believe in what we do
- If you believe, as we do, this is one of the finest places on earth to live
- If seeing is believing, I wish you could be here
- I believe it doesn't have to be this way

- When you really believe in us, we grow stronger and more capable of helping
- Please believe that your donation really counts
- More opportunities to help the causes you believe in most

See also: CONVINCE, PERSUADE

BELIEVER
- I am a passionate believer in
- I believe you are a believer too
- I became a believer the first time I saw this plan in action
- If you're a believer, you'll just naturally want to help
- Turning enormous numbers of people into believers
- All believers must join together in

BELONG
- With your gift you show that you belong with those people who truly care about
- To develop that sense of belonging in our homes and our communities
- Experience the joy of belonging
- To provide healthy alternatives to all those who end up seeking a sense of belonging in all the wrong places
- Everyone needs somewhere to belong
- They desperately want to belong somewhere
- Helping them get back where they really belong
- Each of us belongs to the human family

BENEFACTOR
- You are much more than a nameless, faceless benefactor
- Needing to seek out a new benefactor very soon
- We need all the benefactors we can get
- When you help, you become a benefactor to people who were once utterly without hope
- From the biggest benefactor to the smallest, we welcome you all
- You don't have to be rich to be a benefactor
- So proud to list you among our benefactors

See also: ANGEL, CONTRIBUTOR, DONOR, SPONSOR

BENEFICIARY
- You may also name our organization as the beneficiary of a life insurance policy
- We are all beneficiaries of
- You create untold beneficiaries all around the world
- Please consider making our organization a beneficiary of your will

BENEFIT
- You'll enjoy a number of very special benefits and privileges
- Our activities are designed to benefit all those who
- And the benefits are enormous
- Find out how you will benefit
- Everyone would benefit from this action

- Increasing access to our services could bring more benefits to more people at less cost than any other single method now available
- For the long term benefit of our constituents
- We will all benefit from the savings that arise from
- Able to provide the benefit with negligible involvement for all the added benefits
- Using the added benefits we never thought we'd need
- The real benefit takes place in your head, your heart and your soul
- Discover the benefits of enhanced
- The benefits add up daily
- You can benefit from the following
- And the benefits don't stop there
- Reap immeasurable benefit
- We'll be glad to tell you about some additional benefits and privileges
- To our mutual benefit
- All those who will benefit directly and indirectly
- Bringing the greatest benefit to the most people

Benefit: advantage, well-being, welfare, betterment, improvement, furtherance, advancement, promotion, help, aid, gain, profit, service, use, improve, do good to, be of service to, avail oneself

See also: ADVANTAGE, BLESSING, GOODNESS, HELP

BEST
- With your help, we can provide the very best of
- Devoted to bringing the very best to
- As a national organization, we sponsor only the best in
- We are doing our level best to
- Deserving the very best of help and care
- Sometimes the best you can do is
- One of the best ways to help is
- We fortunate few enjoy the best the world has to offer
- Helping children to be the best they can be
- Challenging each to achieve her very best
- Our supporters are the best
- Truly believe the best is yet to come
- Having the best of all worlds
- Join the best and brightest
- Making it easier to do what we do best
- You'll know what's best for

Best: tops, peerless, perfect, excellent, first-class, crack, superior, unsurpassed, super, unexcelled, choice, superior, select, paramount, outstanding, paramount, capital, peerless, superlative, foremost, first-rate

BET
- Make us your best bet to
- I'm betting on your support
- It's an awfully big bet but we feel we can do it
- They're betting their very lives on your understanding and support

- Betting everything on one nerve-racking roll of the dice
- Here's betting you won't be able to resist

See also: **CHANCE, CROSSROADS, HOPE, DECISION**

BETTER

- Constantly working to make it better still
- With your support, we know we can do even better
- Actually felt better than I had in years – in fact, so wonderful I couldn't believe it
- Better by far to
- Making it a little better each time you give
- Proudly contribute to the betterment of the human condition
- Better you give a small amount than none at all
- Clearly choosing the better way to go
- Nobody knows this better than you and the victims
- Forging ourselves into a better society by helping those who need it most
- There to show a better way
- An appeal to our better selves
- Even better than that is
- Bigger doesn't necessarily mean better
- There has been a visible change for the better

See also: **HELP, IMPROVE**

BIG

- You've got to think big to be big
- It's bigger than all of us
- Growing bigger and better every day
- You have a heart big enough for everybody
- The bigger we get, the more people we can help

BIRTHRIGHT

- A national alliance devoted to protecting our children's birthright
- Future generations are counting on you and me to preserve their birthright
- It's your birthright and theirs too
- A birthright more precious than any other
- A birthright our ancestors fought and died to build and defend
- It would be so easy to lose this inestimable birthright
- Things we take as our birthright others would gladly suffer torments to achieve
- The truth is that these wonderful things are not automatically our birthright

See also: **HERITAGE, INHERITANCE, LEGACY, TRADITION**

BLAME

- Laying blame at our personal doorstep doesn't help anyone
- Time to stop blaming and start putting things right
- We must all take our share of blame for this situation
- Can't blame them for thinking there is no way out
- We don't just sit around and blame circumstances
- We are still blaming the victims, we are still ashamed

See also: CONDEMNATION, FINGER, GUILT, REGRET, SORRY, TURMOIL

BLAST
- Having a real blast
- Watching their hopes get blasted out of the water
- Blast our way through these obstacles if we have to

See also: AMBUSH, EXPLODE, HIT, OVERCOME

BLESSING
- I join all the others in wishing you every blessing for the New Year
- Speedy relief would be such a blessing
- Help those who long for the blessing of relief from pain
- Offering a special blessing upon this gift and those who receive it
- You receive a blessing with each gift you give
- Your participation would add so much to the blessings these people count most valuable
- Can sometimes seem to outweigh the blessings of

See also: ADVANTAGE, ANGEL, BENEFIT, GOODNESS

BLOCK
- Blocking us from moving where we want to go
- Refuse to let this obstacle block our way any longer
- Lack of adequate funding has always been the major block
- The biggest block of all can be solved if you will only work with us
- Blocking our path is a number of serious objections
- Moving as fast as we can to block this disastrous development

See also: DISRUPT, OBSTACLE, PREVENT, STOP, WALL

BLOOD
- The joy of helping gets into your blood
- Tragically, more blood will be spilled unless you
- Such injustices make your blood boil
- To honor those who have already paid with their blood
- The ground has been watered with their blood and their bitterest tears
- Worse than trying to wring blood from a stone
- So important to keep these blood ties from being broken
- To prevent any more blood being spilled

See also: FAMILY, RELATIONSHIP, SACRIFICE

BLOODLETTING
- The bloodletting has got to stop
- Once again, we're in for a bloodletting
- A bloodletting government is bent on slashing the budget
- Struggling to recover from this merciless bloodletting of funds and resources

See also: ATTACK, CATASTROPHE, CUTBACK

BLOW

- Then came the biggest blow of all
- Able to withstand blow after blow without caving in
- Another heavy blow almost put an end to
- All of it adds up to a crushing blow to
- Staggering under the cruellest blow of all
- The blows have fallen, one after the other, but we still have managed to withstand this worst attack
- Grab this chance to strike a telling blow against
- Now is your chance to get in a powerful blow against
- Move quickly to prevent this final blow

See also: FIGHT, HIT, OBSTACLE, PROBLEM, SETBACK

BOMB

- So many people are walking bombs, waiting to explode
- Things seemed to be nicely settled down again when a second bomb went off
- Just when you think you've heard it all, another bombshell drops
- Such courage amidst the bombs and machine gun fire
- An explosive issue, ready to drop like a bomb
- Every one of us is bombarded by
- Help us dodge another bomb

BONUS

- As an added bonus
- The biggest bonus of all would be
- A totally unexpected bonus delighted us last year
- Working toward the bonus of
- Something added to your regular donation would be a wonderful bonus we could use to increase help to
- As a bonus for your increased participation, we are offering you this lovely gift
- The real bonus is the happiness that shows up in their eyes
- Watching them walk away, healthy, happy and safe, is the biggest bonus we could possibly receive

See also: BENEFIT, EXTRA, GIFT, SURPRISE

BOOK

- In the long run, the book is by far the more potent weapon
- To so many, a book is a rare and awesome thing
- Imagine your name in the great book of benefactors
- With just a little more money we could buy books to help educate
- Education is more than just knowledge from books
- Get into their good books
- Help make sure we can book far enough ahead to

BOOST

- With a little boost from your contributions
- Provide a real boost amid tough economic conditions

- Please give us a boost with your donation
- The best boost we have so far received
- Ordinarily self- sufficient people just need a little boost to get back on their feet again
- If you could boost your customary donation just a little bit this year

See also: **ADVANCE, AID, ASSIST, HELP, IMPROVE, SUPPORT**

BOTHER

- Don't bother to read this unless you've decided not to support our cause
- Forgive me for bothering you so soon after your last donation
- Helping those in need is no bother at all
- Not everyone will bother when they see someone sick or homeless in the street
- The end result is worth any amount of bother

See also: **ASK, EFFORT, PROBLEM, STRUGGLE, TROUBLE**

BOUNDARY

- A boundary that cannot be crossed easily
- There is no boundary which can enclose
- Extending existing artistic boundaries
- It knows no social or economic boundaries
- Taking great care to cross no boundaries that shouldn't be crossed
- Breaking the boundaries that previously restricted expansion
- Boundary problems with children, parents and society

See also: **EDGE, LIMIT**

BRAVE

- He's very brave and mature, and even manages to find some humor in his ongoing tribulation
- And you, too, can be part of this brave new world
- You'll be helping one very brave little boy
- Only the bravest dare venture there
- Every day we grow braver in our fight to conquer
- You can help make sure this brave effort does not falter

See also: **BACKBONE, CHAMPION, COURAGE, HERO**

BREACH

- But we've found a breach in that seemingly impenetrable wall
- To pull back now because of lack of money would be a terrible breach of trust
- Help us breach the gap
- An unconscionable breach of ethics and promises

See also: **FAILURE, GAP**

BREAKTHROUGH

- Wonderful breakthroughs have already relieved much suffering
- Breakthrough after breakthrough has brought us to the point where we can help so many
- Instrumental in bringing a breakthrough approach to

- Your dollars help bring the breakthrough suffering people so richly deserve
- More news about this important breakthrough is enclosed
- Poised to achieve the breakthrough we need to conquer
- We haven't found a cure but we're close to a breakthrough
- Some terrific breakthroughs are happening right here, now
- You can help speed those breakthroughs
- This is the single most important breakthrough in fifty years
- In a very dramatic breakthrough
- Patiently stringing together a series of small breakthroughs into our current success
- That huge breakthrough could be just around the next corner

See also: ACHIEVEMENT, ADVANCE, CURE, DISCOVERY, LEAP, RESEARCH, SCIENTIST, STRIDE

BRIDGE
- This network makes a vital bridge between all groups who really care
- The joy of building bridges between human beings
- We'll certainly have to cross that scary bridge when we come to it
- Please help us bridge this funding gap
- Building a bridge of understanding to your door and your heart

See also: JOIN, LEAP, LINK, OVERCOME

BRING
- Proud to help to bring you this service
- Bringing compassionate people together
- Doing our best to bring the best to
- We deeply value everything you bring to this
- Proud of the contribution you bring

BROCHURE
- Please take time to read the enclosed brochure
- The whole story is in the enclosed brochure
- Help pay for distributing this brochure packed with life-saving facts

See also: ADVERTISE, INFORMATION

BUCK
- When it comes to dealing with this problem, the buck stops here
- But it is going to take big bucks to solve
- Often it doesn't take that many bucks to
- It takes courage to buck the system
- A buck or two out of your pocket means so much to someone who is hungry

See also: DEFIANCE, DOLLAR, FUNDS, MONEY

BUDGET
- This year's budget is painting an even more chilling picture
- We are still working on our budget for this year, and frankly, I need to know how much you can help us

- If we can't meet our budget, we can't continue.
- As budget time approaches, we're sending out an urgent appeal for funds
- Sweeping staff and budget cuts once again imperil our survival
- The question of an adequate budget grows more urgent every day we have to wait
- Frankly, our budget has just been hammered
- Proper budgeting is the only sound foundation
- Limited budgets cannot cover any items we want our children to have

Budget: expenses, overhead, operating expenses, costs, estimate, statement, plan, allowance, program, ration, allotment, percentage, quota, share, portion, stockpile, reserves, assets, supply, capital, funds, purse, finances, schedule
See also: ASSETS, FUNDS, MONEY, PLAN, PROGRAM, SHARE, SUPPLY, SUPPORT

BULLET
- This is certainly not a magic bullet
- We've been dodging bullets about this for the past year
- All too often, a bullet is the only answer they get
- To rescue the innocents trapped and terrified, under the hail of bullets
- Shamefully spending money for bullets rather than food and medicine

BURDEN
- Do not wish to place an unfair burden upon
- More burdens than anyone could possibly carry
- Lift the burdens from the backs of the weary and disadvantaged
- There is no crueller burden than
- Helping a family that cannot bear just one more burden
- To make heavy burdens light
- Praying that this burden will slide from their shoulders
- Burdened with a clumsy, bloated administration and hidebound ideas

See also: BLOCK, EFFORT, OBSTACLE, PROBLEM

BUSINESS
- Uniting consumers with charitable and socially aware businesses
- The well being of our fellows is everybody's business
- The true business of life is to see that everyone is respected and properly cared for
- Please make it your business to see that
- Since the very beginning, our business has been helping

See also: BARGAIN, CONCERN, CORPORATE, DEAL, ENTERPRISE, ECONOMIC

BUY
- You don't have to buy anything
- Many don't buy that argument
- You can't buy peace and happiness, but you can sure do a lot toward them with a generous donation

- People there are buying into the belief that

CALL

- You responded to the call
- I encourage you to call our special hotline
- The call for help is ringing out
- People like you are answering the call
- Our dedicated workers respond to calls promptly, saving lives
- Call before the vote takes place
- We calling upon you for assistance
- This could be their last call for help
- It's your call now
- Thrilled to a stirring call to arms
- I'm calling on you today to ask

See also: APPEAL, ASK, CHOICE, DECISION, REQUEST

CAMPAIGN

- We have also begun a special campaign for
- To run our campaign for the next several months we urgently need donations from concerned people such as yourself
- By joining the campaign today you will affirm your belief in a caring country which protects people most in need
- Help our new campaign take wing
- Well equipped to wage an effective campaign to save
- Many of you will have seen our campaign emerge in the press
- Please join our campaign to save
- However you contribute to our campaign to
- Part of an overall campaign to
- The campaign to protect these precious, threatened ideals
- What a difference it makes for our vital campaigns
- Thousands of letter writing campaigns
- Launched a major campaign to rescue
- Will you campaign for fairness
- Allow us to undertake other critical campaign strategies
- The campaign of harassment is increasing
- Campaign to ensure public and parliamentary understanding of
- Subject of an intense worldwide campaign demanding
- To help with special campaigns addressing immediate needs or issues
- Absolutely vital campaign that must succeed
- The effect of a well-organized campaign can be enormous
- Outspoken campaigning on human rights violations
- Only by campaigning very hard can we succeed in
- I'm writing to ask you to join our campaign
- Wage a powerful, two-pronged campaign
- Campaign has grown in scope and intensity
- With outstanding people like you working on our campaign
- Invite you to become part of our annual campaign

- A sizable percentage of campaign funding consists of small individual contributions

Campaign: battle, war, strategy, course of action, operation, manoeuvres, crusade, battle plan, canvass, barnstorm
See also: BATTLE, PLAN, PROGRAM, STRATEGY, WAR

CANDIDATE
- Not the candidate of special interests
- So many candidates qualify for this program
- To support the candidate of your choice

See also: ADVOCATE

CAPABLE
- Whatever you are capable of providing
- An army of capable people are waiting to spring into action
- To show youngsters what they are capable of

See also: ABLE, ABILITY

CAPACITY
- Capacity has suffered under a series of successive cuts and changes
- As long as we never lose the capacity for change
- In an altogether different capacity
- Our capacity to help must learn to match their capacity for suffering

See also: ABILITY, APTITUDE, SKILL, TALENT

CARE
- Enhance our place in the continuum of care
- You care about people
- Because of you, we'll be able to deliver better care
- Appreciation for the care is very deep
- Staunch health care providers
- Help us keep up the skilled and loving care our patients deserve
- Bring up-to-date, integrated care to each individual
- Finally get the competent, humanitarian care they so badly need
- Speedy, compassionate, effective care
- Care tailored to each patient's uniquely complex, individual needs
- Someone cared before it was too late
- When no one else seems to care, we are there
- Take care of yourself in everything you do
- Remained actively involved with her family and her care right to the very end
- Whether it was a hot meal, protection from abuse, a caring smile, friendly conversation, a warm bed or job retraining, we were there
- Poor and middle income people may no longer be able to get the care they need
- I know how passionately you care about
- If not me, who will care
- I know you are someone who cares
- We care too much to let our program suffer such a savaging

- Providing an overall concept of care planning
- Only because you care enough to help
- Please care before it's too late
- A perfect way to show you care
- Come to rely on high standards of quality care
- I am so heartened to know you care
- It all happens because of people like you, people who care, people who take a moment from their busy lives to help those less fortunate
- You'll be showing how very much you care

Care: attention, caution, carefulness, vigilance, watchfulness, concern, regard, mindfulness, consciousness, prudence, awareness, circumspection, care for, watch out for, look after, be concerned for, be solicitous, attend to, deal with, take up, take action on, cherish, love
See also: ATTENTION, AWARENESS, COMPASSION, CONCERN, FOCUS, GOODNESS, KINDNESS, LOVE, NURSE, NURTURE, PASSION

CAREGIVER
- As primary caregiver, I felt helpless and alone in coping
- Gave me back my confidence as a caregiver
- A unique program that gives caregivers a breather and clients a chance for a day of healthy stimulation
- Helping caregivers give time and personal effort to those in need
- Discuss issues from the perspective of both consumer and caregiver
- For caregivers, emotional crises can be the hardest situations
- A caregiver must know how to deal with the impact of the situation upon themselves

See also: ANGEL, HELPER, NURSE, PROFESSIONAL

CARING
- To become the mainspring of creative caring
- Caring individuals who have taken one step closer to getting involved in the issue
- Success is measured in caring
- Without caring individuals like you to support our work, there would be no hope for the thousands of
- Learn to be caring, sharing human beings
- Only because of caring people like you
- Your thoughtfulness, your caring, your compassion is the real key
- True caring is the foundation of our entire system
- After a while, you get practice at caring
- We depend on caring people like you

Caring: kindness, beneficence, benevolence, benefaction, humanitarianism, altruism, philanthropy, charity, almsgiving
See also: COMPASSIONATE, CONCERN, LOVE

CASE
- In over half of all cases we have no idea why
- Predicts that an estimated number of cases occur each year

- Many cases go undetected and unreported
- And these are just the cases that are reported
- Cases undertaken because of suspected maltreatment
- Dealing with a multitude of contentious and demanding cases
- Just in case you haven't been given all the rending details
- The most difficult cases are the emotional scars
- For years, we have been taking on the most challenging cases

See also: **EXAMPLE, HELPER, WORKER**

CATASTROPHE
- I encourage you to do more than wait for a possible catastrophe
- A catastrophe is looming over all our heads
- Unless we act now, an unspeakable catastrophe will strike
- Such policies have proved to be a catastrophe for

See also: **BLOW, CRISIS, EMERGENCY, DISASTER, NIGHTMARE, ORDEAL, TRAUMA, TRAGEDY**

CAUSE
- We'd rather devote your dollars to the cause
- Reflecting on the years of our lives which so many have cheerfully given to our cause
- You are helping the same cause that these famous people so fervently believe in
- The cause remains unknown and there is no known prevention or treatment
- Our cause is a deserving one
- Wherever there was a good cause, she was there
- Have been continually supportive of the cause
- Today, thanks to research funded by people like you, we have many ways to determine the cause of
- If you get a lot of fundraising mail, it can sometimes be very hard to decide which worthy cause to support
- Dedicated to addressing the underlying causes of
- Your involvement with this very worthwhile cause is crucial
- Largely preventable causes
- There's no known cause or cure
- The leading cause of death and adult disability

Cause: reason why, source, root, origin, agent, motive, ideal, idea, question, matter, topic, principle, belief, tenet, purpose, conviction, end, aim, purpose, goal, causation
See also: **GOAL, MISSION, PRINCIPLE, PURPOSE, REASON, ROOT, SOURCE, TOPIC, UNDERTAKING**

CELEBRATE
- That's why, from time to time, we can stand up and celebrate
- We join together in celebrating with you
- We celebrate the appeal to
- As you celebrate this year, please take a moment to consider all of your good fortune
- We're celebrating many years of helping to protect and save lives

- Celebrated each success together
- Celebrating isn't just for birthdays
- Learning to celebrate the everyday achievements and accomplishments
- Learning to celebrate the sheer, irreplaceable joy of life
- It's about celebrating who we are
- Learn to celebrate yourself

See also: SECTION FIVE

CELEBRATION

- Join the celebration
- Your donation amounts to a private celebration of
- Do all we can to make it a celebration of love
- Please join us in the annual celebration of our rich heritage
- Organized national celebrations to encourage the public to celebrate our cultural legacy
- Giving is a great way to make your celebration special

CHALLENGE

- The further challenge facing them is one shared by us all
- With you beside us, no challenge is too big
- Our future depends on the number of supporters who accept this challenge
- You can take on any challenge to
- It's a big challenge and that's why we urgently need the most generous gift you can possibly send today
- Never before have I faced such a challenge
- That's why it's so challenging, so powerful
- One of the most challenging periods our organization has ever faced
- Challenged us to raise an additional sum by means of
- If we can meet the challenge, we will achieve an additional bonus of
- The challenge here is to do something really exciting
- We know you will accept this challenge.
- Now we have a new challenge
- It is this challenge I hope you will help us meet
- Not afraid to accept this huge challenge
- Able to meet the challenge of our rapidly changing world

See also: BLOCK, CHAMPION, OBSTACLE, PROBLEM, PRIORITY, VICTORY

CHALLENGES

- The greatest challenges facing us are
- No idea how to come to terms with the challenges in their lives
- Dealing with very unique challenges indeed
- Join us in the challenges ahead with a tax-creditable contribution today
- I believe it's important for people to understand the challenges faced by families coping with
- To meet the expanding challenges of the twenty-first century
- Remain what it has always been – a joyous place of life and hope amidst life's

   most demanding challenges
- Facing a number of new challenges
- Anxious to take on new challenges and opportunities
- To make a difference in young people's lives by providing the skills to adapt to new cultural, technological and economic challenges
- Confident of our role in the challenges which lie ahead
- Able to understand the difficult challenges facing their sick baby
- One of today's biggest challenges just hit us
- Met staggering challenges with resourcefulness and ingenuity
- How we choose to respond to the challenge
- No challenge is too great
- The challenges we face this year are substantially greater
- Challenges a lot bigger than those of the past
- Many of our successes are certainly being challenged
- Challenges that have helped us grow
- Challenges have overwhelmed them

Challenge: invitation, dare, call, summons, gauntlet, risk, venture, hazard, tough job, puzzle, provocation, ultimatum, obstacle, barrier, frustration

CHALLENGE FUND

- In order to accomplish this urgently needed project, we have established a challenge fund
- Our challenge fund is money that will be devoted exclusively to
- Setting up our challenge fund really tested our mettle

CHAMPION

- Be a champion today
- Help champion those who cannot stand up for themselves
- Help a real champion keep on winning
- You are the champion they're looking to
- Deep down inside you, I know there's a champion
- Championing an unpopular cause sometimes takes courage far beyond ordinary measure
- They're champions in their own way by doing
- Every round is a championship round as far as we're concerned

See also: ADVOCATE, ANGEL, FIGHTER, HERO, SPONSOR

CHANCE

- You decided to give our organization a chance by making a donation
- All they're asking for is a fighting chance
- Well, here's your chance to show how much you care
- You can reduce your chances
- If she had a chance, she would thank you
- If we don't do this now, we won't get another chance to
- So here's your chance to create a difference
- Will you give them the chance they so very much deserve
- Give a child a new chance

- We'll never get a second chance to do something this wonderful
- Now we really have a chance to make lasting positive changes
- Helping those who, because of the unpredictable chances in life, have fallen upon hard times
- We're only going to get one chance to fix this mess
- You'll be giving someone a chance at life itself
- Giving us a chance to know and understand one another
- In order to give men and women everywhere the chance to
- You have a chance if you act quickly
- This is an unprecedented chance to make real progress
- This is your chance to help

Chance: accident, serendipity, possibility, opportunity, prospect, opening, likelihood, occasion, time
See also: BET, OCCASION, OPPORTUNITY, PROSPECT, TIME

CHANGE
- You can sure change things
- We need your help to change all this
- By reaching out with your generosity, you're helping to change
- You've demonstrated your commitment to creating permanent change
- We know that lasting change takes time
- Your donation can create abiding change
- But lasting change doesn't happen overnight
- Helping to bring about enduring change
- I can't change what happened, but I can help others who
- The pain of watching a loving wife and mother change into a completely dependent, terrified person who
- Would change if they could
- With your participation, the rate of change can speed up enormously
- Rapidly, it changed for the worse
- We are working to change all that
- The situation by which political change has received a strong impetus provides many challenges
- I'm sure you'll find it a refreshing change
- Such a tremendous change from
- Your help brings about so many positive changes
- Their special skills and talents bring real lasting change to countries that desperately need it
- Times have changed and so must we
- We have changed so much since this brave venture began
- Change is the only constant
- I'm confident that things will change soon, but right now we need
- What I saw that day made a profound change in my life and my beliefs
- If you like this change, please show your support with a donation
- Together with our funds and technical support, bring dramatic change
- Extraordinary change and unimagined possibilities are offering new hope for the future

- The opportunity to change someone's life for the better
- Challenging, pushing, prodding for change
- If we want this kind of richness, growth and change, we must
- Find the courage to change
- Unexpected changes can upset the even most careful of planning
- While pushing for crucial changes at the international level like the one's I've outlined
- Yes, the changes are incredible
- Change can appear uncomfortable, risky or even terrifying
- Your gift today can change all that
- Have changed a lot over the years
- Probably hasn't changed much in the last one hundred years
- Totally changed their lives
- Change can't be stopped, but it can be shaped to the best advantage
- Consider ways to radically change how we view ourselves
- First, I'll walk you through the most recent changes to
- Change just doesn't happen overnight
- Asking how soon you'll see these changes
- Some of the changes will be very subtle
- Big changes are in the wind
- If changes are not made soon
- You can make big changes
- Because of your generosity we can keep the wave of change going

Change: transform, moderate, temper, alter, correct, modify, convert, mutate, transfigure, retool, remodel, switch, replace, exchange, translate, reconstruct, reorder, recast, reorganize, innovation, novelty, revolution, transition, evolution, conversation, transfiguration
See also: **ALTERNATIVE, CHALLENGE, INNOVATION, OPPORTUNITY, TRANSFORM, RENEW**

CHANNEL
- Provides an immediate and available avenue to channel
- Going through regular channels is proving far too slow
- Please help us channel some resources to those in the most desperate circumstances
- Your are one of our best channels of support

See also: **MEANS, OPPORTUNITY, WAY**

CHAOS
- Out of the milling, despairing chaos our workers bring order, comfort and medical relief
- We cannot let this destructive chaos continue
- Sometimes the best of plans fall into chaos
- Chaos can be an exceedingly creative thing
- Staying calm in the midst of chaos and bedlam
- The situation is rapidly descending toward chaos

See also: **CRISIS, CONFUSE, DISASTER, DISORDER, HAVOC, MESS,**

NIGHTMARE, TURMOIL

CHARACTER
- To reward desire, intelligence and strength of character
- It's not in their character to
- Helping to build character helps build our nation
- Enough character to refuse to submit to this shame
- Developing the kind of character best suited to
- The very character of it precludes
- Changing the very character of

See also: ASPECT, FEATURE, NATURE

CHARGE
- It may be necessary for you to take charge and call for help
- Move the discussion to people taking charge of their own lives so they can prevent
- Reminding again us that we ought to take charge
- You and I are charged with the care of those in need
- Instead, she took charge of her life
- Our workers are take-charge people who get things done
- We find ourselves charged with a grave responsibility
- Everybody is charging more for everything these days

See also: GUIDANCE, LEAD, RESPONSIBILITY

CHARITABLE
- One of the most rewarding charitable commitments you can make
- Let's prove we are truly a charitable society
- There are so many charitable causes crying out – and each one needs your help
- Helping to strengthen charitable organizations such as

See also: GIVING, KINDNESS

CHARITY
- Recognized as the most efficient, reputable large charity in
- Charities especially need more facts
- Faith, hope and charity are virtues that never go out of style – or out of usefulness
- Those left out of society's abundance need your kindness and your charity as much as ever
- Please give to your favorite charity today
- The lesson of charity is one that will last a child for life
- Don't back away from helping a charity you really care about
- Would mean a lot to charities such as ourselves
- Recognizing that many charities have limited funds
- The exponential growth rate in registered charities will almost certainly continue
- More charities must chase an ever-shrinking source of funds
- The charity in our hearts must be matched by the generosity of our pocketbooks
- This is not charity, it's neighborly help

- Positively affected by the kindness and charity we have seen here today
- They want our solidarity, not our charity

Charity: generosity, bounty, munificence, liberality, open-handedness, philanthropy, altruism, humanitarianism, big-heartedness, benevolence, humanity, kindliness, kind-heartedness, compassion, mercy, sympathy, understanding, aid, assistance, bequest, clemency, tenderness, offering, unselfishness, open-heartedness, alms, contribution, legacy, brotherly love
See also: DONATION, GIFT, HELP, KINDNESS, SUPPORT

CHECK
See: CHEQUE

CHEER
- Met, talked, cheered each other on
- In these cases, good cheer is more valuable than rubies
- Cheered the hearts of those who are downtrodden
- So easy to bring a little cheer into the lives of
- Join our cheering section today
- Doing our best to cheer you on to the finish line
See also: BACK, BOOST, ENCOURAGE

CHEQUE
- Please, just sit down and write out a cheque
- Right now, before you go on to other things, please pick up your cheque book and write us a cheque for whatever you can afford
- As you reach for your cheque book, consider this
- Write your cheque and put it in the envelope
- So please, if you can, sit down and write a cheque to
- Please take a moment to write your cheque and mail it, along with your reply memo, in the envelope I've enclosed for your interest and commitment
- Why not send us a cheque for
- The change begins the moment you drop your cheque in the mail
- Please send your cheque without delay so we can take care of the neediest
- You know what you're getting before you write that cheque
- Your cheque means so much to
- Please write your cheque today
- Think about writing us the biggest cheque you can
- If not with a cheque, then with your calls and letters
See also: CONTRIBUTION, DONATION, GIFT

CHILD
- As you read this letter, a child is being abused
- Child abuse can be prevented
- Your gift has helped a child in need
- Child abuse hurts
- It costs the child most of all
- The neglect of even one child is intolerable

- To help a child get the best possible start
- Small fears can loom very big and scary to a child
- Being a child shouldn't hurt
- Imagine how you'd feel if your child suddenly disappeared
- Imagine not being able to keep your own little one warm and fed, safe and dry
- We don't just keep a child alive today, we focus on tomorrow as well
- Unlike most children, this child rarely looks forward to
- To provide a child with the care she needs to survive
- It's about helping, one child at a time
- Help a child feel wanted and accepted
- The worst degradation a child can face
- Watch joy and hope kindle in a child's eyes
- Because of your gift, a child somewhere, perhaps on your very street, won't have to suffer the horrors of child abuse or neglect
- There is help, one child at a time
- It's so difficult, not knowing what's wrong with your child
- Wondering why her child was in such agony
- Imagine that special child in your life needing help and feeling they have nowhere to turn
- A child any mom or dad would be proud of
- Please add a child in need to your holiday list
- When we help a child, we grow too
- Help us give a bright future to every child
- The joy of touching the life of a child just like your own
- Nourishing food and safe shelter changes everything for a child
- Your caring transforms a child's life and the life of his or her family
- You'll also be helping a very brave little child struggling with a burden that would make any grownup shudder.
- The immense satisfaction of seeing a child blossom before our eyes
- Seeing a child's eyes light up with joy and hope
- The agony of not knowing whether your child is dead or alive
- To help a child develop a lifelong love of reading
- Ask a poor child how it feels to go to school hungry each morning
- Begin to change the world for one child
- You will bring shining hope into a child's life
- You can help put a smile on a child's face
- Are you prepared to see this child die

Child: small fry, baby, babe, lad, lass, little shaver, juvenile, youth, infant, chick, junior, toddler, tot, preschooler, tad, youngster, offspring, progeny, chip off the block, minor, nipper, tyke, small fry, adolescent

See also: DAUGHTER, FAMILY, GIRLS, KID, YOUNG, YOUNGSTER, YOUTH

CHILDHOOD
- Needless to say, their childhood was not a happy one
- Not the kind of childhood you dream of for your children
- Childhood innocence ripped away

- Your gift had helped her to experience all that childhood has to offer
- Childhood can be very beautiful
- Childhood isn't always easy
- To experience all the joys childhood has to offer
- So that childhood can remain the sweetest time of life
- Children robbed of their childhood
- Sometimes, childhood itself seems to be disappearing
- Childhood can be beautiful, but it isn't always easy
- You are really giving the gift of childhood

Childhood: infancy, babyhood, flower of youth, salad days, tender years, adolescence, puberty, growing up, teens

CHILDREN

- Hopeful that her children will have a better life
- Hope their children will beat the odds to reach their first birthday
- Please help us help children, the adults of tomorrow, make a better tomorrow for everyone
- The greatest gift of all – children
- Children who would otherwise continue to live alone in their own silent world
- When children are taught to improve themselves and their surroundings, we all benefit
- Every week children and their parents attend therapy sessions
- Sadly, that leaves many thousands of young children waiting for help
- One of the most evil things I think of is the suffering of innocent children
- A leading cause of absenteeism among school children
- Helping children and their parents to better understand and cope with this debilitating disease
- Guidance and counselling to children
- Thousands of children live in the street
- Enough children live in poverty to form another province
- We're providing shelter for homeless children in
- People who have heard the cry and seen the plight of the children
- Helpless, hurting children look to you for help
- Tragically, one quarter are children
- The children are counting on you to come through for them
- The protection of children is our number one priority
- We're committed to saving those children already born
- The children spend just a few hours of their time to raise money for other children
- Do we wonder at the values our children are missing
- The children were thrilled to receive your generous donation
- This project lets children help other children
- So children will pick up a book instead of a gun
- Children are very special to us
- If you believe in helping children strive for a future, please help now
- In their uncertain world, so many children die needlessly

- Children are still major victims of adult wars raging around the world
- Their children are as real as our own
- These are the neglected, abandoned, exploited and abused children of the world
- We should all remember that the world's future is with its children
- Your gift will help make sure that we are here for each of those children
- Taking care of children is important to us all
- Children can learn and grow along with
- In these difficult times, needy children suffer more than most
- As children grow up, safe and secure, a little bit of you goes with them
- Your generosity can double or triple the number of children we save from perishing needlessly
- Suppose they were your own children
- I've lived through my own children's agony.
- Our children are depending on us to
- Millions of children will go hungry today
- These children growing up without even a roof over their heads
- Children are the world of tomorrow
- We can't let these children slip through our fingers
- Your heart can't help but be moved by the terrible stresses more and more children find themselves under
- Promoting the well-being of children should be the highest priority of society
- Children who don't know why, except that it must be their fault
- How many more abused children hide their wounds
- Dedicated to making society a safe, nurturing place for children
- Strong advocate for the rights of children
- These children are counting on you
- Wherever children cry, we want to be there
- So that many more children can get the help they so badly need
- Children too famished even to cry
- These actions hurt you and your children directly
- If you believe in helping children strive for a future
- Guiding my children to a better tomorrow
- Children often exhibit as much interest as adults
- After the program, older children report that they are now making different, better choices for themselves
- The wrenching statistics of children left seriously injured – thanks to their parents
- The importance of learning how to listen to children's complaints, feelings and insecurities
- Threaten that which is most precious to us – our children
- The laughter of children is the sign of our success

See also: CHILD, FAMILY, GIRLS, KIDS, LITTLE ONES, POSTERITY, YOUNG, YOUNGSTERS, YOUTH

CHIP IN
- Whatever you can chip in will be much appreciated
- Bit by bit, people have been chipping in to help

- I'm asking you to chip in what you can
- If everyone chips in, just a little, the accumulated sum will add up

See also: **DONATE, CONTRIBUTE, GIVE**

CHOICE

- The choice is always ours
- The choice of spreading your donation over
- Helping them to make healthy choices every day
- So that people may have a decent, dignified choice available
- A first rate choice
- At this moment of moments, the choice is yours
- Providing a choice for those who have no choice
- In fact, we were forced to make hard choices in the course of a rigorous review process
- You and I have the choice and ability to do something about it
- The choice to help or turn away is always yours
- Our choice is frighteningly simple

Choice: selection, decision, judgement, commitment, differentiation, alternative, option, possibility, answer, solution, way out, substitute, discrimination, vote

See also: **CROSSROADS, DECISION, OPPORTUNITY, OPTION, SELECT**

CHOOSE

- That's why they choose us
- You have the chance to choose
- Emerge re-energized and able to choose
- Please choose to help make life better for
- I'm pleased to announce that you have been chosen
- When you choose to help us, you're choosing to help thousands

See also: **DECIDE, SELECT**

CHOP

- Chopping away at what little is left of
- Once again our funds have been drastically chopped
- So much has already been chopped away
- Chopping at our very foundation

See also: **CUT, CUTBACKS, DOWNSIZE, SLASH, STOP**

CHORUS

- You join a swelling chorus
- A chorus of protest thundered through
- We must raise our voices in a chorus of
- This chorus is beginning to be heard from every corner of the country

See also: **GROUP, SPEAK, VOICE**

CHRISTMAS

- The support of so many caring people has been the finest Christmas gift we could possibly receive

- This Christmas, please open your heart to help others who need your love and kindness
- Your gift today can provide a memorable Christmas for so many children like this little darling
- Support us by making a special donation on behalf of someone on your Christmas list
- It's beginning to look like Christmas
- We're as much a part of Christmas as decorating the tree and family dinners
- Christmas is an important time for us, just as it is for you and your loved ones
- To help make Christmas special for children whose families couldn't afford to make their own wishes come true
- Help make Christmas merry and provide hope for the new year
- Think about the Christmas feast you look forward to every year
- Now imagine Christmas without that feast at all or maybe even without anything to eat
- So this Christmas, be generous with your love, your understanding, your support
- Your gift could bring a family a welcome Christmas dinner and toys
- Please add a child in need to your Christmas list
- A Christmas time double bonus of caring and practical help
- Celebrating isn't just for Christmas and New Year
- With Christmas just around the corner, we wish to tell you
- This year you can give a membership as a gift to a friend or relative for Christmas

Christmas: Yule, Yuletide, Noel, holiday season, Christmas time, Christmastide
See also: CELEBRATION, CHEER, HOLIDAY, SEASON

CIRCUMSTANCES
- Help those in reduced circumstances to
- People are willing to do a great deal to change their lives and their circumstances
- Could end up living their lives in circumstances far lower than they could ever have imagined
- Through an unexpected turn of circumstances, we find ourselves in need of
- We intend to turn these circumstances around
- No one could have predicted these kinds of circumstances
- A profound change in circumstances

See also: ATMOSPHERE, CONDITIONS, SURROUND

CITIZEN
- We exist for you and every other citizen
- We citizens must take this matter into our own hands
- It's up to the ordinary citizen to make sure
- The real essence of what a citizen is

CITY
- In the midst of all the riches of our city, there are people with nothing
- No home, no food, no one to nurture them in this affluent city
- The city as habitat versus the city as resource

- Rural folk need help just as much as city folk
- Another victim of the city's savagery
- In a big, impersonal city, life can be very cruel
- A progressive city can never rest on its laurels

See also: COMMUNITY, NATION, NEIGHBORHOOD

CLARITY
- We are able to see, with ever-increasing clarity
- The clarity of the issue is indisputable
- Explaining, with clarity, exactly what is required

CLIENT
- Our program works with each client for a period of about
- Every one of our clients has unique needs
- Our clients are people just like you
- So that we can better serve our ever-increasing client base
- Serving an increasingly diverse clientele

COALITION
- A coalition funded primarily from the donations of individuals like you
- A coalition forged of dire necessity to fight for
- Naturally, you help make our coalition truly powerful

See also: AFFILIATION, ASSOCIATION, COLLABORATION, GROUP, ORGANIZATION, PARTNERSHIP

COLLABORATION
- This collaboration could be the answer to it all
- If we can all collaborate, this problem could be solved quickly
- You are essential to this fine collaboration
- The result of inspired collaboration
- Replaced with a new-found collaboration of all parties
- The establishment of this collaboration is a real first

See also: COALITION

COLLECTION
- You will help us build our collection
- But maintaining this superb collection is very expensive
- Help protect a collection like no other in the world

See also: ART, ASSET, CULTURE, RESOURCE

COMBAT
- The only way to combat this is through a good national program
- We must be ready, at all times, to combat this abomination
- Once again we're marching into combat
- Every day we tirelessly combat poverty and misery

See also: ATTACK, BATTLE, FIGHT, STRUGGLE, WAR

COMFORT
- To know the inexpressible comfort of
- You never have to leave the comfort of your home
- Help and comfort can be given in so many forms
- To comfort those who are sick, lonely or deeply troubled
- A touch of a hand, a single kind word can be a sorely needed comfort
- Need support, comfort and information to get through a difficult time
- Can bring comfort to those badly in need of

Comfort: alleviate, mitigate, palliate, salve, comfort, soothe, solace, console, succor, assure, reassure, calm, allay, put at ease, quiet one's fears

See also: CARE, COMPASSION, EASE, KINDNESS, PEACE

COMMIT
- Once committed, we refused to be turned aside
- When you commit your gift to us, you're doing so much good to so many deeply in need
- I hope you will once again commit for the coming year
- Continue to commit ourselves to the processes begun at
- We're committed to helping

See also: DONATE, GIVE, PLEDGE, PROMISE

COMMITMENT
- You know the meaning of real commitment
- We rely on your commitment and generosity
- We keep going only through the continued commitment of caring people like you
- We did all this while keeping our commitment to live within our means.
- Please honor your commitment as soon as possible
- Over the years, we've seen a growing commitment to
- Combines with a deep love and knowledge of our history and a commitment both public and professional to the role
- As an individual who has demonstrated uncommon commitment, we are sure you will want to
- I hope you will join me and the thousands of others who have made the commitment to support this vital work all around the world
- Successfully got them to adopt a stronger commitment to
- Commitment springs from a moving personal experience of
- Making the commitment to hold that dream in place
- The government just didn't honor its commitment
- When you become a member you are showing your commitment to one of the greatest of all
- Your commitment to this life-changing work
- We see this as a vital and ongoing commitment
- You may not be able to help us financially but maybe you can make another form of commitment such as your services, storage space, use of meeting space, etc.
- Your commitment keeps the future of the hospital as bright as the past
- With our widely recognized commitment to caring
- Our commitment alone isn't enough

- Takes a special kind of commitment
- We need your commitment as soon as possible
- Your commitment will make a definite difference
- Seeing avenues to express concern and commitment
- The kind of commitment our donors and partners expect from us
- This is a major commitment and it needs major support
- My commitment is stronger than ever

Commitment: pledge, covenant, promise, vow, assurance, obligation, undertaking, responsibility, guarantee, decision, choice, conclusion, stand, determination, loyalty, committal
See also: GIFT, DONATION, HELP, OBLIGATION, PLEDGE, PROMISE, SUPPORT

COMMON

- In an ever changing world, they become a common ground for all of us
- To establish some common sense rules about
- The most basic common decency would dictate
- It's just common sense, isn't it
- We all have so many things in common
- We stand together on common ground
- Share something in common more important than all the problems
- With an eye to the common good
- Helping to further our common cause
- Determine our common goals

COMMUNICATE

- The ability, opportunity and desire to communicate all this
- Trying so hard to communicate their needs
- It is so important to help with communication between
- Communication is the key to all
- Communicating the issues and the needs to you is a very important part of my job
- Keeping the lines of communication open at all times

See also: CONTACT, REACH, SPEAK, TELL, VOICE

COMMUNITY

- We want to become one of your first new friends in this community
- How would you like to give your friends and your community a gift they would really appreciate
- It is important to all our community that we share our bounty with those people who live on the margins of our society
- Working hand in hand with local community leaders
- We've been working together to make our community safe, healthy and economically strong.
- We've fought for funding to help build our community
- Working to make this a better community for you and your family
- What happens to this bit of land affects everyone in the community
- Secured money to help purchase the property for future community development

- Selling our community as a uniquely livable, safe, people place
- What business in the downtown needs above all is more people living in the downtown community
- Something that is reflective of our community
- It's so encouraging to see how the lives of the whole community have improved
- Everywhere there are fledgling community movements
- Your generosity helps support kids in your community
- Keep your community going this winter
- We started it to show that no one is alone in this community
- Your donations stay in the community where you live and love
- Let's face it, your community needs your help more than ever
- Survival skills they'll need in the community
- Ability to cope successfully in the community offers the best promise for public safety and security
- Ability to rejoin the community
- Please send a gift now to help others in our community who are less fortunate
- To secure a future of local and indigenous communities
- What I'm trying to say is that, as long as you are a member of our community, our organization is important to you
- Your financial support directly benefits people in our community
- Working with people and businesses to improve the economic and social conditions of our community
- We've been part of this community for many years
- We've worked together and supported one another in our community
- Community groups like ours are stepping in, doing what must done
- But we've come to realize that it's not enough to just work at the community level
- A non-profit group committed to working with the community to end hunger and improve access to
- Decisions by people who know little of the realities in these communities
- The potential to reach out to our scattered communities
- As well as provide essential services in many communities
- To help communities gain access to the basic necessities of life
- Your gift will enable us to keep working with important community organizations such as
- An important part of our work is in community programs and public relations
- No community is immune from the tragedy of
- A vital part of the community, carrying the spirit of compassion far beyond our doors
- We need your contribution to the community
- The well-bring of the whole community is paramount
- Work with local people and groups to achieve changes in their communities
- Because of you, they are creating stronger communities
- Communities in which their children can live full and satisfying lives
- Most important, you'll make a difference to your community
- Help communities respond locally to
- Uprooted from their communities

- Building a model for safer communities
- A higher degree of flexibility and sensitivity to the needs of the community
- Keeping our community a vital, wonderful place to live, work and raise a family
- For all those who want to live and work in a safe, prosperous community
- What is a community
- Our diverse communities are really interdependent
- Strong communities with influence over local decisions
- Communities give a city strength and stability
- What would our community be like without it
- Won't you join other leaders in our community
- All part of our community
- This community is strongly challenged
- With your active support in your community
- With our continued hard work, our community will enjoy
- Supporting their own community-based initiatives
- Communities actively participating in creating solutions to the problems that affect them
- Recreating communities of mutual support and reciprocity
- Reinventing community
- Our goal is to nurture communities and the economies sustaining them
- Equipping them with the skills to rebuild their former communities
- Injecting new life and energy into communities

Community: neighborhood, district, town, city, metropolis, village, society, public, citizenry, population, fellowship, association, congregation, confederacy, organization, commonalty
See also: COUNTRY, FELLOWSHIP, GROUP, HOME, NATION, NEIGHBORHOOD, PARTNERSHIP, SOCIETY

COMPANIONSHIP
- Who need some help and companionship along the way
- A joyous companionship accomplishing so much
- Your gift is a form of companionship
- A little companionship to lighten a lonely day

See also: FELLOWSHIP, FRIENDSHIP

COMPANY
- You and your company could double your donation
- You may still be eligible through a parent company or an affiliate
- A way to get your whole company involved
- Invite you to keep us company on this inspiring journey

See also: CORPORATE, ORGANIZATION

COMPASSION
- Stand squarely for compassion
- So much misery could be prevented just by simple acts of compassion and responsibility
- When simple compassion moves us to act

- Please have some compassion on these suffering people
- I'm appealing directly to your sense of compassion
- Compassion never flags, patience never wears out.
- Your compassion is deeply appreciated
- Our single most precious commodity is your compassion

Compassion: pity, tenderness, love, gentleness, mercy, kindness, sympathy, consolation, concern, kindliness, tender-heartedness, solace, fellow feeling, understanding, tolerance, humanity, goodness, patience, mildness, ruth, forbearance, long-suffering, indulgence, heart, warm-heartedness, warmth, clemency, benevolence, goodness, consideration

See also: **CARE, CONCERN, KINDNESS, LOVE**

COMPASSIONATE
- Defining us as a civilized, compassionate nation
- Whatever the need, we extend compassionate, healing arms
- I know you have a deeply compassionate heart
- Finding a more compassionate way to make these changes

See also: **CARING, COMFORT, CONCERN, LOVE**

COMPENSATION
- So admire people who give of themselves, devoting their time and effort, without compensation
- The best compensation is the smile on their faces
- Though we can never provide true compensation for the losses they have suffered
- How else are they going to get compensation

See also: **PAYOFF, REWARD**

COMPLACENCY
- We mustn't allow ourselves to get lulled into complacency
- We mustn't allow a deadly complacency to set in
- Complacency is our worst enemy
- Victims of blind complacency

See also: **APATHY, INDIFFERENCE, LIP SERVICE**

COMPROMISE
- Sometimes compromise is valuable
- No compromise is possible here
- Joining in an honorable compromise

See also: **AGREE, CROSSROADS**

CONCENTRATE
- Not to concentrate so much on what had been lost but rather to build on what remained of
- An area we can really concentrate upon
- Beware of concentrating too many powers in one place
- Concentrating all our effort on resolving this situation
- Simply improving powers of concentration can help so much in

See also: **ATTENTION, FOCUS**

CONCEPT
- I believe so strongly in this concept that
- We need to develop a totally different concept to
- This is a glorious new concept that must be developed
- I know you'll be as excited about this new concept as I am
- Once people grasp the concept, they flock to support it
- An introduction to the current concepts, practices and procedures of
- Concepts that clarify and support
- Allowing these concepts to be readily implemented
- A non-negotiable concept
- Helping to understand the basic concepts and principles of human relations

See also: **CAMPAIGN, IDEA, THOUGHT, TOPIC**

CONCERN
- True concern dictates that
- Translate your concern into action
- Responding quickly to national and international concerns
- I must turn to you, a concerned citizen, for help
- Our dominant concern is proper care of the human habitat
- I know you share my concern about
- Have what it takes to make your concerns heard
- It's a critical concern for all caring citizens
- Such concerns have to be swiftly addressed
- During this process, several key areas of concern become apparent
- Really attempted to meet that concern
- Many share the common concern of wanting to know how we spend your contributions each year
- This concern has been growing rapidly
- We believe concerned people like you will prove otherwise
- This years has brought so many additional concerns for
- It's concerned individuals like you who will make the real difference

Concern: worry, regard, care, thought, consideration, attention, caution, pain, vigilance, alertness, prudence, awareness, thought, mindfulness, scrupulousness, anxiety, exactness, precision, duty, responsibility, distress, hurt, bother

See also: **ATTENTION, AWARENESS, CARE, COMPASSION, INVOLVEMENT**

CONDEMNATION
- In spite of worldwide condemnation
- So that rising condemnation can no longer be ignored
- Condemnation lies in the eyes of suffering innocents
- Only the fiercest condemnation will prevent this from continuing
- Add your voice to the growing chorus of condemnation

See also: **BLAME, FINGER, GUILT, REGRET, SORRY**

CONDITIONS

- One of the most misunderstood of conditions
- Such conditions are simply unacceptable to any decent society
- Contend with daily conditions that test their strength, courage and faith in themselves
- For every person released, others remain in deplorable conditions
- Only by addressing the conditions that breed crime can
- Excellent progress under very difficult conditions
- Conditions worsened before our very eyes
- Conditions like these are utterly intolerable
- Even assessing these conditions is difficult
- Helped alleviate some of the worst working conditions in human history
- Able to withstand the worst possible working conditions
- To demystify these apparently incurable conditions
- That will change conditions for the better

Condition: state, phase, circumstance, situation, plight, dilemma, quandary, fix, state of affairs, predicament

See also: ATMOSPHERE, CIRCUMSTANCES, SURROUND

CONFIDENCE

- I was determined to justify their confidence in me
- Help a great bunch of kids grow up with strength and confidence
- Pleased to have your confidence and support
- I can tell you with confidence that your support is crucial
- I deeply appreciate your vote of confidence in us
- It is especially gratifying to know that we've earned you confidence
- We are working hard to gain your confidence in our ability to carry out our mission

See also: BELIEF, FAITH, POWER, STRENGTH, TRUST

CONFIDENT

- Watching them become more confident by the day
- We are confident that, together, we will find a cure
- I am confident that we can achieve this

See also: BRAVE, COURAGE

CONFLICT

- Have you felt that no one understands the conflict you're facing
- To offer the best alternatives to resolve global conflict
- Conflict is not the answer
- Learning as soon as possible to resolve conflict
- I know you receive so much conflicting information about this issue
- The best conflict handling style

See also: BATTLE, FIGHT, STRUGGLE, WAR

CONFUSE

- Stumbling confused amidst the traffic on a busy road

- Growing more confused every day
- Nobody could have been more confused than I was when I first ran into this situation
- We must never get our priorities confused

See also: CHAOS, DISORDER

CONGRATULATIONS
- Send your congratulations today by making out a cheque
- Congratulations on joining our team
- Heartiest congratulations are in order for
- Basking in well-deserved congratulations for such an outstanding achievement

See also: SECTION FIVE

CONNECT
- Get connected
- It all comes down to how well you connect
- We'll do our best to connect you with
- Services must connect with the people who really need them

See also: JOIN, LINK, PARTNER, TOGETHER

CONNECTION
- A lifelong connection to
- Foster a powerful connection between all people who
- When you send your gift, you make a strong connection with
- A deeper level of connection with all family members
- Each new connection has to be carefully developed and nurtured
- The best connection is a lasting connection

See also: COMMUNITY, LINK, PARTNERSHIP, RELATIONSHIP

CONSEQUENCES
- Consider the consequences
- The consequences of not acting are enormous
- Help avert the terrible consequences certain to arrive

See also: FRUITION, OUTCOME, RESULTS

CONSERVATION
- Assisting us to support educational and heritage conservation work
- With just a little more help, we'll be able to save a great deal more
- Asking your help in this huge conservation effort
- Conservation means just that – to conserve
- Conservation of scarce resources is even more important

See also: GUARD, PRESERVATION, PROTECTION, SAVE

CONSIDER
- Just consider how many good things have already happened
- Please take a moment to consider others not so fortunate as
- With so much to consider already

- Please consider making a contribution that truly has the power to change the situation
- Consider this before all else
- I invite your careful consideration of the enclosed
- I ask you to consider one of the many choices
- Here's something else to consider

See also: CHOOSE, DECIDE, SELECT, THINK

CONSULTATION
- Provide expert consultation services to
- After consultation with several colleagues
- This is our consultation with you
- The consultation process can be streamlined and improved

See also: ADVICE, HELP, MEET, WISDOM

CONTACT
- Enables you to contact us from anywhere in the world
- Contact your councillor and the mayor today
- Human contact works the greatest good
- Very few charities have the time or range of contacts for a truly effective
- The unique ability to be in contact with the entire
- Making meaningful contact every day

See also: CALL, INFORM, MEET, REACH, PARTNER

CONTINUE
- It's only with your help that we can continue our work
- We really need you to continue your support
- Making sure we can continue on this promising path to success

CONTRIBUTE
- Please contribute as generously as you can today.
- Please contribute this amount or whatever you possibly can
- But whatever you contribute, please do so as quickly as you can
- Whatever you want to contribute
- Need whatever you feel comfortable contributing
- It's hard to find individuals or groups who will contribute the entire cost
- Contribute a birthday, memorial or graduation gift to celebrate the personal milestone in the name of a special loved one
- You'll be able to contribute your time, energy, experience and skills toward helping
- It's the easiest way to contribute
- You contribute so much more than money when you donate
- However you contribute to our campaign
- Program established to encourage companies and individuals to contribute to funds for

See also: GIVE, DONATE

CONTRIBUTION

- I hope you will make a generous contribution toward
- Your contribution will let us increase the basic level of support
- Has already made a major contribution to
- Please mail in your contribution today
- I want to assure you that your contribution will support programs that really make a difference in the lives of
- So your contribution makes a big difference to them too
- I hope you'll consider our request and make contribution, but if you can't, I hope you'll still be involved
- Your contribution helps us fund the following programs
- Making a significant contribution to improving the future
- If you can make a contribution of $__ or more, you'll automatically receive a subscription to
- Please return this slip with your contribution in the enclosed envelope
- Despite the fact that it was too late for him, he sent a contribution with his note – and apologized that it wasn't more
- Your financial contribution of $__ or whatever you can afford helps ensure the continuation of success stories like this one
- Your contribution will go a long way toward enabling us to give as many children a
- Your contribution will enable us to
- I hope you'll consider our request and make a contribution
- If you can't make a contribution, I hope you will still be involved
- With your contribution of $__ or more, you will receive
- Will you make a contribution of $__ or as much as $__ or more if possible to help fund more
- At the same time, I urge you to make a tax-creditable contribution to support our ongoing activities
- Contribution has recently taken the form of
- As generous a contribution as you can manage
- Please send your contribution today
- We hope you'll make your contribution as soon as possible
- Your generous contribution does so much to help
- Please send your contribution right away
- Our gratitude for your very generous contribution
- Send it with your contribution to help us be better informed
- Peace of mind, knowing that, through your contribution, you are helping those most gravely at risk
- Our way of being accountable for the contributions you make
- Your contribution will allow this successful work to continue
- Not a dime of your contribution will be wasted
- Your valuable contribution is very deeply appreciated
- Delighted if you prefer to make a direct contribution instead
- Your contribution directly enables our dedicated workers
- Your contribution is critical to our success
- We're entirely dependent upon contributions from members and friends

- Working to recruit the major financial contributions needed to meet our ambitious goals
- We can assure our donors that their contributions are carefully and effectively used to
- And we can only do it through the continued contributions of caring people like you
- Your contributions can join together to meet this entire need
- It is provided for by voluntary contributions from people in our community

See also: AMOUNT, CHECK, DONATION, EFFORT, FUNDS, GIFT, MONEY, VOLUNTEER, WORK

CONTRIBUTOR

- The generosity of private contributors has enabled us to
- I know you'll want to be a contributor
- As a loyal contributor, I know you feel strongly in your heart that
- Enjoy the prestige of becoming a leading contributor

See also: DONOR, SUPPORTER

CONTROL

- There are so many things in life we cannot control
- We cannot control where we are born
- Help us get in there before the situation spins utterly out of control
- One of the ways you help control the direction is by giving
- Sooner or later we'll have to take control of this situation
- Strong voices calling for stronger controls

CONTROVERSY

- We never shy from controversy
- How best to help has turned into a raging controversy
- I invite your opinion on this controversy
- The idea has certainly stirred up a lively controversy

See also: BATTLE, CONFLICT, FIGHT, STRUGGLE

CONVENIENCE

- Enclosed is a return envelope for your convenience
- Think of the convenience of giving this way
- For your convenience, I've included a list of
- We can't wait for the convenience of
- More of our donors are choosing this convenient way of supporting
- See for yourself how convenient it is
- Giving early is also a very convenient way of

See also: COMFORT, EASE, EASY, SIMPLE

CONVINCE

- You probably don't need any more convincing
- But I'm sure you are already thoroughly convinced of the merit of
- If you're still not convinced, read the enclosed note from

- I'm absolutely convinced that, with your help, we'll be able to lick this stubborn problem
- The task of convincing a presently indifferent public
- The united force of our conviction will make them sit up and take notice for once

See also: PERSUADE

COOPERANTS

- The second reason is our cooperants
- Proud of cooperants like you
- Our cooperants always come through in the crunch
- No organization could have finer cooperants than ours

See also: CLIENT, DONOR, SUPPORTER

COOPERATION

- Cooperation is the best answer to the conflict
- With the cooperation of everyone concerned, we can
- Bring about this excellent cooperation as soon as possible
- Better cooperation between all parties is certainly one good answer
- Through cooperation, so much more can be achieved

See also: COLLABORATION, PARTNERSHIP, TEAMWORK

COPE

- Too exhausted to cope any more, she is at her wit's end
- We must help them cope
- Your donation is crucial if we're to cope at all with
- The best possible coping mechanism of
- Help those who wonder how they're going to cope with one more disaster
- Learning effective coping skills that will stay with them for life
- Quickly picking up new methods of coping

See also: MANAGE, STRUGGLE

CORPORATE

- Exploring new standards and methods for measuring and encouraging corporate support for the community
- Corporate giving has become one of our mainstays
- So that the entire staff can feel good about corporate giving and participate in the fundraising
- Our corporate donors are our main pillars of support

See also: BUSINESS, COMPANY, ECONOMIC, ENTERPRISE

COST

- As you can imagine, the cost of providing these services is high
- No cost is too high if it saves one life
- What does all this cost
- The cost to those who must bear the brunt is far too great
- Of course, the entire cost of these items far exceeded the total of our annual fund
- The cost of ignoring this problem is disastrous

- For an overall cost of merely
- Most people can't afford to pay the full cost
- It costs as little as $__ to send one child to camp
- It doesn't cost much to help
- The cost is incalculable
- If you could just give us some help with the costs
- It costs us all so dearly
- Help us meet the rising costs of
- It really costs so little to help significantly
- Created by the spiralling costs of
- The financial and emotional costs are enormous
- Help bring skyrocketing costs under control
- Rejected the government's approach of cutting costs for essential health care services
- Working instead to promote less costly community care
- We are working hard to reduce the immediate costs of providing
- It's also important to note that our administrative costs are less than
- In danger of being totally crushed under the increasing costs being foisted upon us
- Tremendous emotional and financial costs
- Must cope with soaring health care costs
- Keep costs down through donated time, space, products and services

Cost: price, worth, value, expenditure, outlay, payment, charge, rate, penalty, sacrifice, demand, valuation
See also: CHARGE, EXPENSE, PRICE, FUND, PRICE, RESOURCE, VALUE, WORTH

COUNSELLING
- Offers counselling on numerous issues to help people solve their own problems
- We can give them food, information, and counselling now, and a chance to have a job and a home later
- A free, confidential counselling service to turn to anytime, day or night
- Supporting and developing core counselling skills

See also: ADVICE, GUIDANCE, WISDOM

COUNSELLORS
- Our counsellors offer warmth, comfort and practical advice in a world that so often appears uncaring and riddled with fear
- A wise, experienced counsellor can make a real change
- Please help us hire and train more badly needed counsellors

COUNT
- The people in need are counting on you to
- I know I can count on you to
- I can't even count the number of times over all these years
- It's not what we have done, but what we will do in the days, weeks and months ahead that will count

- The first thing we must count is the terrible cost of doing nothing
- I'm sure you or someone close has counted on us at some time or other
- Now we're counting on you
- Urgent! I'm counting on you to help so that we can
- Counting on your contribution
- Consider those with very few blessings to count

Count: enumerate, list, tell, number, name, talk, add up, total, include, reckon, take into account, consider, regard, esteem, judge, look upon, matter, have worth, amount, have clout, depend upon, lean on, rely on, reckon on, figure on, trust, believe in, calculate on, interest, weigh
See also: DEPEND, RELY, TRUST

COUNTRY

- We can't let our country down
- The first concern of any country is the shelter and protection of its citizens
- A way for you to actually be part of life in a developing country
- This is a call to stand up for your country
- Sharing the good fortune we are born to in this country

See also: COMMUNITY, NATION, SOCIETY

COURAGE

- Showed staggering courage in spite of her own fears and sense of loss
- I've been humbled by the courage of so many who carry on bravely despite their pain
- The faith and courage to carry on after all they've been through
- Individuals with courage and conviction to overcome tremendous hardships
- Courage isn't always obvious
- The greatest courage is often the unseen kind
- Their courage is an inspiration to us all
- Confronted her own life with patience, courage and cheerfulness

Courage: valor, bravery, heroism, stout-heartedness, boldness, gallantry, audacity, fearlessness, dauntlessness, self-assurance, intrepidness, staunchness, steadfastness, heart, hardiness, mettle, backbone, spirit
See also: BACKBONE, BRAVE, CONFIDENT, HERO

CRACK

- Rescuing those who have already cracked under the strain
- Will soon crack under this enormous burden
- So no one else falls through the cracks
- Help us crack this stubborn problem
- I'm afraid the cracks are beginning to widen
- The cracks in the system were soon apparent

See also: FAIL, FAILURE, GAP, NEED,

CREATE

- We must nurture the capacity to create
- We created thousands of jobs

- You are helping to create something worth fighting for
- Your gift helps to create a whole new life
- Out of this disaster, help us create something beautiful

Create: beget, engender, invent, originate, make, produce, fashion, fabricate, design, devise, conceive, develop, construct, build, erect, shape, mould, forge, imagine, dream up, envision, establish, initiate, inaugurate, arrange, start, launch

CREDIBILITY

- Far more important is the credibility this gives
- Stretch their credibility with absurd claims
- The credibility and exposure have allowed us to
- The support of caring people like you adds enormous credibility to

See also: BELIEF, CONFIDENCE, CREDIT, TRUST

CREDIT

- We must give credit where credit is due
- The credit goes to you for responding so promptly and so generously
- Credited with pulling the situation out of the fire
- People like you really deserve all the credit
- Our credit is rapidly running out

CRIME

- Striking at the roots of crime is more productive than harsher prison terms
- Nipping crime in the bud
- It's a crime what is happening to these deserving people
- Indifference to suffering is the worst of crimes
- Social unrest, crime and violence are also increasing
- It's a crime, what happens to some through no fault of their own

Crime: transgression, wrong, harm, violation, offense, misdeed, outrage, disgrace, abomination, scandal, shame, felony, law-breaking

See also: ABUSE, BLOOD, HURT, OUTRAGE, SHAME

CRISIS

- In a crisis, when moments count, we're able to
- Now that crisis is rushing upon us, we need your help more than ever
- Because of reduced fundraising revenue and increased expenses, we were faced with a financial crisis
- Once again we must rush in to deal with overwhelming crisis
- This crisis indicates that we must educate as many as we can to be aware of
- If it weren't for groups like these and the support of people willing to help, many lives would have been lost during this crisis
- The urgent need for help in a crisis situation
- Precipitated a new crisis
- Able to deal swiftly and competently with crises
- Just not prepared to weather this financial crisis

Crisis: emergency, point of no return, turning point, extremity, disaster, pass, climax, moment of truth, catastrophe, zero hour, deadlock, crunch, trouble, difficulty, mess,

muddle, scrape, imbroglio, impasse, strait, standstill, calamity, exigency, pinch, tragedy
See also: CATASTROPHE, DISASTER, EMERGENCY, MESS

CRITERIA
- Calculated according to the strictest criteria
- Making sure they meet the very highest criteria
- Changes in criteria have vastly improved standards
- No-holds-barred criteria allow for no compromise in quality
- Changing the criteria by which they are judged

See also: MEASURE, STANDARD

CROSSROADS
- Now, at this critical crossroads in your life, we need your generosity and your support more than ever
- A true crossroads of the world
- We have come to a crossroads and must carefully choose the right path
- Helping those who stand at a vital crossroads in their existence
- As they stand at this crossroads, they urgently need your help

See also: CHOICE, DECISION, DIRECTION, OPTION

CRUEL
- It's not only unnecessary, it's cruel
- Cruel circumstance holds them in its grip
- You can help extricate them from this cruel dilemma

CRUELTY
- It's hard to look such cruelty in the face
- Deliberate cruelty to animals is an ugly reality
- Cruelty in any form is intolerable
- The cruelty of having choose which of your children gets to survive
- Violence and cruelty are a fact of life in any large city
- How can we be party to the cruelty of leaving these desperate people without help of any kind

See also: ABUSE, AGONY, PAIN, SUFFERING, TORMENT, TORTURE

CRUNCH
- Now that we're down to the crunch, you've just got to help
- When it comes to the crunch, we rely on you
- You always help us out in a crunch

See also: CRISIS, EMERGENCY, SQUEEZE

CRY
- Must hear those who cry out to us
- Crying out to us for help and comfort
- Stop the cries of suffering people
- If only you could hear their pitiful cries for help

- Sometimes we just want to cry out

See also: **APPEAL, BEG, CALL, REACH, SHOUT, VOICE**

CULTURE

- If we don't do better, we may not be able to speak of a distinctive culture before long
- Our culture is a rich and unique
- Doing everything possible to protect this rare and unusual culture
- Radically changing how this is viewed in the culture
- Believe in its relevance to our culture
- Considered crucial to cultural survival
- Possess traditional knowledge of their culture
- Preserving something that has been special to so many cultures
- The cultural dimensions will highlight
- A culture closely examined
- Learning how to promote a training culture

See also: **ART, COLLECTION, EDUCATION**

CURE

- Then there's the biggest dream of all – that of a cure
- Give priceless hope while we tackle the challenge of finding a cure
- There is no miracle cure for this troubling condition
- With your help, we can find cures and better treatments for
- But there's no cure yet
- They need your help – and they need a cure.
- So many people desperately need your help to find a cure for their affliction
- We have a mission – to find a cure
- Wouldn't you want your own dear ones to have a cure should they be struck down
- Your gift will truly help bring us closer to a cure
- Told me I could personally help find a cure
- How can we stop when our ultimate goal is the cure
- Future potential to eventually secure a cure
- Remains relentless in its search for a cure
- Working together, we will find a cure
- And most of all, offered hope for what they need most – a cure
- A cure, the only way to have a normal life again
- We need a cure – and we need your help
- We must all renew our efforts to find the cure
- Dedicated to finding a cure for
- We don't know the cause and still don't have the cure
- Expand our search for a cure
- Hope that vital research will find a cure
- They urgently need your renewed support to help find a cure
- All across the country, brave people are waiting for the answer, the cure that will release them from the suffering
- I wish I could tell you that we know how to cure every one of the many forms of

this disease
- This is something we must change if we are to find a cure in the foreseeable future
- Looking for effective treatments and a cure for this killer disease
- There is a cure, we just have to find it
- We depend on you to help us find the cure
- The fact is, most of these diseases cannot be cured and many are fatal
- It's hard to wait patiently while somebody looks for a cure
- We can't find the cause, we don't know the cure
- Await your help in finding a cure that will finally end the disruption, unpredictability, stigma – and most of all, the pain.

Cure: remedy, curative, relief, corrective, correction, restorative, antidote, healing, therapy. recovery, answer, reparation, medication, preventative
See also: ADVANCE, BREAKTHROUGH, LEAP, RELIEF, SOLUTION

CURTAIL
- Brutally curtailed by lack of funds
- Far from curtailing our activities, we are going to expand them
- Shortages have seriously curtailed our efforts and moved us to ask for an emergency donation to

CUT
- Believe that to control the deficit they must cut back on social services essential to all citizens
- And now we've even had to make cuts in some vitally needed services
- Can't stand any more cuts without serious damage to our future
- Cuts we are already struggling so hard to absorb
- We've already absorbed funding cuts in all areas of
- You're worried about all the drastic cuts to
- They're making these cuts for one reason and one reason only
- And that means more and deeper cuts
- Dumping these cuts on the most vulnerable people
- Irresponsible cuts mean universal suffering for
- Tell them to stop their cuts and keep their promises
- Massive cuts to social programs are creating personal disaster for this community
- Cuts to programs will affect all poor people – young and old alike
- Cuts which affect all of us, but which also deeply affect the quality of life of those most in need
- You have a chance, before these cuts take effect, to raise your voice
- Rather than trying to better the lives of poor people, the government is bringing in even more ruthless cuts
- At a time when our country is looking to cut back its aid to developing countries, we need you now more than ever
- We're expecting much deeper cuts to our grants
- It's quite frightening to think how further cuts in funding could affect the very programs and services you enjoy so much
- Cuts to social assistance are creating a growing number of people in our city who

are desperate and who have no resources
- The recently announced cuts to so many social services have put a staggering load on us
- Deep cuts to social programs will hurt us all
- Major cuts which are going to affect every segment of our society
- But given the recent provincial cuts, it is becoming much more difficult
- It's quite frightening to think of how further cuts in funding could affect the very programs
- Forcing these deep cuts on the most at-risk people isn't necessary
  – it's cruel
- Promised that any cuts would respect the special role of
- These cuts are probably the worst crisis we have ever had to face
- We are concerned with our ability to absorb any more cuts
- Irresponsible cuts mean unnecessary suffering for
- Refuse to see it mangled out of recognition by disastrous budget cuts
- This is the unkindest cut of all

Cut: slash, gouge, sever, slice, dismember, shorten, abridge, saw, chop, curtail, retrench, cold-shoulder, mutilate, mangle, abbreviate, eliminate, reduce, diminish, cut down on, ease up, halt, stop, switch off, desist, discontinue, cease, interrupt, disown, reduction, slowdown, deletion, omission, abatement, excision, trim, lop off, carve away, restrict

See also: AXE, CURTAIL, DOWNSIZE, REDUCE, SLASH

CUTBACKS
- And the cutbacks are already happening
- It is especially difficult in light of recent cutbacks to funding for these irreplaceable programs
- But a recent program of cutbacks in social spending imposed by
- These cutbacks had drastic consequences
- Right now, with current government cutbacks, and the threat of more on the way
- Government cutbacks are always threatening to reduce the number of people we can help and now it's more precarious than ever
- With cutbacks and a growing load of people to help, we may be forced to turn away people like
- With your help, we can carry on despite government cutbacks

CYCLE
- Yes, you can help break this vicious cycle
- Help them escape the bottom of the cycle
- The cycle will just continue unless you step in now
- The cycle of nature has been badly disrupted

DAGGER
- Have that cruel dagger hanging over his head
- A sight that pitiful is a dagger to the heart
- Keen and deadly as the blade of a dagger

DAMAGE
- Take action before any more damage is done
- Your much-needed gift will help prevent damage to delicate environments
- I know you are as appalled at this damage as I am
- Yes, with your help, we can repair the damage
- Very swift action is required for damage control

See also: ABUSE, HURT

DANGER
- Increasing personal danger because of these assaults
- With danger swirling all around her
- By far the most profound danger facing millions
- We've also seen shocking growth in the dangers they face
- Reckless , dangerous plans have caused
- Some of the greatest dangers are things we take for granted
- Very few things are more dangerous than this
- Treading a very dangerous path

See also: AMBUSH, JEOPARDY, RISK, THREAT

DARKEST
- In my darkest hour, your words brought hope
- The darkest time, just before the dawn
- The darkest scenario would be
- Help bring light and comfort into the darkest corners

DAUGHTER
- Her loving daughter is upfront about what the program means to her mother
- So that daughters will have a better chance than their mothers had
- A daughter any parent could be proud of
- Daughters need to have equal treatment
- Daughters often bear the brunt of caregiving for their elderly parents

See also: CHILD, FAMILY, GIRLS, WOMEN

DAY
- Eventually, that happy day will come
- Every minute of every day is precious
- Start your day with
- Everywhere, every day, we work to
- Every day counts to those in pain
- In the momentous days leading up to
- The days ahead will be some of the most challenging
- So many wonderful happenings sprinkle our days
- Just can't wait for the day when
- Getting through, one day at a time
- You really made my day

See also: MOMENT, TIME

DEADLINE

- We're desperate to meet this deadline
- Unless we meet this deadline, thousands will suffer
- Deadline time is rapidly approaching
- If this deadline is not met, we won't get another chance
- Please help us meet this unalterable deadline
- Because of this onrushing budgetary deadline, your gifts are needed within the next three weeks
- Often, we are working to deadlines of weeks, days or even hours
- Could you please send your gift before the deadline

See also: **BOUNDARY, LIMIT**

DEAF

- Can no longer turn a deaf ear
- How can we remain deaf to their cries for help
- Deaf to the strongest appeal for change

See also: **APATHY, COMPLACENCY, INDIFFERENCE**

DEAL

- A good deal, and a good deal more
- Here's the deal
- Have I got a deal for you
- The straight deal is this
- To help those who have got a raw deal in life
- We'd sure like you in on the deal

See also: **BARGAIN, BUSINESS, COLLABORATION**

DEAR

- Maybe even someone very dear to you or to me
- Protect principles dearer than life itself
- A cause very dear to all our hearts
- The price of freedom is often very dear
- Nothing could be dearer than
- Your participation is very dear to us
- Ignoring this threat will cost us dear

DEATH

- Death stalks them, day and night
- It's so hard to come to terms with the death of even one
- So many of those deaths could have been prevented if only
- Just a little aid and comfort can sometimes mean the difference between life and death
- Escalating deaths resulting from these serious ailments
- Resulting in millions of needless deaths annually
- Designed to reduce the number of needless deaths from

See also: **END, LOSE, SICK**

DEBATE

- I'm sure you'll be mightily interested in the debate about
- When people are dying, we don't have time to debate
- We're for debate and against silence
- Rife with often bitter debate
- Determined to be leaders in this crucial debate
- We face an enormous debate about
- To focus debate on developing solutions to
- One of the most divisive debates ripping apart our society
- The time for planning and debate has ended

DECIDE

- Yours to keep whatever you decide
- We must decide quickly or else face the prospect of
- Faced with such a choice, could you decide
- Someone who may decide to join us in our important work

See also: CHOOSE, CONSIDER, SELECT

DECISION

- Your recent decision to join our family of donors shows that you care about people
- Open the door to public participation in the decision-making process
- This decision was very controversial
- Making many routine decisions regularly
- The shocking decision jerked me right out of my chair
- Make the right decision now
- This decision might have the most rewarding and important consequences for the rest of your life
- Helping our donors narrow their decision making
- Whenever we find ourselves hesitating over a decision
- They become unable to make decisions as before
- The decision you make will affect the lives of thousands
- Learning to make better decisions
- I look forward to your decision about

Decision: determination, resolution, resolve, commitment, conclusion, judgement, verdict, decree, purpose, tenacity, persistence, ruling, order, command, edict, evaluation, consideration, settlement, making up one's mind, decisiveness, spirit, will-power, firmness

See also: CALL, CHOICE, OPTION

DEDICATED

- Dedicated to getting results
- No one could be more dedicated than
- Our dedicated staff and volunteers have been working day and night

DEDICATION

- To honor the long time dedication of

- Honoring their dedication with a large donation
- Reach someone who shares your dedication to long-term solutions for the many difficult problems
- Her constancy, her devotion to her tasks, her sunny nature, all of which set an example of dedication which has inspired us all to become better people
- Persistent dedication to the cause coupled with great common sense and a penetrating wit
- This selfless dedication has helped so very much to
- Could only have been accomplished with incredible dedication
- Dedication isn't enough
- If all it took was dedication, our organization could run for the next hundred years
- Unfortunately, dedication doesn't pay the bills
- Tireless courage and dedication only work if they are backed up by adequate resources

Dedication: devotion, fidelity, faithfulness, allegiance, adherence, surrender, fealty, consecration, commitment, loyalty
See also: DETERMINATION, FAITH, LOYALTY

DEED
- Aggressive support in word and deed
- Hurry before the deed is done
- By our deeds shall we be known
- Salute people who perform good deeds with little publicity or fanfare
- Such kind, useful deeds are within reach of everyone

See also: ACTION, EVENT

DEFEAT
- Show that we will not accept defeat
- In the end, they defeated the biggest enemy of all
- With your help, we can turn this defeat into a shining victory
- Helping them rebound from this cruel defeat

See also: BEAT, LOSE, OVERCOME

DEFENCE
- You join thousands of others roused in fierce defence of our
- The best defence is an immediate offence
- Vigorously leaping to the defence of
- You are part of our defence plan

See also: GUARD, PROTECTION, WALL

DEFEND
- Feel strongly we must defend
- We must defend our interests against
- It's up us to defend them
- Close ranks with us in defending
- It's our turn to defend these noble traditions

See also: **GUARD, PROTECT, SAVE**

DEFENDER
- Authorities were harassing defenders even as
- You join thousands of other staunch defenders of
- Giving the best support we can to these courageous defenders

See also: **ADVOCATE, CHAMPION, HERO. SPONSOR**

DEFIANCE
- Parade their defiance and flaunt their disregard for
- Made this progress in defiance of grave difficulties, including strong opposition from
- Standing tall in proud defiance
- Gross defiance of the rules has brought everything to the brink of disaster

DEFICIENCY
- We've lived with failures and deficiencies of the system
- To make up these deficiencies, we ask for your donation
- Given so many deficiencies, the advances are all the more admirable
- The biggest deficiencies must be addressed at once

See also: **CRACK, DISABILITY, HANDICAP, GAP, NEED**

DEFICIT
- A modest user fee would wipe out the deficit
- Struggling to reduce the deficit
- Simply can no longer sustain a deficit position
- So that we don't fall into a deficit position

See also: **CRUNCH, CUTBACK, LOSS, REDUCTION**

DEGRADATION
- So they won't have to suffer the pain and degradation so many have suffered in the past
- Mocked and violated through physical and mental degradation
- Racing to prevent further degradation of this fragile environment
- The threat of degradation to the system is very real

See also: **CONDEMNATION, DESPAIR, LOSS**

DELAY
- We know how much misery each delay costs
- Attack this problem without delay
- Mailing your donation now will give us a reasonable margin in case of unforseen delays
- The least delay could prove fatal
- A delay at this late date would be disastrous
- It is crucial that we be able to act with a minimum of delay

See also: **BEHIND, LATE**

DELIGHT
- I wish you could see the delight on their faces
- The unending delight of helping
- I'm delighted to be able to tell you that
- Your contribution is a source of such delight

See also: HAPPINESS, JOY, PLEASURE

DELIVER
- You can help to deliver
- Our charge and sole focus is to deliver skills, information, techniques and ideas that will help
- Your support is the only thing that can enable us to deliver this urgently needed help on time
- It's imperative that we keep up with and deliver on those needs

Deliver: transfer, provide, hand over, pass on, turn over, transmit, send, remit, forward, launch, liberate, free, release, protect

See also: BRING, PROVIDE, SEND, SUPPLY

DEMAND
- The demand for our services is ever greater
- But we can't keep up with the demand
- Only you can help us meet such overwhelming demand
- Please help us meet the increasing demand for
- In order to meet the demand from our participants, we need your
- In all cases, we demand an end to
- At a time when demand is skyrocketing and staff drastically reduced
- Year after year, the demands on our services grow
- These demands shouldn't drive anyone away
- Respond to conflicting but equally important demands
- With so many demands on your time and generosity

See also: ASK, NEED, REQUIRE

DEMOCRACY
- Democracy is the heart and engine of genuine development
- To the point where democracy itself is threatened
- Nurture increased democracy with your gift
- Only with democracy will this oppression be finally stopped

See also: COUNTRY, GOVERNMENT, NATION, PEOPLE, TOGETHER, UNITE

DEPEND
- You can depend on us to protect the services that are important to you
- Success depends on all of us
- Depending on some form of social assistance
- I hope you understand just how much we depend upon your ongoing support to continue the fight against
- Those in need depend on us – and we depend on you

- A large number of investigative teams now depend on us

See also: COUNT, RELY

DEPTH
- Can't have such breadth if it is at the expense of depth
- People very far out of their depth
- Depends not on the depth of your pocketbook but the size of your heart
- We keep sounding amazing new depths of caring
- For those who are touching the depths

DESERT
- We can't desert them
- Deserted in their hour of direst need
- Your help turns deserts into gardens

See also: ABANDON

DESERVING
- You never know which deserving person your donation will give a lift to this year
- So many deserving people waiting their turn
- No one is more deserving than those awaiting our help
- With so many deserving causes competing for attention, it's heartbreaking to choose

See also: IMPORTANT, VALUE

DESPERATE
- Called in a desperate attempt to get the help she needs
- Feeling utterly helpless and desperate
- This is the kind of desperation that drives people to
- Desperately in need of our assistance
- Never before have I seen such desperation
- Desperately hoping that help will come soon

Desperate: pressing, urgent, compelling, critical, crucial, perilous, precarious, serious, fatal, grave, deadly, shocking, intolerable, distressing, woeful, despairing, wretched, inconsolable, downcast, forlorn, dangerous, severe, abject

See also: CRISIS, EMERGENCY, STRESS, URGENT

DESPAIR
- So many ways to get people out of the cycle of poverty and despair
- A faith in humankind that transcends despair
- No one should suffer this kind of despair
- You can turn despair into hope so easily

Despair: hopelessness, dismay, discouragement, depression, dejection, defeatism, gloom, sorrow, melancholy, misery, wretchedness, distress, grief, anguish, desperation, tribulation, trial, ordeal, heartache, lose hope, give up, surrender, quit, throw in the towel

See also: GRIEF, MISERY, PAIN, SORROW, SUFFERING

DESTINY
- Discover how destiny decided that
- We can make our own destiny
- Their destiny is in your hands
- It must have been destiny that set us on this path
- Help a people struggling to control their own destiny

See also: END, FATE, GOAL

DESTITUTE
- Traumatized and instantly destitute
- Destitute of ideas and moral fibre
- They are the truly destitute of the world

See also: HOMELESS, LOSS, POOR, POVERTY

DESTROY
- Stop them from destroying the kind of place we've always been proud to call home
- Destroyed by unthinkable criminal acts
- Lives can be destroyed in a moment
- To help them rebuild what has been so tragically destroyed
- Now all we've built can so easily be destroyed

See also: ABUSE, ATTACK, DEVASTATE, VIOLENCE

DETAILS
- Happy to give you all the details
- Here's how to get full details quickly and easily
- These grim and graphic details only emphasize how
- For more exciting details, please read our newsletter
- A plan of action worked out down to the final detail

DETERIORATION
- The effects of such a deterioration in living conditions will last far into the future
- You can see the shocking deterioration for yourself
- It is so heartening to see the deterioration reversed

DETERMINATION
- Her sad, poignant letter filled us with determination to work even harder, even faster, to stop this misery and do it as soon as possible
- Renewed determination and continued efforts are needed
- Such determination deserves to be rewarded with our help

See also: CONCENTRATE, DRIVE, ENDURE, FOCUS, LOYALTY, PERSISTENCE

DETERMINE
- Asking you to help us determine the true cause of
- We are determined not to give in
- We are only becoming more determined than ever to

- Determined to get help into the most inaccessible places

DEVASTATE
- The whole family was devastated
- In spite of the devastation, we're still here and we still need you
- Overcome the emotional devastation caused by

See also: CATASTROPHE, CRISIS, DISASTER

DEVELOPMENT
- Has been in joint development
- Development is steadily moving in
- Embarking upon the development of
- A startling new development on the scene is
- Devoted exclusively to comprehensive personal development
- Striving to represent every area of personal development
- Favorably disposed to be involved in the development of such programs
- Keeping you better informed with regard to overall developments

See also: ENCOURAGE, EXPAND, GROW, PLAN

DIAGNOSIS
- When we finally got the diagnosis, none of us could believe it
- Confront this grim diagnosis
- For people facing this kind of diagnosis, support is the first priority
- The diagnosis indicates that we need to have help from you

DIE
- They don't have to die
- He was sure that he was dying
- Many more will die in the coming months
- So many die in terror at the hands of
- They died in silence, alone and forgotten
- The agony of watching her children die in her arms, one after another, was too much for her
- Others are dying as you read this
- Too many people are still dying from this illness
- People are literally dying for lack of the simplest help
- The heartbreak of having to say goodbye to a dying loved one
- The central objective of helping patients die with dignity and comfort

Die: expire, pass away, pass on, lay down one's life, give up the ghost, bite the dust, end, breathe one's last, die away, vanish, disappear, stop, cease, decease

See also: DEATH, GRIEF, LOSS

DIFFERENCE
- Your involvement makes an incredible difference
- Each one makes such a big difference.
- You make a difference between failure and success
- It means the difference between adequate and outstanding

- Making a difference today, for a better tomorrow
- The difference in every case was
- See the difference we have already made
- Show the difference our efforts individually and collectively make
- You may not think your donation makes a difference but, believe me, it does
- It can make all the difference for those at the bottom of the scale
- One person can make a difference
- An immeasurable, life-changing difference
- The difference is working with
- The difference in every case was
- The difference is who gets to run their lives
- This is where you can make a stunning difference
- Here's your chance to create a difference
- Won't you join us and help engineer a world of difference
- Your involvement makes an incredible difference

Difference: contrast, improvement, distinction
See also: CHANGE, GAP, IMPROVE

DIFFERENT
- Why is this cause different
- Yes, we march to a different drummer
- Now it's time to try something different
- Looking at this problem in a whole different light

DIFFICULT
- Our supporters realize how difficult it is to
- It was probably the most difficult thing I've ever done in my life
- The skills and techniques of dealing with difficult people
- As you can see, I find it difficult to begin
- Could be very difficult in the long run unless you help now
- Nothing is more difficult than facing those people with nothing to give

See also: CHALLENGE, HARD, STRUGGLE

DIFFICULTY
- Among those who have the most difficulty these days
- My difficulty in writing often stems from a certain amount of rage and frustration
- Experience difficulty in many areas
- A chance to escape the awful difficulties of

See also: BLOCK, OBSTACLE, PROBLEM

DIG
- Dig deep into your pockets
- So please, dig down deep and help
- Help us dig in and get the job done
- Those who dig deepest often have the most modest of means to help
- Dig down and find those few extra dollars

See also: REACH, SEARCH

DIGNITY
- Helping people keep their dignity and independence
- Your gift helps preserve the basic human dignity of
- When all they have left is their dignity

Dignity: nobility, honor, worthiness, worth, respectability, repute, gravity, reserve, human value, self-esteem, self-respect, self-regard

DIRECTION
- Once again we are asking for your help and direction in maintaining the high level of service
- Give more direction to take control of
- So they don't go galloping off in the wrong direction
- Time to take a new direction, offering new possibilities and new hope
- New directions beckon
- Moving in the right direction to attain that goal
- For all those seeking a new direction in their lives
- Careful not to pull in opposite directions

See also: CHOICE, DECISION, OPTION

DISABILITY
- Major disabilities from aging, illness or injury
- With help and encouragement people can overcome the gravest disability
- Turning every disability into a shining asset

See also: DIFFICULTY, DISADVANTAGE, HANDICAP, LOSS

DISABLED
- Rehabilitation and independence to the disabled
- You're helping the disabled declare independence
- So many will benefit from our health and rehabilitation services
- Without your generosity, the whole system could be disabled

DISADVANTAGE
- People with disabilities are at an even greater disadvantage
- Decidedly at a disadvantage
- Would be very disappointed if, through lack of funds, we were forced into a position of disadvantage
- Disadvantaged families have abusive situations more often than economically stable families
- To permit ourselves to know and understand the problems of the disadvantaged
- Never allow ourselves to dismiss the disadvantaged as being of no importance to us

See also: DIFFICULTY, DISABILITY, GAP, HANDICAP, LOSS, OBSTACLE, PROBLEM

DISAPPEAR
- Refusing to let these courageous people disappear
- One by one, without our help, they'll just quietly disappear

- The dismay of watching our main support disappear

DISAPPOINT
- So that no one, child or grownup, will be left disappointed
- How can we disappoint the children
- I know you won't be disappointed
- The first disappointment only made their resolve stronger

DISASTER
- Disasters rarely give warning
- In vital day-by-day operations and in confrontation with unforeseen disasters
- It's an exciting new idea that helps them when natural disaster strikes
- Disaster after disaster has swept over this war-ravaged area
- The disaster would be utterly unprecedented
- The looming disaster doesn't have to be inevitable

Disaster: calamity, catastrophe, crisis, emergency, tragedy, dreadful accident, shock, blow, bad luck, ill fortune, mishap, misfortune, mischance, misadventure, glitch, reverse, setback, comedown, cataclysm, convulsion, spasm, upheaval, debacle, breakdown, collapse, adversity, affliction, ruin, trouble, hardship, ill wind, fiasco, setback
See also: CATASTROPHE, CRISIS

DISCIPLINE
- To develop self-discipline and work habits that serve for a lifetime
- To learn the disciplines of better living
- Disciplines to save resources and live thriftily

See also: ORDER, PLAN

DISCOURAGE
- We shall not be discouraged by
- Discouragingly, nothing showed up
- In the midst of all the discouragement, a strong helping hand
- It's so easy to feel discouraged
- Don't be discouraged by the unprepossessing appearance

DISCOVER
- Have been fortunate enough to discover a way to make a real change in these people's lives
- Discover the joy of giving
- Now that you've discovered us, I know you'll help
- Working very hard to discover the real truth

See also: FIND, LOOK, SEARCH

DISCOVERY
- The discovery that's taken this country by storm
- We're right on the edge of major new discoveries
- Scientific discoveries lead to more effective care, shortens hospital stays and

saves health care dollars

Discovery: perception, discernment, finding, realization, invention, innovation, idea, breakthrough, concoction, leap, find, recognition, unearthing
See also: ADVANCE, BREAKTHROUGH, CURE, SOLUTION

DISCUSS
- To feel comfortable about discussing the issue that is most troubling
- I have something really important to discuss with you
- Supplemented by lively, thought-provoking discussions
- Providing ample opportunity for discussion and critique

DISEASE
- We can't forget the staggering numbers affected by this dread disease
- I'm writing to you about the world's worst disease
- A definitive look at our war against disease
- The most neglected disease in
- We must give our scientists the tools they need to finally defeat this awful disease
- Yet thousands who suffer from this disease are waiting and hoping
- It's not a regrettable but incurable disease
- It's a disease that can lead to frustrating memory loss and frightening confusion
- Thanks to your ongoing support, more and more people with this disease can lead a near normal life.
- Everyone dreams of the day when this disease will be gone
- Terrifying both to those with the disease and the families who so dearly love them
- This disease affects millions of people
- Despite the relentless grip of this disease, they never lost their courage, their dignity or their sense of humor
- This disease is something you should never have to live through alone
- Many diseases are not preventable no matter how careful you are
- Do you believe that this disease is inevitable for all those who get it
- So malnourished her body just couldn't fight off disease
- These diseases are the major cause of childhood illness and account for the deaths of
- Every day, thousands of children die from simple, preventable diseases
- So often contaminated, the source of many deadly diseases

Disease: Malady, sickness, illness, disorder, ailment, complaint, affliction, bug, abnormality, ill-health, unhealthiness, infection
See also: ILLNESS, PAIN,, SICK, SUFFERING

DISILLUSION
- Now is not the time to become disillusioned about
- We won't give in to disillusion
- Can't bear to see such fine people fall prey to disillusion
- These days, it doesn't take long to become disillusioned with

DISORDER
- Finally find a cure for this terrible disorder
- More than ever, we need your help in fighting this dreadful disorder
- So many live with the unpredictability of these cruel disorders

See also: CHAOS, CONFUSE, HAVOC, ILLNESS, MESS

DISREGARD
- Blatant disregard is shocking
- It's hard to disregard such suffering
- Begging you to please, please do not disregard this warning
- Fatally disregarding the signs

DISRUPT
- Nothing disrupts our activities more than
- It disrupts their education, derails their social lives, cripples their attempts to find and keep work in today's fiercely competitive environment
- To counter those doing everything they can to disrupt
- Our plans have been severely disrupted by

DISTINCTION
- An uncommon distinction that should not go unnoticed
- Naturally, we make the fine distinction that
- Has served with distinction and courage for so many years

DISTRACT
- Nothing can distract us from our goal
- A grief-stricken mother, distracted and sobbing
- Work steadily even in the midst of the worst distractions

DIVERSITY
- Helping to foster vital natural diversity
- Without enough diversity, the whole system will collapse
- Diversity means both a healthy economy and ecosystem

DO
- Here is a way for you to do something about this critical problem
- We can do this, and much more
- I want to do something about it
- I'll bet you've been meaning to do it for years now
- What can you do right now is
- Here's how you can do something positive about it
- That means we should do something about it now, while we can
- Because of you, we can do it
- It's easy to do
- You can do a great deal
- They do it themselves, painfully and agonizingly slow
- All she ever wanted to do was live an ordinary life

- Help us show what we can really do when
- Do it for yourself
- There is only so much they can do alone
- How are we doing
- Do it now, please
- It can be done

Do: perform, execute, discharge, work out, bring about, engineer, make happen, achieve, attain, finish, complete, prepare, create, act, proceed, manage
See also: ACHIEVE, ACT

DOLLAR
- Every dollar will be used creatively, innovatively and efficiently to produce
- Every dollar you donate will be shared with your association to support a local undertaking vital to you
- Every dollar counts, every dollar is precious
- Each dollar you give works so hard
- One dollar does the work of two
- Every dollar you give is matched by
- Give a dollar for every year you've lived
- Because of your dollars, someone can go home – healthy again and loved
- It also one of the world's most efficient at putting your dollars to work where they're needed most
- Without your dollars, these programs could no longer exist
- Your dollars will be put to work immediately to provide services
- Making sure our very best people are minding the dollars
- Each dollar you give brings us another step closer to final relief – the cure we so desperately seek.
- Because your dollars make our work possible
- Your dollars are put to such good use
- Your vitally needed dollars will help do the job
- Although critically important, those dollars alone have never been enough to sustain our services
- It's hard to measure in dollars, but not in smiles
- But only dollars can ensure your continued satisfaction and participation you now enjoy
- Your dollars today will help secure an enlightened future tomorrow
- Look at how far your dollars go
- See the hope your dollars buy
- Frankly, we need more dollars in our mailbox
- Look at the good work your donation dollars can do
- Look to people like you to help us provide the dollars we need to continue
- Our only source of support is voluntary dollars of people like yourself

See also: CONTRIBUTION, DONATION, FUND, GIFT, MONEY

DOMESTIC
- Still more disturbing facts about domestic violence are leaking out
- To boldly ask the questions that uncover domestic violence

- Children who witness domestic violence are more likely to become abusers themselves
- Dedicated to stopping the huge economic and psychological cost of domestic violence

DONATE
- By donating today, you can help make life better for people who
- Donate if you can
- Find it hard asking a person to donate his or her hard-earned money
- There is no better way to donate than to give monthly
- Looking to you to donate generously

See also: CONTRIBUTE, GIVE, VOLUNTEER

DONATION
- Please help us with a donation today
- Please send along your donation to
- Beyond that, however, is the fact that your donation, be it great or small, will mean so much to those in need
- Your donation will go a long way in helping those who need it most
- I know that every one of you will do the best you can to assist us with a sacrificial donation
- So be a friend and make a donation to
- Sometimes, you may ask yourself whether making one donation can possibly make a difference
- Please stand on guard with a single or monthly donation today
- Your donation will be used wisely
- Think of what your donation could mean to a hungry child
- Your donation goes further
- Your donation will make a difference
- Please help and send your donation today
- I hope you can make a donation of
- As generous a donation as you can manage
- Your generous donation will help continue the superb programs and services you expect and enjoy from
- If you would like to make a personal donation, please call
- Your donation, great or small, will mean so much to those in need
- Your donation also goes right to the services that people need to keep their dignity and independence
- Donation of as much as you can possibly afford
- A simple donation will help us deliver urgently needed help to men, women and children right across our city
- It's as easy as completing and returning your donation form in the enclosed postage-paid envelope
- Your donation brings us just a little closer to the day when
- Please make a donation today
- I want to assure you again, that your donation will truly mean a difference in the

quality of help we can continue to offer
- Our lifeblood is really the individual donations made by concerned, caring people such as yourself
- If you're unable to give monthly, please consider a one-time donation
- Your donation moves us closer to the dream
- By making a donation you are helping to
- Donations from caring people like you are the very heartbeat of our organization
- A memorial donation would honor them greatly
- Donations come in all shapes and sizes
- In making your donation, you'll be helping those working so hard to provide a better life for
- We also requested an additional donation for our work in
- To make a donation or find out more about us, please contact
- Please make a donation to support this effort, even if you've already made your annual renewal gift to
- I urge you to make a generous donation right now giving someone hope
- Your donation, at work with gifts from other caring people, will give us the ability to help thousands
- Your donation is part of a larger force, the force of independence
- If so little money does this, imagine what a larger donation can do for these desperate people
- Your donation assists with so many national endeavors of
- Your most recent donation was deeply appreciated
- By making a donation now, you are helping us build
- Where does my donation go
- Your donation is spent frugally and effectively
- You'd see your donation touching lives, one at a time
- And that's why we need your donation so urgently
- Donations continue to arrive by mail and phone, along with letters of encouragement and steadfast loyalty
- Cash donations are critical but your time is also valuable
- Your donation will make it possible for
- The suggested donation is
- Please complete and mail the donation form attached to this letter
- Rest assured every cent of your donation goes to work where needed most
- If you prefer a single donation, please send whatever you can afford

See also: **CONTRIBUTION, DOLLARS, CHECK, FUND, GIFT, MONEY**

DONE
- Can anything be done
- The deep satisfaction of knowing what you have really done
- Working long and hard to get the job done
- We've done all this and more
- There's so much to be done – with your help
- Just want to done with this trying situation once and for all

DONOR

- The immense value of an informed donor
- The first reason behind our success is our donors
- Without the unwavering support of our donors, none of our projects would ever get off the ground
- With limited government funding, we rely on generous donors like you to keep up our lifesaving work
- And since not all donors can continue to support us year after year
- Donors like you did not let us down
- Thanks to thousands of loyal donors like you, firmly committed to helping us provide
- Currently seeing caring donors like you pitch in a little more during these tight times
- You are so much more than just a kind-hearted donor
- Find a deep personal joy in becoming a donor
- Enthusiastic support from committed donors has helped us grow

Donor: patron, giver, donator, contributor, supporter, benefactor, backer, angel, grantor

See also: **BENEFACTOR, FRIEND, PARTNER, SPONSOR, SUPPORTER, VOLUNTEER**

DOOR

- Opening the door to the workplace for so many
- Open the doors to public participation
- Before this door of opportunity is closed forever
- Help us keep our doors open for another season
- With your caring support, we can open the door to the
- To prevent this from turning into a revolving door
- Your continued support is needed to keep the doors open

See also: **ACCESS, CHANCE, OPPORTUNITY**

DOUBT

- Determined not to let these dreams become blurred with doubt
- Refuse to succumb to doubt that we can change these awful circumstances
- It's not at all unusual to have these doubts
- To stop being plagued by swarming doubts
- Calming their doubts and assuring them their life is now safe
- We cannot remain mired in self-doubt
- If you are still in doubt, just take a look at the statistics I've enclosed

DOWNSIZE

- Regretfully, a decision has been made to downsize the program
- Unfortunately, it's impossible to downsize the need
- Massive downsizing and restructuring, job burnout and a need for new challenges
- Without strong donor support, we could be downsized

- Don't let this crucial program become a victim if downsizing

See also: **CUTS, CUTBACK, LOSS, REDUCTION, SETBACK, SHORTFALL, SLASH**

DRAGON
- Sometimes the opposition can look like a dragon
- Determined to slay these dragons
- The problems are like so many dragons lying in wait

DRAIN
- Physically, emotionally and financially drained
- Our resources are all but drained away
- The will to act can sometimes be easily drained away by
- All this effort must not just go down the drain

DRASTIC
- This means drastic cuts in
- Even that amount has shrunk drastically
- It's time for swift and drastic action

DREAD
- Thanks to the generosity of people like you, so much of the dread has already been removed from the
- I dread to imagine what might happen if we don't get enough funds together in time
- We've been dreading this all along
- Some look forward, with dread, to another day of life
- Help prevent something we even dread to think about

See also: **ANXIETY, FEAR, STRESS, TERROR**

DREAM
- This dream can become a glorious reality if we all work together
- Our million dollar dream
- This must not remain an impossible dream
- A dream perhaps achieved only once a century
- Help fulfil a dream
- Our dream is to have all children safe and happy
- Our dream was born out of the experience of hundreds of people over many years
- We dream of a day when sick, suffering people won't be abandoned to the harsh indifference of
- It's not an unattainable dream
- I guess some dreams do come true
- The opportunity to achieve the dreams they truly deserve
- Making dreams a lot more than just wishful thinking
- Turning dreams into a vision of fulfilled desires

- Reaching out to create new dreams
- Only you can reach for your dreams
- We must give our youth ways to fulfil their dreams
- No longer an impossible dream
- Gifts they could only dream of
- The end of a dream

Dream: vision, hope, desire, invention, visualization, daydream, whimsy, imagination, idea, aspiration, goal, aim, conceive, dream up, envision, imagine, fantasize, fancy, must, suppose
See also: AIM, HOPE, GOAL, IMAGINE, STRIVE, VISION

DRIVE
- This fundraising drive is our most important ever
- You provide the drive that gets things done
- The need for a cure is the driving force behind our work
- Please participate in our paper drive to pay for new computers

See also: ENERGY. FORCE, MOMENTUM

DROUGHT
- As the drought worsens, human lives hang in the balance
- Relentless drought scourged the already tortured land
- Choked by drought, their hopes and their livelihood withered away

DRUG
- Desperately need help after finishing a drug and addiction program
- The drug of cold indifference
- Our researchers are developing new drugs that can limit the number of
- More and better new drugs are just part of the answer
- If you could just help a little to defray the prohibitive cost of these lifesaving drugs

See also: BREAKTHROUGH, CURE, RESEARCH

DUCK
- Duck and run for cover
- No one can duck these kinds of consequences
- We duck but we can't hide
- Making sure they can't just duck out on us

DYNAMIC
- Let's replace this with something much more dynamic
- A new dynamic has totally revitalized the organization
- Dynamic action is exhilarating and freeing

EAGER
- I want you to know how eager I am to
- Heartwarming to see so many so eager to help

- So eagerly awaiting your response
- Everyone asked has been very eager to do their bit to

EARLIER
- The earlier the better
- I got this news to you earlier than usual
- The situation has become worse much earlier than expected
- The earlier we get help to them, the sooner they mend

EARTH
- The Earth is a beautiful wet blue ball
- You and I and all of us must care for this Earth we dwell upon
- Wonderful to see the new crop springing green from the earth

See also: ENVIRONMENT

EASE
- Please help ease the torment of
- Your compassion helps ease
- The ease of giving is unmatched
- Longing for only a few moments of ease

EASY
- It's easy and it makes a difference
- I'll show you how easy it is to help
- Helping is easy and quick to do
- If you'll help, the rest is easy

See also: CONVENIENCE, SIMPLE

ECOLOGY
- We must always think about ecology first
- Our first concern must always be the ecology
- I know you care deeply about the effect on the ecology
- Incredible beauty and ecological significance

See also: EARTH, ENVIRONMENT, NATURE, NURTURE

ECONOMIC
- Support projects and businesses that will bring economic growth and stability to our communities
- Is a key economic asset, generating tourist dollars
- Higher education has become absolutely essential to everyone's economic survival – and young people know it
- This program also makes great economic sense

See also: ASSET, BUDGET, BUSINESS, CORPORATE

ECONOMY
- They're using the economy as an excuse to gut our programs

- The economy is certainly rocky these days
- Fearing the economy is in collapse
- We don't have to tell any of you how tough today's economy is

EDGE
- A definite edge that makes all the difference in personal life
- Come with me on a journey to the far edge
- Help rescue those teetering on the edge
- Without your help, we're slowly being pushed to the edge of disaster

See also: ADVANTAGE, BENEFIT, BOUNDARY

EDUCATE
- The historically honored place reserved for the educated person in our society has disappeared
- Unrelenting in our efforts to educate the public about a desperate need
- The more people we can educate about this condition, the better our chances of beating it
- Our mission is to educate bright, financially needy students
- Our goal is to create awareness and educate people about

See also: INFORM, LEARN, TEACH, TRAIN

EDUCATION
- Our hearts swell with pride at the greatly increased numbers of youth eager to work so hard and sacrifice so much for a university education
- To safeguard their higher education, our next generation needs so much
- Today, a college education is not a passport to lifetime security
- To promote every success in educational endeavors.
- Education is the only ticket to success
- Education doesn't stop with a graduation ceremony
- Sadly making education and values appear to have no connection with getting what they want
- This education initiative drastically reduced the number of
- Like most here, she could not contribute toward her education
- A new plan for education
- Education is the only permanent answer to the problem
- Without the benefit of a practical education that your dollars can help to provide
- You'll also help us provide education programs for individuals, their families, health professionals and the general public.
- Deprived of the education that would change their lives
- Help ensure continuing education
- With your help, we can beam a vast variety of curriculum-based courses for students to see in the classroom and receive an education
- Education programs to help prevent further spread of disease
- Thank you for allowing so many worthy young men and women to have a quality education

See also: GUIDANCE, INFORMATION, SCHOOL, TEACHER,

UNIVERSITY

EDUCATIONAL
- Yet what have our governments done in response to so much hope, so much effort to gain the educational tools needed to face an ever shifting, ever more demanding future
- Participants get formal and informal training from a variety of self-help courses, educational credit courses and skills training courses
- A lifeline for continuing educational excellence
- Conducted in any communities, these programs provide educational sessions and social interaction for adults suffering from
- Perhaps the best indication that our educational systems are failing us is the explosive growth of

EFFECT
- Resolve to have an effect upon
- The powerful effects of compassionate people in action
- In addition to the direct effects of
- Effects of mind-boggling and rapidly expanding breadth
- The far-reaching effect is fantastic
- Your response has an immediate effect upon the lives of people at risk
- The damaging emotional and psychological effects have been well documented

EFFECTIVE
- You can help us become even more effective
- I'm convinced our efforts are so effective because
- You'll be effectively providing delicious lunches for those who otherwise might not eat at all
- A swift and effective effort was mounted
- To increase their personal effectiveness in every possible way

EFFICIENCY
- We also pride ourselves on our efficiency
- We pay a great deal of attention to the efficiency of the system
- With just a little more funding we could increase our efficiency twofold
- Simplicity and efficiency are the hallmarks
- We try our very best to be cost-saving and full of efficiency

EFFORT
- You can help with this important effort
- But they are also a vital effort on behalf of our fundraising program
- No effort is too much
- Intensive effort has gone into the entire operation
- We are striving to promote this effort
- A consistent effort has been made to reach students and other segments of society with our message about

- But they are also a vital effort on behalf of our fund-raising program
- Requires a concerted effort on the part of all
- Your unselfish efforts are helping them to
- As a part, you can be proud of this extraordinary effort
- Can we count on you to be part of this effort
- Let's make this a unanimous effort
- Help bolster efforts to improve
- Your efforts are bearing fruit
- The hard work and dedication which characterize their efforts on behalf
- Now you and I need to safeguard these efforts
- Efforts of many years have paid off
- The personal efforts and support of people like you have been invaluable in helping to preserve and enhance
- We support them in their efforts
- Proof that many of our efforts are now bearing fruit
- If so, I applaud your efforts
- We need to redouble our efforts right away
- At the forefront of national and international efforts to
- Your efforts really pay off with spectacular results
- Special opportunity to celebrate efforts to heal the planet
- Enable us to continue efforts that have already accomplished so much
- Please choose to support our efforts
- Persist in our efforts to reach the day when this disease no longer threatens
- We attempt to learn from these efforts
- We support efforts to challenge obstacles to change

See also: ACTION, BURDEN, EFFORT, STRIVE, STRUGGLE, WORK

ELDERLY
- The elderly put out their shaking hand to you
- Meets the many difficulties of old age, working hard to maintain elderly persons in their own familiar communities
- Dedicated to meeting the needs of elderly people in our city
- A desperately needy elderly person
- A poverty-stricken elderly person who has so very little
- In-home visits and meals to the elderly bring daily help and cheer
- Ensuring the elderly in this community do not fall though the cracks
- Many of you may want to keep your donations going to services for the elderly; indeed we hope you do

See also: OLD, SENIORS, WISDOM

ELEMENT
- The most explosive element in this heady mix is
- So that all the elements can work smoothly together
- The most important element is your participation
- All the elements are just waiting to be put together – with your help

EMBARRASS
- Some people have to be embarrassed into action
- Don't be embarrassed
- Almost an embarrassment of choices

EMERGENCY
- Deal quickly and competently with emergencies
- It also provides an emergency source of food
- In case of emergency, you should know what action is absolutely essential

See also: CRISIS, DESPERATE, DISASTER, URGENT

EMOTION
- The emotional costs of caring for someone with this illness are incalculable
- Relies heavily on our workers for emotional support and encouragement
- The emotional response was overwhelming
- Intense emotional states experienced by both patient and caregiver
- Learning to effectively manage their own emotions
- Focus on the provision of physical, emotional and spiritual support

See also: DELIGHT, DESPAIR, EMBARRASS, EMPATHY, FEAR, FEELING, HAPPY, JOY, JUBILATION, LOVE

EMPATHY
- Prompting awareness and empathy
- If you have the least empathy at all for these unfortunates
- Empathy is the most powerful of motivators
- Rapidly developing empathy for the cause

EMPHASIZE
- We cannot emphasize too much the urgency
- I've never really emphasized the importance of
- Choosing which needs to be emphasized is often the hardest part

EMPOWER
- By giving freely, you empower yourself
- Empowering individuals, families and communities to pursue the best within themselves
- Please help empower thousands of other disadvantaged people in developing countries by giving your gift today
- In it, you'll get a real glimpse of what your funds do to encourage progressive social policy and empower low income people to speak out
- To empower and enrich one or more aspects of
- Empowering children to reach for a happy future

ENCOURAGE
- I want to encourage you to try
- Should encourage us to fresh action

- In the past, your support has encouraged us so much
- I encourage you to comment on our programs
- Individuality is encouraged
- Encourage each of us to give a little – and help a lot
- With such encouraging results to show, I'm now asking you to help a little more
- Please encourage as many of your friends as you can to act

Encourage: hearten, reassure, cheer, buoy up, stimulate, animate, boost, invigorate, give a shot in the arm to, urge, exhort, egg on, impel, induce, persuade, inflame, instigate, stir up, inspire, approve, promote, advance, forward, endorse, sanction, incite, energize, motivate, galvanize, electrify

See also: CHEER, HEARTEN, SUPPORT

ENCOURAGEMENT

- This project offers much encouragement to those struggling with
- Cheered by the unwavering support and encouragement of
- Found the encouragement and empathy we needed
- Just a little bit of encouragement can go a very long way
- To help just one more child in need of hope and encouragement

END

- Put an end to this problem once and for all
- To end the misery permanently
- Always keeping the greater end in sight
- To avoid hitting a few dead ends
- Tries hard to make ends meet by working two jobs
- We're trying our best to make ends meet, but it's a difficult struggle
- Must question their ends in this activity
- Once again we must ask whether the ends justify the means

See also: CUT, DESTROY, GOAL, MEANS, PURPOSE, RESOURCE, STOP, TARGET

ENDANGER

- It's no surprise that these magnificent creatures are now endangered after being so drastically reduced
- Even more will be endangered if we don't soon change our destructive ways
- People like you could become an endangered species
- Only you can help keep them off the endangered list

See also: JEOPARDY, RISK, THREATEN

ENDING

- Help us bring about a happy ending for
- A different ending if you and I are willing to make a personal commitment today to fund
- A huge step toward ending poverty and illness in this region
- But you can change the ending of this story

ENDORSEMENT
- Your gift is also your endorsement
- The happy smiles and changed lives are our best endorsement
- Humbly asking for your endorsement

ENDURE
- They endure through the most daunting of
- You name it, I endured it
- Your enduring support is our mainstay

See also: PAIN

ENEMY
- Something you wouldn't wish on your worst enemy
- An implacable enemy of all poverty and suffering
- Battling the enemies of freedom every day
- Help us defeat a dangerous and aggressive enemy

ENERGY
- The real energy is coming from people like you
- Her gift of energy and loyalty have been of immeasurable value
- The movement is gathering energy and speed
- We can pool our energies together to increase
- To free blocked energy for more creative use
- With such high energy behind us, we can reach everybody

See also: DYNAMIC, ENTHUSIASM, POWER, STRENGTH

ENOUGH
- Enough is enough
- As if we didn't get more than enough now
- Not enough is being done about this grave situation
- Without your help there simply won't be enough to go round
- It's not enough that you give only once

ENSURE
- Please help ensure that this great program has a future by writing a generous donation check right now
- Ensure there is no restriction on the level of gift
- Working so hard to ensure this ongoing success
- Only you can ensure the continuation of this wonderful institution

ENTERPRISE
- An enterprise that promises enormous rewards
- Please support us in undertaking such a brave and daring enterprise
- To direct this enterprise of such tremendous importance

See also: ADVENTURE, BUSINESS, UNDERTAKING

ENTHUSIASM
- The fruit of boundless enthusiasm
- The result should be renewed strength and enthusiasm for us all
- Respond with enthusiasm and creativity to
- You enthusiasm and generosity is the fuel that makes it all run
- Discovery and enthusiasm highlight this program

See also: DELIGHT, EMOTION, ENERGY, EXCITEMENT, JOY, PASSION, RAPTURE, STIMULATE

ENTITLED
- No wonder so many feel entitled to
- You are entitled to know the true facts
- You are entitled to the great feeling that comes with
- Everyone should be entitled to the basic necessities of life

ENVIRONMENT
- Helping to rehabilitate a fragile environment devastated by years of war, drought and famine
- Expansion of this plant would have serious health and environmental effects on our community.
- Without conducting environmental studies or examining the alternatives
- In a tough new environment, we need your commitment more than ever
- Help save the environment by taking action now
- Discuss and agree on solving some of the worst, large-scale environmental problems
- Personally committed themselves and their nations to taking specific, positive steps to heal the environment and prevent further decline
- As a valued supporter, I'm sure you're as concerned as I am about the effects of such additional stresses on these precious, special environments
- Protecting and preserving our natural environment has always been a priority
- An even greater emphasis on learning to protect our fragile environment
- Working to promote sustainable agriculture and education while living in harmony with their delicate environment
- These touching letters from children tell what the environment means to them
- Please try to save the environment with us
- The pressing need to address complex environmental problems
- Those countries that want to improve their standard of living without damage to the environment should receive financial support
- Providing a warm, loving environment
- At last find a safe environment for
- The effects of additional stresses on our precious natural environments
- A positive impact upon the environment through determined effort
- In an environment that is constantly supportive
- Provide a new and dynamic environment that will encourage and inspire increased activity
- To survive, prosper and grow in this changing and challenging new environment

- Building a complete positive, productive environment that supports efforts to grow and change
- We thrive in a challenging environment
- A nurturing and energizing environment
- Able to recognize the factors in the environment that

See also: ANIMAL, ATMOSPHERE, EARTH, HOME, SURROUND, NATURE, NURTURE

ENVIRONMENTAL

- Environmental devastation caused by these projects is of grave concern
- Having an environmental conscience is more than just a fad
- Environmental concerns must always have first priority

EQUALITY

- Which works with individuals and organizations to foster equality and freedom, safeguard cultures and communities, and protect the environment
- Always working toward complete equality
- Equality of the sexes is the key to progress in these communities

ERADICATE

- Continuing the fight to eradicate one of the major pollutants
- Breathe a sigh of relief when this problem is eradicated
- Just want to eradicate this age old scourge

See also: CUT, EXTINCTION, PREVENT, STOP

ESSENTIAL

- Absolutely essential to our success
- Must not hack back essentials
- Your support is the utterly essential component
- Even the bare essentials might soon be beyond reach

See also: BASIC, NECESSITY, NEED

EVENT

- This particularly significant annual event would be a good opportunity to try this idea out
- Two significant events have just occurred that will change the situation
- We would pleased to hear from anyone offering to organize a fundraising event
- So much hinges on your participation in this fundraising event
- Influence the course of human events

See also: ACTION, DEED, OCCASION

EVERYBODY

- Everybody knows about
- Everyone is too busy to stop for a moment and help
- That means everybody is affected, including you and your family

EVERYDAY

- They have continual trouble with everyday activities such as eating and walking
- Just everyday people making big changes for the better
- It's everyday actions that really count

EVERYTHING

- Since everything else has been tried, this is the last resort
- We do everything we can to help
- Leaving everything up to you

EVIDENCE

- Brings impressive evidence to support this claim
- Unfortunately, there is mounting evidence that
- Hard evidence for the official claims is lacking
- This accumulation of evidence is a strong indication that

See also: EXAMPLE, PROOF

EVOLVE

- To help the situation evolve significantly
- Evolving toward a better way of doing things – and a better society
- Evolved into one of the finest centers anywhere

See also: CHANGE, CREATE, DEVELOP

EXAGGERATION

- This is not an exaggeration
- All exaggeration aside
- Please don't imagine that I'm exaggerating the need

EXAMPLE

- That's just one example
- These young people need an example to follow
- Here are some examples of what your donation will do
- Another frightening example comes from
- The following are prime examples of
- This work is just one example of the dozens of practical projects your donations support
- Teaching them to lead by example
- You can help set a fine example by responding quickly

EXCELLENCE

- A world class center of excellence
- Dedicated to the pursuit of excellence
- Celebrating their excellence as students, alumni, faculty and staff
- Strongly committed to excellence
- Motivating our children to pursue excellence
- Ensure continued excellence and strength in teaching

- To ensure continued excellence and strength in
- To communicate excellence and quality
- By providing a margin of excellence
- So that excellence can always be recognized and rewarded
- Their evolution to excellence

Excellence: nobility, greatness, distinction, superiority, preeminence, transcendence, worth, value, quality, perfection, supremacy, virtue, merit, strong point, exaltation

EXCITEMENT

- Make sure you're part of the excitement
- Share the excitement
- Wish you could see the excitement on the faces of the children
- Shivers of excitement running down my spine
- They could barely contain their excitement

See also: DELIGHT, ENERGY, ENTHUSIASM, FEELING, PASSION, THRILL

EXCITING

- Nothing is more exciting than the feeling of
- This is the most exciting advance since
- I have the most exciting news to tell you
- Support the exciting programs planned for the coming year

EXECUTIVE

- Executive decisions are often the hardest
- Your executive works very hard to
- Our executive is always in the spotlight

EXISTENCE

- Their very existence is threatened regularly
- In fact, they are fundamental to our existence
- Tied inexorably to the existence of a
- So that children do not have to merely cling to existence
- Help turn mere existence into vibrant life

EXPAND

- As you can see, we've been expanding steadily
- Since then we have expanded to include
- It feels so good to expand heart and mind
- Helping individuals who want to expand their knowledge and practical skills
- Allowing us to develop and learn how to expand
- Resulting in significant expansion

See also: DEVELOP, GROW

EXPENDITURE

- We have done all our work with a minimum of expenditure or overhead, relying

on volunteers
- Trying to keep our expenditures in line with our income
- Our biggest expenditure cannot possibly reduced in any way

EXPENSE
- Imposes heavy expenses upon us
- We have saved some considerable expense by
- After having gone to all the expense of

See also: COST, FUNDING, MONEY

EXPERIENCE
- First hand experience of the significance of
- Banked a lot of experience
- To expand on our experience can have a positive impact upon
- What makes this experience so gratifying is
- Surely you've had similar experiences with
- Take a moment to share a little of my own experience with you
- I'm telling you today, as one who has had first hand experience
- Provide an experience that will stay with them the rest of their lives
- Every day we learn more from experience
- Many have likened this awful experience to being buried alive
- Personal experience is so important
- The experience was very meaningful
- Experience the joys of giving
- Had a chance to experience a different kind of
- You may have had an experience like the one I had several years ago
- Working to make this more than just a one-shot experience
- My experience has been terrific
- We've banked a lot of experience
- Honed by a lifetime of well-distilled experience
- Gain precious first hand experience with
- Appealing to all levels of experience
- The experiences are terrifying
- Offering one of the most challenging experiences ever

Experience: feel, meet, encounter, perceive, observe, sense, undergo, go through, endure, suffer through, understand, learn about, discover, appreciate, wisdom, knowledge, learning, common sense, enlightenment, event, episode, ordeal, occurrence, happening, adventure, transaction

See also: APPRECIATE, FEELING, GUIDANCE, LEARN, MEET, KNOWLEDGE, WISDOM

EXPERT
- Efficient and highly expert
- Just think about the incredible coming together of these experts in so many fields
- Rub shoulders with experts and ask the questions that are uppermost in your mind

- Guided by some of the foremost experts
- Despite firm assurances from the experts in these matters
- Under guidance from the very best experts in the field

EXPERTISE

- Benefiting enormously from this expertise and courtesy in
- Someday you or someone you love could need the expertise and the kindly warmth of
- The combined expertise represented by this group is truly phenomenal

See also: COUNSELLING, GUIDANCE, KNOWLEDGE, WISDOM

EXPLAIN

- First, I must explain why your help is so crucial
- Let me explain why I now feel it urgent to launch this global campaign
- Working hard to adequately explain in this short letter
- Let me try to explain in the simplest terms possible
- I'll explain more about this in a minute
- To explain what it is and how it came into existence

EXPLODE

- I have to get something off my chest before I explode
- Exploding old myths that prevent the acceptance of new ideas
- Stop the situation before it explodes in our faces

See also: BLAST, CRISIS

EXPLOITATION

- Stop the unspeakable exploitation
- Can no longer tolerate the unconscionable exploitation of the poorest and weakest
- Back the women who will no longer stand for such exploitation

See also: ABUSE, BATTER, CRUELTY, NEGLECT, SUFFERING

EXPLORE

- Must have the freedom to explore
- Explore the thrilling possibilities of us
- To explore this in much greater depth
- Explore your heart to find how deeply you really care
- Exploring more and better ways to compliment
- As we explore so many exciting new avenues of action
- We are also committed to exploring new approaches

Explore: examine, scrutinize, survey, search, check into, research, look into, investigate, probe, go into, review, study, take stock of, feel out, inquire into
See also: DISCOVER

EXPOSE

- Give notice that their actions have been exposed

- We've exposed savage regimes to international condemnation
- Such corruption, once exposed to the eyes of the world, must wither away
- Exposing children to art and music at an early age really pays off
- Good exposure to the fact

EXPRESSION

- And we conduct public awareness campaigns about freedom of expression
- Please help us fight for freedom of expression by joining
- To encourage the full expression of

EXTINCTION

- Do we want to be responsible for one more extinction
- Wavering on the edge of extinction
- Extinction is more than a real possibility
- Fallen into a sad extinction of rights

EXTRA

- Go the extra mile
- We can no longer afford all the extras
- It's that little extra touch that counts
- An extra smile warms a heart and costs no money

See also: BENEFIT, BONUS, GIFT

EXTRAORDINARY

- Extraordinary needs require extraordinary generosity
- You can make an extraordinary difference
- You have responded with truly extraordinary kindness and warmth
- Ordinary people doing extraordinary things

See also: AMAZE, SPECIAL, WONDER

EYE

- And now readily catch the eye of
- So we can keep a close eye on this situation
- When I look into the eyes of those who struggle so hard
- Is it any wonder most people simply turn a blind eye?
- No one can turn a blind eye to such suffering
- This really opens your eyes

See also: ATTENTION, SIGHT

FACE

- One look at her careworn face tells the entire story
- Her face showed how hard her life had been
- The changing face of need
- Dare to look directly into the grim face of need
- Presenting an ever changing face to the world
- To better reflect the changing face of

- I've seen time and again how faces ravaged by terror and desperation become transformed
- The many bleak faces of need, fear, hunger and want

FACT
- And that's not just opinion, it's an indisputable fact
- Here are some startling facts you should be aware of
- We give the bald facts without bias
- The fact is, it doesn't always work that way
- Hard facts, important insights and actual case studies from leading experts prove that
- Here are a number of crucial facts to convince you
- Proven facts cut through the prejudice and misinformation
- Yet the sad fact is
- I do not recount these facts to be morbid or to be sensational
- I want to share these facts with you
- If these facts touch your heart, I hope you'll listen to what I have to say
- Some painful facts about
- Learned a lot of grim facts in a hurry
- Must never lose sight of this sobering fact

Fact: item, detail, point, particular, component, element, feature, factor, truth, certainty, reality, actuality, data, information, the score, verity, incident, phenomenon, event, episode, naked and unvarnished truth
See also: INFORMATION, KNOWLEDGE, PROOF, TRUTH

FACTOR
- What factors determine a decision to advance
- Your support is a major factor
- Factoring everything in

FAIL
- We cannot allow them to fail
- Please don't fail us in this unprecedented crisis
- No one can fail to understand the implications
- Now is not the time for courage to fail or resolution weaken

FAILURE
- Failure to do so will necessitate
- The greatest failures and shortcomings to date are
- You help can turn this failure completely around
- To people who have known nothing but failure, understanding and encouragement are priceless things

See also: BREACH, DESPAIR, GAP, LOSS

FAIR
- It isn't fair that those so innocent should suffer so much

- Striving to be very fair in the distribution of this aid
- Only wanting the judgement to be fair
- Neither fair nor free

FAIRNESS

- I know you're a person committed to fairness and to justice
- Haven't underestimated how much you're willing to work for fairness
- Total fairness is the keystone of this program
- It's all about basic fairness

FAITH

- It's your faith in a noble cause that keeps
- In faith that the necessary funds will be provided
- Has shaken many people's faith in the system
- We ask you to base your support not on blind faith but on hard facts
- Once again, we have faith in your kindness and generosity

See also: BELIEF, COMMITMENT, HOPE

FAMILIES

- Helping families cope with stress, poverty, violence
- Too many children grow up in troubled families where good role models and good advice are hard to find
- Dramatic difference in the lives of the families behind those headlines
- The difference is helping families move from makeshift shelters to
- Reach out to the struggling families who need it
- But I believe we can help struggling families regain their sense of power and self esteem by giving them access to
- They needed help, just as so many families do
- To ensure families get the support they so desperately need
- When you come right down to it, it's families that really count
- For those of us with a roof over our heads, food to eat and loving families to nurture us
- You're keeping families together when you give
- People who battle every day to find ways to feed their families
- Helping families get back on their feet

FAMILY

- Spotted a family in serious distress
- Today, that family is functioning again
- When this affliction strikes, the whole family suffers
- And they agonize – one family at a time
- Delivered right to a struggling family's door
- The receiving family itself will then pay part of the cost
- How the ravages of this disease affected the whole family
- Please think about the torment this family is experiencing
- This means thousands of family members will be affected

- A complete family support service designed to meet the unique needs of parents and children in the home, school and community
- Meeting poverty, violence and unemployment head-on with a wide variety of family services
- Please give a mother the means to feed her family
- As part of our donor family, we'll let you know what's happening
- I feel that my children and I are very much a part of a larger family.
- We want you to remain part of our family
- Now, more than ever, we need the support of all our donor family
- Whatever your choice, you're part of our family
- The dedicated volunteers who make up our family
- Almost as though you were an unseen member of that family
- Without home, family or friends
- Like being part of a large, caring family
- Perhaps has helped you or someone in your immediate family through a tough time in their lives
- Every day counts to a family trying to survive
- I feel that my children and I belong to a much greater family
- The tools to handle the needs of each family member
- The crushing financial sacrifices of the one income, one parent family
- You and I can't afford to have adults without help suffer from unemployment and family pressures
- The family of humankind
- Let me tell you about a family I know
- You may wonder how a family copes

Family: household, brood, kin, kinsfolk, parentage, descent, folks, kith and kin, tribe, clan, race, branch, pedigree, species

See also: CHILDREN, COMMUNITY, FRIENDSHIP, HOME, NEIGHBORHOOD, MOTHER, PARENTHOOD

FANCY
- Not just a whim or fancy, but enduring help
- It's not fancy, but it's theirs
- Our service hasn't a single fancy frill

FARMER
- We would not be able to tell farmers about these simple farming methods without your continued support
- Women farmers working small plots are the backbone of the economy
- Grassroots support starts with helping subsistence farmers

FATE
- Only you can change their frightening fate
- Never accept a fate like this
- Fated to fail – unless you step in now
- The fate of millions lies in your hands

See also: **CHOICE, DESTINY, FUTURE**

FATHER
- Without a father for so many of the formative years
- Working to get the fathers involved too
- Fathers who only want to do the very best for their children

FAVOR
- So won't you please do me the favor of responding
- Returning this great favor by
- May I ask a favor of you
- Must not favor one plan or the other

FEAR
- Even the names trigger fear
- Fear, anxiety and denial may hinder
- Living in constant fear
- Fears will be calmed
- Must not allow themselves to be paralyzed by fear
- Together, we are shattering the unreasoned fears that still exist about
- Create a facility where people from all walks of life are able to encounter their inner fears
- Try to capitalize upon our fear and anxiety about crime and violence
- Fear of change can stop us dead in our tracks
- Boldly breaking through the fear
- Most fears are really about what might happen, not what is happening
- Discovering where these fears really originate
- Finally lifts the veil of fear
- At least you can attach a name to your fears
- Like so many others, he had his fears
- Fear can be replaced with pride and joy

Fear: fright, dread, alarm, terror, horror, dismay, apprehension, misgiving, distrust, qualm, worry, concern, consternation, trepidation, panic, suspicion
See also: **DREAD, HORROR, NIGHTMARE, TERROR, THREAT**

FEATURE
- Another very popular feature has been
- The most important feature of this plan is
- Let me explain the very best feature to you

See also: **ASPECT, CHARACTER**

FEED
- That feed an ever increasing percentage of the poor
- Looking to us to be fed and housed
- Feeding on this idea, a whole new notion has developed
- To feed so many hungry is an enormous undertaking

See also: **DEVELOP, GROW, NURTURE, SUPPORT**

FEEL

- If you feel the way I do about
- It feels really good just to help out
- You'll feel so good about helping
- How would you feel if one of your loved ones were
- You feel terrific knowing that your gift helped
- Like you, I feel passionate about
- You can feel the changes happening
- Feel the difference for yourself
- Wait until you feel the pure satisfaction of helping
- Imagine how they feel, faced with such devastation

Feel: sense, intuit, have a hunch, feel in one's bones, know, apprehend, perceive, see, note, discern, understand, comprehend, sympathize, empathize, commiserate, pity, weep for, lament, bleed for, experience, touch, go through, bear

FEELING

- The confident feeling of "I can do anything"
- That glorious inner feeling
- Such a good feeling fills you
- A breakthrough in expressing their true feelings
- Nothing can replace that wonderful feeling in your heart
- Share the special feeling
- It is important for us to be able to express our feelings
- The fellow feeling was marvellous
- Get that joyful feeling deep down inside you
- Tools to effectively communicate feelings

See also: **EMOTION, SENSE**

FEES

- We have to scramble just to find the fees
- Our fees are very reasonable, especially when you compare what they give you, with those of other organizations
- Unless people like you help, we will be forced to raise our fees
- In order to prevent fees from shooting out of reach
- Can't allow fees to be an obstacle to those who so brilliantly deserve

See also: **COSTS, EXPENSE**

FELLOWSHIP

- All of which has leavened our fellowship and
- How can we build on the remarkable outpouring of fellowship
- Please join in our fellowship by
- Your fellowship is an integral and essential part of our effort

See also: **AFFILIATION, FRIENDSHIP, PARTNERSHIP**

FIGHT

- Working with us in this fight
- A leader in the fight for
- Fight to save and enhance
- Really believe it's a fight we can win
- We can't fight this alone
- You can fight back against the specific factors that contribute
- Able to continue the fight for all of us
- Fighting against poverty and hunger, we offer not words, but deeds
- Built by people who knew how to wage a fight
- Now another fight is needed
- With you beside us, this fight can be won
- We can't fight the sword alone
- I should emphasize that our fight is more than a matter or principle – it's a fight to preserve life
- Don't have to fight for the care and consideration they deserve
- Brilliant people are trained and chafing to join the fight

See also: ATTACK, BATTLE, STRUGGLE, WAR

FIGHTER

- She was a fighter
- Such gutsy fighters deserve our support
- Back a fighter all the way

See also: ADVOCATE, CHAMPION

FINANCE

- Must ensure financing for our next project
- Helping us get our finances in shape
- Only you can help us finance this emergency operation

FINANCIAL

- With tremendous financial pressures reshaping the types of
- Your financial support helps maintain an irreplaceable lifeline
- Your financial gift is a vital key to wiping out this appalling
- This also means we have no financial safety net
- We continually require financial support
- Your financial support is much appreciated as we battle
- Due to financial constraints, we fall far short of meeting the need
- We asked you to help us through an unusually difficult financial time
- The mailings we send give you an opportunity to show your ongoing support with a financial contribution
- We are asking you to support this fund so that we can achieve a permanent financial base that will allow us to continue to
- We can't count on them to make the same financial pledge as before
- This time of year we need a financial boost for the work ahead
- But that requires a strong financial base

- The financial squeeze we're in right now isn't just our problem, it's your problem too
- Your financial support is the very tap root of our
- Your financial contribution of $__ or $__ or whatever you can manage
- Your financial encouragement means so much
- A concocted financial crisis appears to be winning over votes
- We continually require financial support from individuals like yourself to maintain our important public service programs
- We're continually battling to overcome the financial gap created by the impact that spiralling costs and increased competition have had on our shrinking base funding
- Contributed significant financial support toward preserving our
- I assure you that your financial support will be used effectively so that our cause can grow across
- That's why I'm hoping you'll join with me in making a financial commitment to this outstanding organization
- On their behalf, I am asking you to send a financial gift today
- By supporting our programs financially, you help save people like
- And we can only do it with your financial help
- Your financial support will help us share your views and ideas with all interested parties
- From a purely financial perspective
- Working hard to ensure the long term financial viability of
- If the financial situation is dismal now
- Knowing where we stand financially at any given moment

See also: **BUSINESS, COST, DONATION, FUNDING, GIFT, MONEY, SUPPORT**

FIND
- Trying to find out what was wrong with
- Find out how you can help
- The more we find out, the more we realize the urgency of
- I know you will find a way to support this effort

See also: **DISCOVER, SEARCH**

FINGER
- We must stop the finger pointing and get to work together
- Able to put our finger on the exact cause and remedy
- Tie a string around you r finger to remember us
- Finger the culprit immediately

See also: **BLAME, CONDEMNATION, GUILT, JUSTICE**

FIRST
- We're proud of this very important first for us
- First on our list is
- Will always be first with us

- For the first time anywhere, we have brought together a group more impressive than
- Research like this is leading to first-of-its-kind treatment

See also: **LEADER**

FIRST NATIONS
- What the place meant to the First Nations from the start of time
- Sense the meaning of the land to First Nations people and everyone else who has been exposed to it
- Our First Nations have much to teach us

FIT
- It'll be a close fit but we can do it
- Doesn't always fit into our world, the world we know
- In order to fit closely with other organized activities
- Please fit us into your annual giving plan
- Everything fits together beautifully

FIX
- There are no easy fixes for this problem
- Quick fixes don't work in parenting
- If we don't fix this, who will
- There is really only one way to fix such an unfortunate situation
- Have figured out a low-cost way to fix this

FOCUS
- Had a sharp focus on this problem due to her understanding of
- In the fall, there was a lot of focus on
- Now we must focus on action
- Our current focus is on
- We must shift the focus to
- Focusing on the most common problems found in
- Sometimes there just seems to be too much to focus on
- So that patients can focus on getting better
- A razor keen focus on the heart of the issue
- A strong appeal for people to make a major shift in focus from waiting to see what happens to taking major action
- Our main focus is to work for the release of
- Can become a vital focusing point for
- Maintaining focus despite all the obstacles that get in the way
- Focusing our efforts on very specific area
- One of the main focuses of our work concerns

Focus: converge, unify, bring together, concentrate, unite, zero in on, axis, center, central point, core, heart, marrow, crux, navel, rivet, stress
See also: **ATTENTION, CONCENTRATE**

FOLLOW-UP
- In order to pay for even the most basic follow-up
- Immediate follow-up action was called for
- The problem is that there is little or no follow-up
- What we need is follow-up and consistency that can finally be provided

FOOD
- The result is a food box brimming with freshness and goodness delivered to a struggling family
- Find ways to feed families healthful food with dignity and self reliance
- People who are able to survive with dignity are those who can provide nourishing food for their own families
- Just when money and food are often running low, we deliver
- Food that will help children grow up healthy, strong and vibrant
- Left not only in a worse financial predicament but there wasn't enough food to go around
- When the harvest is poor, they have to use every ounce of rice and wheat for food, otherwise they'd starve
- Food and health care to the homeless
- A hot meal and good food can make all the difference

See also: **LIFEBLOOD, MALNUTRITION, NURTURE, SUSTAIN**

FORCE
- A vibrant new force came into their lives
- Powerful forces are working to destroy everything we've built up with so much hard work
- No on understands the forces at work better than
- What you and I can do to stand up against the destructive forces of evil
- Symbolized the most powerful force shaping all of us
- External and internal forces unseen in this century come into play
- Our primary goal is to become a leading force in
- This organization is the driving force for

See also: **DRIVE, ENERGY, MOMENTUM, POWER**

FORECAST
- Let us work you into our forecast
- We're showing the forecast for the next
- With your help we can change this glum forecast
- Since you've been pitching in, forecasts have improved dramatically

See also: **FUTURE, POTENTIAL**

FOREFRONT
- We are at the forefront of the issue of
- Continues in the forefront of global efforts to improve the lives of poor people
- Your partnership keeps us in the forefront

FORESIGHT
- With foresight and wisdom, our ancestors created
- Continued foresight is needed
- With enough foresight, we can keep on course no matter what difficulties are thrown at us

FORGET
- We must never forget where we came from or how far we've come
- Makes us forget the hardship and see the beauty
- Please don't forget that
- We can forget at our peril
- I will never forget the heart wrenching sight
- In case you've forgotten

Forget: fail to remember, disremember, slip one's mind, lose sight of, overlook, pass over, escape, miss, pass by, omit, let be, let alone, take no notice of, ignore, neglect, write off, dismiss, close one's eyes to, wink at

See also: ERADICATE, LOSE, OVERLOOK

FORM
- You will note that on the enclosed form that you have the opportunity of making a gift to the
- Take a moment to complete the enclosed form and return it to me with your tax-creditable cheque for $__ or more if you can possibly manage
- Mail your enclosed form today
- To decide which form your assistance will take

FORMAT
- This has been altogether the best format for
- We hope to revise the format soon of
- Fitted successfully into a stripped-down, streamlined, modern format
- The new format has proved exceedingly efficient

FORTUNATE
- Help those less fortunate than yourself
- We who are so fortunate must think of others who are not
- Very fortunate to have had so much assistance
- Your help is one of the most fortunate things happening to these people
- So fortunate to have you as one of our donor family
- When you think how fortunate each of us really is
- Those less fortunate than you

See also: LUCKY

FOUNDATION
- Building a solid foundation on which to fulfil their lives and their relationships
- Acquire a solid foundation for
- Foundation for healthy development and learning

- A streamlined, financially sound foundation ensures continued growth and service for
- Donors like you make a firm foundation
- Acting like individual bricks in a foundation
- Help us build a firm foundation for

Foundation: fundamental, basis, groundwork, fundamental principle, source, root, grounds, reason, rationale, cause, motive, occasion, base, ground, substructure, founding, setting up, footing, institution, establishment
See also: BASIC, NECESSITY

FOUNDED

- That's why our organization is even more important now than when it was founded so many years ago
- Ask yourself what your beliefs are really founded upon
- Founded upon strong and unalienable principles
- Well-founded guidelines have produced success

FREE

- Help, free of charge, to those who need it
- I hope you will feel free to visit us
- You've helped free thousands of
- Finally free to do as they please
- Those of us who understand what it is to be truly free
- To be finally free of this debilitating problem

Free: independent, self-governing, self-directed, liberated, emancipated, rescued, unhampered, voluntary, unconditional, generous, liberal, unbound

FREEDOM

- To secure immediate and unconditional freedom
- Our freedoms remain in peril
- A place in which to move beyond fear into freedom
- The joy of finally arriving in this great land of freedom and opportunity
- The freedom to choose is a very precious right
- Will give us a lot more freedom in that area

Freedom: liberty, independence, emancipation, release, relief, scope, elbow room, privilege, right, leisure, sincerity, candor, naturalness, autonomy
See also: AUTONOMY, INDEPENDENCE, PRIVILEGE, RELIEF

FRIEND

- Has been a longtime friend of
- A friend in need is a friend in deed
- You are a treasured friend
- Become a lifelong friend
- Be a friend to those without anyone else to rely upon
- That's why we need to encourage new friends like you to join us
- Become one of the best friends they'll ever have

- As a friend you'll discover a world of other friends who
- Friends interested in volunteering and fundraising
- It couldn't happen without friends like you who care so much
- Wouldn't be there if it weren't for friends like you
- With the help of our many friends and members
- We depend more than ever on loyal friends like you
- Last year, thousands of volunteer "friends" like you contributed over
- Join the growing number of friends who support
- Please ask your friends to get involved too
- Winning friends all over the world
- Honest caring is the best way to win friends
- We consider you one of our old friends and would not, under any circumstances
- We're looking for a few hundred friends to help us raise money
- Sure could use a little help from its friends
- The thousands who suffer from this condition need caring friends like you to help them improve their lives
- Please join friends and neighbors in supporting

Friend: booster, confederate, pal, admirer, supporter, acquaintance, champion, companion, sidekick, buddy, confidante, ally, alter ego, soul mate, helpmate, peer, colleague, compatriot, confrere, associate, coworker, cohort, collaborator, helper, assistant, advocate, patron, benefactor

See also: CAREGIVER, DONOR, FAMILY, HELPER, PARTNER, SUPPORTER

FRIENDSHIP
- They are so hungry for friendship
- The comfort of new friendships
- Now is the time to join together in enduring friendship
- We value your friendship enormously
- Building friendships, building support

See also: CARING, COMMUNITY, FAMILY, PARTNERSHIP

FRIGHTEN
- What frightens us most is that
- To stop being frightened of the possible consequences
- Hard work and persistence do not frighten us
- Standing firm in the face of this frightening situation

See also: ALARM, WARNING

FRONT LINE
- Has been on the front lines for many years
- Your donation goes directly to front line workers
- This battle isn't all fought on the front lines
- We stand shoulder to shoulder on the front lines
- Please back our courageous front line workers with your generosity

FRUITION
- I applaud you for your help to bring this to fruition
- To bring these research discoveries to fruition
- With so many projects so close to fruition, we just can't stop now for lack of funds

See also: CONSEQUENCES, OUTCOME, RESULTS, SUCCESS

FRUSTRATE
- I'm so frustrated I can't even think straight
- I can certainly relate to their agony and frustration
- Help overcome the frustration of not being able to give enough help
- Must not let this unexpected obstacle frustrate our plans
- If you've been frustrated about not being able to do anything personally about this problem, here's a way
- To reduce the frustration of dealing with difficult people

See also: PREVENT, STOP

FUNCTION
- How it functions and what affects it
- Without your support and encouragement, our organization could not function
- Our organization has so many important functions
- It is responsible for so many vital functions

FUND
- Every dollar of that fund represents precious new hope for
- Every day, with your assistance, the fund moves toward its goal
- Relying on friends like you to fund this noble venture
- Protecting this fund must be a strong priority
- A fund not just of money, but of expertise and enthusiasm
- Desperately short of funds
- Funds need to be increased significantly
- Once again, funds are getting short
- Vital funds slashed away just as demand is skyrocketing
- A calamitous withdrawal of funds
- Handling the funds provided by supporters of our work is a responsibility we exercise with care and pride
- The remaining funds went to support many other urgent `projects including
- However, we are able to provide less than half of the funds urgently requested annually, simply because we do not have the money for this life saving work
- Slashing away at the funds that are the very underpinning
- Including the funds needed to start
- There are no funds presently available for
- Funds are so scarce at this time of year
- Our funds are limited but our work is limitless
- In order to provide the necessary funds

Fund: endowment, accumulation, pool, reserve, store, supply, nest egg, savings, treasury, cash, asset, money, grant, capital, means

FUNDING
- The sad fact is, we receive relatively little funding compared to other
- So more of our funding can be directed toward programming
- Most importantly, we want you to know that gifts from individuals like yourself account for almost all of our funding
- Funding the further enhancement of
- With no end to funding cuts in sight
- Our government funding has steadily decreased
- We back them up with funding and technical support
- We receive only a limited amount of funding from
- The importance of private funding to support our programs cannot be overestimated
- Lack of proper funding leaves us so frustrated
- We receive our funding from people like you
- Just think of how much it would mean to the lives of so many if we had the funding to make this service available to everyone who needs it and is eagerly waiting for it
- Our funding is limited but our work is limitless
- When more funding would go so far to solve the problem
- Even as funding shrinks alarmingly, need increases every day
- We receive no government funding
- Funding cutbacks are putting even greater pressure on our services
- Just one of the ways we hope to meet this year's funding needs
- Successfully lobby for increased funding

See also: CONTRIBUTION, FINANCE, MEANS, MONEY, RESOURCE, SUPPORT

FUNDRAISER
- This annual fundraiser is open to the public
- Your services as a volunteer fundraiser are deeply appreciated
- Our fundraisers work so hard

See also: FRIEND, VOLUNTEER, WORKER

FUNDRAISING
- Today, I want to take a few moments to tell your more about our fundraising program
- The major part of our fundraising is done by mail and by phone
- I also want you to know a little more about how our fundraising initiative works
- The task of fundraising is becoming extremely difficult
- Determined to take a practical, organized approach to fundraising
- Asking people to give not money, but time to help in our fundraising effort
- In fundraising, time can be even more valuable than money
- Practical tips to solve your fundraising challenges
- Organize a fundraising effort to amass a war chest

- Note your very successful fundraising efforts last year

FUTURE
- Plot our course for the future
- Only you can keep the future glowing
- Together, we can keep the future bright for those who need it most
- Immense pride in our past and hope for the future
- Help foster the future through new
- I'm enthusiastic and optimistic about the future
- Give them back a rosy, promising future
- Everyone knows the problem has grim consequences for our future
- You'll have a part of their future as they grow strong and self-sufficient
- A dream for the future is to build
- As a bonus, you'll have a chance to impact the future of
- Thought-provoking predictions for the future
- A future for every child
- Chance has given them a bleak and uncertain future through no fault of their own
- Allowing us to face our future as a nation
- Giving you a say in the future
- We would be sacrificing our future
- Make sure our children have the skills they need for the future
- When you give, you're giving a gift that builds for the future and works for today
- It can deny them the brighter future our kids take for granted
- Whose future will be brighter because of you
- Your help is critical to our future
- The level of service you will expect in the future
- This is our future being lost
- Denied a say in their own future
- We're working for a better future by helping people become self-sufficient
- Changed from being strong and independent into people who couldn't imagine a future with any sort of hope
- The future looks even brighter
- Now we invite you to play an active role in our future
- Help strive for a pain-free future
- A future packed with new challenges, a passion for a very different life
- Our future is in your hands
- Setting the way the world will work in the future
- It gives me such great hope for the future
- Help us invent a whole new future
- Invent your future by what you decide today
- You're looking at the face of the future
- Inspiring thousands of people to create a more powerful and purposeful future for themselves
- Charting a future with dreams and true desires guiding the way
- Delivering the future to
- Change now for a better future

- Forging a different future from the present they inhabit
- Invites the participation and assistance of those who share this vision of the future
- Embraces the future with action and hope
- We ask you to join us in this option of hope for the future
- Embracing the future enthusiastically
- We will not mortgage our future
- Support future generations with a stroke of your pen
- Because their future is your future

See also: DESTINY, FATE, FORECAST, FORESIGHT, HOPE, TOMORROW, UPDATE

GAIN

- With your backing, we're making steady gains
- You have nothing to lose and everything to gain by
- You have such a lot to gain by helping
- Help them gain a little more hope each day

GALVANIZE

- Galvanized by the need for
- Galvanized by the sight of
- Provided the shock needed to galvanize people into useful action

See also: MOTIVATE, STIMULATE

GAME

- Helping to win a very dangerous game
- This isn't any game we're involved in
- The game is just getting interesting

GAP

- We are continually battling to overcome the financial gap created by
- Every year, the gap between the rich and the poor gets wider
- But, as usual, the leaders could only come up with stop-gap measures
- It's up to each one of us to step into the gap and increase our support
- Committed to bridging the gap that separates people who
- Thanks to you, we can bridge the gap between
- Filling major gaps in the system
- Dedicated to overcoming the funding gap by asking your participation
- Closing the gap between what government programs offer and what human service and environmental organizations desperately need
- An initiative to do our part and fill the gap
- We need you to help fill that gap
- We're rapidly closing the gap
- Stop-gap measures are not enough

See also: BREACH, FAILURE, SHORTFALL

GENERATION

- Now a younger generation is itching to follow in their footsteps
- The movement is being fuelled by generational changes
- Another generation rebels at the thought of
- A generation that prides itself on individuality and freedom
- Passed from one generation to the next
- Give pleasure to later generations
- To last for generations to come
- Give today so that future generations – your children and mine – can finally live free of this agonizing scourge

GENEROSITY

- Should you be able to extend your generosity to
- As a non-profit organization, we rely on the generosity of donors to a great extent
- Your generosity can help keep the fight alive and well
- Through your generosity, we can conquer
- It's your generosity that's easing pain and giving them fresh hope
- Your generosity will help the helpless, feed the hungry and provide assistance to those who need it
- Thanks to the ongoing generosity of caring people like you
- Your generosity means we can continue to make a difference
- Thanks to your generosity
- Your generosity means to much to so many
- Your generosity helps give the gift that's needed most
- We count on the generosity of people like you to help save those lives
- Your unselfish generosity means a lot
- Hundreds have responded with generosity and warmth

GENEROUS

- With the help of many generous people like you, we are dedicated to
- Please be as generous as you can
- I know you are a generous person
- Please give generously today
- Won't you please be generous
- We hope you will be generous in this emergency
- The more generous you can be, the more people you help
- I urge you to be a generous as you can
- I encourage you to give generously
- Appealing to a generous and loving heart
- Give in to a generous impulse
- To those who are generous of spirit, our profound thanks
- Generous people trust us with their donations
- Please be as generous as you possibly can
- Let that generous feeling steal over you

Generous: charitable, bountiful, benevolent, munificent, liberal, big-hearted, open-handed, humanitarian, altruistic, unselfish, public-spirited, good, noble, kind,

kindhearted, unstinted, lavish, free, unrestricted, ungrudging, ample, obliging, considerate, accommodating, hospitable, abundant, rich, copious, rich, bounteous, overflowing, plentiful
See also: CHARITABLE, GIVING, HELPFUL, KIND

GENIUS
- Sometimes you feel that a playful genius is at work
- The genius of this plan is that
- It doesn't take a genius to understand the possible consequences of
- You never know where the next genius will be nurtured

GESTURE
- The gesture has proved quite futile
- Much, much more than just some grand gesture
- There isn't a better gesture you could make than to give

GIANT
- Destined to be one of the giants
- We stand on the shoulders of giants
- Help us take a giant step forward

GIFT
- Your gift brings relief and a cure that much closer
- Will you be a Good Samaritan by sending a generous gift
- An equally valuable gift is given in return
- In response to your gift, hearts are moved
- Send your gift now before you put this letter aside
- And will you please consider sending a gift to
- And of course, if you can send a gift of any amount, your generosity will be a tremendous help to us
- In this time of urgent need, if you could find it possible to add to the amount of your previous gift, so many more could be helped
- A simple but crucial gift
- By giving a generous, tax-deductible gift of compassion
- No matter how large or small your gift may be, it is deeply valued
- Your tax-deductible gift will allow us to reach more people and involve them in our campaign
- Your gift of whatever you can afford will make a big difference
- Your gift to us is a gift of warm clothes and hot food to those who are cold and hungry
- Your gift will help send even more
- Your gift will help our member groups to
- Thanks for your time, concern, and gift
- Bring help to those who need it with a generous gift today
- Although we have no set fee, consider that a gift of $__, $__ or whatever you can afford will make a substantial difference

- Your gift reaches out to so many
- Your very special gift cannot come to soon
- The gift of your kind assistance
- Your gift will be at hard at work and will ensure
- Your gift will enrich the lives of
- Your gift is an act of kindness
- Your gift will be used wisely
- Your gift is greatly appreciated
- Please consider a gift of $__, $__ or even $___
- Your gift means so much to so many
- Your gift holds the key
- The gift that keeps growing
- Your gift makes such good sense
- Your gift enables us to continue
- Your gift is so important to what we can do in the next quarter
- A gift straight from your heart is the most valuable
- Help give the gift that's needed most
- I urge you to send your gift as soon as possible
- Please send the largest gift you can
- Your tax-deductible gift will make a lasting difference
- Please send your much-needed gift today
- With your gift, you'll be touching a life in a crucial way
- You'd be surprised how far your gift will go
- Will you help by sending a gift of
- Send a single gift of
- Your gift will help us send out thousands of information packages
- Your gift, of any amount, will help
- Or maybe at this time you could help even more with a gift
- By sharing your gift, you will help us provide
- That's why I must ask you if you could give a special gift
- One that is perhaps a little more than your usual gift
- With your gift, we can treat so many more
- Your gift directly affects the quality of
- Your gift will have a tremendous impact on
- Every gift is important and appreciated
- Send us the form; we will verify your gift and do the rest
- Every gift is important
- Many of you were generous enough to go one step further by making an extra gift during the year
- Make your special gift right this minute
- Even if you have already made your annual renewal gift, I hope you will make an extra gift for whatever amount you can afford
- Gifts from our donors are responsible for so much of what we've been able to accomplish
- One of the greatest gifts you can give yourself and your family
- A gift of any size will be greatly appreciated

- Please help keep hope bright by making a year-end gift to
- Believe me, every gift is needed and appreciated
- A gift of $__ or whatever you can afford will help strengthen our efforts on your behalf
- We are very happy to receive gifts-in-kind of equipment or goods
- Please be sure to include a special gift
- Here are some examples of what your gift can do
- The greatest gift you can give
- Is the most precious gift you can give
- Because of your generosity, they'll receive gifts they could only dream of
- Please put a generous gift on your "to do" list this week
- Please send your gift today to support brave and resourceful people working for justice and long-term change
- Your gift will touch so many lives

Gift: assistance, support, aid, kindness, generosity, contribution, donation, pledge, sponsorship, resources, alliance, investment, involvement, endowment, bequest, present, offering, premium, benefit, bonus, charity, alms, gratuity, grant, subsidy, allowance, handout, bestowal, almsgiving, largesse

See also: CARING, COLLABORATION, COMMITMENT, COMPASSION, CONTRIBUTION, DEDICATION, DOLLARS, DONATION, GENEROSITY, HELP, MONEY, OFFERING, SACRIFICE, SUPPORT

GIRL

- More girls and boys want to join than ever before
- But you and I can help these little girls – and thousands like them
- Despite her terrible disability, just longing to be one of the girls
- It's especially important that young girls receive this boost of confidence early in their lives
- Be there for this girl and her family, providing education, comfort and support, assuring sufferers that they weren't alone in their misery
- Education for girls is especially crucial
- To finally give girl children the same advantages as their brothers
- Helping girls shake off ingrained cultural disadvantages

See also: CHILDREN, FAMILY, KIDS, YOUTH, WOMEN

GIVE

- Give them something they could never give themselves
- You can give, too
- If you don't have anything to give at this time, it's okay
- Whatever you give will come back to you many times over in satisfaction and joy
- Every cent you give will be spent on
- Contribute to the cause and give a share
- Please give as much as you can afford
- Give an amount that is meaningful to you
- Give more if you can, or give less, but give
- When you give, what are you doing?

- Give as generously as you possibly can
- Regardless of the amount you can give, it will help
- The more you give, the more help we can extend
- To all of you who give so graciously time and time again
- Now, more than ever, please give
- Something has to give
- Give – so you can sleep at night
- Remember, it is better to give than to receive
- The more you give, the more help we can extend
- Please give whatever you can afford
- Give more than thanks
- Tremendous willingness to give
- My gift is the opportunity to give
- If you don't give, who will

Give: present, bestow, donate, contribute, turn over, award, hand over, vouchsafe, grant, leave, supply, shell out, pay, dish out, allot, allocate, mete out, distribute, apportion, dispense, offer, manifest, yield, consign, surrender, relinquish, furnish, endow, entrust, invest, provide, afford, impart, communicate, deliver, confer, empower, enable, authorize, expend, put out, pitch in

See also: **BACK, COMMIT, CONTRIBUTE, DONATE, FUND, PLEDGE, PROMISE, PROVIDE, SUPPORT, VOLUNTEER**

GIVEN

- This seems like such a given here in
- Such sickening conditions do not have to be a given
- Assumed this to be a given and not negotiable

GIVING

- Giving is as easy as completing and returning the enclosed donation form
- That's why I keep on giving
- The gift of giving
- That's why I hope you'll keep on giving too
- We know you won't stop giving after your first gift
- Your gift will keep on giving to those in need

GLOBAL

- With a global framework being established
- Finally realize this has global implications
- Working hard until these changes are global
- You can be part of a network that is truly global
- A global problem, a global response

See also: **COMMUNITY, EARTH, INTERNATIONAL, WORLD**

GO

- Where does it all go
- If you wonder where it all goes

- We really couldn't go on without you
- To ask where we are going

GOAL

- Thanks to the support of concerned people like you, we can work determinedly toward that goal
- Suggesting ways in which our organization can be reformed and transformed to meet this goal will be a continuing priority project in the coming months
- Help us reach our goal
- Our primary goal is to promote increased public enjoyment and use of the area
- With your help, we can reach this goal
- Our goal is to find better ways to treat disease and, through research, to find a cure
- Our ultimate goal is to stop, and eventually reverse
- Our number one goal
- Our goal is to prove the pen is mightier than the sword
- We need your financial help to reach this goal
- Our goal is to make sure we do it right
- Please help us towards that goal with a generous gift
- Please help us reach our goal of universal access to
- The goal of all our good work is to make
- The goal of the program is to help people understand the crucial link
- An alliance of people with a common goal of caring
- If every family gave a little, we could reach our goal
- You are the first to know about these special goals set by our staff
- But in order to accomplish these goals, we need the support and understanding of the community
- Help us achieve our goals and help us do even more
- In order to achieve these goals, we are committed to funding more
- First-hand tips on setting and achieving goals
- It's easier to get where you're going when you learn to set goals
- Setting and redefining personal goals
- These are the goals of the Annual Fund
- No finer goals are possible than these
- Our program sets achievable development goals
- To help us carefully examine her goals
- Here are just a few of our goals

Goal: intent, purpose, aim, intention, end, ideal, object, objective, target
See also: AIM, DECISION, DREAM, END, PURPOSE, TARGET

GOOD

- Good times begin with a call to
- Does so much good for others
- Remembered and respected for the good you do others
- Unfortunately, the good feeling I had lasted only until I found out the hard reality
- Do something good today

- Oh boy, does it feel good to
- It really feels good to have helped so many
- And I know you'll feel good about that
- Our workers are very good at what they do
- Chances are good that one of those saved is someone you know or love
- Feel good with good reason
- Doing the least harm and most good
- Please be good enough to
- Give till it feels good

GOOD DEED

- By our good deeds we will be remembered
- It only takes one good deed to make a difference
- A good deed today will really make you smile
- Your opportunity to do a good deed today

Good deed: sustenance, favor, blessing, grace, sponsorship, auspices, good offices, kind regard, fosterage, furtherance, advancement, advance, advantage, welfare, maintenance, ministry, ministration, restoration, boon, good deed, kind deed, good turn, subsidy,

GOOD WILL

- Persuade people of good will, such as yourself
- And please, share that good will by supporting
- Such good will, supported by your kind donations, can truly work wonders

GOODNESS

- Truly brimming with goodness
- Thank goodness for an organization that
- Determined to support the forces of goodness in this world
- Please have the goodness to
- Reap hundredfold the goodness that you sow

See also: GENEROSITY, KINDNESS

GOVERNMENT

- Unlike many other charitable organizations, we neither seek nor accept government support
- Add to that a financially strapped government forced to reduce funding
- As governments deal with swelling deficits and declining revenue
- If we don't get the support we need to offset government cutbacks, more budgets may face drastic reduction too
- Provided an opportunity for all levels of government to work together to create a revitalized waterfront
- The government has argued that pubic opinion supports its position on social program cuts
- The government gambled that you and I will let the poor get poorer
- But there's still time to influence the government's course of action and turn

things around
- Had an effect on making the government think twice about disastrous budget cuts
- Crimes committed by governments against their own citizens
- All this was sanctioned by the government
- The recent election of government more sympathetic to
- Pressed our government to maintain and strengthen its commitment to keep funding this crucial program
- We can no longer rely upon the government to protect
- Government dollars are shrinking
- Today, government support has been hacked so badly we're struggling just to maintain
- Can no longer count on government programs
- At the same time, uncertain government funding is creating difficulties
- Information on government actions affecting charities you'll find nowhere else
- The government has completely reneged on its promise to
- Looking for other ways besides government to obtain needed dollars
- More than the government can do

Government: administration, guidance, management, authority, dictatorship, parliament, congress, regime, command, rule, leadership, reign, presidency, statesmanship, regulation, supervision

GRANT
- To help those we have targeted this year, we must match these grants dollar for dollar with contributions
- That's why these grants are so important right now
- It's terribly important to take two things for granted
- We must not take such progress for granted
- Don't take this organization for granted

GRATEFUL
- I am grateful to you all for your interest and support
- We are particularly grateful to
- No one could be more grateful than those who have received such essential help
- Please accept our grateful thanks

Grateful: indebted, thankful, obliged, appreciative, beholden, under obligation, fulled with gratitude, pleased, agreeable

GRATIFY
- None more gratifying than
- In order to gratify this wish
- Here's a way to gratify your natural desire to help
- Imagine the gratification you will feel when you give
- Feel an immense sense of gratification in the fact that

GRATITUDE
- Runs high with emotion and gratitude

- Whisper their soft gratitude for this great gift of love
- We cannot really express in words our deep gratitude to you for
- Asked me to extend personal gratitude for

See also: APPRECIATION, THANKS
See also: SECTION FIVE – SAYING THANKS

GREETINGS

- I am pleased to extend my warmest greetings
- Greetings to our many loyal supporters
- Warmest greetings on another holiday season as we ask your help
- A wonderful way to add to your greetings is to include a donation

GRIEF

- Grief is a normal, natural response
- So much grief could be saved if only a little more money were available to spend
- Learning how to develop a healthy response to grief
- To join in working through grief and anger
- A way of expressing your grief and condolences
- Grief that only the closest friends can understand
- Many friends can share this grief

See also: LOSS, PAIN, SORROW, SUFFERING, TEARS

GRIEVE

- I grieve every day, thinking of the potentially meaningful years that have been stolen from
- Millions around the world are grieving
- No sight is sadder than that of a grieving mother
- To those who have suffered grievous harm, help must be extended

GROUND

- They become a common ground for all of us
- Breaking new ground every day
- This ground-breaking program offers enormous possibilities
- To help those ground down by life's difficulties
- Working hard just not to lose ground
- Gain ground inch by hard-won inch

See also: BREAKTHROUGH, EARTH, PROGRESS, WORLD

GROUP

- Finally found a group of people who knew what he had been through and what he needed
- You're part of a very special group
- A large and enthusiastic group of supporters
- One of the first to form a support group in our province so families could learn how to cope
- For people who think a group working together is much

more exciting than separate individuals battling each other
- Sorting out the roles and rules of group interaction
- Presenting several models of self-help groups
- Through supportive group sharing
- Also working more closely with target groups
- Our membership includes groups as diverse as

See also: **COMMUNITY, FAMILY, GROUP, PARTNERSHIP**

GROW

- We can provide them with a chance to grow up to be confident, caring people and future leaders
- They grow a little food to feed their families.
- Helping people grow inside
- You'd be astonished at how just a little help lets them grow and change
- Growing our organization is like growing a plant
- Our support is growing dramatically
- Feel the compassion growing in your heart
- Watching such trends with growing concern, we turn to you
- Growing up is a lot more complicated than it used to be
- When we help them grow, we grow too
- Never question the ability to grow and improve

See also: **DEVELOP, EXPAND, INCREASE**

GROWTH

- To enhance personal growth
- In fact, only by slowing this alarmingly rapid growth can we
- To reach our goal through steady growth
- The explosive growth of
- This accounts for the phenomenal growth of
- Know that your donation, no matter what the level, nurtures, supports and encourages the growth of
- Offering the opportunity for personal growth and development through
- A dynamic vehicle for self-growth

GUARANTEE

- No guarantee we won't be left holding the bag
- When you give, we guarantee deep satisfaction
- A rock solid guarantee
- Help provide the most basic guarantee of safety
- Your gift is your guarantee of caring
- In order to guarantee ongoing programs, we need your help

GUARD

- You'll be guarding your own rights to the hard-won institutions that make our country what it is today
- Stand on guard beside us by

- To guard against creeping indifference
- You can help us guard against
- To fiercely guard such hard-fought progress

See also: ARMOR, CONSERVATION, PRESERVATION, PROTECT, SAFEGUARD, WALL

GUIDANCE
- Receptive to guidance from adults whom they know, like and respect
- They desperately need guidance and leadership
- Sound guidance in this matter is the first priority
- Including the scope, breadth, practical advice and guidance offered in

See also: ADVICE, COUNSEL, EXPERIENCE, HELP, WISDOM

GUILT
- The guilt of having survived when so many others did not
- Horrible guilt swept over him for having passed such a dread burden to his own innocent child.
- Instead of just sitting around feeling guilty, why don't we
- Guilty of the lesser sin of
- Guilty of indifference
- Guilty of spreading a deadly virus

See also: BLAME, CONDEMNATION, REGRET, SORRY

HABIT
- Identifying healthier, life-long skills and habits
- How can we go back to our old, comfortable habits
- Such habits of thought will now have to be abandoned
- Make regular giving a healthy habit
- Get into the habit of helping
- Teach your children the habit of donating early

HAND
- Because no one is there to lend them a hand
- Needing a helping hand just to get by
- Please lend a hand today
- By lending a hand and sending a tax-creditable donation to
- Your gift is a real helping hand to a child striving for independence
- Yes, I will extend a hand to
- Will no one extend a hand to help
- Will you reach out a hand to aid and assist
- I'm hoping you're the one person who will extend a helping hand
- The hand that helps the most
- Last year, we gave a hand up to more than
- Please lend a hand today
- Suffered so much at the hands of
- Held hands and laughed with joy

- Tended them with loving hands
- Kind words and helping hands make all the difference
- Deserving a big hand for doing so well
- To hold your hand when you feel scared about
- Always looking toward others for support and a helping hand
- Maybe it's time to join hands for this journey
- So much material has already passed through our hands
- Without your help, our hands are tied
- Come with open hands

See also: **AID, ASSIST, HELP, OUTREACH, REACH**

HANDICAP

- Struggling under such a tremendous handicap
- Handicapped by lack of resources
- Won't be stopped no matter what the handicap
- You can help remove this unnecessary handicap

See also: **DISABILITY, DISADVANTAGE, OBSTACLE, PROBLEM**

HANDLE

- We must increase our capacity to handle the most difficult cases
- If your budget can handle it, please add a little more to your regular donation
- Have handled the matter in a most exemplary manner
- Can deal with even the most hard to handle

HANDWRITING

- The handwriting is on the wall
- No matter how fancy the handwriting, the message is as grim
- A plea for help in shaky handwriting

See also: **MESSAGE**

HAPPEN

- It could happen to you
- Something that could happen to any of us
- Hope bad things don't happen to you and your family
- But it is happening here, every day
- Something exciting is happening across the country
- This was happening while, just a little way away, a much more significant event was shaking foundations
- Particularly concerned because we see what is happening to people in the places where we work
- What happened there is happening in many other countries too
- When you renew your support, we'll let you know what's happening.
- Not something that might or could happen – it's already happening

HAPPINESS

- Giving a second chance at happiness

- Wishing you happiness, love and laughter
- Despite so many disadvantages, nothing stops their happiness from shining through
- Nothing can outshine the hope and happiness in their eyes

HAPPY

- Help make happy endings come true for
- Discover that the more you help others, the more happy and satisfied you are with your own life
- Full of youth, adults and seniors who are happier, safe and healthier
- At this happy time of year, I'd like to share some of our success stories with you

Happy: delighted, glad, pleased, elated, satisfied, thrilled, cheery, cheerful, sunny, jubilant, overjoyed, laughing, smiling, light-hearted, blithesome, carefree, easy-going, breezy, exultant, fortunate, lucky, opportune, prosperous, correct, flourishing, fitting, appropriate, essential, rewarding, satisfying, exhilarated, apt, good, hilarious, valuable, advantageous, seemly, ecstatic, gleeful, jubilant

See also: DELIGHT, JOY, LUCKY, PLEASURE, SMILE

HARD

- It's just too hard to refuse the help they needs so desperately
- Since the death of her husband, she finds it so hard to go on
- Have fought for this too long and too hard to stop now
- Life can be very hard for those without access to basic
- Attitudes are hardening everywhere
- Hardest of all is wanting the simple daily comforts that everyone else takes for granted

See also: CHALLENGE, DIFFICULT, STRUGGLE

HARDSHIP

- Hardship will be lessened
- It helps caregivers who are facing desperate hardships
- The greatest hardships can be overcome with your assistance
- Those enduring terrible hardships often ask very little
- Free them from a life of unrelenting hardship

HAVEN

- Offers a warm, family-centered haven for the battle ahead
- A haven of peace and caring in the midst of a merciless environment
- Help us keep this haven of safety in this turbulent world
- See it as a haven of joy and safety

See also: HOME, RESCUE, SAFETY, SHELTER

HAVOC

- Know only too well the havoc these rending upheavals can cause
- In the midst of an unbelievable amount of havoc
- Caused dreadful, sudden havoc to thousands of innocent lives

- Funding cuts are playing havoc with crucial long term plans and goals

See also: **CATASTROPHE, CHAOS, DISASTER, MESS**

HEAL

- Heal the wounds of poverty and abuse
- In many instances, the physical body heals but not the psyche
- The healing has at last begun
- Always increasing our knowledge of the healing process
- Let's write a prescription for being healed

HEALTH

- To keep the population in good health is a top priority
- Play a leading role in health care delivery
- Creating ever new responsibilities for the health care professional
- Introducing the most basic concepts of mental health
- Transformed the way people look at health and medicine
- Determined to remain healthy, wealthy and wise
- Where it will threaten our health and our children's health

HEAR

- The best chance to meet and hear
- Please let me hear from you today, if at all possible
- We'd also love to hear from you about this issue
- I'd really like to hear from you and your family
- We hope to hear from you as soon as possible
- We need to hear from you by
- Please let us hear from you very soon
- I look forward to seeing you and hearing your ideas
- Please let me hear from you today
- Through word of mouth we have heard that
- Have you heard about
- I can hardly wait to hear from you
- Don't believe everything you hear

See also: **COMMUNICATE, INFORMATION, UNDERSTAND**

HEART

- Sympathetic ear and understanding heart
- Surely no cause is nearer to our hearts than
- I know your heart rushes out to
- And I'm hoping you'll see it in your heart to help us make a difference
- You have only one heart, and you can't live without it
- I must tell you, from my heart to yours
- Deep in my heart, I know
- Unfortunately, much of the world seems to have a heart of stone
- Only a heart of granite could turn away
- That's why I'm hoping you'll open your heart

- Surely no cause can be nearer to our hearts
- What I see every day would break your heart for I know it breaks mine
- If these sad facts and stories touch your heart
- Find it in your heart to send a generous gift to
- I hope you'll find it in your heart to help generously
- Our workers are the very heart of
- Touch a heart today
- Staggering grief when a beating heart finally stills
- Let me tell you something that may break your heart
- Our hearts go out to you
- Trying to gut the very heart of
- Where are our hearts in this
- Look deep into your heart and find the truth
- Tiny hearts set on winning
- Something close to everyone's heart
- Express what's most dear to your heart
- Make room in your heart for
- Our heart goes out to every one of them

Heart: soul, spirit, gut, feeling, sensibility, sympathy, passion, concern, kindness, courage, bravery, mettle, spunk, core, center, essence, goodness
See also: CARE, CONCERN, COURAGE, GOODNESS, KINDNESS, LOVE, PASSION, SPIRIT

HEARTEN
- Tremendously heartened by
- You can hearten a suffering family
- Your participation is heartening to all of us here

Hearten: inspire, invigorate, encourage, hearten, buck up, pluck up, bear up, build up, buoy up, boost
See also: CHEER, ENCOURAGE

HECTIC
- It's been a hectic year
- No matter how hectic, the rewards always greatly outweigh the
- We just can't keep up this hectic pace without some help from

HELP
- Please help us now
- Your help means so much in finally putting an end to this anguish
- Active, practical help
- Won't you please help once more
- How can I help
- I need to know how much you can help us
- That's how you can help
- We must turn to you for help
- Your help is needed today

- Will you help
- How could you not help
- We'll need your help to be there for so many people
- Help us meet the ever-increasing demand
- You can help so many
- Help us help others
- Help us make progress
- Help fill the need
- Your help is so essential
- Please help
- Your help means so much to
- You can help by making a gift of
- You can help today by writing a check
- Your help is vital
- Help us beat the odds
- Help us succeed
- Help make this vision a reality
- Help make this shining dream come true
- Your help, gift, donation, counts so much
- We can really use your help right now
- Your help is great news
- Without your help, the suffering will continue
- So many are depending on your help
- We need your help and need it fast
- So very many beg for your help
- We need your immediate help
- Please help save these people
- Help us continue
- Help sustain
- Your gift will help launch so many programs
- They need our help urgently
- Helps provide so very much
- Your support, along with that of so many generous fellow citizens, can help, really help
- We're inviting you to help
- This letter is our invitation to help
- We look forward to your help
- Please help us reach out
- Help us make it happen
- Please extend a helping hand
- It's such a beautiful way to help
- We simply cannot do it without your help
- Help us go the distance
- Help us provide hope and guidance
- Here's what you and I can do to help
- Here's how you can help

- You helped raise the money to make this such a success
- Along with the help of so many others
- Help put people back to work
- Help us back a winner all the way
- You'll be helping thousands
- You can help with a generous donation to
- With the help of people like you
- We do it with the help of many friends
- Help those who can't help themselves
- Help us wage a nationwide campaign to
- With your help, we'll make sure that even more people have something to be thankful about
- Without our help, who knows where they'd be today
- But we still need help from you
- So who will you be helping
- Without you, getting help would be just a dream
- In twenty years we've helped a lot of people
- But to continue, we need your help
- Please help ensure that our programs have a future by writing a generous cheque right now
- Your help is needed – and it's needed now!
- I'm writing to you with an urgent request for help
- We really need your help
- With your help, we can continue to provide
- Helping those who cannot help themselves
- Helping others help themselves
- Because right now we really need your help
- Your help is the critical ingredient
- We know that, with your help, we can succeed in improving
- And right now you can help twice as much
- If it weren't for people like you, we wouldn't be able to help as many
- That's why we urgently need your help today
- Here's how you can help in a very specific, personal way
- We just wish we could do more to help
- Each year we help more than a million individuals
- Prepared to help the needy in so many ways
- Frankly, we need all the help you can give, and we need it as soon as possible
- Please, won't you help them today.
- Help us keep going, please
- Won't you help too
- I think I've found someone who can help
- You and your family can help in several ways
- You've helped to make this one of the most successful
- How can you help – please make a contribution of $25, $50, $100 or more
- This is why your help is so important
- But without your help, it can't be done

- There are things each of us can do to help

Help: join in, pitch in, aid, befriend, oblige, abet, accommodate, lend a hand, chip in, lend oneself to, lift a hand to, collaborate, unite, team up with, come to the rescue, expedite, facilitate, hasten, bolster, boost, underwrite, intercede, share, enhance, ameliorate, benefit, help out, provide, assist, serve, be of use

See also: BACK, BENEFIT, CARE, ENCOURAGE, CONTRIBUTE, DONATE, FUND, GIVE, HEARTEN, REACH, SERVE, SUPPORT, VOLUNTEER

HELPLINE

- The helpline is designed to answer your questions
- The helpline is really a lifeline to many who call
- Awareness and effectiveness have greatly increased due to the installation and expansion of our helpline

HELPER

- Without a helper like this, we never could have
- But the best helpers are people like you
- In order to finance our many volunteer helpers

Helper: laborer, personnel, staff, crew, work force, gang, team, helpmeet, assistant, right hand, supporter, benefactor, faculty

See also: CAREGIVER, FRIEND, VOLUNTEER, WORKER

HERE

- Here when others need us
- Getting there from here
- Here's the best way to help
- Firmly grounded in the here and now
- We have to look at what's happening right here

HERITAGE

- Halting the degradation of our heritage by
- An example of our invaluable heritage that was in need of repair or in danger of vanishing
- All proceeds will be devoted to this heritage preservation effort
- Our prized heritage must be protected and cared for
- To keep our living heritage
- You'll also be part of a movement protecting one of the proudest parts of our heritage
- Places that remain vibrant, living symbols of our heritage
- Our own driving commitment springs from the importance of our rare national heritage
- Become a "friend" of our heritage today
- You and I must work together with government to conserve and protect our unique natural and cultural heritage
- The personal effort and support of people like you have been invaluable in

helping to preserve and enhance our heritage
- Closely involved with the local heritage community and its efforts to promote appreciation for
- To protect our unique natural and cultural heritage
- Protect our heritage now and into the future

See also: BIRTHRIGHT, INHERITANCE, LEGACY, MEMORIAL, PAST, TRADITION

HERO
- These quiet, courageous people are the true heroes
- Please support a local hero
- Get ready to thrill to a most unlikely hero
- Now you can be a hero too
- Imagine spending time with your personal heroes every day
- Saluting all the unsung heroes who keep the world going
- The pain of seeing many of their heroes tarnished during their lifetime
- Not all heroes fly or morph
- Just one of the many heroes taking part in
- Kids should be inspired by real-life heroes

See also: CHAMPION, DEFENDER, FIGHTER

HEROIC
- These heroic people have suffered for generations
- The most heroic thing I've ever seen was
- To support people making heroic efforts to better their lives

HESITATE
- Please don't hesitate to send whatever you can today
- She who hesitates is lost
- No one would hesitate a moment to help if they could only see
- Whatever you do, do not hesitate

HIGHLIGHT
- A highlight of each season is
- On a positive note, one of the highlights of the year was the news of
- Hearing from you is a real highlight of our campaign
- I just want share some of the highlights of the past
- Help us highlight their hard work and dedication

HISTORIC
- The historically significant interiors
- Few people have had the opportunity to enjoy the beauty and the historical significance of
- Contribute to a truly historic moment
- To maintain our historic role as care providers

See also: BIRTHRIGHT, INHERITANCE, LEGACY, TRADITION

HISTORY
- How different history would be if only people had
- Keep our living history alive
- For the first time in human history we have the chance to
- This is a very great moment in the history of
- We'd like to think these threats are ancient history, but unfortunately, they're not
- Now you can become part of this history too
- You can help make history
- For the first time in our history, there's a real chance of beating this problem
- Helping to make history every day
- A new phase of human history is beginning
- There's some real history here

See also: HERITAGE, LEGACY, MEMORIAL, MEMORY, PAST, REMEMBER, REMINDER, TRADITION

HIT
- We've already taken hits, big hits
- Your gift last year was a tremendous hit
- Putting forward hard hitting, no nonsense remedies
- Hoping it will be a great hit

HOLIDAY
- Would like to take a holiday from pain and suffering
- We get no days off during the holidays
- I hope you will act in the spirit of the holidays to help
- I hope you will act in the spirit these joyful holidays
- Please use these holiday gifts with our warm wishes
- With the holidays rapidly approaching, there's no better time to consider the needs of those less fortunate
- The holidays are for making people happy
- The holidays are right around the corner
- Holiday greetings and best wishes for the New Year
- May this beautiful holiday season bring you many special joys
- May the simple joys of the holiday season be with you always
- Wonderful holiday season
- Love and joy this holiday season
- The best part of the lovely season
- Best wishes for a bright and beautiful season
- Relish and enjoy the warmth and goodwill of the holidays

See also: CELEBRATE, CHRISTMAS, SEASON

HOLIDAY SEASON
- Please include us in the list of agencies you plan to help during the holiday season
- The holiday season always strains our resources to the limit
- Please use the enclosed holiday gift with our warm wishes

- In this holiday season, you can be there in spirit
- On behalf of all those you've helped, I wish you a pleasant and memorable holiday season
- Just in time for the holiday season

HOLISTIC
- To enable people to remain in their homes and communities as long as possible while having access to holistic health care
- A non-invasive, holistic approach used in many hospitals today
- So many people turning to a more holistic form of medicine

HOME
- To help build the kind of place we're proud to call home
- A cheerful, loving home for those who can never leave.
- Founded compassionately as a home for
- Even more afraid they'll have to return to an abusive home
- Such a great need for a home they can call their own
- We can declare that this is our home
- Hammer home the gravity of the situation
- And we are beginning to see the effects here at home too
- On the home front, we have the machinations of
- The state of our earth, the only home we will ever know
- These grim facts were brought home to us in a very shocking manner
- Occupying the very center of our home
- The community we love is our home

Home: dwelling, residence, domicile, habitation, habitat, lodging, nest, living quarters, accommodations, housing, roof, location, place, house, farm, cabin, cottage, shack, hovel, hearth, household, homestead, home sweet home, shelter, retreat, refuge, asylum, domain, territory, birthplace, motherland, sphere, journey's end, native soil, abode
See also: COMMUNITY, FAMILY, SAFETY, SHELTER

HOMELESS
- Your gift is a warm bed to the homeless, a warm smile and outstretched hands to the lonely
- The homeless people you've seen huddled on air gratings will soon be joined by hundreds more
- Many homeless are mentally ill
- Your support will provide a warm meal, counselling, and medical attention for many homeless men and women this winter
- A refuge for homeless people where they can get a hot meal, a cup of coffee and see a familiar face
- With your donation, we can continue to offer a warm, safe refuge for homeless people on the streets
- Hundreds of homeless men and women are coming to us for help and comfort
- It's time to befriend the homeless

See also: DESPERATE, DESTITUTE, POVERTY, STREET

HONOR
- I'm delighted to inform you of a special honor
- This unique honor is yours
- Please honor these brave people with your support
- I'll never forget the honor of helping
- Honor your loved one in a very special way

HOPE
- I know just how heart-moving that look of dawning, wrenching hope can be
- A philosophy based on humanity and hope
- Today there's hope, real hope
- Hope for the simple happiness that you and I enjoy daily
- Amidst the heartbreak there is so much hope
- Hope when reform is promised, disillusion when things fall through
- When hope is all but crushed
- Call our lines for hope in their darkest hour
- Give the precious gift of hope today.
- Give the gift they need the most: hope
- The gift you give today is an expression of hope for
- Your help will give them hope
- We fervently hope you will consider giving
- With your support, we can provide hope and comfort for victims of this cruel lottery
- Your financial support today means precious hope to
- You are their only hope
- Your help is their only hope
- Please help keep hope alive
- We know you want to share that hope
- Give the gift of hope, love, encouragement, shelter, safety
- We hope you will accept the challenge
- Beacon of hope amidst the darkness of hopeless suffering
- Real hope means all of us working together.
- There's real cause for hope
- We very much hope that
- Nothing is more tragic than to discover once-shining hopes now dumped upon the trash heaps of life
- Keep the covenant of hope
- Watch hope kindle in a child's eyes
- They are a symbol of hope for
- Bring a ray of hope into their lives
- Giving them a sense of hope and belonging
- Yielded more real signs of hope than ever before
- Represent the front line of hope for the hopeless
- Many experiencing their first glimmer of hope in years

- Real hope means all of us working together.
- Need the hope progress brings
- Give the precious gift of hope today.
- So long as we have the will and the resources, there's reason to hope
- Plummeting hopes in this area have caused no end of
- These words echo the hope people in need share with people who care
- Please help the thousands of sufferers who wait and hope – and long for a normal life
- Or some comment that indicates they are part of our hopes and dreams
- Also raises our hopes but, at the same time, it demands our devoting energy and resources to

Hope: desire, wish, longing, expectation, yearning, dream, craving, hankering, anticipation, ambition, belief, go for, trust, conviction, faith, have faith in, confidence, assurance, prospect, promise, expectancy
See also: BELIEF, FAITH, DREAM, FUTURE, PROMISE, WISH

HOPELESS
- It's not a hopeless picture
- Thousands of people don't have to imagine – they know what it's like to be hungry, to be alone, to feel hopeless
- Stop feeling hopeless about
- Shaking off the helpless, hopeless attitude
- It's hard because poverty often breeds hopelessness
- Hopelessness is a creeping, insidious poison that paralyzes and destroys
See also: ABANDON, DESPAIR, DESPERATE, SUICIDE

HORIZONS
- The wide horizons solution
- Climbing up far enough to see the horizon at last
- Always seeking to extend our horizons
- Able to see the broader horizon
- Here's something to expand your horizons
See also: POSSIBILITY, PROMISE

HORROR
- Despite public horror and revulsion
- Help stop the horror by supporting our work as much as you can
- This is one horror we can do something about
- We could only look on with horror as
See also: DISASTER, FEAR, NIGHTMARE, TERROR

HOSPITAL
- Partnership between hospital and community
- A great hospital relies on the power of one – and that one is you
- You become a partner in a world-renowned hospital

HOUSING
- Wind whipping in through cracks in the walls of their housing
- Rats and roaches from bad housing running over the baby's bed
- Housing without running water, or heat, or electricity
- Rain leaking monotonously though their housing's broken roof

HOW
- How do we do it
- Here's how it works
- Asking not how, but why
- Left wondering how on earth we're going to accomplish this
- The inevitable question is how do we manage it

HUMAN
- Relate to real, live, warm human beings
- Things that undignify and humiliate human beings
- Resources to meet the human service needs of families and communities
- Genuine human compassion is the answer
- Human assets are the most precious

HUMANE
- While it's human to care, it is truly humane to share
- The only humane thing to do is
- The truly humane among us can not stand by while such suffering takes place
- Under these circumstances, a quick death would be humane

See also: **CARE, KINDNESS**

HUMANITY
- A benefit to all humanity
- Humanity has been waiting a long time for this idea
- Reaching out to humanity, not partisan interest
- Compassionate humanity is the foundation of this movement

See also: **PEOPLE, POPULATION, WORLD**

HUNCH
- I have a hunch about you
- I had a hunch about the largeness of your heart, and I was right
- Certainly going on more than just a lucky hunch

HUNGER
- Hunger will be satisfied
- Every day thousands die of hunger
- In a world full of plenty, hunger is an unnecessary evil
- Help fill an abiding hunger for dignity and respect
- They are hungry every day
- Hunger is a persistent problem

- A partnership that will make a lasting impact on hunger in this city
- Your donation goes a long way towards meaningful solutions to hunger
- Hunger is once again rearing its ugly head

See also: **FOOD, MALNUTRITION, NEED, WISH**

HURT

- They are hurt and suffering
- Be most hurtful to those adults and children living below the poverty line, including many who visit food banks or are homeless
- They hurt just as much no matter what they're called
- Though they are silent, you can see the hurt in their eyes

See also: **ABUSE, AGONY, PAIN, SUFFERING, TORTURE**

HYSTERIA

- The hysteria surrounding those early years was something I'll never forget
- Able to think clearly when the hysteria subsides
- The worst kind of hysteria is the cause
- Must not give in to mindless hysteria

IDEA

- A great idea is worth supporting
- The idea is simple
- This idea, too, is an excellent one
- So that you have a better idea of how things work here
- It seemed like a good idea at the time
- Great ideas are our real capital
- Our best idea ever
- Now you can participate in a magnificent idea
- Turned an improbable idea into a lovely reality
- We bring you new ideas and news of a great possibility
- A healthy and vibrant cross-fertilization of ideas
- An astonishing number of new ideas
- Now let me tell you about a fabulous idea
- Here are some ideas to help you help
- Such a wonderful opportunity to pool ideas about
- A treasure house of innovative health ideas that will turn worry and fear into real hope for millions
- Encouraging a creative and honest exchange of ideas with people like yourself
- An idea whose time has certainly come
- You can feel the greatness of this idea in our world and our community
- From an ambitious idea, this organization has grown into a new phenomenon
- No one can resist an idea whose time has come
- Unquestionably, an idea whose time has arrived
- The idea is a very simple one
- An idea with stunning potential
- Isn't it great to see such fresh, practical ideas

- Giving participants the opportunity to work with their own ideas

Idea: notion, thought, concept, conception, perception, surmise, observation, theory, conjecture

See also: ADVANCE, CONCEPT, INFORMATION, INNOVATION, INSPIRATION, THOUGHT

IDEAL
- An ideal we all should live by
- What ideals will we put before our children
- Living up to the high ideals of all those who have gone before us
- In order to create the most ideal of conditions
- Ideally, this is what we must achieve
- Finding again the shining ideals of our youth
- You too, can support the ideals of
- At one time or another, we've all dreamed of the ideal life

Ideal: perfect, model, pinnacle, peak, height of excellence, acme, example, exemplar, archetype, prototype, original, consummate, supreme, absolute, fabulous, faultless, best, goal, objective, mark, paragon, apotheosis, nonpareil

See also: AIM, GOAL, MODEL, OBJECTIVE, TARGET

IDENTIFY
- Urgent that we accurately identify those at risk so that preventative measures can be taken immediately
- It is so important to identify and correct the causes of this problem
- The importance of our identity as designated by
- To quickly identify the cause and bring about a solution

IGNORANCE
- Ignorance like this can make you want to scream
- Roll back the dark curtain of ignorance
- Ignorance is the greatest enemy
- Falling victim to ignorance every day

See also: APATHY, INDIFFERENCE, NEGLECT, SILENCE

ILL
- It means that should he ever fall ill, he won't have to face the distress and humiliation that has already twisted the lives of his siblings
- Those most ill must be treated first
- Compassion for those too ill to help themselves
- Reach out to those who are poor, ill and alone

See also: DISEASE, PAIN, SICK

ILLITERACY
- Lead the fight against illiteracy and the life of poverty that goes with it
- Illiteracy is a crippling but often invisible handicap
- Rescue those among us shrouded in illiteracy

- Can't afford illiteracy about this issue

ILLNESS
- I sincerely hope you never have to suffer from this illness
- Though illness can strike anytime
- Shocking sudden rise in this illness
- Too embarrassed to talk about their illness
- Need so many special services because of their illness
- You'll be supporting the largest medical research foundation dedicated to research into this grim illness
- One of the highest rates of illness in the world
- Is not rare to find such illness there
- The illness strikes between the ages of
- We don't know who the illness will strike next, or when or why
- Years after the diagnosis, the illness struck again
- She discovered she had this dreadful illness
- Afraid of catching this mysterious and fatal illness
- Sliding ever deeper into this frightening, baffling illness
- Help more people reach a stage where their illness stabilizes
- Works hard to ensure that people with this illness receive the services and medical treatment they need to live as productive a life as possible
- This illness is a life sentence
- One of natures cruellest, most debilitating illnesses
- Trapped helplessly by a terrifying illness

See also: DEATH, DISEASE, SICK

IMAGE
- We all remember seeing the distressing images of
- Images burned forever into our minds
- Painful images haunt us and move us to action

IMAGINATION
- Through the use of vision and imagination we can
- The only limit is our own imagination
- This is where we put your imagination to work
- Stretch your imagination to see the shining result
- Please use your imagination

See also: IDEA, INNOVATION, INSPIRATION, PASSION

IMAGINE
- You can almost imagine a day when
- Imagine how it would be if all this needless suffering were wiped out
- It's time to imagine a totally new approach
- Can you imagine what it would be like to
- Imagine what it does to a family

See also: CONSIDER, PICTURE, THINK

IMMEDIATE
- That's why I'm writing to ask for your immediate help
- Urgent and immediate
- The situation requires an immediate response
- Your immediate response to this appeal could save the day
- I need your immediate help to make sure
- Our immediate needs are very pressing

IMMUNE
- No social strata, no cultural group, no neighborhood is immune
- Immune to the temptations of
- How could anyone be immune to such a sight

See also: **DEAF, INDIFFERENCE, PROTECT, SAFE**

IMPACT
- The crippling impact of this disease
- We too want to examine and draw attention to the impact of these institutions
- Help each and every donor to make more of an impact with their gift
- We tried to limit the impact on our action and advocacy efforts
- Saw the potential impact of
- The impact has been swift and hard
- Something that's making real impact on thousands of
- Impact upon our shrinking base funding
- Has the potential to create an unprecedented impact on
- No one can fail to see the positive impact this program will have upon
- The most important factor in reducing the impact of
- Has a direct impact of people as well as wildlife

See also: **EFFECT, HIT, POWER, VIOLENCE**

IMPARTIAL
- We must remain impartial to do our work effectively
- We operate in this way so that we can remain impartial
- To ensure impartiality in all cases, we accept no funds from
- It is our mission to work impartially on behalf of

See also: **JUSTICE**

IMPLEMENT
- If this new arrangement is implemented
- Must be implemented as quickly as possible
- Doing everything we can to implement

IMPORTANT
- There's something important about this I think you should know
- It's important to all of us here to know that people like you are with us
- Because there's something very important I think you should understand
- It's important to me, and to all of us here, to know that people like you are with

us all the way
- This is especially important as
- I can't tell you how important it is that you and others help our fellow workers carry out these tasks
- Never has it been more important to
- This is especially important
- The process of finding out what is really important to them
- Surely nothing can be more important than
- I know you understand the importance of our work
- I can't think of anything you could do that would be more important

Important: significant, critical, of great consequence, vital, crucial, grave, serious, sober, momentous, pressing, urgent, imperative, priority, mattering, necessary, essential, valuable, remarkable, prominent, outstanding, noteworthy, of merit, weighty, major, principal, mighty, formidable, commanding, distinguished, notable, substantial, influential, inestimable, invaluable, top-level, grand, esteemed, respected
See also: DISTINGUISHED, NECESSITY, URGENT

IMPOSSIBLE

- It is often impossible to tell whether this worsening is caused by
- Nothing is impossible if you come to our aid
- Caught up in seemingly impossible circumstances, they nonetheless

IMPRESSION

- What a way to make a good first impression
- Making a very lasting impression on these people
- We hope this story has made an impression on you

IMPROVE

- Lighten the load and improve their life
- The quickest way to improve matters is
- Constant improvement must always be our aim
- Creating a constant environment to support the improvement that results in a better life
- As each day passes, there is further improvement

Improve: Ameliorate, better, prosper, benefit, avail, advantage, stand in good stead, be useful/profitable, come in handy
See also: ADVANCE, BETTER

INACCESSIBLE

- Because of the generosity of donors like you, these things are no longer inaccessible to
- Without your help, the simplest basics could be inaccessible
- Something once thought inaccessible is now possible

INACTION

- We have seen first hand the results of such inaction

- So easy to fall into inaction
- Inaction will be the worst possible course
- Inaction and indifference is the cause of so much evil

INCENTIVE
- A real incentive for you to send us your donation right away
- We're making available special incentives to make your giving easier
- Our new incentives program is working very well
- Continued success is a real incentive for everyone

INCEPTION
- We are very proud that, from its inception, we never wavered from our several resolves
- The tone was set at its inception
- Your chance to be in on this from the very inception

See also: BEGINNING, INNOVATION, INITIATIVE, SEED, SPARK, START

INCIDENCE
- The incidence is among the highest in the world
- After several incidences, the pattern began to emerge
- Helping to cut back the distressing number of incidences

See also: EVENT, HAPPENING, OCCASION

INCOME
- I want to underscore that all income from our program will go entirely to the charity we support
- A small portion of your income, as a donation, would be tremendously appreciated
- Your gift will help increase the income needed to
- Investment income from the funds will be used to assist

See also: BUDGET, FUNDING, MONEY, RESOURCE

INCREASE
- Help increase the number of calls we answer
- Guarantee and a dramatic increase in
- Providing the necessary tools and behavioral skills to dramatically increase quality of life
- There's an alarming increase in the prevalence of
- The increasing number of people who want to help
- Even if you prefer not to increase your support at this time

See also: EXPAND, GROW, INFLATION

INDEPENDENCE
- Gave back the independence she thought she had lost forever
- Please take a moment now to help others regain their independence
- A real helping hand to a child striving for independence

- Found new freedom and independence through the use of
- You don't think about your independence until you lose it
- A fierce desire for dignity and independence

See also: **AUTONOMY, FREEDOM**

INDIFFERENCE

- Indifference just might kill us all
- The biggest challenge is smashing the indifference
- Indifference has allowed the problem to reach this crisis
- Indifference is the greatest crime
- Children are suffering right now because of our indifference

See also: **APATHY, COMPLACENCY, DEAF, LIP SERVICE, NEGLECT, NUMB, SILENCE**

INDIVIDUAL

- There are individual stories and feelings behind those newspaper headlines
- I know you are a warm and caring individual
- An example of the difference a single committed individual can make
- Almost all our work is financed by concerned individuals like you
- Individuals who believe in the artistic vision of
- We rely heavily on individual donations to help us continue our work
- The government repays gifts of money given by individuals
- A way to help people, one individual at a time
- Each individual contribution – yours, for example – is very important
- Though each individual case is different, they are all equally deserving
- Our hope is that individuals like you will find it in your hearts to help take responsibility for
- If each individual helps just a little, we can win
- Remember that each individual is precious, unique and has unalienable rights
- Recognizing you as an informed individual

Individual: single, sole, lone, separate, distinct, solitary, particular, special, unique, singular, extraordinary, select, nonconformist, maverick

INFLATION

- Like you, we've suffered over the years from inflation and higher purchasing costs
- Suffering from an overblown inflation of claims
- Climbing inflation can wipe out gains in a very short time

INFLUENCE

- Use their influence to try and save more
- To counter so many negative influences
- They are the least politically influential people on earth
- One way you can really exert influence is by your participation
- Wielding influence from within

INFORM

- To make sure you are better informed about
- I really want to inform you about
- The urgent necessity to inform all parties about
- There will be other opportunities over the coming months to keep you informed about
- To understand why and how you can stay informed about
- Created specifically to keep people like you informed
- Our newsletter informing you about current events in
- The finest of ideals inform their every action
- We'll keep you informed through special communiques and reports of how we're doing and other important issues affecting

Inform: appraise, tell, let know, impart, relate, notify, advise, brief, acquaint, report, broadcast, instruct, teach, enlighten, illuminate, disclose , let know
See also: CALL, COMMUNICATE, CONTACT, REACH, SPEAK, TELL, VOICE

INFORMATION

- As the information ages rushes upon us we must regroup
- The information that could change a life
- This information may save your life or the life of someone dear to you
- I wonder if, in the meantime, you would allow me to send you the most fascinating information about
- To ensure that our clients have the most current information and entertainment available
- Most of us depend on the printed word for invaluable information
- But we are asked for more information than we can supply with our current level of funding
- Read the information, make up your own mind about
- Give the information and the means to make responsible choices about their lives
- You'll continue to receive our newsletter bringing you the latest information about
- If you would like more information, please write to us
- Ensure that reliable information is released to the rest of the world
- With your renewed membership we'll be able to keep sending you the most up-to-date information about
- You'll receive the journal packed with current medical information as well as notices about activities and meetings in your area
- To make these stories public information
- Provide information and support on a confidential basis to
- To act as an information clearing house for member societies
- These programs provide vital information and tools to learn
- You'll hear about activities and educational meetings in your area – news and information from other members.
- You'll continue to receive our newsletter bringing you the latest information
- How do we arm ourselves with solid, accurate information on the issues to help

us make intelligent decisions
- An information source you can't do without
- I'm reproducing the letter here for your information
- A little bit of information about ourselves
- But I hope, too, that you will find them an important source of information about the work we do
- It contains valuable information to make you more aware
- Contact our office for information on this as well
- Buried in the midst of this information onslaught, you will find
- We must get the information we need in order to
- Less and less able to make sense of information from the outside world
- Studied the most recent information in groups
- Stay tuned for more information
- Thousands seek the information and support that we provide
- Provide them with information they can use immediately so they do not have to suffer the pain of
- Information crucial to people like
- This information will be updated weekly
- Never blindly accept the information served up to us
- I'd like to send you more information
- This vital source of information is free with your donation
- Provide the most important, leading-edge information you can receive at this critical point in time
- Information they need to improve and manage their lives
- Information vital to stopping or preventing
- Please take the time to consider the enclosed information

Information: data, facts, knowledge, input, news, tidings, report, account, message, communication, notice, instruction, advice, tip, lowdown, scoop
See also: **COMMUNICATE, COUNSELLING, IDEA, KNOWLEDGE, MESSAGE, NEWS, POLICY, PRESENTATION, RESEARCH, VOICE**

INGREDIENT
- The biggest ingredient is the love and care we all show
- With your help, we can provide all the essential ingredients for
- Help us provide the missing ingredient

INHERITANCE
- Either way, 100% of your gift will directly support our national inheritance
- Help us build a splendid inheritance for our children
- Without you, their inheritance will be pain and desolation
See also: **BIRTHRIGHT, HERITAGE, LEGACY, TRADITION**

INITIATIVE
- Please join us in the very important initiative
- Your initiative will get the whole project going
- This year, we will be writing you in the spring, summer and fall to talk to you

about some of the key initiatives under way
- We could see it was a remarkable initiative and we acted quickly
- A bold yet sensitive initiative
- Exercise great initiative and teamwork to raise

INJUSTICE
- Unfortunately, there is still widespread injustice in the world
- While injustice lives, we can never stop fighting
- This shocking injustice cannot be allowed to continue

See also: ABUSE, CRUELTY, EXPLOITATION

INNOCENT
- You're afraid that innocent people are being hurt
- Protecting the most innocent and the most vulnerable is our mandate
- None of us is totally innocent in this regard
- The battle isn't dimming childhood innocence

INNOVATION
- Ensuring our national reputation for innovation
- We're counting on you to support this far-sighted innovation
- It is innovation that carries society forward
- Making the leap from need to innovation

See also: ADVANCE, IDEA, RESEARCH

INSIGHT
- Help give practical insights and advice
- Unique insight into traditions that
- Share the pleasure that comes from new insights
- Keen insights into our future
- Developing insight into the causes and diagnosis of
- These strategic insights have changed everything
- Gain valuable insights into
- Your thoughts are invaluable to us in providing personal insight and motivation

Insight: perception, intuition, understanding, discernment, knowledge, sagacity, farsightedness, common sense, judgement, vision, clarity, sense, wit, indication, information, distinction

INSPIRATION
- To inspire and challenge with their experience and insights
- A never-ending inspiration for us all
- Where does inspiration come from
- Drawing inspiration from their efforts

Inspiration: revelation, incentive, encouragement, prompting, exhortation, spur, goad, influence, incitement, spark, instigation, awakening, stirring, arousal, revival, rally, brightness, warmth, reassurance, comfort, confirmation, revelation, enlightenment, awareness, instruction, teaching

INSTITUTION
- We can't watch treasured institutions taken apart before our very eyes
- A venerable institution with a caring heart
- Not just an institution but a place where lives are mended and joy restored
- A grand institution growing weak as nourishment is steadily withdrawn

See also: ASSOCIATION, FOUNDATION, ORGANIZATION

INTEGRATE
- Discover how you helped someone integrate fully into the life and work
- So many parts to integrate into a seamless whole
- Help many agencies put forth an integrated effort
- Integrate yourself into this exciting effort

See also: CONNECT, JOIN, LINK

INTEGRITY
- I think of integrity, leadership and self-reliance, moral courage, concern for others and spirituality
- Commitment to integrity and values forms the basis of our philosophy
- Preserving their personal dignity and integrity
- Please honor their integrity by

INTELLECTUAL
- The academic and student projects described above are vital to the intellectual and community life of
- This is not just some abstract, intellectual concern
- Intellectual excellence is our unswerving goal

INTELLIGENCE
- At a time when the ability of human intelligence to meet its problems is being tested as never before
- Displaying intelligence through the choices we make
- Approach this challenge with intelligence and compassion

INTEREST
- That means the best interest of us all.
- It might interest you to know that
- An utterly absorbing view of
- You have a vested interest in our future
- I know you'll find plenty to interest you.
- If you know of anyone who would be interested in helping, please call
- Once again taking an interest in the world around him
- We know you take a personal interest in everything to do with
- I know you are deeply interested in
- We know that you share with us a deep interest in the welfare of
- It will be very interesting to watch how
- We must get interested in

- Encouraging students to explore their own areas of interest at their own pace
- Able to gain the cooperation of a wide variety of often disparate interests
- Further our humanitarian interests

Interest: advantage, moment, concern, consequence, significance, benefit, profit, service, avail, use, worth, value, behalf, business, stake, involvement

INTERNATIONAL
- Is one of the leading international development agencies
- Need to understand how international cooperation makes the world better for all of us
- Internationally proven
- To help fight increased international pressure to reduce protection of
- Working internationally to get them to comply with anti-poverty promises it made at
- You can help solve this truly international problem

INTERVENTION
- Our timely intervention resulted in a call for
- Intervention in the form of a very welcome cheque
- Specific intervention is necessary to de-escalate the situation

See also: ACTION, COUNSELING, HELP

INVEST
- Invest proudly in
- Invest for yourself, you children and your great grandchildren
- If we want the impact to be positive, we must invest time and effort now
- Invest an hour or two in a people-friendly activity
- Why not invest in
- Invest gloriously in our heritage
- Invest for yourself, your children and your great grandchildren.
- You'll be investing in better lives
- Your invitation to invest
- You don't have to be a millionaire to invest in
- Investing in a secure future is what you do when you
- When you contribute, you invest in the future

Invest: put money into, venture, lay out, support, patronize, subsidize, back, commit, place, empower, endow

INVESTIGATION
- You donation will help us expand our investigation of
- Investigation into the causes and cures for this condition is needed quickly
- In-depth investigations cost a lot of money

INVESTMENT
- It's hard to find a better investment
- Achieve the most mileage from your investment

- Your investment is vital
- It's the best foreign investment you can make
- You couldn't make a better investment
- Your gift is a great investment
- That's our idea of investment
- This is probably one of the best investments you could ever make
- So our commitment, and your investment, is long-term
- What a tremendous investment for all
- This is a very long term investment
- You know a good investment when you see one
- Gives you a great return on your investment

INVITATION
- I extend a very special invitation for you to join us in
- You invitation to visit us
- Please regard this letter as your personal invitation to

INVITE
- I'd like to personally invite you to
- I'd like to invite you to become a part of it
- You are heartily invited to join in
- Inviting you to make a contribution
- I invite you to examine the harsh facts and consider a donation

INVOLVE
- We need to involve ourselves a lot more in
- Please, I want you to get involved now
- That's why I decided to become involved
- That's the reason I'm involved in
- We have to get involved because a lot of other people won't
- I almost didn't get involved because I didn't understand what it was about or what was at stake
- I'm asking you to get involved in any way you can
- That's why I need you to get involved right away
- We believe that getting involved is important
- That's why I am so actively involved in
- If you wish to become involved, we welcome you
- We believe getting involved is vitally important
- Heavily involved in causes such as

INVOLVEMENT
- We hope to deepen the involvement of caring and committed supporters like you
- You involvement will be a joy
- Its success depends on your involvement
- Steadily increasing our extensive involvement with

IRONY
- The sad irony of it all is
- The most diabolically ironic twist to all this is
- To lose out now would be the final irony

ISSUE
- A very popular issue
- Have you wanted to express yourself and resolve an issue and not known how or where you could go to do so
- Now, let me turn to some of the issues we've been focusing on in recent months
- Issues that children and youth bring to home, school and the community
- We can't be divided on this issue
- Sorting this issue out is very important
- The issues concern all of us very much
- Addresses and clarifies issues our constituents most consistently face
- We'll forward your concerns to those who can make a difference on this burning issue
- The refinement and focus of each issue is outstanding
- If there's an issue you deeply care about, now is the time to say so
- You can make such a difference on this issue
- Linking a number of pressing issues to
- Provided perspective on a multitude of issues
- Others, who feel as passionately about these vital issues as you do, stand beside you when you help
- Speaking out on these issues through news releases and radio, television and newspaper interviews
- The most important, the most intriguing, interesting, challenging issues
- Learning another, better way of dealing with contentious issues
- We all have issues to face in life
- Some issues we just don't recognize soon enough
- Carefully guided opportunity to explore life issues in a safe setting
- Leading edge issues require leading edge answers
- Keeping abreast of these very significant issues
- Let me outline the issues

Issue: question, problem, poser, challenge, idea, topic, bone of contention, moot point, political football
See also: IDEA, ISSUE, MATTER, QUESTION, TOPIC

JEOPARDY
- Virtually all social programs may be in jeopardy
- Double jeopardy if we miss now
- I know you understand just how much jeopardy these children are in
- Snatched from jeopardy in a nick of time
- How can we leave them in such jeopardy

See also: DANGER, RISK, THREAT

JOB

- It's a job we love
- Help get the job done
- The tough job of helping to
- Your support can make our job a lot easier
- I have the job of convincing you that
- But it's a big job and we can only do it with your help
- We help people find jobs through
- Cuts the job down to size
- Help us do a far more extensive job
- Your generous gift will help us get the job finished

Job: undertaking, work, business, task, chore, matter at hand, activity, venture, performance, role, achievement, enterprise, mission, employment, occupation, livelihood, living, calling, vocation, profession, trade, craft

See also: ACTIVITY, MANDATE, LABOR, MISSION, PURPOSE, ROLE, UNDERTAKING, WORK

JOIN

- I really need you to join us now
- Join the battle, help us defeat the enemy
- So please, join us today
- We'd like you to join us
- I urge you to join us
- Why not join us in helping to
- For every one of you who joins, the cause advances
- Please join the fight
- If you'll join us, you'll be helping to
- I want you to join me so much that I've put together this package
- To further encourage you to join us, I'm going to
- By joining us, you play a direct, personal role in helping all those who so desperately need
- I urge you to join us in this nationwide effort
- By joining, you will become part of a worldwide movement to
- Won't you join us and help make a world of difference
- By joining, you help so many
- In return for joining us for one year, you will receive
- All available to you when you join
- That's why I'm asking you to join as a new member today
- Today, I'm asking you to join me in the fight by making a tax-creditable donation
- Please join me and others from coast to coast with your financial support for
- I hope you will give serious thought to joining others in supporting
- Since you first joined the ranks of those caring individuals who
- That's why we have recently joined together to
- There are so many benefits to joining
- Joining us is a way you can help in a meaningful way
- When you join, you'll receive a free subscription to

- Join forces to solve this stubborn problem
- We sincerely hope you can join us

Join: unite, join together, link hands, connect, bridge, attach, consolidate, combine, merge, ally, league, join forces, team up, go along with, enrol, band together, affiliate, associate, throw in with, cooperate, collaborate, sign up, sign on, enlist, enter into, cast one's lot with, participate, contribute, mingle, mix
See also: COMMUNITY, CONNECT, GROUP, MEMBER, PARTNER

JOINTLY

- Have jointly developed a vital program
- Operating jointly, we've done twice as much
- By acting jointly, we double the impact and effectiveness

JOURNEY

- Her journey home is often a terrifying one
- Join us on journeys of the mind and imagination
- The journey is a long one but full of hope
- Offering a creative, personal journey
- Your gift is the first step in their journey to a brighter future

Journey: travel, progress, tour, excursion, trek, expedition, passage, transition, transit, way, course, route, roam, migrate, proceed, pass

JOY

- The joy of creativity
- Remember the joy, the pride, the bursting confidence
- Just imagine the joy it will bring to
- As you can plainly see, nothing stops her happiness and vivid imagination from coming through with joy
- There are spontaneous tears of joy when
- Your gift makes you part of the joy when they finally rush into one another's arms
- Think of the joy you will give
- Discover new joy by joining us to
- You can just feel the joy welling up in your heart when you help

Joy: pleasure, enjoyment, happiness, delight, gladness, felicity, bliss, ecstasy, cheer, excitement, thrill, gaiety, buoyancy, serenity, tranquillity, exhilaration, frolic, fun, festivity, celebration, elation, glee, rejoicing, laughter, optimism, merriment, exaltation, transport, rapture
See also: CHEER, DELIGHT, HAPPY, HAPPINESS, JUBILATION, PLEASURE, SMILE

JOYFUL

- Feel a wonderful, playful, joyful delight
- We go joyfully forward
- With joyful hearts we see people's lives improve

JUBILATION
- Practically danced with jubilation at
- Jubilation spread rapidly from home to home
- Almost indescribable jubilation at final success

JUBILEE
- Silver jubilee special appeal
- Make every day a jubilee day
- Help us celebrate this very special jubilee year

JUSTICE
- By requesting that those responsible be brought to justice
- The most basic sense of justice demands that
- So that justice and fairness prevail, we must throw our support behind
- Justice gives a voice to the dumb
- You share our concern with social solidarity and global justice

Justice: fairness, fair play, equity, fair-mindedness, impartiality, tolerance, neutrality, rightness, objectivity, goodness, sincerity, virtue, uprightness, integrity, probity, retribution, nemesis, truthfulness, candor, compensation, recompense, adjudication, ruling, statement, opinion, finding, propriety

See also: FREEDOM, IMPARTIALITY

KEY
- Giving the key to open up all the things they want and need in life
- Your help and participation is the real key
- You're holding the key in your hand right now
- This is clearly the key to it all

See also: ANSWER, CURE, SOLUTION, SOLVE

KID
- A good kid who's going through a very tough time
- I wish you could hear the glee of inner city kids at play
- Especially important as kids grow up and prepare for the big job of making a living and raising families of their own
- Problems far to big for little kids to handle
- Give these kids a chance to escape a life of poverty, hunger and disease
- Kids in distress don't deserve such treatment
- Helping kids make the right decisions
- Keeping kids in school, giving them a nourishing breakfast and lending an ear when things go wrong
- You're giving kids a chance
- Help kids learn sharing and caring
- Thank you for helping us help kids
- We can't let our kids down
- After you've worked with abused kids as long as I have, you begin to think you've heard it all

- At times, kids need incredible strength to resist these dangers
- Thousands of kids end up on the streets – with no ambition, no hope
- A place where kids can laugh and learn and sing and dance
- There are thousands of kids living on the streets

See also: **CHILDREN, FUTURE, GIRLS, LITTLE ONES, POSTERITY, YOUNG, YOUNGSTERS, YOUTH**

KILLER
- A once dreaded killer and thought to be eradicated, is on the rise again
- Help stalk a killer
- Will soon turn into a killer unless stopped early

See also: **ABUSER, BLOOD, DAGGER, DANGER, HUNGER, RISK, THREAT**

KINDNESS
- Kindness and an understanding heart are always on duty
- With kindness and encouragement, he turned his life around
- Benefit so greatly from your kindness
- Your kindness is so deeply appreciated

See also: **CARING, COMPASSION, CONCERN, GOODNESS**

KNIFE
- Under the knife once again
- Taking a knife to what little remains
- The knife is poised to make terrible cuts

See also: **AXE, CHOP, CUTS, DAGGER, REDUCE, SLASH**

KNOW
- But what do I know
- We are, of course, well known for our
- You need to know that
- Did you know that
- While it's true that most people know something about what we stand for, we still have to
- You may not even know that
- Letting you know what our organization means in your area
- I know this only too well
- You may be interested to know that
- We'll let you know how your donation has been used to help save lives
- We don't know why but we mean to find out
- Knowing more about this is vital to understanding how we can ensure the end of
- People urgently need to know about
- And who knows the true situation better than
- Can you imagine the agony of not knowing
- We want you to know you were with us
- All of you know only too well

Know: fathom, understand, get the hang of, realize, comprehend, discern, penetrate, recognize, get the picture, be aware of, appreciate, distinguish, discriminate, acknowledge, grasp, perceive, think, recall
See also: **APPRECIATE, REALIZE, RECOGNITION, UNDERSTAND**

KNOWLEDGE
- Our workers have intimate knowledge of the countries where they work
- Utilizes your knowledge which only you, as a caring parent, can bring to the consultation about your child
- We use our extensive knowledge to advise
- Providing the next generation with the knowledge and skills that will help them build a future – our future
- Knowledge will help us in adversity
- Designed to build a firm base of knowledge about
- A good deal of knowledge and a sense of humor to share
- Never before has there been so much certainty that revolutionary new knowledge is just over the horizon
- Knowledge that could bestow the unbelievable blessing of a normal life upon people now trapped in a hell of
- Must make use of this precious new knowledge
See also: **CONCEPT, IDEA, INFORMATION, NEWS**

LABOR
- The many years during which so many of us have labored on behalf of
- Not matter how difficult, our work has always been a labor of love
- All the dedicated labor is finally paying off
- Keeping giving – so that all this loving labor is not in vain
See also: **EFFORT, WORK**

LABYRINTH
- Rescued from this horrifying labyrinth
- At times can feel as though you're lost in a labyrinth of
- The labyrinthine politics are almost too complicated to follow
See also: **CHALLENGE, MYSTERY, PUZZLE**

LANDMARK
- This promises to be a landmark year
- Please help us save this very unique local landmark
- To stop these wonderful old landmarks from disappearing at an alarming rate

LAPSED DONOR
See: **SECTION SIX**

LAPSED MEMBER
See: **SECTION SIX**

LATE

- It's not too late to put an end to this fiasco
- We may be too late for one victim, but we don't have to be too late for others
- And perhaps keep us from being too late for someone you love
- With your help, it's never too late
- As the saying goes, better late than never

See also: BEHIND, DELAY, PROCRASTINATION, STOP

LAUGH

- When you see it, you don't know whether to laugh or cry
- Help to make them laugh again
- Certainly nothing to laugh about

See also: DELIGHT, HAPPY, JOYFUL, SMILE

LAUGHTER

- Bring laughter into sorrowful hearts
- Precious as the ring of carefree laughter
- The children's laughter is so infectious
- Help bring the laughter back
- Finally able to hear laughter once again

LEAD

- It's only natural that we should take the lead in this important area
- Join us in the lead
- If we're to remain in the lead we need your help
- Our organization has always been one of the leading defenders
- Committed to leading the nation in undergraduate education as well as research and scholarship
- Leading the pack will be our privilege and our goal
- Leading edge concepts evolving constantly

LEADER

- Help us remain an indisputable leader in this field
- A farsighted group of community leaders joined together to form
- Ambitious, public-spirited leaders
- Today, there's an urgent need for new funding to recruit and train leaders and expand our programs right across the country
- Only the strongest and most visionary leaders could have created a concept where
- Coupled with the guidance of extraordinarily gifted leaders
- Discovering the process of making a leader

Leader: pacesetter, mover, motivator, ringleader, bellwether, vanguard, pioneer, explorer, ground breaker

LEADERSHIP

- Assumes active leadership in

- Their role is to provide leadership in discussions on a national level
- To increase and improve leadership amongst our youth

LEAGUE
- Now there are many others in the same league as
- In league with other oppressors
- Putting them in a league of their own

LEAP
- Leaping straight into the twenty-first century
- It's not much of a leap to realize what must be done next
- We've made vast leaps since we wrote to you last
- Suddenly advancing in quantum leaps
- Has made giant leaps forward in the last fifty years

See also: ADVANCE, BREAKTHROUGH, PROGRESS

LEARN
- We tried to learn everything we could about
- Ask you to listen and learn
- They need to be given the opportunity to learn about the values that can turn them into responsible, productive citizens
- I hope, for the sake of our youth, we never stop learning
- We can learn so much from these brave people
- A chance to learn to strive to do their best and respect others
- Saying yes to learning
- Making the best place for young people to learn
- Learn how and why and when to use
- Striving constantly to learn
- A hands-on learning project
- Learning lessons of compassion, thrift, generosity and kindness
- I just know that once you learn about it, you'll be excited too
- A way to learn more than they ever dreamed possible
- To help you learn more about this complex problem, I'm sending you details
- You can also take the time to learn
- I know you've shared the joy of learning all your life
- Lifelong learning is essential for both career fulfillment and personal growth
- Designed to assist in determining your learning goal
- Have you always been intrigued by learning
- Compatible with the many different learning styles of
- A learning experience to cherish for the rest of your life
- Yet they want so desperately to learn
- When will we ever learn
- Giving kids the nutrition they need to learn
- So bad, it's impossible for many of these children to learn
- So saddened to learn

Learn: realize, comprehend, grasp, perceive, see the light, apprehend, get the picture, ascertain, determine, detect, discover, bring to light, uncover, get the idea/picture, latch on to, glean, pick up, get wind of, get the lowdown, understand, gather, tip off, hear of, memorize, study, be aware

See also: **DISCOVER, EXPLORE, REALIZE, UNDERSTAND**

LEGACY
- Precious, unassailable legacy
- Only with your help can we preserve for tomorrow this priceless, fragile legacy entrusted to our care today.
- Please consider leaving a legacy in your will as a gift to
- Inheriting an unparalleled legacy
- Sometimes you can't see the legacy you leave
- Trying not to leave a legacy of pain
- After you have made provision for your family and friends in your will, consider leaving the residue of your estate as a legacy
- You can leave, as legacy to help others, an item of property
- Please continue that legacy of caring

See also: **BIRTHRIGHT, HERITAGE, POSTERITY, TRADITION**

LESSON
- This is not a lesson we want people to learn
- A bitter lesson we don't want to have to repeat
- The lessons of the past have not been lost
- Help teach the precious lessons of kindness, honesty, peace and cooperation
- A loving lesson in life
- We must benefit from these very hard lessons
- A lesson we do not want to have to learn a second time

LET
- We can't let up now
- Please don't let this happen
- If you'll just let us, we can do so much

See also:: **ALLOW**

LETTER
- This is no ordinary letter
- I know you're the kind of compassionate person who will read this letter very carefully
- I'm writing you this special letter because I'm extremely worried
- By writing a letter to the right person, you can help get results
- I think that, after reading this letter, you'll understand why I'm convinced that we're heading for trouble of awesome proportions
- Please give now, before you set this letter aside
- In my last letter, I mentioned to you that
- Just reading a letter from someone we've helped confirms that
- Your letter prevents more disastrous funding cuts before they happen

- This brief letter, only a few poignant lines long, stood out from the rest
- I'm having a great deal of trouble writing this letter to you
- In the few days it took for you to receive this letter, hundreds died
- I hope you'll read this letter very thoughtfully
- Please answer this letter of love and concern
- This letter is not an appeal
- Please don't throw this letter away
- With high hopes, we're dropping this letter in the mail to you
- Please don't put my letter aside
- If you can, please mail back the slip enclosed with this letter
- You can, and you should, take action today
- Please read this letter carefully and send your donation today
- That letter saved my life
- Please take a moment to sign the enclosed personalized letter to
- That's the reason my friends and I are passing out this urgent letter
- You have been chosen to receive this letter because
- The purpose of this letter is to ask you to contribute
- Thank you for taking the time to read this letter

LETTERS

- Supporting us with your donations and letters of praise
- One of the liveliest and most provocative letters you will ever read
- We get hundreds of letters about this in any given week
- Normally, I hate writing letters, but today I just can't wait to tell you about
- I do know that I've mailed a great many letters to people like you, people much like my own close and good friends
- If you've recently sent in your annual donation, and our letters have crossed in the mail, please accept our thanks
- This letter is the most important we've ever sent to you

LEVEL

- Will also support those wishing to acquire and maintain the highest level of health possible
- Level by level, we mean attain our objectives
- Demand a level playing field
- To maintain these levels of excellence, we need your help

LIFE

- Much improving care and the quality of life
- Lead a happy and fulfilled life
- Aimed at making the most out of life for
- Restoring life for so many
- Another way to celebrate life
- Destroying the integrity of human life
- This place literally saved my life
- More than I've ever done in my life

- Feels he is literally running for his life
- Please send your gift to touch the life of someone who needs you, now and throughout the year
- Please share a gift of $__ to help make a difference in the life of a
- The very symbol of life
- Supporting efforts to turn lives around is vital to rehabilitation
- Help give them a chance to turn their lives around
- Life isn't all champagne corks
- Struggling with the tensions of modern life
- The quality of life for those affected depends on the success of each of our member agencies
- The very breath of life
- They come from all walks of life
- Helping people improve their own lives
- Her life now has every chance of turning around
- When it comes to making life easier
- Learning the life skill they need to survive and even thrive in their own world
- Thousands more young lives have been saved
- Working to improve the quality of life for everyone who lives here
- We felt as though we'd been given a second chance at life
- It may save your life or the life of a loved one
- No chance at a normal life without your help
- A normal life, something she never knew existed
- For a long time he thought his life was over
- With our help, he had a brand new lease on life
- Went home with a brand new chance at a normal life
- This simple service can mean the difference between life and death
- You'll be touching a life in a crucial way
- When life hangs by a single fraying thread
- Every life is so very precious
- Life became very difficult
- The terror of seeing chunks of your life begin to disappear
- You can touch a life today
- But, at the same time, to carry on with life
- Until the day they found our service, they thought their lives were over
- A way of life for one horrific year
- With millions of factors in the delicate combination that makes life possible
- The web of life is under threat
- Working hard to preserve the diversity of life on Earth
- Provide a winning new life for
- Would that make a change in your life
- Life has been far from simple
- What would that do for their outlook, motivation and approach to life
- Able to go out and take up a normal life again
- Accepted as just part of life
- Life is a journey

- Finally able to live life on their own terms
- Being offered a second chance at life
- You can give him his life back
- Not content to let such a sad life just happen
- Creating a better life for all
- More such people can live productive lives

Life: existence, being, animation, lifestyle, way of life, lifeline, creation, nature, liveliness, vivacity, spirit
See also: EARTH, ECOLOGY, NATURE, SPIRIT

LIFEBLOOD
- They are definitely our lifeblood
- Your gifts are the very lifeblood of this noble enterprise
- Without enough money, the very lifeblood of our organization will drain away

LIFELINE
- A thin, tough, unbreakable lifeline
- Help throw a lifeline to those most in danger
- This precious lifeline is slowly fraying
- Your donations are the lifeline that keeps it all going

LIFT
- Give such a lift to
- Lift up out of hopelessness and misery
- Lift them up from where they have fallen, exhausted and full of despair

LIGHT
- Shedding relentless light upon this hidden subject
- Like light from the face of a rescuing angel
- Suddenly feeling light and free from care
- Let our light be a beacon by which all may steer

LIMIT
- The horizon is not the limit
- Accept no limits
- Please don't limit your contribution
- Refuse to endure such painful limits

LIMITATION
- No limitations are set
- Limitations are only obstacles to be overcome
- Determined not to let such limitations stop us

LINK
- A direct link to the world's highest decision makers
- One of the few links to the world as they know it is

- We an all become links in a strong, unbreakable chain
- Seeing how they link up to form a foundation for

See also: CONNECT, JOIN, PARTNER

LIP SERVICE
- Merely paying lip service to the concept of
- Simply paying lip service to its promise to open its doors to the world
- Lip service is not enough

See also: APATHY, INDIFFERENCE

LISTEN
- Learning to really listen
- We listen to your concerns
- When we listen carefully, we very soon discover
- Sooner or later, someone is going to listen
- Listening is our specialty
- Develop sensitive listening and focusing skills
- Giving the unconditional gift of listening with your heart open
- To listen, to hear, to understand

See also: ATTENTION, HEAR, UNDERSTAND

LITTLE ONES
- Right now, there's a little one who really needs your help
- Saddest of all are the little ones who don't understand why it hurts so much
- Untold other little ones hide their wounds
- Please remember all the little ones depending upon your help

See also: CHILDREN, KIDS, YOUNG, YOUTH

LIVE
- Really couldn't live without them
- Striving to live more richly
- Give so that more may live
- Must live in utter despair
- Lives in fear that she may be the next victim

Live: exist, have being, breathe, survive, be alive, cling to life, subsist, hold on, persevere, persist, endure, flourish, thrive, exist

LIVES
- Lives remain at stake
- Aren't these lives worth any price
- Help those whose lives are living nightmares
- I passionately believe that people's lives must be more than just a game of chance
- With your help, we can save even more lives
- The comfort of going to bed knowing you've helped save so many priceless lives
- The greatest danger to young lives
- Claims thousands of young lives every day

- Young lives are at risk
- Missed sharing so much of their precious early lives.
- The tender lives of young people
- So many depend on us to help save their lives
- Enriching lives in so many ways
- Our aim is simple: to save lives and ease suffering by providing
- Our efforts have already saved the lives of thousands of people
- The help they need to take control of their lives
- The joy of helping others build new lives
- And have their lives changed forever
- Now you have the opportunity to save even more lives by making a tax-creditable contribution to
- Help to keep on putting shattered lives back together again
- Every day you hold so many lives in your hands
- Their lives were painfully changed in the space of minutes
- All of us strive to make the most of our lives
- Leave to resume their lives as independently as possible
- Cuts short the lives of thousands

See also: CHILDREN, WOMEN, PEOPLE, YOUTH

LIVING

- Wondering fearfully how he'll be able to go on making a living
- Provide a decent standard of living for all
- Make everyday living very difficult or even impossible
- Try living on less than the price of a haircut
- It's all about living life to the absolute fullest

LOBBY

- We lobby governments, organize petitions, send letters, faxes and postcards to appeal for
- Your gift helps us run ads setting out alternatives and lobby the government
- While that lobby may be extremely vocal
- Lobbies and runs of advertising to make sure

Lobby: pressure group, interest group, agents, representatives, solicitors, influence, affect, persuade, move, promote, talk into

See also: ADVOCATE, CONVINCE, MOVE, PERSUADE

LONELY

- Lonely and upset and needing comfort
- Lonely, distressed, homeless and unemployed men and women get the counselling, referrals and support they need to find a brighter future
- To fill a lonely, empty heart with love

See also: ALONE, PAIN

LONG

- Has always been there for the long haul

- Looking long and hard at the choices
- Longing for the touch of a kind hand
- Settling in for a very long fight

LOOK

- They look forward so eagerly to
- Just have a look at a page or two of the enclosed brochure and you'll see for yourself
- We have to take a long hard look at what these policies really mean
- It's time to take a realistic look at

LOSE

- So what do you have to lose
- What a shame to lose out in the long run simply for lack of funds
- I'm so afraid we'll lose them if you don't help

LOSS

- A net loss to us all
- Fear the loss of something we all take for granted
- Without enough support we face the irreparable loss of
- With your help, we can prevent further losses and regain lost ground
- Assisting others in dealing with loss
- Loss is their daily bread
- Help to understand such profound loss
- Can empathize with this loss

LOST

- A treasure once believed lost to us forever
- You or I or someone very dear to us could be the helpless, the hopeless, the lost souls of tomorrow
- Let me try to explain what has been lost
- Found them wandering in the street looking lost and terrified

LOVE

- The love is freely given
- Love alone can't fix this problem
- Love thy neighbor
- Our gifts are one way to show our enduring love for one another
- Love is not enough
- There are so many ways to show your love
- Thanks for helping to spread love around
- Put your love to work today
- Make loving care a daily experience for so many
- Won't you share your love with
- Your love is the most generous gift of all
- Slowly, a child discovers what it is like to be loved

- Help us show them how much they are loved
- The best parts of life are little acts of kindness and love given to others
- Here's how you can share your love with the children who need

Love: fondness, affection, devotion, attraction, regard, warmth, adoration, friendship, closeness, passion, yearning, emotion, ardor, rapture, romance, concern, sympathy, caring, solicitude, affinity, harmony, amity, concord, brotherhood, tenderness, good feeling, appreciate, relish, embrace, enjoy

See also: COMPASSION, CARING, CONCERN, GOODNESS, KINDNESS, PASSION

LOYAL

- One of the most loyal and imaginative supporters of
- No one has been more loyal than our donors
- Our organization is always staunchly loyal to the highest principles of service

LOYALTY

- I want you to know that your loyalty helped all of us face a tough year with renewed energy
- Your loyalty is paramount for our survival and growth
- Our loyalty is unchallenged
- Your unwavering loyalty has encouraged us to
- Year after year, we appreciate your steadfast loyalty

See also: COMMITMENT, HONOR, PLEDGE

LUCKY

- We're really lucky to have what we've got
- Lucky enough to be involved
- Countless others aren't so lucky
- Reminded how lucky we really are
- They consider themselves so lucky to have even the simplest items

See also: FORTUNATE, HAPPY

MAIL

- Since we can't mail to everybody
- Very soon we'll contact you by mail
- That saves thousands of dollars in mailing costs, leaving more money for our core programs
- You can help us reduce our mailing costs with one simple action
- Contributions received make this one of our most successful mailings of the entire year
- I'm mailing this to you as quickly as possible to ask for your help

See also: CONTACT, POSTAGE, SEND

MAILBOX

- Look for upcoming issues in your mailbox
- The answer is right there in your mailbox

- Your mailbox is a tremendous source of help and information

MALNUTRITION
- Has declared that there are thousands of children suffering from malnutrition as a result of increasing unemployment
- Malnutrition is a scourge that must be wiped out
- The gaunt, sallow face of malnutrition

See also: FOOD, HUNGER, NURTURE

MANAGE
- Anything you can manage will be greatly appreciated
- If you could manage to dig just a little bit deeper
- With your help, we might just manage to make it

See also: ACHIEVE, AFFORD

MANAGEMENT
- Must understand the importance of good management
- Relying upon management that is experienced and credible
- Sometimes the best management is the least management

MANDATE
- Has much enhanced its mandate
- Although it's outside our mandate, we still want to help
- Only you can help us carry our this important mandate

See also: MISSION, PURPOSE, RESPONSIBILITY

MATCH
- Why not match the amount
- Allow a rapid matching of donated good and services with needs indicated by appeals for assistance
- We can help you find the right match
- Whatever amount you give will be matched by
- I urge you to match the contribution of a struggling family so that
- Hundreds of companies actively encourage their employees to support charities by offering to match their gifts
- Let me tell you how you can double your money via matching funds
- That few can match
- Each and every gift will be matched, allowing you to double the impact
- To help us, they will match each dollar raised with an additional dollar
- With the match, your donation doubles
- I hope you'll be able to match your last gift or increase it slightly

Match: twin, mate, double, parallel, equal, keep pace with, keep up with, reproduce, duplicate, compare, correspond, complement, harmonize, blend, coordinate

MATCHING GIFTS AND FUNDS
- Gifts to education through incentive matching gift programs

- Allows for all donations to the funds established to be matched by the government
- Participated in such programs, resulting in matching gifts providing extra
- A generous friend has promised us a matching gift
- That means your gift will be automatically doubled by matching funds
- Remember, your gift is automatically matched, dollar for dollar
- Your contribution is matched many times more by government, private donations and institutions and other development organizations
- You'll be helping twice as much through matching gifts
- Whatever amount you give will be matched by a 2-to-1 ratio so even a small amount will become greater
- Remember, whatever amount you decide to donate, however great or small, will be matched by a minimum gift of
- Your gift qualifies our organization to apply for matching funds from
- Please indicate if your gift will be matched by your employer
- Want to thank you for using our matching gift program
- This matching gift will be directed to
- Just think of the difference your annual gift can make thanks to these matching funds

See also: **SECTION SIX, SECTION EIGHT**

MATERIAL

- Material of the first quality, thereby enhancing its effectiveness both with members and the public
- We must develop more materials for free distribution to
- Must first be free of material wants
- We ask you to examine the enclosed material closely, then make a donation
- A constant flow of information and material supports

MATTER

- Nestled at the heart of the matter
- Able to see what truly matters in life
- Without the right help, nothing else matters
- Several matters have begun to arouse our concern
- Bringing you up to date on several matters

See also: **CONCERN, ISSUE, PROBLEM**

MEANING

- Inject renewed meaning into
- The meaning is very clear
- Suddenly we can see afar more poignant meaning in all this
- We know you will instantly understand the meaning of this

MEANS

- Managing to exist on the skimpiest of means
- Only people like you can give us the means to carry on

- Please place the means to help within our reach

Means: way, resource, step, shift, resort, measure, working proposition, artifice, device, contrivance, expedient, stopgap, makeshift, method, substance

See also: ABILITY, FUND, METHOD, RESOURCE, WAY

MEASURE
- Measuring our success by your generous response
- Polls show that most people, and I am one of them, support these measures
- We might have to take the most drastic of measures
- Stop these measures from being implemented
- After much consideration, the very best measures to take are
- Won't settle for less than their full measure of
- Half measures are no good here
- The best measuring stick is the one you provide

MEDIATION
- Mediation skills are now being used in many diverse areas
- To provide mediation where dispute resolution is needed
- Mediation is a more harmonious way to resolve grievances

MEDICAL
- On the other hand, special medical studies show that
- To help rush medical help to areas of greatest need
- Fund medical advances and save threatened lives
- Giving priority to individuals who require acute medical treatment

See also: CURE, DISEASE, RESEARCH, SCIENTIST

MEDICINE
- A celebration of the science and art of modern medicine
- Love and laughter are always the best medicine for
- To help provide basic food and medicine
- A few inexpensive medicines can do so much good

MEET
- Though you'll probably never have a chance to meet any of these courageous people
- Meeting their needs is everything
- I wish you could meet just one of those you've helped

MEETING
- I have had the privilege of meeting hundreds of you who
- The meeting is critical
- Meetings that allowed people to get to know one another and increase their resolve and dedication to support the
- A joyous meeting of minds and hearts

MEMBER

- The best way to help is by becoming a member
- By becoming a member, you contribute to an organization dedicated to the active, ongoing welfare of
- With a gift of $ __, you can become a founding member of
- Please become a founding member today by sending in your tax-creditable gift
- We want very much for you to remain with us as a valued member
- The importance of your role as a member is more critical than ever
- If you become a member now, you'll receive a free gift
- I look forward to welcoming you as a member
- I invite you to join as a supporting partner and member
- Protect your investment and share a well-deserved sense of satisfaction by becoming a privileged member of
- Now we invite you to become a member of our family
- Feel the pride of becoming a founding member today
- As a member, your donation will go straight into programming
- Please support us by joining as a new member today
- Become a member right now
- You've been a faithful member since
- If you enrol as a member, you will receive
- If you've been a member before, you know about member benefits
- Because you're a member, you've already done your part
- It is an area where the ordinary member can do the most to support the
- As a member, you're probably aware of dozens more stories of
- In a member-get-member style
- Help us help others – become a member today
- Even if you choose not to be a member, please consider a modest gift

See also: **PARTICIPANT, PARTNER, WORKER**

MEMBERS

- Every year, new members join, confident we're looking out for them wherever they go
- Without members, outreach would be impossible
- Please respond to the call for members and donations today
- Members support the crucial work each month, automatically
- The addition of new members is always an exciting development
- The original core members remain staunchly active
- A special offer for members and friends of
- As always, I urge each of you to encourage new members to join
- If each of us could contact a friend, I'm sure we would attract new members
- Members are the backbone of our organization
- One of our members was the inspiration and guiding force in
- Support from individual members will allow us to
- But we can't do it without supportive members like you
- As members and friends of
- Such an influx of new members will obviously strengthen us in our own work for

- Again and again, members keep telling us
- By gaining new members, we can improve the quality of
- Our members rely on the flexibility of
- As members, you are part of a very important group of individuals
- Exploring ways to ensure members receive maximum benefits from our program
- A key part of the program is the information our members provide
- Making sure members are given sufficient time to respond
- Such situations allow us very little time to contact members
- Providing sufficient information so that all members understand
- Over the past year, a large number of our members have asked to look at services which
- It is our intent to provide equal opportunity to all members
- These are solid members

See also: SECTION SIX – LAPSED MEMBER

MEMBERSHIP
- Through your membership, you've joined other caring people providing invaluable support to
- Did you know that membership provides a real bonus for us as well as for you
- We cannot help but be the richer for your membership
- They will be given a complimentary membership for one year
- After that time, they will be asked if they wish to renew and keep up their membership
- Enjoy a longstanding membership in
- No hidden obligations in our membership
- I hope you will send your membership donation today
- One of the most important of these initiatives is membership
- Your personal support, through your membership donation, will help us continue to provide
- Simply complete and return the enclosed membership contribution card, indicating your payment option
- Membership drawn from the community at large
- Our membership campaign is now in full swing
- The benefits of membership have never been greater
- Your membership will make it the best year ever
- Membership can mean a lifetime of memories
- Only with your membership and increased support can we meet our goals
- Membership points the way
- Membership offers you a historical perspective
- Take the minute necessary to complete the enclosed membership application
- Please renew your deeply-appreciated membership in
- Please renew your membership today – and add a donation if you can
- It is absolutely essential that we increase our membership to continue the idea and practice of
- You've been specially nominated for membership in this very prestigious group
- Your membership fees cover everything

- A name already familiar to a good portion of our membership
- The membership has grown until the branch has become the strong organization it is today
- Through your membership, you've joined other caring people providing invaluable support to
- Your deeply-valued membership has now expired and we need you.
- That's why each membership is vital
- Your deeply valued membership has expired
- Seeking comments and suggestions from our membership to enable us to provide better service
- Membership is not about making the numbers, its about protecting
- Make a membership donation of
- Membership is really basic to
- A look at a few of those making up our membership family
- Because of your membership dollars
- It benefits you and everyone if our membership is strong
- Here is a membership message from
- On whose behalf your membership will protect
- Your membership will also bring you
- If you're able to make a larger gift, I'll be delighted to send you some very attractive membership benefits
- A membership you'll always be proud of
- By contributing $ ___, you'll become a supporting member
- Please give us instructions for your membership
- Activate your membership – respond right away
- If you have a question about membership, please feel free to contact
- In recognition of your membership contribution, you'll receive
- Help us by responding today with a generous membership contribution
- Your membership tells how much you appreciate
- Your membership is expiring very soon
- The rewards of membership are priceless
- Learn how you can step up your membership to the next level
- You may wish to include a special gift with your membership
- We have wonderful ways to thank you for your membership pledge
- I hope you will decide to activate your membership

Membership: allegiance, admission, belonging, adherence, club, association, body, group, company, society, fellowship
See also: SECTION SIX

MEMBERSHIP RENEWAL
- You can help defend freedom by renewing your membership
- Your membership renewal will not only support our work
- Membership renewals are handled separately
- Let me tell how crucial your membership renewal is to the children in need

See: SECTION SIX

MEMORIAL
- A donation to help others is one of the finest memorials you can make to someone you love
- Memorials are a special way to contribute
- Give as a memorial to all those who have gone before

See also: **HONOR, HISTORY, REMINDER, TRADITION**

MEMORY
- Donate in memory of a loved one
- So that their memory will not die
- A splendid way to perpetuate the memory of a family member
- Our hearts are full of wonderful memories
- Quiet pleasures and happy memories
- Help wipe out all the bad memories
- We rekindle memories of your student days
- Memories to inspire them when they again face the difficulty of
- Creating a unique treasury of memories
- Help wipe out all the bad memories
- Hard as I try, I'll never be free of those haunting, terrifying memories
- So many warm memories of

See also: **HERITAGE, PAST, REMEMBER, REMINDER**

MESS
- It's up to us to clean up the mess our society has made
- One more heart-breakingly tragic mess dedicated workers must clean up quickly
- A way to leave no mess behind ourselves

See also: **CHAOS, HAVOC, DISASTER**

MESSAGE
- That's the message I'd like to leave you with as I sign off
- This is an urgent action message to people like you who are concerned
- What does it take to get this shocking message across
- Help us spread the message
- A noncommercial message from
- The message really boils down to this
- To maintain a strict focus on loyalty rather than diluting its message
- Now, more than ever, we need this message to be heard
- Read this important message only if you've decided not to join
- The message we spend hard-earned dollars to get across
- We can send a clear message that this will not be tolerated
- Will send a powerful message that will be heard

See also: **COMMUNICATE, INFORMATION, REACH**

METHOD
- Learn better methods to
- The move away from traditional methods of delivering aid is accelerating

- Our methods are constantly improving
See also: MEANS, WAY

METICULOUS
- Meticulous supervision at all times
- Meticulous craftsmanship
- Utterly meticulous in our planning

MIND
- With this in mind, we have decided to add our own special
- It's time to make up your own mind about
- So that the mind and heart can work together
- We have to keep an open mind about the uses
- Make up our own minds instead of swallowing ideas whole
- Here is one way you can speak your mind and be heard
- So many ugly ways to shatter a mind
- Reach them while their minds are wide open
- Allowing our bodies and minds to recharge and rejuvenate
- The leading minds of the country have contributed
- A gathering of the most brilliant minds on earth
- Rubbing shoulders with the brightest minds in the world
- I mind very much about needless suffering
- Open your mind, open your heart
- Hope you'll keep us in mind for the future

Mind: intellect, soul, spirit, inner being, genius, intelligence, brain, wit, perception, sanity, senses, reason, common sense, judgement, sentiment
See also: AWARENESS, CARE, MEMORY, THOUGHT

MIRACLE
- Your gift can help bring the miracle that rescues
- Parents call it a miracle and we agree
- Miracles are taking place regularly at
- I hope you will make sure miracles keep happening with your support
- Miracles do happen
- Amazing miracles occur every day
- Make a miracle happen, give generously
- You can make a miracle happen with a stroke of your pen
- Only through your support can science work its miracles
- At that moment, we can all believe in miracles
- Your donation will help bring a miracle into the lives of so many
- A miracle is just waiting to happen – maybe to you
- It becomes easy to believe in miracles when you see what just a little help can do
- Seems like a kind of miracle
- Miracles are worked by folks like you

Miracle: marvel, wonder, spectacle, prodigy, wonder work, phenomenon, rarity, curiosity, supernatural event

See also: AMAZE, WONDER

MIRROR
- Hold up a mirror to our nation
- Our actions are only a mirror of our real selves
- Be able to look into the mirror with a clear conscience

MISCONCEPTION
- Fight through a thicket of misconceptions
- Our biggest challenge is to change the misconceptions and fear that surround
- This damaging misconception must be cleared up at once

See also: MISGUIDED, MISTAKE, MISUNDERSTAND, WRONG

MISERY
- We can't let the misery drag on when
- Living in constant misery because of this disease
- Help put an end to the misery today
- Millions will be facing hunger and lonely misery, poverty, alcohol and drug abuse, unemployment, depression and family violence

See also: ABUSE, DISEASE, PAIN, SUFFERING, TORTURE

MISGUIDED
- Often misguided policies or sheer lack of money cripple efforts
- Those with good but misguided intentions
- Misguided efforts to help have already caused so much damage
- Please save us from such misguided people

MISSION
- I'm announcing a mission so urgent, so huge that we cannot undertake it without the extraordinary help of caring people like you
- Our mission is to extend help, and then hope
- Our mission is to supply basic human needs, provide personal counselling and undertake the spiritual and moral regeneration and physical rehabilitation of all persons in need who come within its sphere of influence regardless of race, color, creed or sex
- Because you share in our mission to
- Like so many others, I'm dedicated to achieving our mission
- Additional programs compatible with our mission are constantly being developed
- Must first provide a program to give itself the strength and sense of mission it needs to carry out its role

See also: CAMPAIGN, MANDATE, PURPOSE, REASON, RESPONSIBILITY, UNDERTAKING

MISTAKES
- If we avoid the usual mistakes
- In order to correct past mistakes we must move quickly

- Supporters have the mistaken impression that we have already won

Mistake: inaccuracy, error, blooper, blunder, misjudgment, misapprehension, gaffe, misreading, breach, transgression, misdeed, indiscretion

MISUNDERSTAND
- But please don't misunderstand
- To set straight all those who might misunderstand
- We regret any misunderstanding that may have arisen
- What a relief to clear up such misunderstandings

MOBILIZE
- We need to mobilize our elected representatives to respond to this grave threat
- If we're to mobilize in time, we must have your help
- Mobilizing every last scrap of support to help
- You are one of those I'm hoping to mobilize
- Only a rapid mass mobilization can work

See also: INSPIRATION

MODEL
- Creating an excellent model for all to follow
- Modelled on the actions of giants before us
- No longer can we use outdated models in our efforts to meet this challenge
- A model in which donating money is the driving force
- Aggressively promoting this model to help close the gap between
- Has given us an excellent model to realize our dreams
- A growing belief that this is the model to follow

See also: EXAMPLE, GOAL, IDEAL, MODEL, OBJECTIVE

MOMENT
- Please, don't let another moment go by
- I hope you'll just take a moment to look at the enclosed
- Please spare a moment from your busy life
- Take a moment now, while you're thinking about this
- There isn't a moment to spare
- Hoping to see the big moment when
- Please take a moment right now to
- Every moment of life is precious
- At this very moment people are waiting and suffering
- When moments count
- Ready to act at a moment's notice
- Appreciating the many small, celebratory moments of life
- Life is full of special moments
- Help make this moment golden
- Why not help make this a moment to remember
- One of the most moving moments was

MOMENTUM

- Please help us maintain the momentum with a donation today to
- In order to get up enough momentum
- It's not enough merely to have momentum
- So exciting to see and feel the momentum building
- With enough momentum, nothing can stop us
- Please do not let valuable momentum die
- Your gift will give the momentum to save our heritage

Momentum: impetus, drive, impulse, force, energy, thrust, driving power, speed
See also: DRIVE, ENERGY, FORCE, POWER

MONEY

- We don't get big money from major players
- But it also takes money to get things done
- Money you couldn't invest better in your community
- How to make so little money stretch so far
- It takes a lot of money to fund the vast range of
- Needless to say, all this costs money
- Your support will help us save money now by
- That's why we have set out to increase the amount of money we can give to research and educational programs
- When you consider the time and money that must go in
- It may be the best money you've ever spent
- We direct the money to where it is most needed
- The seed money your gift provided gave birth to
- Now we have to find the money from somewhere else
- Their parents had no money to pay for medical care
- When we see all the urgently needed things we could do if we had the money, we grow very frustrated
- I don't just mean sending money, as important as that is to our efforts
- That money was used to support
- Our work takes money, lots of money
- The money raised through this effort will ensure that more people than ever will receive
- We had to say we simply did not have the money that would allow them of offer these vital services to
- Wouldn't it be better to spend some of the increasingly scarce money on preventing
- It's like a savings account for money
- They have to borrow the money at crippling interest rates
- It will turn out to be the best money you've ever spent
- Making your money go much further
- The answer, of course, is money
- Better than money in the bank
- Put your money where your eyes are
- Worth more than all the money and material things in this world

- You don't have to give a lot of money

Money: cash, currency, greenback, pocket change, coin, dollars, bucks, loot, dough, moolah, boodle, profit, funds, donation, resource, gift

MONITOR
- An easy, effective way to monitor the most innovative, challenging and unconventional viewpoints
- Every action is monitored closely
- Carefully monitoring every aspect of how our program is carried out
- You can become one of thousands of monitors

MONTHLY GIVING, SUSTAINING DONOR
See also: SECTION SIX – MONTHLY OR SUSTAINED GIVING

MONTH
- A month can seem like ten years when you're cold and hungry
- If you give only one month out of every year, you will still be helping enormously
- Month after month, they toil away
- The importance of our work in the critical months ahead
- Every month the situation gets worse

MORAL
- Maybe there's a moral here
- It's our moral duty to
- Obviously the only moral thing to do is
- Moral people everywhere can't help but feel outrage
- Providing an unshakable moral base for our youth

See also: IDEAL, MODEL, PRINCIPLE, STANDARD

MORE
- But it does so much more
- But there's far more to it than that
- No matter how difficult, you can always manage a little more
- There's a whole lot more to
- But even more than that
- But so much more must be done
- There are hundreds more urgently in need of help
- Yes, we still must ask for more

MOSAIC
- Bring together a mosaic of culturally diverse work
- A mosaic of services all making a image of
- Fit the pieces of the mosaic together into a picture of love and caring
- Each of you is a vital piece in the great mosaic

See also: CHOICE, DIVERSITY

MOTHER

- Strongly urge that mothers with young children take control of their children's health
- A young mother races to the hospital, heart pounding, terrified her baby will die in her arms
- I'm writing to you today as a mother
- As a mother, I know the joy of holding a newborn close to my heart
- Tragically, many mothers are forced to raise the children they love in these awful conditions
- The simple happiness of a mother being able to watch her children safely at play
- Give a mother the right to have her next baby at time when it has a chance to live
- The pain of a mother whose child is teased at school for wearing shabby clothes
- The Earth is a loving, nurturing mother to us all
- We see mothers crying every day
- What can a mother do when her children desperately need food and there is none
- A mother's tears have given us the courage to ask you to

See also: **CHILDREN, EARTH, FAMILY, GIRLS, NATURE, NURTURE, WOMEN**

MOTIVATE

- Really motivated by
- Designed to get you motivated
- Items that support one another for motivation, treatment and prevention
- Highly motivated people, like you, can work wonders
- Giving a very powerful motivation to

See also: **DRIVE, GALVANIZE, INSPIRATION, MOMENTUM, STIMULATE**

MOUNTAIN

- Rearing before us like a mountain
- Now is the time to start moving mountains
- Climbed more mountains than she can remember
- The view from the mountain top is worth the climb

MOUTH

- Spoken out of the mouth of truth
- Putting food into hungry mouths
- Their mouths are full dust
- Truth from the mouths of babes
- Time to open up our mouths and speak up
- Mouths open in silent, anguished cries

MOVEMENT

- But the movement has become even more relevant
- Even if you've never been in a movement
- Your gift will make you part of a national movement made up of compassionate

individuals who believe it is wrong to target a country's poorest and most disadvantaged members

- The movement is made up of thousands of determined individuals, each taking action
- The movement is truly massive
- The greatest mass movement of people since
- Need you to join us and be part of this important movement

Movement: cause, action, activity, proceedings, advance, drive, crusade, fundraiser, coalition, front, grass-roots movement, course, trend, campaign
See also: ACTION, CAUSE, DRIVE, IDEA, MOMENTUM

MOVE

- Right now, while you are reading this, far-reaching moves are being planned
- Moves that will affect us all profoundly, including you
- It may be time for you to get moving
- Move out of your chair right now and help
- Working together, we can move a mountain

See also: ACT, ACTION, DECISION

MUCH

- But there's still so much that needs to be done
- Never too much to ask
- Much, much more than that
- So little can do so much

MUTUAL

- Turn to each other for mutual support
- Transformed into a mutually agreeable arrangement
- I assure you, the feeling is mutual
- With your help, our mutual goal is in sight

See also: MATCH, PARTNERSHIP, TOGETHER

MYSTERY

- The sudden increase/decrease remains a troubling mystery
- Despite significant differences, the mystery has almost been solved
- To help unravel the mysteries of
- The way to help these people is no mystery

See also: CHALLENGE, LABYRINTH, PROBLEM, PUZZLE

MYTH

- Nothing but a myth of gargantuan proportions
- Points the ways and dispels myths
- Here's your opportunity to separate the myths from the reality
- Blows the lid off the myth that
- Help shatter harmful myths and misinformation that damage lives

NAME
- You can now proudly add your name to the roster of supporters
- Caring in more than just name only
- Your name has been suggested as one who might wish to support our vital efforts to

See also: SECTION EIGHT – NAME EXCHANGE, ADDRESS VERIFICATION

NATION
- Access to cultural institutions which bind us as a nation
- Now they seek to build new, democratic nations
- The process of nation-building never ends
- New challenges confront the community of nations
- Our nation is traditionally generous, especially at this time of the year

Nation: country, tribe, clan, race, dynasty, public, society, community. state, republic, public, commonwealth, federation, realm, kingdom
See also: COUNTRY, PEOPLE, POPULATION, SOCIETY

NATIONAL
- A matter of the gravest national importance
- A national program not funded directly through
- Preserving this institution is a matter of national pride
- This is our largest, most urgent national appeal yet

NATURAL
- With your help, we can all take care of our country's stunning, irreplaceable natural beauty
- It's only natural to want to help
- The natural world is the only world we have

NATURE
- Working together with Mother Nature herself, making her a friend
- Some people are bound to shrug and say it's just the nature of the beast
- Poor farmers everywhere are at the mercy of nature
- Learning what it really means to live in harmony with nature
- Consider a gift of a different nature
- Build a future in which human beings live in harmony with nature
- Nature is never predictable

See also: EARTH, ECOLOGY, ENVIRONMENT, NURTURE

NAYSAYERS
- Help us prove the naysayers wrong
- If we listened to the naysayers, we'd never get anything done
- Too many naysayers are trying to sabotage this project

See also: DESPAIR, HOPELESS, NO, REJECT

NECESSITY

- With the desperate need for necessities looking us in the face
- Though sad at its necessity, we once again admire the adroit action in bringing about
- A matter of necessity
- Help those who don't even have the bare necessities
- I'm sure you can understand the urgent necessity for
- Gives people who truly in need the hope and the means to provide the basic necessities of life for their families

NEED

- Meeting people at their point of need
- We're there wherever human need cries out for help and comfort
- Times might change, human need doesn't
- We don't just deal with local need.
- Up to date on timeless need
- Stretching into every conceivable area of human need
- Ever mindful of the need for
- I didn't know what was in there, but I really needed help
- The need for our help is growing every day
- However, our need is great and our need is NOW!
- Because the need is now so staggering
- More sorely needed than ever before
- There's never been such a tremendous need
- It will go a long way in helping those who need it most
- Always there when you need us
- I can't stress the need for your help enough
- You have never been more needed
- It's hard when you need so much
- They needed our program more than ever
- They can now do that because we were there for them in their moment of need
- But there are so many others who need us now
- The need is growing greater every day
- It's hard to imagine a need this great
- The need is exceedingly urgent
- To help us with a very special need
- We're not going to pull any punches about how much we need
- I quickly became convinced that there was a need for
- Fill this gaping need
- We need you urgently
- Filled with aching, gnawing need
- We must respond to this escalating need
- A tiny fraction of what's desperately needed
- It meets practical needs with a personal expression of love and caring
- How do you sift through so many urgent and pressing needs
- The needs of the children are more important than any others

- Who else needs your help
- Learning how to ask for what we need
- When you need us, we're there
- The growth of need has been explosive
- Their hands outstretched in naked need
- Simply because we were not aware of your needs
- So many different problems, so many needs to fill
- Overwhelmed by all the needs that cry out to be filled
- Need your help to get us through this special period of need

Need: demand, requirement, necessity, requisite, obligation, charge, duty, essential, indispensability, want, lack, dearth, default, insufficiency, shortcoming, crave for, yearn for, necessity

See also: ASK, CRY, DESTITUTE, HOMELESS, HUNGER, NECESSITY, POVERTY, SCARCITY, WANT, WISH

NEGLECT

- Neglect is the most common form of abuse
- We won't stand for the continued neglect of our
- How satisfying to repair signs of neglect and foster a new flowering
- Now subject to the most shameful neglect
- We can't let this neglect go on
- The most important yet most neglected aspect

See also: APATHY, INDIFFERENCE, POVERTY

NEGOTIABLE

- Assumed this to be a given and not negotiable
- The basics are simply not negotiable
- Learning the difference between what's negotiable and what's not

NEGOTIATE

- Negotiating is one of the essential skills of life
- As we negotiate the tricky road of life
- Help us negotiate a very difficult course
- It's now possible to negotiate considerable improvements

NEIGHBOR

- We've long enjoyed good relations with you, our neighbor and friend
- The true meaning of being a neighbor
- Neighbors helping neighbors
- Knew I just had to reach out to my neighbors and friends
- You may not know the names of the neighbors you'll help
- As one of your neighbors, I'm a great believer in
- To be there for thousands of your neighbors who
- We're easily located to help you and your neighbors
- Let's start with the thousands of your neighbors who came to us for help last year
- As caring family members and good neighbors, you and I can't afford to have

people without proper care
- Tells everyone you helped neighbors by making a tax-creditable gift
- What your neighbors are saying
- It's hard to turn your back on those who are your neighbors
- Serving our elderly or ill neighbors faithfully

NEIGHBORHOOD
- We've been in your neighborhood a long time
- Now we are being told that our neighborhoods and the people who live there must do more
- I am a neighborhood friend
- To give hundreds of neighborhood young people a future to look forward to
- There to make our neighborhood a better place, and we can only do it with your financial help
- The goal of all our good work is to make our neighborhood a great place to live for everyone
- We'll always be a city of neighborhoods
- Carefully nurturing our neighborhoods
- So that neighborhoods receive flexible, sensitive responses to their local needs
- Try to imagine your neighborhood without it
- If you change your neighborhood, you have changed the world

See also: COMMUNITY, FAMILY, GROUP, HOME, PARTNER, STREET, TOGETHER, UNITE

NERVOUS
- It's time to get nervous
- We're getting very nervous about
- When funding drops to these low levels, even we get nervous

NET
- With a disintegrating social safety net, it is more important than ever that we relearn essential skills
- Netting a great increase in donations this year
- Dangerous as walking a tight rope without a net

NETWORK
- We are expanding our network of
- Energetic networking greatly increases our capacity to help
- A strongly meshed network covering the entire area
- You are part of a network that spans most of the globe
- Building a fully integrated network to develop, manage and promote
- Sometimes we have to take a networking break

NEW
- We're offering so many new ways to help
- New season, new growth, new beginnings

- So new we can't predict anything about it yet
- Something new under the sun
- Something new is going on here
- Here's a new one
- Something new every day

NEWCOMER
- But these newcomers are finding it more and more difficult
- Help these newcomers before they run afoul of
- I welcome you if you're a newcomer to helping
- We might be newcomers but we're sure willing to learn

NEWS
- There isn't much you can do to make bad news "good", but you can do something to make certain we aren't caught off guard and unprepared when trouble strikes
- It's time for some really uplifting news
- Here's even better news
- The encouraging news is that you can reduce your chance of contracting illness
- To get an indispensable overview of news and issues that affect
- The news is good on all fronts
- This may be the best news of all
- The news out there is not cheerful
- The appalling news seems to keep growing
- Behind this bad news there's lot of good news
- Bad news headlines that besiege us every day
- Here's the good news about the fight to preserve
- Generated a lot of news coverage
- Our newsletter will provide you with good, solid news about
- I have some great news for you
- Because of you, we'll be able to convey some really wonderful news
- A focal point for the latest breaking news, events and points of interest in our sector
- I come to you with hopeful news
- Stunned by the news
- News that touched us to the quick
- Deal with the tragic and upsetting news

See also: INFORMATION

NIGHTMARE
- Having the unspeakable become a living nightmare
- I, for one, don't want anybody to have to live with the nightmares that still recur
- These nightmare conditions are killing thousands
- Struggling to hard to emerge from this nightmare

See also: CATASTROPHE, DISASTER, HORROR, SUFFERING, TERROR, TORMENT, TRAUMA, UNTHINKABLE

NO
- We had to say no to so many urgent requests for
- How can we bear to say no to the children again
- Let's stand together and say a resounding no to this outrage

NORMAL
- Your caring support of our research program means that thousands have the prospect of a normal adult life.
- Hoping desperately that someday soon, they'll have a normal life
- Almost forgotten what normal is

NOTICE
- I want to give you advance notice of some great new programs
- Make them sit up and take notice
- It's time to notice the poor and homeless who are almost invisible
- I've really noticed how much you care about

NOW
- If not now, when
- Now is the time to do it
- We must act now when conditions are so right
- There is no better time than now to intervene

NOWHERE
- So many, heart-breakingly, had nowhere else to turn
- Often, there is nowhere else for them to go
- Nowhere is the need more great
- Sometimes wonderful things just seem to come out of nowhere

NUMBER
- Numbers like that make us very nervous
- No matter how we juggle the numbers, we have to ask your help
- At first, we were certain that we couldn't have got the numbers right
- There are a great number of ways you can help
- As these staggering numbers show, this is probably the greatest threat yet
- From there, the numbers appear even more compelling
- You only have to add up the numbers to see

NUMB
- So overwhelmed we can go numb to the needs
- We can get numbed so easily
- Combat the numbing effect of such a large catastrophe
- The reality of all can be truly numbing to the mind

NURSE
- Slowly nursing a spindly baby

- Nursed, encouraged, loved and looked after
- Tenderly nursing this new program along

See also: CAREGIVER, HELPER

NURTURE

- We nurture the smallest change for the better
- Nurtured like a tiny seedling that will one day be a giant redwood
- Stretch out a nurturing hand

Nurture: tend, remedy, restore, nourish, mend, cure, make whole, bring round, revive, rejuvenate, rehabilitate, set on one's feet, feed, maintain, sustain, take care of, cherish, tend, cultivate, foster, promote, boost, encourage, strengthen, support, advocate, advance, give a leg up, lend a hand, stimulate, further

See also: FOOD, HELP, NURSE

OBJECTIVE

- Please help us achieve our objectives
- Help in planning, defining and implementing our objectives for
- Our objective is annual funding for our program
- Determined to reach these objectives, I'm asking you to

See also: AIM, GOAL, IDEAL, MANDATE, MISSION, TARGET, UNDERTAKING

OBLIGATION

- A real sense of obligation drives this program
- You might feel it's your obligation to
- If we're to meet our obligations, we must have your help
- Please remember you are under no obligation to send a gift

See also: COMMITMENT, PLEDGE, PROMISE

OBSTACLE

- Only one obstacle stands in our way
- To bravely overcome all obstacles
- This is one obstacle we must surmount

See also: CHALLENGE, PROBLEM, OPPOSITION, PUZZLE

OBVIOUS

- It is painfully obvious from events that occurred
- When we look beyond the obvious, we often see the real truth
- The solution is fairly obvious

OCCASION

- On this very special occasion of our
- Please rise to the occasion
- On this occasion, we are really counting on you
- I understand that this does happen occasionally

See also: ACTION, EVENT, HAPPENING

ODDS
- Against all odds, achieving something special
- Improve your odds against
- The odds are in your favor
- Let's increase the odds for these courageous people

See also: CHANCE, OPPORTUNITY

OFFER
- No pie in the sky for us – we offer something concrete and valuable
- A truly extraordinary offer
- If this offer sounds unusual, please read on
- A very special, tempting offer
- An offer of exceptional value
- So that we can offer them so much more than they get now
- An offer you can't refuse

Offer: proffer, tender, hold out, present, extend, recommend, sacrifice, offer up, bid for, proposal, proposition, approach, advance, overture, submission, suggestion

OFFERING
- Your offering to help us reach those poverty-infested areas will be appreciated
- An offering of love and compassion
- Every offering is deeply appreciated
- We'd like to ask for your offering because the need is so great

See also: GIFT, CONTRIBUTION, DONATION, PLEDGE

OFFICIAL
- By the very state officials entrusted to protect their lives and liberty
- It's official; we need your help
- The reality turned out to be quite different from the official story

OLD
- Help for older folk in need
- A deserving older person
- Old people are denied the peace they've earned because of
- While older folk are being forgotten by others, we step in to help
- Older folks need your help today more than ever
- Unless you are old and lonely with no one to care for you

See also: ELDERLY, SENIORS, WISDOM

OPINION
- We plan to barrage the government with public opinion
- We must have a large number of opinion polls to have an impact
- We're waging a large public opinion campaign helping to secure
- You are making your opinion loudly heard on this matter when you
- So that your opinion can be heard
- It is our unanimous opinion that you

- Your opinion is very important to us
- Your opinions are needed on whether the cuts to these programs should go ahead

See also: IDEA, THOUGHT

OPPONENT
- We're up against a huge opponent
- Their opponents include a phalanx of frightening health problems
- If we can all work together, no opponent is too overwhelming
- We've licked tougher opponents before

See also: ENEMY, OPPOSITION

OPPORTUNITY
- Provides that opportunity for people from all walks of life
- Please take this opportunity
- Opportunity to care for their children the way they need to be cared for
- Finally, we face a historic opportunity to address problems that lead to
- Gave me the opportunity to work for change
- To see that no one is denied equality of opportunity
- I sincerely hope you'll take this opportunity to join us in
- Now we have the opportunity to service directly
- Inspire our friends, patients and families to be a part of an opportunity
- So that everyone can have the opportunity to enjoy
- So again, we offer you the opportunity to
- Once again we welcome the opportunity to deal with you directly
- We just can't afford to miss this opportunity
- This might be our final opportunity to save
- An ideal opportunity to promote
- History has just presented us with an unprecedented opportunity
- We have a golden opportunity to repeat the same miracle
- Few people have enjoyed the opportunity to fully appreciate the beauty and historical significance of
- Provides an opportunity to hold group support sessions for people with
- Opportunity to deepen and enhance your involvement
- Grateful for this wonderful opportunity
- Happy and proud to have this opportunity
- Challenging you to share in this exciting opportunity
- Did you know there is an opportunity for you to help
- Making sure you haven't already missed a valuable opportunity to
- At every available opportunity
- New opportunities arise every day
- Don't miss this golden opportunity to
- Even more sponsorship and exhibit opportunities
- What's so exciting is the opportunity to reach more people than ever with information they need
- Creating yet more opportunities for you to collaborate
- You know, there are a lot of great opportunities out there

- Making sure everyone has the same opportunity
- Increasing the ability to make use of those opportunities
- Empower us to grasp the new opportunities
- Why not take this opportunity to increase your support

Opportunity: opening, right occasion, possibility, favorable moment, good time, golden chance, contingency, stroke of luck, break

See also: **CHANCE, FREEDOM, OCCASION, OPTION, POSSIBILITY**

OPPOSITION

- Rest assured of our firm opposition to any such scheme
- You join a fiercely united opposition to
- Help us overcome this vigorous opposition
- Let us have no illusions about the strength of the opposition

See also: **OBSTACLE, PROBLEM**

OPPRESSION

- Constant struggle to free themselves from oppression
- Found everywhere oppression flourishes
- I know you hate oppression as much as I do
- First, we must stop the horrendous oppression

See also: **ABUSE, EXPLOITATION, SUFFERING**

OPTION

- We must assess our options
- Wide range of options corresponding to the particular needs of
- Providing simple time and cost efficient options to help your community
- You might feel your options are limited
- In order to finance these very special options, we must
- Carefully weigh the options
- We have no other option but to ask you

See also: **CHOICE, CROSSROADS, DECISION, OPPORTUNITY, POSSIBILITY**

ORDEAL

- My own ordeal started when
- An ordeal such as you or I could not imagine
- Every day is an ordeal for these suffering people
- Help so that they will no longer have to endure such an ordeal
- No ordeal could be greater than this
- No one chooses to turn living into such a grim ordeal

See also: **DISASTER, ILLNESS, NIGHTMARE, PAIN**

ORDER

- It's a tall order, but we must try
- We look forward to receiving your orders at
- Progressing in orderly stages

- The first rule is to establish order and calm

ORDINARY
- It's ordinary people who really have the power to
- This is no ordinary appeal
- We are something out of the ordinary
- Step out of the ordinary
- Nothing is ordinary here

See also: **NORMAL**

ORGANIZATION
- No compendium could possibly cover all the life and works of an ever-busy national organization
- Efficient organization makes your dollar go farther
- Ranks among the largest non-profit organizations working in this field
- Our grassroots, front-line partner organizations
- As a young organization, we are very honored to receive
- We are the only national not-for-profit charitable health organization dedicated solely to finding a cure or effective treatment for
- Our organization has completely re-invented itself
- Perhaps you support other organizations which help
- Long-standing reputation as a national organization that is truly representative of the poor
- Unlike many organizations, ours receives no government funding
- Each organization has its own unique needs and goals
- Organizations that must meet certain criteria to receive a donation

See also: **ASSOCIATION, COMMUNITY, CORPORATE, FOUNDATION, GROUP, MEMBERSHIP**

ORGANIZE
- You've be surprised how quickly something can get organized
- Organized resistence can be easily overcome
- Organized to demand government support and funding for

OTHERS
- Others may want to do both
- You, along with thousands of others
- When we help others, we're really helping ourselves
- It's time to really focus on the plight of others
- So that others can enjoy some of the basics of life we take for granted
- And for the others we are helping, please send a gift today

OUTCOME
- Without our help, the outcome is all too predictable
- A successful outcome is much more likely to
- Your donation is the best, most powerful way to influence the outcome

- Influencing the outcome for the better
- This happy outcome is a direct result of your help
- I cannot express how happy I am about the outcome of our appeal

See also: CONSEQUENCES, END, PAYOFF, RESULT

OUTCRY
- Confronted by a concerted public outcry
- Add your voice to this outcry
- Only a universal outcry will really stop this from happening

See also: CRY, MESSAGE, SHOUT, VOICE

OUTLOOK
- To be there for people just when the outlook is bleakest
- The outlook changes daily
- Those you helped have a much improved, optimistic out look on life
- Whether's there's real hope or not depends on your outlook

See also: ATTITUDE, OPINION, SITUATION

OUTRAGE
- Must respond with the moral outrage required to stop this hideous crime against
- The outrage fuels our determination to make real changes here
- Do something about an outrage that affects us all
- No decent human being could allow these outrages to go on
- It's nothing but an outrage, pure and simple
- I'm sure you're just as outraged as the rest of us

See also: ABUSE, ANGER, HORROR, NIGHTMARE

OUTREACH
- Give as much as you can so that more vital outreach programs can be developed
- But outreach to the community depends on this annual appeal
- Outreach to everybody most in need

See also: REACH OUT

OUTSPEND
- Currently, we are being badly outspent by the
- The opposition is outspending us three to one
- Just because they outspend us doesn't mean they will win

OVERCOME
- To face and overcome each difficult time as it arises
- You can overcome anything with enough faith and encouragement
- Help us overcome lack of participation from government and business

See also: BEAT, DEFEAT, SOLVE, SUCCESS, WIN

OVERLOOK
- I remember thinking how easy it would be to overlook the needs of

- We can't overlook such manipulation
- Must not overlook the hidden factors
- Help us make sure no one, no matter how despairing or in pain, is ever overlooked

OVERWHELM
- Hopelessness would have overwhelmed us
- The sheer numbers can overwhelm
- Triumph against overwhelming odds and opposition

OWE
- We owe it to them and to ourselves
- At the very least, we owe them respect and basic consideration
- No one owes more to donors like you
- They owe you their very lives
- Owing our very best efforts of their behalf

See also: OBLIGATION, RESPONSIBILITY

PACE
- Change now comes at a dizzying pace
- The pace of change is steadily accelerating
- To speed up the pace of discovery
- Only you can help us keep pace with the need

See also: PROGRESS, SPEED

PAIN
- Lived through the pain, never crying or complaining
- Stayed strong through the pain
- Has already experienced more pain that you and I will know in a lifetime
- Unspeakable pain is often a daily fact
- Painful horrors we can barely think about
- Only the pain is predictable
- When searing abdominal pain first gripped her
- The pain striking anywhere, any time
- No one should have to live with the pain
- The pain is excruciating
- Painful, chronic, frustrating illness
- Unpredictable, sometimes daily bouts of pain
- So many waiting and hoping as they endure their pain
- No one should have to face the pain these children must
- Only after suffering through months of excruciating pain
- The pain is almost impossible to look at
- Remember, only the pain is predictable
- Going into the pain is how I learned to handle it
- Of course that didn't stop the pain or other symptoms

Pain: smart, hurt, sting, ache, soreness, twinge, smart, discomfort, stab, throb,

torment, torture, grief, agony, misery, woe, suffering, heartache, despair, wretchedness, unhappiness, despondency, distress, disquiet, worry, anxiety, care, desolation, trouble, tribulation, trial, curse, ordeal, burden, bitterness, annoyance, fret, bother, sorrow, wound, cut, affliction, curse, scourge
See also: **AGONY, DESPAIR, HURT, NIGHTMARE, ORDEAL, SUFFERING, TORMENT, TORTURE**

PANIC
- They swallow the panic and don't tell a soul
- We mustn't panic about the frightening size of this problem
- Panic can stampede people into terribly wrong decisions
- Imagine the panic of first hearing this dread diagnosis

See also: **DREAD, FEAR, HORROR. RISK, TERROR, THREAT**

PARENT
- Surely more than any parent should have to bear
- To help a desperate parent before the first blow is struck
- Respond to the desperate look in a parent's eyes
- Parents desperately looking for help, new skills and ideas
- Bringing hope to frantic, heartbroken parents who have waited so long
- Alarmed parents fighting down that awful stab of fear
- Practical information for parents
- Those parents who struggle so hard and love their children as much as any of us
- These little ones look to their parents for safety and comfort
- No one can put a price on the worth of being a better parent
- We show parents how to
- Learning to appreciate parents more
- Nothing compares with the magic bond they have with their parents
- Making children closer to their parents

See also: **CAREGIVER, COMMUNITY, CHILDREN, FAMILY, KIDS, MOTHER**

PARENTHOOD
- Dealing with the emotional issues around visitation rights, child support, spousal expectations and single parenthood
- The grave responsibilities of parenthood sometimes weight them down
- People taking their parenthood very seriously

PARENTING
- Developing adequate and effective parenting resource materials
- Supporting them with parenting skills
- Parenting is the most important skill of all

PARKS
- Your proud gift helps our national parks and historic sites remain world-renowned

- Tell us how we can further champion our national parks and historic sites.
- Your help is needed to ensure our national parks and historic sites remain the vibrant, living symbols we all so deeply treasure
- We can no longer rely solely on government to protect the world's finest national park system
- Your gift of $__ or more helps us continue to protect our national parks now and into the future
- We are all helping to preserve and protect our cherished, irreplaceable national parks and historic sites
- The parks are precious and unassailable and not to be touched
- Yet even as we labored to make our parks and national sites better and better, the government has been slashing away at the funds that are very underpinning of our parks system

PART
- We have already taken part in hundreds of
- We must all do our part to
- Doing your part makes you feel such satisfaction
- We're asking you to take part in this glorious effort
- You'll know you're doing your part to ensure that
- All of us must do his or her part to secure our liberty
- Now you can be a part of it
- We want you to remain a vital part of it

See also: COMMUNITY, JOIN, PARTNER

PARTICIPANT
- Encouraged to become an active participant in
- Participants will learn how to help and support others
- Offered according to the needs and wishes of participants

See also: COMMUNITY, MEMBER, PARTNER, VOLUNTEER

PARTICIPATE
- In fact, we now have thousands participating in actions to
- Your participation is crucial to
- We're delighted to say your participation helped reconstruct
- We welcome your participation enormously
- Success requires active participation by all parties

See also: ACT, JOIN, GROUP

PARTNER
- We need you to be a partner in this important work
- You are the perfect partner
- Be a perfect partner with
- Clasp hands with us, become a powerful partner
- I'm inviting you today to become a partner in
- Only with partners like you can we keep this promising progress going

- Through the generous support of many partners
- Working together with our financial partners and supporters
- In co-operation with our local project partners

Partner: comrade, ally, aide, colleague, associate, companion, helpmate, helpmeet, co-worker, copartner, consort, confrere, sidekick, crony, friend, buddy, mate, collaborator, participant, contributor, participator, confederate, conspirer, abettor, accomplice, accessory, financier, funder, subsidizer,
See also: DONOR, FRIEND, HELPER, TEAM, VOLUNTEER

PARTNERSHIP

- We forge partnerships between
- Through these partnerships, we all share common concerns and work together on solutions to global problems
- A partnership with you is all important
- Your partnership with us is a precious gift
- It is a partnership that will not only help a family feed their children
- In partnership with people around the globe
- It's a partnership where everybody wins
- We hope you'll accept this partnership offer
- Won't you join us in this remarkable partnership that keeps
- Through these partnerships, we all share common concerns and work together on solutions to global problems
- Please join a remarkable partnership
- Our partnership represents a commitment that will survive well into the future, not only benefiting
- What a comfort to know your partnership has helped it grow ever better and better
- Keeping our partnership firmly anchored in
- Your partnership is an indispensable part of our tradition

Partnership: alliance, association, friendship, participation, merger, sponsorship

PARTY

- Now that the party is over, you and I have to pay for the cleanup
- Join the party, reap the benefits
- Now you can be a major party to this renewal

See also: COMMUNITY, GROUP, LOBBY

PASSION

- Their struggles, their passion for life
- Something you can have a real passion for
- Driven by a passion so powerful that
- Fulfilled dreams require passion
- Foster a burning passion to succeed
- Allowing us to reveal a passion for the dreams that truly matter
- Without your passion and involvement, this idea would never have grown so strong

- Our fears and our passions surely have the same source

See also: **CARE, DRIVE, EMOTION, FEELING, INTEREST, LOVE**

PAST
- I can only try to put the past behind me
- You've always been there in the past, supporting us with your donations and letters of praise
- Even more than in the past, we need your participation
- The sad past does not equal a hopeful future

See also: **HISTORY, LEGACY**

PATH
- If we keep taking this path we will soon discover
- Helped set thousands of youngsters on the right path
- The courage to depart from the well-travelled path
- Creating our own path
- I hope you will choose to walk this path with us
- Sometimes there are so many paths to choose from
- So many paths, you end up standing still

PATIENT
- And each patient clings to precious, hungry hope for a better life
- Dedication to patients is paramount
- Provides many services that address the needs of patients, families and the public, including
- Ensuring that patient needs always come first
- A very satisfied and grateful patient says thank you

PATTERN
- A disturbing new pattern is emerging and we must try to change it as soon as we can
- More pieces of the overall pattern begin to appear
- Unlearning old patterns of behavior
- Following that same pattern, we too can have a success

PAYOFF
- The payoff is so big
- Such a modest investment for such a huge payoff
- The payoff comes in pure love

See also: **OUTCOME, RESULT, SUCCESS**

PEACE
- Ever closer to finally achieving the simple peace and joy you and I enjoy every day
- Plant the seeds of peace today
- Encouraging that support is the single most valuable thing you or I can do to

    foster international peace and justice
- Known at home and abroad as a force for peace
- Peace is a blessing none of us can take for granted
- The priceless treasure of peace and prosperity
- Help the country to remain peaceful
- Achieve peace of mind through
- Solutions for your peace of mind
- It's really all about peace of mind for themselves and their families
- What we all truly want is peace of mind

Peace: harmony, peacefulness, respite, relief, tranquillity, orderliness, serenity, serendipity, accord, compatibility, amity, detente, friendliness, cordiality, fellowship, good will, unity, rest, ease, comfort, quietude, stillness, hush, repose
See also: HAPPINESS, ORDER

PENNY
- We don't receive a penny from
- Every penny counts
- For mere pennies a day, you can give aid and comfort
- Costs a few pennies more than a cup of coffee
- Mere pennies to you, but life and death to them
- You'll appreciate how every penny helps and how much it achieves
- Every penny you can spare helps us

See also: DOLLARS, DONATION, GIFT, MONEY

PEOPLE
- It's time to use the power of the people
- We are these people and they are us
- People offering a hand to people in need
- People who really believe that
- Allow us to reach even more people and involve them
- People who have worked all their lives to
- Lately, so many other people have been asking us for help
- So many people down there need us
- We expect as many, or more, people to come to us for help this year
- More people than ever are hurting
- Thanks to outstanding people like you
- May be forced to turn away people in need
- The people who are there when help is needed
- Suffering people who have nowhere else to turn
- These are real people with hopes and dreams, mothers and fathers, children and grandchildren just like you and me
- Become one of the many people who make it possible
- They really do depend on people like you and me
- Active people like you are a very special breed
- What these people are doing sometimes approaches insanity
- We can't let these people down

- Some people just never seem to have any luck
- People everywhere are preparing for
- Helping to create a people-to-people delivery system
- People who may someday support our work as well

See also: **COMMUNITY, FAMILY, GROUP, HUMAN, HUMANITY, MEMBER, SOCIETY, VOLUNTEER**

PERSISTENCE
- Asking for your persistence in helping to attack this difficulty
- If I'm persistent in asking you for a contribution, it's because we must ensure that
- The most persistent of problems can be solved

See also: **DETERMINATION, LOYALTY**

PERSON
- So that one more person can be saved from the agony of
- Making sure yet another person can be released from
- We'd like you to meet an amazing person
- I want to make sure not one single person who asks for our help gets turned away
- Dignity of the person is one of the first things we address
- Maybe you can't be there in person, but you can be there in spirit
- If only you could be there with us in person, you could see the joy for yourself
- Finally convinced they are worth something as persons

See also: **COMMUNITY, HUMAN, MEMBER, VOLUNTEER**

PERSONAL
- How you help is often a highly personal thing
- On a very personal level, I am concerned for individuals who have contracted this horrifying disease
- I want to approach you about a very personal concern
- Let me tell you about a personal experience

PERSPECTIVE
- I hope, from your perspective, we did not let you down either
- A startling new perspective on yourself and the universe around you
- Bring to the table a singular perspective
- Enthusiastically sharing her perspective
- Bringing you a unique perspective on the world
- No other organization brings the same broad perspective

Perspective: outlook, view, viewpoint, overview, position, stand, vantage point, attitude, way of thinking

See also: **IDEA, OPINION, OUTLOOK, VIEW**

PERSUADE
- Help us persuade others to
- No one has to be persuaded about the urgency of the need
- I hope I have managed to persuade you

- If we can just persuade a sufficient number of people to contribute
- One look at this scene ought to persuade the hardest heart

See also: BELIEVE, CONVINCE

PETITION

- Your signature on this petition will help enormously
- If you can't send a contribution now, for whatever reason, I hope you'll still sign the enclosed petition to show your concern for protecting
- I have signed the petition to remind the government that all citizens have the right to
- Our petition is approaching thousands of names
- I need you to sign the enclosed petition and return it quickly
- A successful petition drive requires your signature
- Along with your signed petition, I'm asking you to contribute

See also: ASK, COUNT, DEMAND, JOIN, PARTICIPATE, REQUEST, SURVEY

PHILOSOPHY

- Profound understanding of the philosophy underlying
- We've embraced this philosophy in our choices
- Live every day by this shining philosophy
- If you share this same philosophy you'll understand the need to act
- To find a philosophy that really works

See also: CONCEPT, CONCERN, IDEA, OPINION, STRATEGY, THOUGHT, THEORY

PICTURE

- Do you get the picture now
- As you can see from the picture I have enclosed
- Just picture the joy you will help bring
- This where you enter the picture
- You are also part of this larger picture
- Your participation can change the whole picture
- Just picture this

See also: IMAGINE, SEE

PIECE

- Pick up the pieces
- When everything is falling to pieces
- Put the pieces carefully in place
- Overjoyed to find another piece of the puzzle

PLACE

- A place to relish instead of a place to fear
- The unimaginable luxury of a place of their own
- Help make this the greatest place in the world to live

- Always have first place in our hearts

PLAN
- When you join the plan you receive
- A plan urgently needed on this troubled planet
- Such a marvellous plan
- The best laid plans sometimes need a little help
- Lacks a carefully designed plan to
- Here's how this amazing plan works
- Unless they hear from you, this dreadful plan will go ahead
- Letters come almost every day praising the plan
- I'm letting you know the plan ahead of time so that you can fully participate
- Work to establish the best possible plan to meet needs as they arise
- We may have to shelve our plans for more ambitious projects
- The plan runs totally counter to

Plan: scheme, arrangement, design, grouping, layout, organization, pattern, configuration, proposal, project, prospect, conception, purpose, view, intent, ambition, intention, hope, aspiration, map, ground plan, model, sketch, draft, chart, look ahead, arrange, line up, work out, schedule, block out, propose, strategize, devise, develop, frame, construct, envision, mastermind, contemplate, outline, draw up, plot, fashion, shape, concoct, intend, measure

See also: CONCEPT, IDEA, ORGANIZATION, STRATEGY

PLANET
- Just as concerned about this planet as you are
- We can succeed in preserving a livable planet for our children and grandchildren
- On notice about the real dangers that threaten our fair, fragile planet
- If you love this planet, act now
- Creating hope for the future of our beautiful blue planet
- We just don't have another planet we can move to
- The planet is shrinking every day – and so are our chances of survival

See also: EARTH, ENVIRONMENT, GLOBAL, WORLD

PLANNED GIVING
- Please contact us for a free pamphlet on our planned giving program
- Make planned giving part of your life plan
- Planned giving makes the most sense in these circumstances

See also: SECTION SIX – MONTHLY OR SUSTAINED GIVING

PLANNING
- We must do some planning now for those who
- Participation in the planning is crucial
- The strategic planning process must be
- The planning is all important
- Insisted we have a say in the planning process

PLAY

- Playing for keeps
- I'm afraid it's not child's play we're involved in
- In order to avoid playing into the hands of
- This idea plays well
- Come play with us

PLAYER

- The really big players rolled the dice
- If we're to be genuine players in this game, we must
- You can be a real player too
- Working hard to become a major player in

PLEA

- Please don't ignore our plea
- My plea is that you join me and more than a million compassionate human beings worldwide in the urgent work of
- How can such pleas be ignored

See also: APPEAL, ASK, PETITION, REQUEST

PLEASE

- Please, please do it now
- And please hurry
- You'll be so pleased with the progress to date
- Saying please very strongly

PLEASURE

- I take especial pleasure in calling your attention to
- I hope I will have the pleasure of counting as one of our supporters
- Together, we can share that simple pleasure with
- Often take for granted the enormous pleasure of
- With the greatest of pleasure, we learned
- You can imagine their pleasure when they discovered
- Through your gift, you are sharing one of life's greatest pleasures with someone who is

See also: DELIGHT, HAPPINESS, JOY, SMILE

PLEDGE

- We wait eagerly for your pledge
- But how about those pledge drives
- Please take a moment to return the enclosed pledge card
- If you will only pledge even a modest amount
- You can donate the full amount of your pledge
- Whether you pledge $20 or $200, it all goes toward
- What could be more appropriate than pledging
- If enough people pledge, we've made it

- Make a pledgetoday
- Pledging mutual loyalty and cooperation
- If you wish, you can make a one time only pledge of

See also: **GIFT, CONTRIBUTION, DONATION, COMMITMENT, OBLIGATION, PROMISE**

PLIGHT

- Become transformed as they realize somebody is providing genuine, practical, immediate help for their plight
- The plight of fellow human beings
- Hearts were moved by such a sad plight
- Imagine yourself trapped in the same plight

Plight: condition, situation, state, shape, circumstance, position, emergency, crisis, exigency, pinch, squeeze, pickle, bind, tight spot, corner, problem, trouble, hornet's nest, hot water, complication, mix-up, deadlock, stalemate, impasse, standstill, mess, jam, scrape, tangle, quandary, dilemma, muddle, kettle of fish, stew, hole, fix

See also: **CATASTROPHE, CONDITIONS, CRISIS, DISASTER, MESS, PREDICAMENT, PROBLEM, SITUATION, SQUEEZE**

PLUG

- Don't let them pull the plug on this urgently needed
- Rushing to plug the gaps in the system
- Allow me to put in a plug for a good cause
- Plugging along through every difficulty

POCKET

- Being asked to reach into your pocket and donate
- Please, please dig just a little bit deeper into your pocket
- Just a little something from you pocket is very welcome

POLICY

- We also know that such a policy carries a high price
- Looking to support a policy of reaffirming and strengthening
- Working hard to put a sound policy in place
- All policy options are carefully explored in
- Framework to develop guidelines for such a policy

See also: **IDEA, PLAN, STRATEGY**

POLITICAL

- Clear that this was a political move following
- We are not affiliated with any political party
- Every day people are murdered by governments for their political beliefs and activities
- Pushing for a political solution to this
- The only real solution must be a political one

See also: **GOVERNMENT, NATION**

POOR

- Poor people are the last to be heard and the first to suffer
- Now imagine, for a moment, being poor
- Unique work of bringing the voices of the poor people directly to the politicians
- Tragically, for the world's poorest people, this was a losing proposition
- I know that, like me, you think it shameful to target the poorest people in society to shoulder this unfair, crushing burden
- The poorest and most vulnerable

See also: DESTITUTE, HOMELESS, PAIN, POVERTY

POPULAR

- Its many links to popular culture
- This has proved one of the most popular ways to give
- This is not a popularity contest but a serious undertaking
- The right action is not always the popular action
- Helping to make this worthy cause more popular

POPULATION

- To keep pace with the aging population
- We need a population equipped to cope and thrive
- That number is growing due to our aging population
- Taking emergency measures to deal with the population explosion
- Strategies for interacting with special populations are prime considerations
- Only a small percentage of the population is aware that such information exists

Population: residents, inhabitants, citizens, citizenry, populace, folk, head count, demography, commonalty

See also: CITIZEN, COMMUNITY, GROUP, HUMANITY, PEOPLE, SOCIETY

POSITION

- A run down on the position which they felt as favorable at the moment
- Able to position ourselves to do the most good
- Will put us in a very strong position to
- If you are at all in a position to help, please do so as soon as you can
- We take this position in hopes that you will quickly respond
- Placed in the uncomfortable position of having to

See also: OPINION, POLICY, SITUATION

POSITIVE

- Every effort is made to provide a positive experience for
- How good it feels to take positive action as a
- Your actions in supporting us have already had a positive effect on government thinking
- Overall, I hope you feel positive about the important work you were a part of
- Hundreds of lives will be positively affected by your kindness

Positive: sure, certain, sound, definite, unequivocal, categorical, indisputable,

confident, assured, real, veritable, optimistic, hopeful, promising, cheering, sunny, heartening, inspiring, encouraging, favorable, propitious, profitable, good, affirmative, salutary, genuine, authentic, solid, substantial, practical, beneficial, convinced
See also: ENCOURAGE, HAPPY, HEARTEN, JOY, YES

POSSIBILITY
- Such a possibility is utterly mind-boggling
- Help to discover the stupendous possibilities in
- One of the few possibilities to prove feasible for the future of
- A possibility no one has even thought of before
- I know you're as excited as I am about such a possibility

See also: CHANCE, CHOICE, DREAM, OPPORTUNITY, OPTION, POTENTIAL, PROSPECT

POSSIBLE
- Your donation will help make it possible for us to get urgently needed aid through on time
- With you help, we'll be able to do everything possible to
- The only way to make it possible is with the support of people like you
- Believe it really is possible
- You gift will help make it possible for more children to
- In order to make this possible, please mail your gift today
- All this is made possible by
- We need your participation to make this possible
- Information about our work and how your gifts make it all possible
- Dreams become possible here every day – because of you
- You make it all thrillingly possible
- In those days, you'd never have believed it possible
- You make it possible for others to do the same
- You helped make possible this result
- This program has made it all possible for
- Although everything possible was done to
- Make all this possible by giving generously
- Not possible on a daily basis

Possible: probable, likely, odds-on, promising, hopeful, feasible, workable, attainable, obtainable, performable, within reach, affordable, realizable, conceivable, perceivable, understandable
See also: ABILITY, EASY, ENSURE

POSTAGE
- The postage is prepaid to make it more convenient for you to give
- Help us save money on postage by
- For the cost of the postage alone we could
- Postage alone could severely deplete our funds

See also: ADMINISTRATION, CONTACT, LETTER, MAIL, MAILBOX,

SEND

POSTERITY
- Provide for our posterity
- Out of regard for our posterity
- Posterity will make the final judgement

See also: **CHILDREN, FUTURE, HERITAGE, LEGACY**

POTENTIAL
- Uncover the hidden potential
- We must reclaim all that wasted potential
- The potential to achieve our goals and objectives
- A potential solution could be just around the corner
- Such explosive potential must be directed and developed
- A constantly expanding potential
- A leading authority on the development of human potential
- Help them improve their self-confidence and realize the potential in their lives

See also: **CAPACITY, FUTURE, POSSIBILITY**

POVERTY
- Help relieve the curse of poverty
- To help children growing up in the grip of poverty and suffering
- The patterns that keep people living in poverty
- So many ways to get people out of the cycle of poverty and despair
- Struggling for jobs, shelter, food and dignity while living below the poverty line
- Anti-poverty action fund
- Those are just the statistics – which don't show the real face of poverty
- Your donation brings us just a little closer to a day when poverty with its shame and wasted potential is eliminated for good
- Living in poverty and barely getting enough to eat
- Stuck in the cycle of poverty
- Trapped in grinding poverty and oppression
- Adults and children otherwise locked into a life of poverty and disease
- With the support of thousands like you, we work with people around the world, helping them tackle the root causes of poverty in their communities
- Many of the root causes of poverty are beyond community control
- Has predicted that the next generation will be smaller, have poorer health and be less intelligent that today's population as a result of malnutrition caused by extreme poverty
- You can help turn poverty into self-sufficiency
- Still living in abject poverty
- Fair trade ensures people don't have to live in poverty
- Transcending the stark reality of poverty

Poverty: indigence, penury, impoverishment, neediness, privation, destitution, penecilessness, pauperism, mendicity, mendicancy, beggary, distress, difficulties, straits, lack, want, bare cupboards, dearth, default, scarceness, scantiness, skimpiness,

starvation, poorness
See also: CRISIS, DESPERATE, DESTITUTE, HOMELESS, SUFFERING

POWER
- Truly has the power to change lives dramatically for the better
- In embracing the concept of power to the people
- Gives them the power to
- What we need is not the arrogance of power but the strength of our vision
- As always, the ultimate power rests with you, the people
- Asserting the timeless, matchless power of goodness
- I urge you to use whatever power you possess

See also: DETERMINATION, DYNAMIC, STRENGTH

POWERLESS
- We are powerless to help them without you
- No longer powerless but strong and free
- Because of you, these people are no longer powerless
- Refuse to be powerless in this situation

See also: DESPAIR, HOPELESS, POOR

PRACTICAL
- In a practical, hands-on way
- No theory, just genuine practical help
- Looked at from a practical point of view, this is the only useful method
- The kind of practical, serious help people really need
- Stating the situation in the most practical terms

See also: USEFUL

PRECARIOUS
- And now things are more precarious than ever
- Living the most precarious of existences
- In this most precarious of times, please help

See also: DANGER, RISK

PREDICAMENTS
- Predicaments such as these happen every day
- It's hard to imagine a worse predicament
- With your help, we can rescue these people from their predicament

See also: PLIGHT, SITUATION

PREDICTABLE
- It seems that things used to be a lot more predictable
- If we don't help now, a sad outcome is predictable
- Less predictable now than ever before
- The arrival of catastrophe is never predictable

PREMIUM
- Premiums are a way of inspiring you to call us with your pledge
- Right now when funds are a premium
- When you increase your level of giving, you will receive this lovely premium as a token of our appreciation

See also: BONUS, GIFT

PRESENCE
- You presence will be felt the first time those suffering people taste the nourishing food and cover their shivering limbs with warm clothing they have received from
- So that we can remain an ongoing presence in
- Her indefatigable presence coupled with her natural enthusiasm and deep loyalty
- The presence of vigilant caregivers makes all the difference

Presence: closeness, proximity, existence, force, influence

PRESENTATION
- A full presentation concerning how to prevent
- This beautiful presentation piece is yours in thanks for your donation
- A presentation guaranteed to move you

See also: INFORMATION, SHOWCASE

PRESERVATION
- Your generosity means our volunteers can continue to make a difference in the preservation and protection of
- We demand the preservation of
- The preservation of these programs is now our primary goal

See also: DEFEND, SAVE

PRESSURE
- Because one gift or one action added to thousands of gifts or actions can create the kind of pressure that makes people listen
- Your letter will help us keep the pressure on and show that
- Pressure from us successfully resulted in
- To put pressure on the world's leaders to protect
- The more people act right away, the more pressure authorities will feel
- The pressures facing people today are unprecedented
- With increasing pressure for government to curb spending
- The pressure is on in a very major way

See also: CRISIS, SQUEEZE, URGENT

PRESTIGE
- The excitement and prestige of
- By joining now, you can enjoy all the prestige of
- Bringing all their prestige to the service of
- You become part of this enormously prestigious organization

PREVENT

- The most important thing we can do is to help prevent these horrors from happening to someone else
- Work to prevent this happening to other people like myself
- Prevent innocent children from being enticed into
- To simply preventing it from the start
- Finding out how to prevent
- Even a small donation from you can do so much to prevent this bane

Prevent: block, impede, obstruct, hamper, halt, arrest, restrain, check, put a stop to, inhibit, intervene, interrupt, frustrate, foil, thwart, retard, delay, veto, disallow, bar, prohibit, override, balk, repress, contravene, hold back, forestall, preclude, stamp out, baffle

See also: BLOCK, OVERCOME, STOP

PREVENTABLE

- This horrible scourge is fully preventable
- Going after the preventable things first
- So many things are so easily preventable

PREVENTION

- But prevention through educational and personal awareness is just one side of our story
- Invest in prevention by giving today
- Our very first concern is prevention of
- Prevention is the watchword you and I go by

PRICE

- For less than the price of restaurant meal you can pay for the immunization of
- Prices are soaring every day
- The price of not acting now will be very high
- They have paid a terrible price and now its up to us to help
- Although these goals are actually priceless, we find ourselves paying

See also: CHARGE, EXPENSE, COST, VALUE, WORTH

PRIDE

- Show your pride in our work by making a generous contribution to
- We can look at them with pride.
- Provide generous helpings of pride and self esteem
- Pride, dignity and self reliance are the goals
- We can look at them with pride
- They dish out pride along with the nutritious food
- Feel your bosom swell with pride as you watch them begin to revive and thrive

Pride: self-esteem, self respect, pride and joy, treasure, jewel, glory in, bask in, boast, strength, self possession, dignity

See also: CONFIDENCE, DIGNITY, SHOWCASE, TRADITION

PRINCIPLE
- We must stand firm on principle
- We can't ask them to compromise such cherished principles
- Our adherence to these principles and time-honored standards
- A quest for living principles
- Reaching backward to the principles that made this country what it is
- Principles that made the people who they are

See also: CONCEPT, IDEA, IDEAL, MODEL

PRIORITY
- I know all of this is a priority for you
- Giving the very highest priority to
- It's still a top priority
- It remains one of my major priorities
- They've rarely been a world priority
- They're our first and only priority
- Giving your gift and your wishes first priority
- People are always our number one priority
- Our first priority is the complete financing of

Priority: urgency, precedence, seniority, rank, preference, primacy, preeminence, superiority, supremacy, importance, weightiness, consequence

PRISONER
- Remains a prisoner of conscience because of
- To secure the release of prisoners of conscience
- The families of prisoners need your support
- Many former prisoners have contacted us to thank us
- Free the sad prisoners from misery and oppression

See also: DESPAIR, FREEDOM, LIMIT, TORTURE

PRISON
- Volunteers have been visiting men and women in prisons
- Trapped in a terrible prison of poverty and despair
- Help them escape from the prison of their own minds
- Life itself can turn into a prison for those with this disease

PRIVILEGE
- Your support has been a great privilege for us and we sincerely hope you will continue in the future
- We are so privileged to be working with
- We are extremely privileged to have as
- Wonderful additional privileges that can be yours to enjoy

See also: FREEDOM, SPECIAL

PRIZE
- Help us grasp the biggest prize of all

- Prizes encourage students to engage in research on the
- One of our most prized successes is
- By far and away the best prize life offers is the chance to work hard at work worth doing

See also: **BONUS, MIRACLE, PREMIUM, SUCCESS, WIN**

PROACTIVE

- Become proactive today
- Proactive people are taking the lead now
- Because you became proactive, opinions were changed

PROBLEM

- Help us do something about this shocking problem
- Have you ever faced such a problem yourself
- We've already shown that we're real problem solvers
- My problem is that I must do this without being able to speak to you directly when there is so much to be said
- A way to put right this problem that has been allowed to develop
- A problem that affects far too many struggling families
- We are particularly concerned about these problems because
- Once the problem is found, we can bring the newest and best treatments to bear
- We haven't always had this problem
- Of course, they've always struggled with this problem
- So we can continue to focus on solving this problem
- To finally put paid to this problem
- At first glance, you don't really see the problem, but soon
- A program to help you understand the problem
- Wrestling with the really tough problems of
- Recognizing the problem doesn't guarantee a solution
- Finding new answers to old problems
- Help prevent this problem before it starts
- However, there is a very serious problem that you've probably followed in the media
- Our skilled staff is trained to handle these problems
- We seek to connect people around the world to work together on solutions to problems that affect us all
- Social problems, conflicted relationships between parents and children, and concerns that relate to education
- In the face of serious environmental and social problems like
- The problem is rapidly being compounded by
- Looking at an old problem with new, compassionate eyes
- Face problems that many of us couldn't begin to imagine
- All of these are problems you could help stop
- Their work in unravelling the problems of
- There doesn't have to be a problem
- We can't give this problem to someone else

Problem: question, mystery, riddle, poser, predicament, quandary, plight, pickle, hornet's nest, difficulty, trouble, affliction, handicap, disadvantage, inconvenience, nuisance, pest, headache, bother, vexation, hassle, annoyance, incorrigible, intractable, blight
See also: **CHALLENGE, DIFFICULTY, LABYRINTH, MYSTERY, OBSTACLE, PUZZLE**

PROCEDURE
- Matters are progressing satisfactorily according to procedure
- So that it's not just a matter of procedure
- Radically different from our ordinary procedure
- Forced to undergo all manner of humiliating procedures
See also: **ACTION, GUIDANCE, POLICY, STRATEGY, WAY**

PROCESS
- Presided over the complex, often frustrating and certainly very time-consuming process of
- It doesn't need to be a painful process
- We just can't rush this delicate process
- A logical and subsequent step to refining the process
- Whether this process would best deal with our current concerns
See also: **ACCOMPLISH, ACTION, STRATEGY WAY**

PROCRASTINATE
- It's not right to procrastinate in the face of such need
- In many ways, it's so easy to procrastinate
- The results of procrastination are appalling
- In this case, procrastination will prove a real killer
See also: **BEHIND, DELAY, LATE**

PROFESSIONALS
- Geared to the public and to health care professionals
- Our professionals are the finest
- You'll be supporting professionals who care deeply about

PROFIT
- Defeat the short-sighted profit seekers and those who would have mangled the programs out of all recognition
- The profits will be in human happiness and human advancement
- The courage and wisdom to finally put people before profit
See also: **BENEFIT, BONUS, GAIN**

PROGRAM
- We have carefully designed the program to
- To set up a customized rehabilitation program
- Outline a common sense program based on the latest research

- Program that supports so many devoted volunteers
- Recruited to participate in this completely voluntary program
- With all the benefits this program has for
- There's just no other program like it
- What we need is a common sense, fair and compassionate prevention program that gets to the heart of the problem
- Our program is the only one of its kind in
- Launching a program to clean up our
- But the program gave me much more than that
- Our program is active and effective
- The best program we've ever developed to solve this problem
- Our public program has been a success and must continue to be
- This program is the perfect foil to
- This once proud program is rapidly being reduced to scrap
- The programming is designed to support the never-ending search for the best
- Program of activities and displays leading up to
- This very cost-efficient program depends heavily on

Program: agenda, slate, protocol, listing, guide, menu, prospectus, syllabus, scheme, plan, design, project, approach, system, method, procedure, performance, show, platform, creed, principles, plank, order of business
See also: AGENDA, APPROACH, CAMPAIGN, OFFERING, PLAN, PROCEDURE, SYSTEM, STRATEGY, WAY

PROGRAMS

- You fund programs that meet a broad-based spectrum of human need and extend throughout the length and breadth
- Special programs that make life livable again for so many in the hospital's care.
- Our programs endeavor to make the best life possible for
- One, our superior programs and, two, the assumption that we'll always be there
- Steadily developing forward-looking programs
- Refuse to let our programs be mangled out of all recognition
- Programs that provide all of us with security
- These programs are affordable
- Programs that protect all of us
- We really could not live without these programs
- You know how much social programs help all of us every day
- Imagine that the social programs you rely on are no longer there
- Publicizing the real, human face of social program cuts through
- While the social programs our grandparents fought hard to build for all of us are dismantled before our eyes
- Let me stress, a gift from you today will mean quality programs can continue
- Insightful and entertaining programs
- Stimulating, refreshing, educational, cultural programs
- Other programs could be cancelled completely
- Some of our other landmark programs deserve applause
- These social programs form the very fabric of society

- To maintain and enhance social programs that are part of our heritage
- Protecting the social programs that have taken a lifetime to build
- Every day you and I benefit from social programs
- The agenda of some members is to actually shred these programs
- Together, you and I can show that most people want our social programs improved, not dismantled
- This program will supplement our objectives, not replace them
- Your contribution supports programs with meaning and purpose
- Our programs save thousands of lives every year
- But some of our key programs were affected
- One of the most exciting and useful programs around today
- I'm not sure I'd be around today if it weren't for their wonderful programs and support
- Supports these efforts through an extensive development of programs, products and services
- Increasing public awareness through education and advocacy programs
- Need you support to maintain and expand our programs
- Special programs that make life livable again for so many in the hospital's care.
- Our programs endeavor to make the best life possible for
- Our programs are under way right now
- Cut some programs so others, considered top priority, remain protected
- Committed to a range of programs to meet your needs
- A broad program of services
- This program really works
- A very special program is in development right now
- Most of our programs are insufficiently funded

PROGRESS
- And, thanks to folk like you, we've made so much progress already
- I'm proud of the progress we've made already, but there's still much more to do
- Significant progress was made
- Yet progress is being blocked by a few
- We must keep the progress going.
- We need your help to maintain desperately needed progress
- Wonderful progress, yes – but there's still so far to go.
- Progress is a team effort and we need you on our team.
- So much progress has been made that major advances are likely in the near future
- The key to progress is in your hands
- So we can make immediate progress on these and other pressing problems
- You can help make measurable and significant progress a reality by supporting the work of
- If we can persuade more people of good will such as yourself to support our efforts, we'll make even greater progress in the future
- Makes progress possible on the most challenging issues of our times
- We need your help to maintain desperately needed progress
- Expected to surpass all progress made in the past century

- This progress is possible for one reason – research
- We've made such extraordinary progress
- This is startling progress
- We have witnessed the hard won progress of our project partners being threatened by decisions made thousands of miles away
- During this time, these groups have made much progress
- Its progress and popularity are on a steady rise
- I'm happy to report we are making progress
- Progress is only possible when individuals care enough

Progress: improvement, rise, promotion, step forward, breakthrough, stride, gain, growth, development, discovery, invention, creation, finding, advance, innovation, betterment, upgrading, expansion, amelioration, recovery, progression, forward movement, headway, forging ahead, gaining ground, pushing ahead, pressing on, leaping forward, work up, come along
See also: ADVANCE, AHEAD, BETTER, BREAKTHROUGH, DISCOVER, EXPAND, FOREFRONT, GAIN, GROWTH, IMPROVE, LEAD, LEAP, RESEARCH

PROJECT
- Contributions were assigned to this year's accessibility project
- Conceived as a project to aid in funding the further enhancement of
- I just know that this valuable and exciting project is something worth keeping and encouraging.
- See what a difference this project has made to the many people involved
- Each project is making all the difference in the world for these struggling people
- Others may want to assist this new project
- Conceived as a project to aid
- With your help, a critical project has already been completed
- Continue this longstanding project
- A small project that has had a big effect on the lives of
- Let me tell you about some of the projects your generosity has helped pay for
- Our cooperants have helped implement effective projects like this
- People need to know their projects won't be abandoned when funding runs short
- We can't continue to offer these life-giving programs without your help
- Already many critical projects have been completed
- Hundreds of important field projects are awaiting your support
- Already, hundreds projects critical to us have been completed
- Projects that make a concrete difference in the lives of those we serve
- Many critical projects are only half completed
- Many more projects must be put on hold – and even that costs money
- There are many programs and projects that are assisted by and, in some cases, exist because of your donations
- Supports major community building projects and programs that would not be possible without your annual contribution
- Help us continue the life-saving research projects we fund

See also: PROGRAM, UNDERTAKING

PROMISE
- Here's a promise we must keep
- Tell them to keep their promises
- We can't let them break their promises to
- There is so much promise in their futures

Promise: assurance, word, vow, word of honor, profession, contract, bond, obligation, pact, covenant, declare, state, vouch for, betoken, signify, presage, foreshadow, indicate

See also: COMMITMENT, HOPE, OBLIGATION, PLEDGE, UNDERTAKING, WORD

PROMISING
- Help promote these very promising breakthroughs
- Never before have we seen such promising developments
- Something as promising as this cannot be overlooked

Promising: positive, favorable, hopeful, auspicious, fortunate, cheering, anticipated

PROMOTE
- Help us promote the success of
- The very best way to promote our ends
- Nobody can promote this better than
- Promoting peace, economic recovery and better health care

Promote: set up, get going, further, advance, cultivate, elevate, forward, advocate, favor, persuade, incline, dispose, bend, coax, ply, pave/clear/open the way, run interference, boost, encourage, press for, push for

See also: ADVANCE, DEVELOP, NURTURE

PROOF
- What better proof of what can be achieved when people like you team up with government
- Your donation will be the proof we need
- You can provide with real proof of your concern by giving

See also: EVIDENCE, EXAMPLE, TRUTH

PROPOSAL
- I am writing to register my support for the government's proposals on
- The proposals are not the whole solution but will, if they become law, help prevent
- Introduced proposals only to see them weakened or withdrawn under pressure
- Please so help ensure that the current proposals actually succeed
- We must ensure that the proposals contain meaningful provisions to make sure
- Let us put to you a very modest proposal

See also: IDEA, GRANT, PLAN, PROJECT

PROSPECT
- At work creating long-term prospects far brighter than those

- What better prospect than this can there be
- With you on board, prospects look ever so much more hopeful

See also: CHANCE, OPPORTUNITY, OPTION

PROSPERITY
- Help start the spirit of prosperity flowing toward
- Basking in the comfort of prosperity
- Our first priority is to jump-start prosperity
- A little prosperity can produce miraculous changes

See also: ABUNDANCE

PROSTITUTION
- Prostitution is not a voluntary career choice
- To prevent the shameful prostitution of these ideals
- Young girls handed over to a life of prostitution

PROTECT
- Protect the programs that protect you
- Not if we wanted to protect our
- To protect yourself and the ones you love
- To protect against any eventuality, we must
- So many still need to be reached and protected
- You and I must work together to conserve and protect
- To protect and improve
- Protect, not destroy
- Our effort to protect must not stop for lack of funds
- Mobilized to protect
- Protecting our most precious places

Protect: defend, guard, safeguard, guard against, champion, stick up for, preserve, conserve, cherish, shelter, screen, secure
See also: DEFENCE, GUARD, SAFEGUARD, SHELTER

PROTECTION
- Further endangering their protection
- Preservation and protection of
- Help extend a broad shield of protection to the vulnerable
- Restore protection for threatened

PROTEST
- Perhaps you protested
- We held mass meetings to protest and started counter moves to weaken
- Received more calls of protest than any decision in the last few months
- Stand up and protest these thoughtless measures

PROUD
- We are proud to present

- I'm proud to say that we're seeing more and more promising treatments that can prolong and add quality to life
- Please join in one of our proudest moments
- Very proud of our first quarter century
- Our organization can now proudly boast a new
- Which we can be proud to call our own
- You have a right to be proud of yourself

PROVE
- We prove it over and over again in
- Has proved itself repeatedly
- A way to prove how very much you care
- Your donation can prove to be one of the best investments ever

PROVIDE
- By donating, you helped provide
- Look forward to continuing to provide the best
- Helping them by providing

PSYCHOLOGICAL
- What never goes away is the psychological damage
- Looked at from a psychological angle
- Give a tremendously important psychological boost

PUBLIC
- I am asking that you focus on public interest and support that interest
- We know the public does not want this
- I've also seen greater public support as each day passes
- Where public and private responsibility become one and the same
- So that the public face and the private can be the same
- Raising public awareness of the importance of
- Creating public forums about the diverse aspects of
- Always serving the public good
- Public service of the highest kind is always our goal

Public: common, communal, national, joint, general, collective, civic, proletarian, comprehensive, widespread, extensive, popular, plebeian, accessible, unrestricted, shared, open to all, available, free access, unconditional, open, overt, conspicuous, prominent, common people, masses, voters, citizens, society
See also: CITIZEN, COMMUNITY, GROUP, HUMANITY, PEOPLE, POPULATION, STREET

PURPOSE
- Has adhered consistently to its purpose however much it might have hoped to have done even more
- You and I share a common purpose – to make the most out of life
- Never wavered from this purpose despite hard times and constant assaults

- Develop and work on their life's purpose

See also: AIM, GOAL, TARGET

PURSUIT
- Continued our relentless pursuit of
- Pursuit of excellence is everything
- Pursuits have proved most beneficial in rehabilitating our many clients

PUZZLE
- A painful puzzle that's yielding up to science
- Dedicated to solving the stubborn puzzle of
- The puzzle is how to
- There is little time to stand puzzling at the crossroads

See also: CHALLENGE, LABYRINTH, MYSTERY, OBSTACLE

QUALITY
- Please help us continue the quality of services and programs that are there for these and many others
- Committed to the highest quality
- Their quality of life is getting better by the month
- It's all part of the quality with which we lead our lives
- Help for people like you who care about quality of life

Quality: level, importance, distinction, worth, value, merit, standing, fineness, degree, attribute, condition, kind, sort, excellence, bent, supremacy, advantage, capability, dignity, notability

QUESTION
- Looking for an answer to this astonishing question
- A really big question is whether there is any way to really prevent
- Recent reports call into question their ability to manage their responsibilities
- Sometimes it's only the question of a few dollars more
- Should you have concerns or questions about
- How can we leave such urgent questions unanswered
- Please call us if you have questions.
- The answer to this and many other questions is obviously murky
- The questions we need to ask and keep finding answers for
- These questions will remain unanswered unless we act
- Bring your questions and an open heart
- It's all about questions and exploration
- All your questions answered
- Please, let me ask you a question
- Time to ask some soul-searching questions

See also: ASK, ISSUE, PROBLEM, REQUEST

QUESTIONNAIRE
- When you complete the enclosed questionnaire, you are helping us find out how

to become even more cost effective
- Invaluable information from your questionnaire
- You help us find ways to free up even more funds when you fill out the enclosed questionnaire

RANGE
- A very broad range of matters
- A wide range is explored
- Ranging from one end to the other
- To get an idea of the enormous range of the problem

RANKS
- Their ranks are rising while help for them continues to decline
- Now you can join the ranks of those who help regularly
- Don't let them join the ranks of the downtrodden

RAPTURE
- Rapturously happy at the outcome
- To watch the rapture on their faces is reward enough
- The rapture of seeing your child suddenly bloom with health

See also: DELIGHT, HAPPINESS, JOY, PASSION, SMILE

RAVAGE
- Helpless and alone in coping with the physical, psychological and emotional ravages of this disease
- Help repair the ravages of time
- Lives are being ravaged right and left

See also: DAMAGE, HURT, PAIN

REACH
- Can you help them reach more by giving a donation of
- It's so important to reach them while they are still reachable
- We want to stretch and grow and reach for the sky
- And with your help, I know that we can reach more people
- By sending your gift today you can help us reach hundreds of people with education, support and practical assistance
- Here's how you can reach us
- Now within our reach is the ability to
- You can now reach us more easily and quickly through
- We can't reach them unless you help us
- If you would like to help us try to reach those who
- Every single day, thousands try to reach us

See also: COMMUNICATE, CONTACT, RANGE

REACH OUT
- Whereby we have reached out to all

- Please reach out right now
- That's why I'm reaching out to you today
- If a frightened child reached out to you
- Reaching out to thousands waiting for your help
- Please, will you reach out to them with a caring gift
- Help us reach out to them quickly
- Reaching out to help these people is a lot easier than you think
- Please, won't you help us reach out to others by giving us your support
- In reaching out to others, I hope you find a deep personal joy and satisfaction
- Please reach out to men, women and children struggling to survive
- Please reach out compassionately and help those so much in need
- We are reaching out to large numbers of voters

See also: **CARE, HELP, COMMUNICATION, CONTACT**

READ
- And if you would, please read on to learn about
- Please read this letter immediately
- Elsewhere, you will read about the history and achievements of
- I hope you'll take a moment to read the letter I've enclosed from

READY
- We must be ready to
- When you're ready
- Are you ready for this
- Almost ready to give up
- We're ready for your donation now
- Ready and waiting for you to join in

REALITY
- It's up to us to deal with the hard realities
- It's a terrible reality that's all too familiar to those who
- These are everyday realities in dozens of places
- Refusing to let someone else's reality take over

REALIZATION
- A number of people were involved in the realization of this project
- The real shock when the realization struck
- When the realization sinks in people rush to help

REALIZE
- When they realize we actually mean to help, their faces light up all over
- It's takes a while to realize the vast scope of
- I know you realize the gravity of this situation
- Didn't realize there was anyone else like us until we found

See also: **UNDERSTAND**

REASON
- If, for any reason, you wish to
- There is absolutely no reason that
- There's still reason for you to get behind this organization
- There is no morally acceptable reason for it
- There is a reason for everything we do
- The reason you support us in the first place
- Whatever the reason, one thing is sure
- I'll settle for telling you about one reason
- A well-reasoned, thoughtful approach to living
- Whatever your reason, it is urgent that you join with others
- Three reasons why you should contribute
- For reasons of race, sex, religion, or nationality, people are exploited or ignored
- And so, for all of the above reasons, I'm asking you
- I could give you thousands of reasons why you should care about
- There are several excellent reasons for
- We still have major reasons for concern and these are

See also: **GOAL, PURPOSE, THINK**

REBUILD
- Together, we can rebuild
- Rebuilding can be a long, deliberate business
- Rebuilding lives is our business
- To help rebuild as quickly as possible

RECEIVE
- Many supporters tell us how much they like receiving
- Remember, it is better to give than to receive
- We'll be very grateful for whatever we receive
- You really receive much more than you give
- Satisfying to know you are passing on some of what you have received

RECOGNITION
- That have earned the recognition of our peers
- The shock of recognition can be very disturbing
- Not looking for fanfare or recognition
- Only a clear recognition of this pressing need can ensure

RECOGNIZE
- So badly mangled we can't even recognize it
- Oh how great it feels to have our hard work recognized
- I gratefully recognize your loyal commitment over the years to helping those who so urgently need
- Take pride in recognizing so many faithful supporters such as yourself
- Recognize and react
- Your generosity will be recognized

- You may not recognize

Recognize: identify, make out, honor, apprehend, perceive, endorse, sanction, approve, validate, regard, distinguish, show appreciation for, respect, point out

See also: APPRECIATION, CELEBRATION UNDERSTAND

RECOMMENDATIONS
- Must act quickly on these fine recommendations
- We have made several recommendations about
- Basing our recommendations on creative application of cutting-edge technologies

RECONNECT
- Helped them reconnect with
- Reconnect the broken pieces
- Striving to reconnect with our finer selves

RECONSIDER
- If you've decided to say no to helping feed hungry children, please take a minute to reconsider the urgency of this need
- Asked to please, please reconsider
- Reconsidering your annual gift and adding to the amount

RECORD
- A very remarkable record of achievement
- Just check our record to date – you'll be impressed
- Not smug satisfaction with the record
- No matter how excellent the record, we can always improve it – with your help
- Put yourself on the record – with a generous donation

RECOUNT
- What I have just recounted to you is true
- Each story, haltingly recounted, clutched at our hearts
- I cry each time I recount this wrenching tale

See also: COMMUNICATE, INFORM, SPEAK, TELL, VOICE

RECOVERY
- Provides step-by-step guidance on the long, often frustrating, road to recovery
- Your help makes their recovery possible
- Thanks to you, their recovery was swift and complete
- It's about staying committed to making a recovery

See also: CONSERVATION, PRESERVATION, SAVE

REDUCE
- Aim is to reduce the incidence and impact of
- Nothing can reduce the importance of this consideration
- We can't reduce the suffering without money

Reduce: retrench, cut back, lessen, shorten, abbreviate, limit, curtail, nip, restrict, truncate, mitigate, ease, abate, assuage, slacken, rein in, slow down, clip, chop, slash, trim, boil down, shorten, bring down, scale back
See also: **AXE, CUT, CUTBACK, DOWNSIZE, SETBACK, SHORTFALL, SLASH**

REDUCTION
- Already, we're in our fourth year of grant reduction
- Further reductions will prove disastrous for all concerned
- One more drastic reduction we must struggle with

REFLECT
- When we stop a moment to reflect upon
- When we pause to reflect about
- Ought to reflect those changes for the better

See also: **CONSIDER, THINK**

REFORM
- Battle to reform misconceived laws
- Pushing through long overdue reforms
- Help protect those who battle so courageously for reform
- We're setting out to reform the entire system

See also: **BETTER, CHANGE, IMPROVE**

REFRESHING
- Isn't it refreshing to find such a new point of view
- Refreshing changes have let in light and air
- How refreshing to realize people like you will give whole-hearted support

REFUGEES
- Helping newly returned refugees organize to regain
- Refugees from poverty and oppression
- Any one of us could be these refugees
- Refugees are not just faceless fugitives from terror

REFUSE
- We never refuse to help, so please don't refuse us
- We never refuse to help because of money
- How could anyone refuse to reach out
- I know you won't refuse your support after you hear the entire story

See also: **PREVENT, STOP**

REGRET
- We regret any misunderstanding that may have arisen
- Suffer profound regrets about
- How much better to help now than have regrets later

- What will you regret when you look back on your life

See also: APOLOGY, SORRY

REHABILITATE
- So rehabilitating individuals can return to the community with maximum independence
- Working to rehabilitate them, one child at a time
- With you help, we can rehabilitate even the most seemingly hopeless

REHABILITATION
- Our rehabilitation team works hard to
- Take up the slow, unflagging work of rehabilitation, restoring life for so many
- Our rehabilitation goal is to allow individuals to adapt to limitation
- A safe, supportive environment for rehabilitation
- Enabling caregivers to work more comfortably and effectively with rehabilitation clients and their families

REIN
- Keeping a tight rein on
- Getting them to relax their grip on the reins
- Rein in this galloping deterioration
- The reins are firmly in your hands

See also: CONTROL, PREVENT, STOP

REJECT
- Terrified of being rejected
- If you reject these unfortunates, who will help them
- Reaching out to the despised and the rejected of this earth
- Please don't reject this appeal

See also: BLOCK, REFUSE

REJOICE
- Greeted by general rejoicing
- Let's rejoice in all the sick who have been healed
- Now we can rejoice in the splendid success of

REKINDLE
- Help rekindle the dying flame
- Rekindle the fervor in a thousand breasts
- Rekindles the excitement of

RELAPSE
- Each time we hoped he was in remission, only to have him relapse
- The heartbreak of an unexpected relapse
- We've greatly reduced the number of relapses
- Never again relapse into indifference

See also: **FAILURE**

RELATIONSHIP

- Very concerned about our long-term relationship with
- Without your help, our relationship will be jeopardized
- For many years we've had a close relationship with
- We cherish good relationships with our supporters
- Effect on their relationship to other members of the team
- An ongoing relationship continues to exist
- To overcome difficulties in creating and sustaining a relationship
- A relationship based strategy that is the best in the field
- Serving to build the relationship between
- Revolutionizing the relationship between
- Is our future relationship inevitably tied to
- To finally have the relationship they have always dreamed about
- Always enjoyed a close working relationship with
- A relationship that truly touches the heart
- Providing the tools to develop the closeness and trust needed in a relationship
- Creating passion, understanding and excitement in a relationship
- Learning how to foster deep, satisfying relationships for all involved
- Creating a positive relationship with
- Allowing for more meaningful relationships
- Getting a handle on the most influential relationship
- Learn the dynamics of a helping relationship

See also: **COMMUNITY, FAMILY, FRIEND, PARTNER**

RELAX

- At last, people can relax and take a relieved breath
- Working to relax these suffocating restrictions
- Never relax our alert vigilance

See also: **PEACE, STOP**

RELIEF

- Tormented thousands long desperately for relief
- Feel the relief and comfort of knowing that you did your part in helping to cope with this critical emergency
- Now they look to us all for relief
- Each dollar you give brings those afflicted another step closer to final relief.
- With things the way they are, who wouldn't want a little relief
- Bringing relief by making this problem manageable
- Such a welcome relief from the bleakness
- Working very hard together, can offer desperately needed relief to
- Finally breathing a sigh of relief
- With family incomes stretched more each year, who wouldn't yearn for relief
- Every day of relief means
- But temporary relief is not a cure

- Tormented thousands long desperately for relief

Relief: mitigation, ease, alleviation, consolation, calming, relaxation, rescue, deliverance, support, succor, aid, redress, remedy, assistance, support, liberation, extrication, reinforcement, treatment, balm, softening, respite, break, reprieve, remission, escape, ministration

See also: COMFORT, EASE, HELP, RESPITE, SUPPORT

RELUCTANCE

- Must overcome this reluctance to
- We will be forced, reluctantly, to
- We have never been reluctant to help

RELY

- Who will people like us rely on
- Those in need are relying on you
- We're all relying on your help
- We rely on the support of individuals and organizations to continue our research and education programs

See also: COUNT, DEPEND, FAITH, TRUST

REMEDY

- Waiting for the final, blessed remedy to be found
- I know you will help us remedy this situation at once
- There is only one sure remedy for such woes
- What can we do to remedy these mistakes

See also: CURE, EASE, MEDICINE, RELIEF

REMEMBER

- You may remember me
- How fondly we remember
- Remember the first time we wrote to you about
- You'll remember that
- We all remember reading about
- Please remember those you have already helped
- And remember, your gift could help enrol another student
- Remember what it was like when
- Please remember to tell your friends and neighbors
- Long be remembered for

See also: HISTORY, MEMORY, PAST

REMIND

- To remind you that
- Time to remind ourselves of the benefits of
- Every once in a while we are reminded of what is really important
- Like to remind you that we still need donations

Remind: prompt, cue, put in mind, call up, jog the memory, refresh the memory, put in mind of, hint, suggest, clue in, intimate, suggest, recall

REMINDER
- A reminder to all of us to continue the fight for
- The sooner we receive your gift, the fewer reminders we will have to send out
- A chilling reminder that the threat has not changed
- If the donor does not respond to the first renewal, they receive additional reminders later in the year

See also: LEGACY, MEMORIAL, TRADITION

RENEW
- Please renew your commitment today by sending a gift to
- When you renew your support, we'll let you know what's happening
- By renewing your support for
- Help renew belief in human compassion and concern
- Please renew your membership today – and add a much-needed special donation
- Won't you please renew your membership right away
- Your renewed help is vital to
- We need you – please, won't you renew
- When you renew your membership, know that in addition to supporting the our critical work, you have access to the most up-to-date information about
- Please read this only if you've decided not renew your
- It's such a pleasure to number you again among our renewed
- I take a deep satisfaction in our renewed relationship
- It's a great feeling to renew our friendship
- In order to carry out our commitments, we will need the renewed support of every one of our donors
- If you still share our commitment to this vital work, I'm sure you'll renew your support for
- Your renewed gift funds vital research now
- Continue to help, if possible, by renewing your commitment to the preservation of this precious heritage
- Please renew now. I hope to hear from you soon
- Once again, you'll be making a very vital difference when you renew
- Today, I hope you'll renew your commitment to
- You have chosen us in the past so I hope you'll renew once again
- Please renew now, before it's too late
- I hope you will decide to renew your support before the year end
- I urge you to renew that vital commitment before
- Your renewed commitment keeps us going
- So many need your renewed support today.
- Your renewed compassion holds the key to so much hope
- Please take a moment to renew now
- Thank you for pledging to renew your support immediately for the important work of
- Your renewed support now will fund our ongoing work to

- Please renew our ability to help
- I hope you will take a moment to renew your support
- That's why we really need you to renew

Renew: resume, recommence, start afresh, begin again, start over, revive, reestablish, resurrect, bring back, reshape, reconstruct, regenerate, refresh, recharge, refurbish, rehabilitate, revamp, resuscitate

See also: REBUILD, REHABILITATE, RESCUE, RESTORE
See also: SECTION SIX – RENEWAL, LAPSED MEMBER, LAPSED DONOR

RENEWAL

- Join with us in the spirit of renewal
- Your early renewal helps us move ahead quickly with our work
- I'm writing today to ask you to continue your support into the coming year by making your annual renewal contribution
- Our annual renewal campaign is the cornerstone of our fundraising initiatives
- We likely received your donation after we prepared the list for renewal mailing and were not able to remove your name from the list in time
- Your renewal gift will do so much to help us on our way
- At the beginning of the year, we ask each of our donors for an annual renewal gift
- An early renewal is greatly appreciated
- Your early renewal will help us get off to a strong start at the beginning of the year
- If you make your renewal contribution right now, you won't receive any of our reminder letters
- In addition to our annual renewal drive, we usually invite our supporters to help with
- I look forward to receiving your renewal donation in the near future
- The season of hope and renewal has returned
- Please make your renewal gift today
- Your annual renewal donation matters – a lot
- With major advances so near, your renewal means so much
- I'll say my piece about your renewal quickly and clearly
- Remain in effect for your renewal
- I send my first renewal letter about this time each year
- The bulk of the money we raised came through annual renewal gifts like the one I'm asking you to make today
- I urge you to consider making your renewal gift now so that
- I have first to remind you that your renewal of affiliation is now due
- Send me acknowledgment of renewal
- Please send in your renewal today
- Just a reminder that your membership is due for renewal shortly
- I'll just say my piece about your renewal very quickly
- You can still mail your renewal, the earlier, the better
- We will appreciate you mailing your renewal as soon as possible
- Each renewal represents a real person to us, not just a name on the list

- Your renewal plays a very crucial and valued part in the battle to
- Your renewal brings us one step closer to final victory
- Naturally, I hope this will mean that we will be hearing from you very soon with your renewal
- It's renewal time again
- Have been so looking forward to your renewal
- The children are counting on your renewal

See also: GROWTH, RECOVERY, RESTORATION, REVITALIZATION
See also: SECTION SIX – RENEWAL, LAPSED MEMBER, LAPSED DONOR

REPERCUSSIONS
- Without any apparent repercussions
- Suffering the most dreadful repercussions
- You can help lessen the repercussions

See also: RESULT

REPLY
- That's why I want you to reply to this letter today
- May we look for your reply by return mail?
- Please mail your reply by sundown
- Everything depends upon your reply
- How you reply to this appeal will make all the difference

See also: ANSWER, ACKNOWLEDGE, COMMUNICATE, RESPOND

REPRIEVE
- Each dollar you send means a little bit more of a reprieve
- For them, without your help, there will be no reprieve
- Please help us give these doomed creatures a reprieve

See also: EASE. PROTECT, RECOVERY, RELIEF, RESCUE, RESPITE, RESTORE, SAVE, SPARE

REPUTATION
- Our reputation is firmly established
- Our reputation is our guarantee
- Over the years earned an international reputation for top-flight programs
- Enjoys the reputation of being one of the finest in the

REQUEST
- This request is only one part of our ongoing program to
- Last year, we received requests for far more help than we had available
- This is the first time we have received such an unusual, urgent request
- We're still able to fund less than half the total requested
- Resulting from so many requests for
- Please consider this request seriously
- Your special requests will be gratefully honored

See also: APPEAL, ASK, BEG, PLEA, PETITION

RESCUE

- Program to identify and rescue them as soon as possible
- The success of this rescue is desperately important for
- Many daring rescue missions funded by concerned, compassionate people like you
- Join the rescuers today

Rescue: deliver, bail out, save, hold out a hand, snatch from danger, come to the aid, rescue, reprieve, bring off, salvage, preserve, conserve, spare, redeem
See also: AID, ASSIST, HELP, REACH, SAVE

RESEARCH

- The deeper we research, the more hope we find
- Modern research costs money, a great deal of money
- All money raised for this fund goes directly into basic cause and cure research
- Thank you so much for helping our research leaders carry on their very vital investigations
- Despite exciting advances, research remains scandalously underfunded
- Champions research into chronic illness and old age
- Research to alleviate a lifetime of excruciating, ongoing misery
- Thank you so much for helping our research leaders carry on their very vital investigations
- Without your help to expand our crucial research, thousands face a
- Your gift to our research hastens the day when anguished parents no longer have to watch their baby writhing in pain
- We need you on our research team today
- Depending on you to fund the research that will finally put an end to their misery
- To make sure the research and other information available is adequate for forecasting
- After a lot of research and plain hard work
- We support research into the causes and treatment of
- Only more medical research can help us achieve our goal – and research costs money
- This particular research project has really aroused my excitement
- Research projects to discover effective new treatments
- Support medical research into all kinds of disease
- There's never enough money to fund the highest caliber research conducted in
- We're firmly committed to expanding our research
- Your continued support will increase research efforts and awareness to help reduce the suffering caused by
- We sponsor only be best in research
- Help ensure that research remains a top priority
- To keep up world-class research
- We are committed to funding a million dollars on medical research projects in the upcoming months.
- Saving lives through research
- Through research, answers are found

- Your donation helps us invest in research to improve health and advance medical care
- None of our research could happen without the help of friends like you
- That's why it's so important to continue funding life-saving research
- Your gift is already at work helping sponsor more life-saving research like that under way
- We owe it to them, and to ourselves, to help fund even more of that kind of vital research
- More research is the key to a fuller understanding of the many different kinds of
- Provide support for research and education into the causes, diagnosis, prevention and treatment of
- Provide funds for investigators who are involved with research projects in hospitals, universities and research centers
- I'm writing to you today to ask for your help in expanding research into what causes this devastating condition
- To help fund more intensive research into the causes of
- The more research there is, the more hope there is of
- With more research there is real hope of discovering what causes
- You are backing research of a quality second to none
- In spite of the tremendous progress we are making, the need for research continues
- Extensive research has identified
- Developed this groundbreaking research in concert with
- As I write this, pioneering research is under way on such things as
- Recent research funding cuts make our work – and your support – more critical than ever
- You see, funding for one half of all research comes from us
- The research and education we're funding is paying off
- Prompting exciting new research on preventing
- With such promising research underway
- Join us on the leading edge of research and development
- Can't measure the impact of impending research discoveries
- Due to the increasing volume of life-saving research projects
- Could only provide a small percentage of the required research dollars last year
- We provide more research funds than the governments combined
- Just look at the research institutions we support
- Commitment involving strong dedication to research
- No other type of research has saved so many lives
- Such vitally important research is saving thousands of lives right now
- This research has produced extraordinary advances in the fight against
- Without research there is no cure

Research: investigation, inquiry, analysis, study, scrutiny, fact-finding, probe, exploration, assessment, appraisal, search, quest, survey, review, examine, seek out, track down, explore

See also: ADVANCE, BREAKTHROUGH. CURE, DISEASE, DISCOVER, INVESTIGATION, MEDICINE, PROGRESS, SCIENTIST, SEARCH, STUDY

RESEARCHER

- Every day our researchers challenge prevailing wisdom
- Our grants are designed to encourage more researchers to choose the field of
- Our researchers are actively contributing to the remarkable progress
- Researchers across the country are working together to begin testing these promising new
- Being watched closely by researchers around the world
- We must give our researchers the resources to find out why it's happening – and stop it cold
- This excellence is the result of funding talented, productive researchers

See also: SCIENTIST, SPECIALIST, WORKER

RESOLUTION

- Make helping others your first New Year's resolution
- Adamantine resolution brooking no change
- Your help in the resolution of this issue is paramount
- Despite these obstacles, our resolution must not falter

See also: ANSWER, END, OUTCOME, RESULT

RESOLVE

- Resolved in a positive way
- Help us resolve this thorny issue by giving
- Marching forward with unshakable resolve
- Right now our resolve is being mightily tested
- A test of resolve we can not fail
- Only strengthens our resolve

See also: OVERCOME, SOLVE, SOLUTION

RESOURCE

- More than ever, we need a solid support resource we can count on
- Suddenly becoming a wonderful extra resource
- Pitch in your resources to
- Actively searching for the resources that can produce these changes
- If resources are not available to provide top quality programs
- To learn more about this issue, consider the following resources
- To be effective, we must have the resources to
- Please give us the resources we need to
- There's a lot to do and we'll need all the resources possible
- Our resources were severely strained during the crisis
- Please give them the resources which are so much in need
- Carefully choosing where our resources are used
- But to be effective, we must have enough resources to keep the pressure on
- You know we'll have to muster up all our resources to continue these successes next season
- Help us focus our resources on the welfare of others
- They've seen their resources shrink far more than those of others

- It's only a matter of finding the resources
- But in order to continue as a leader in this important work, we must have the financial resources
- And today, as resources become scarcer and the environment meaner
- All they ask is the resources to finish the job
- Due to dwindling financial resources
- Must do all this with very limited resources
- Given the funding resources, we can do it
- Your contribution will help us expand our resources

Resource: support, backup, backing, help, aid, source, reserve, supply, wealth, funding, income, holdings, gains, profits, money, cash, assets, invention, resourcefulness, ingenuity
See also: ASSET, BACKING, CONTRIBUTION, DOLLARS, DONATION, FUNDING, GAIN, HELP, MEANS, MONEY, SUPPLY, SUPPORT, WAY

RESPECT

- Our work has been respected for many years
- Rest assured of our continued respect
- All they ask is the basic dignity and respect
- Respect for the minority
- A lack of respect for human life unprecedented in the history of this continent
- The wonder of just being treated with caring and respect

Respect: esteem, regard, reverence, praise, approval, veneration, admiration, appreciation, adoration, approbation, awe, value, deference

RESPITE

- Families who desperately need respite from the hardships of their life
- To give just a small, precious respite to
- Your gift will provide just a little more respite

See also: COMFORT, EASE, HELP, RELIEF, REPRIEVE

RESPOND

- When you respond, you are taking a firm stand for
- Please respond generously
- Please respond today
- That's why responding to our appeal, along with sending us your contribution, is critical
- You responded in the past so I know you'll respond now
- That tells us you're responding to the hard work and high standards we put into every
- Please respond as quickly and generously as you can by writing a cheque today to help us continue the progress we have made over the last many years
- You responded to the call
- We respond with a resounding, "Yes!"
- This tells us you are responding to the hard work and high standards we put into
- I hope you respond soon

- I hope you'll respond positively to my request
- Must examine why we respond the way we do
- Pleases respond quickly and generously
- I hope you will help us by responding today
- Please respond right now while it's fresh in your mind

Respond: answer, reply, confirm, come back with, counter, rejoin, react to, acknowledge, notice, recognize, salute, reciprocate, return, sympathize with, be moved by, touched by, affected by, feel with, empathize with, understand, feel for, share in, correspond, be caught up in, partake, participate, engage
See also: ACKNOWLEDGE, ANSWER, RECOGNIZE, REPLY

RESPONSE
- Remember, we need to receive your response in the next few days
- If we can significantly boost response now, we'll be able to help so many
- We need a really strong response to this appeal
- Develop an effective response
- Your response is a direct hit with us
- I'll be waiting anxiously for your positive response
- Your response is vitally important
- Your response is invaluable, not only for your much-needed
- We have rarely had so great or positive a response to anything
- The response has been beyond our most extravagant hopes
- Your immediate response will help us keep the pressure on
- The thousands of responses governments receive from caring people round the world give notice to
- Analyze the responses and convey the most pressing concerns
- Individual responses are confidential
- We've had a most remarkable response
- An eloquent and moving response to the power of love
- I never thought such a response possible

RESPONSIBILITY
- All of us have to assume responsibility for
- Despite all the responsibilities of profession, family and other commitments, he continued to serve
- Far too busy juggling responsibilities to
- The vast scope of our responsibilities
- Tossing the responsibility over to
- It is the responsibility of every one of us
- We take our responsibilities very seriously
- Share in the responsibility – and the rewards

See also: JOB, MANDATE, MISSION, REASON, ROLE, SPONSOR, UNDERTAKING, WORK

RESPONSIBLE
- Accurate and responsible

- The only truly responsible thing to do is
- Refuse to be responsible for this fiasco

Responsible: accountable, answerable, reliable, dependable, guilty, obligated

See also: COUNT, DEPEND, RELY, RIGHT

REST
- The rest is up to you
- There can be no rest until this problem is solved
- To find rest and peace at last is a seemingly unattainable dream

RESTORATION
- Ongoing restoration activities
- Participate in the restoration of its original grandeur
- The restoration of peace and security is paramount

RESTORE
- Restore competence and sanity
- Working very hard to restore confidence in
- Experience the joy and satisfaction of seeing health finally restored
- Just to restore some balance and safety to their lives

RESTRAINT
- Even though we have exercised the utmost restraint in this matter
- Current budgetary restraints make it all but impossible to
- With the added pressure of severe government restraints
- Working to get restraints lifted as soon as possible

RESULTS
- To achieve maximum results
- These results have not been easily won
- Awesome results are proof that your donation works hard
- Now looking for results in a different arena
- Enhances and improves the results all round
- There simply isn't a more cost-effective way of obtaining guaranteed, professional results
- Results have rebounded beyond all expectations
- The pressing need in their lives for more effective results
- Focus on planning for effective results
- These terrific results reflect the high standards of our program
- Able to accomplish these incredible results because of two vital factors
- Help achieve these awesome results
- The results are exciting
- Back a program that really gets results

See also: ANSWER, FRUITION, OUTCOME, PAYOFF, RESEARCH, RESOLUTION, RETURN, SOLUTION, SUCCESS

RETURN
- Please return the enclosed form as quickly as you can
- To help the situation return to normal
- Many people have rushed their donation to us by return mail

REVENUE
- Over the next few years, we must generate more than twice as much of our own revenue as now, through merchandising and other initiatives
- An important part of our total revenue comes from friends like you
- We cannot survive, unfortunately, without a steady stream of revenue
- We need to significantly boost revenue to
- Chop crucial dollars away from revenue
- Last year we promised that some surplus revenue would enhance the
- That's why we must try to hard to find additional revenues through donations

Revenue: income, receipts, funds, money, remuneration, allowance, yield, gain, return, fee, finances, wealth, substance, means, wherewithal, capital, cash, wages, proceeds

See also: **BACK, DONATION, FUNDING, GIFT, RESOURCE, MONEY, SUPPORT**

REVIEW
- Each item comes under continual and intense review
- A rigorous review process which dealt with every aspect of our operations
- To proudly review the achievements of the past year

REVITALIZATION
- Committed to the revitalization of our region
- The revitalization of these initiatives can only happen with your participation
- Only with immediate revitalization can this city survive

See also: **GROWTH, RECOVERY, RENEWAL, RESTORATION**

REVOLUTION
- There is a revolution going on in
- Take part in this exciting revolution
- A revolution in thinking has turned us upside down
- Naturally, this has caused a revolution inside and out
- The survivors of this revolution will be those who can

REWARD
- Our reward is those grateful, radiant smiles
- Finding abundant rewards in
- Watch the rewards soar as
- Measure the reward in lives changed
- A greater reward than you could ever imagine
- Found her work so rewarding that
- Rewarded with a warm feeling in your heart

- You know you've done the right thing – and that's reward enough
- Rewarded by knowing you saved a life
- The reward is merely icing on the cake
- Continue to reap the reward
- You will feel so deeply rewarded
- To do more, achieve more, enjoy more of life's rich rewards and satisfactions
- The rewards have been unbelievable

See also: ACKNOWLEDGE, APPRECIATE, COMPENSATION, GIFT, HONOR, PAYOFF, SATISFACTION, TRIBUTE

RIDE

- Sometimes it's a tough roller coaster ride
- Ride to the rescue immediately
- Recently, we've been getting a pretty rough ride

RIDICULOUS

- Going to ridiculous lengths to get some help
- Don't be ridiculous, they said, nobody can achieve such a thing
- Taking ridiculous measures to make a point
- Caught up in a truly ridiculous standoff

RIGHT

- Right away/ right now
- It's just not right
- A crucial right, the right to determine treatment for a loved one
- Both a need and a right for all
- The fundamental right of every human being to
- Standing on guard for the fundamental right to
- I know you're someone who believes everyone has a right to food shelter, and a life with dignity
- The universal right of all
- Their unalienable right to
- New threats to human rights that require our immediate attention
- Must place our rights beyond the reach of
- Fighting for your rights
- We believe that you and thousands of other people will stand up for your rights and the rights of your fellows
- To promote the very best human rights work
- Let's talk about basic rights denied to many of our fellow human beings
- Promotes all internationally recognized human rights through
- Help – because it's the right thing to do
- Teaching participants how to stand up for their rights
- If you don't fully understand your rights, you could end up

RIGHT: good, fair, principled, just, impartial, correct, equitable, moral, ethical, honorable, spot on, unfailing, absolute, accurate, exact, true, valid, sound, faithful, perfect, sensible, desirable, title, just claim, privilege, possession, ownership,

authority, power, justice, prerogative, honest
See also: GOOD, JUSTICE, PRIVILEGE

RISK
- Put their lives at risk every time they
- Must abolish this grave public risk
- The public is at risk
- The danger already posed to the public
- The risk is ever present
- The risk is all ours
- Who is at greatest risk of contracting
- Thousands are at risk because of
- Puts millions more at risk
- The risk is simply not acceptable
- Carry their own serious risks
- For starters, you can find out about the risks of
- Sustained by people willing to take risks
- Sometimes, you just have to risk going out on a limb for what you deeply believe
- We're working every day to reduce your risk of
- If you are knowingly at risk
- To find out whether or not you are at risk
- One of the leading risk factors for
- Lower your risk for illness today
- Find out whether or not you are at risk
- The risk is still significant
- To boldly take these risks
- A risk-free way to give
- Deserve enormous credit for daring to take these risks
- One of the biggest risks is right in our back yard

Risk: peril, hazard, danger, vulnerability, jeopardy, uncertainty, chance, liability, imperilment, insecurity, unpredictability, plunge, long shot, speculation, endanger, expose, menace, threaten, play with fire, dare, venture, gamble, attempt, go for broke, throw caution to the winds, adventure
See also: CRISIS, DANGER, JEOPARDY, THREAT

ROB
- Would rob children of their last crust
- Shamefully robbed of their ability to
- Must not be robbed of their one chance to

ROLE
- Credited with playing a critical role in getting
- Appreciate the key role we played in moving toward a saner, safer
- We're asking you to take a very active role in
- Playing a leading role in re-establishing
- Play an active role in our future

- You can play an important role in protecting
- Taking a leading role in
- Has played a crucial role in providing
- By participating, you can help strengthen our role in the movement for human rights
- There was another role to play in
- Must keep pace with our changing role in
- To promote expanded professional roles
- Primary role is to liaise with
- You play a crucial role in improving the lives of
- Certainly playing a very central role in

See also: RESPONSIBILITY

ROOT
- Helping us get to the root of the problem
- Vigorously root out the causes
- It all starts with a strong root

See also: BASICS, CAUSE, SOURCE, REASON

RULE
- At the end of the day, if sensible rules can't be laid down, the house will collapse and we'll all be losers
- If we don't do something, they'll be allowed to make up their own rules
- Making sure all parties play by the rules
- The rule of law must always be foremost

RUSH
- Because of donors like you, we're able to rush help in at once
- Once again, we must rush to the rescue
- We really have to rush the process
- Rushing to beat this very grim deadline

SACRIFICE
- Even in her despair, she sacrificed to help save others from the same cruel fate
- So much for such a small sacrifice
- Share in the sacrifice
- Willing to sacrifice so much so that others could benefit

See also: BLOOD, DONATION, COST, PRICE

SAD
- I'm sad to report to you that
- Wait until you see one of these sad little faces light up
- Sad looks that could move the hardest heart
- How sad it would be if such a heroic struggle were in vain
- Sadness transformed into radiant delight

See also: DESPAIR, GRIEF, HOPELESS, MISERY POOR, POWERLESS,

SORROW, SUICIDE

SADISM
- Every day our workers steel themselves to receive yet more maimed, traumatized victims of human sadism
- It's sheer sadism to leave people in such conditions
- It's hard to believe that such sadism can exist, yet it does

See also: ABUSE, CRUELTY, PAIN, SUFFERING, TORTURE

SAFE
- Provide a safe atmosphere where people can express their innermost feelings and develop trust in themselves
- Really needed a safe, supportive place to keep clean
- When we can finally make this region safe for
- It is now safe to assume that
- Together, we create a safe haven open to all in need

Safe: secure, defended, sheltered, guarded, sound, out of the woods, home free, invulnerable, intact, bulletproof, guaranteed, in the bag, reliable, harmless, innocuous, unassailable, out of harm's way, safe and sound

SAFEGUARD
- Our brave workers risk personal harm to safeguard others
- Working hard to put ample safeguards in place
- Safeguarding our investment in these fine programs
- The first to safeguard real freedom of choice

See also: DEFEND, GUARD, PROTECT, SHELTER

SAFETY
- It is a public safety issue and that's why we
- How are we going to buy the most amount of safety
- Imagine what would happen without such a safety net
- This has raised concern about the safety of
- Is committed to taking all steps possible to ensure the safety of

See also: COMFORT, EASE, PROTECT, SANCTITY, SECURITY

SANCTITY
- Every day, every minute, the sanctity of human life is mocked and violated
- One place where sanctity is protected
- The sanctity of these vital programs will be breached
- Protecting the sanctity of principles and ideals

SATISFACTION
- Do it for the satisfaction
- The satisfaction doesn't stop there
- Feel the satisfaction of doing your part to
- A new path to inner satisfaction, a connection with our forgotten self

- I know you'll feel an ever-increasing sense of satisfaction
- I know you will experience great personal satisfaction in knowing that, through your gift, you are sharing
- The genuine satisfaction of knowing how much you have helped
- Such a great rush of satisfaction from

SAVE

- We must save them before they slip away altogether
- Maybe you can't save thousands, but you can save one
- By this measure alone we can save an enormous amount of money
- It's an easy, convenient way to save money, time and the environment
- Most of those who died could have been saved if only
- This represents a very significant saving
- Thousands of lives have been saved through work made possible by
- Lifetime savings are quickly depleted because of the extraordinary costs involved in the care of people with

Save: protect, secure, shield, safeguard, keep safe, conserve, keep up, preserve, sustain, maintain, carry over, reserve, lay away, put aside, store up, squirrel away, amass, economize, cut costs, tighten one's belt, prevent, forestall
See also: CONSERVE, DEFEND, RESCUE, PROTECT, REPRIEVE, SPARE

SAY

- Here's what people are saying about
- You have only to say the word and
- Who's to say what might have happened had no one intervened

See also: COMMUNICATE, REACH, SPEAK, TELL, VOICE

SCALE

- On a larger scale
- Nothing on this scale has ever happened before
- The scale of suffering is stupendous
- Scaling down the damage
- Your participation determines the scale of the project

SCARCITY

- The appalling scarcity of supplies can keep even the strongest down
- With such scarcity comes dreadful want
- In danger of losing all through a scarcity of funds
- A terrible scarcity of even the most basic necessities
- Out of scarcity can flow astonishing abundance

See also: DESTITUTE, HUNGER, LOSS, NEED, POVERTY

SCARE

- I don't want to scare you, but
- We're very scared that this program will disappear without your help
- We were scared to death by the very word

- I was scared out of my mind
- Underneath the pretense, she's really very scared, lonely and confused

See also: **FEAR, HORROR, PANIC, THREAT**

SCAR
- So very often, the scars will never heal
- Scarred and battered, but not beaten
- Emotional scars hurt just as much as physical ones
- Salute the scarred veterans of life's battle

See also: **ABUSE, PAIN**

SCENE
- I hope I never have to see another tragic scene like this
- I was deeply touched by a recent scene during the
- Thanks to your support, we can be on the scene in hours
- Scenes of overwhelming joy and emotion

SCHOLARSHIP
- Provide scholarships for bright, eager young people who are prepared to work hard and care for others
- A scholarship to change the future of some deserving student
- Sound scholarship must always form the foundation of our thinking and research

SCHOOL
- Nobody likes to learn in the school of hard knocks
- I think that helping this school is our only chance for
- Schooled in such disciplines
- Helping to build schools in a wilderness of ignorance
- Going back to school to learn sound basics

See also: **EDUCATE, LEARN, TEACH, UNIVERSITY**

SCIENCE
- We're putting all our trust in science to solve this problem
- Only science can give us that relief
- We can't always turn to science for a quick fix
- Science has already unlocked secret after baffling secret

See also: **CURE, DISCOVER, RESEARCH, SEARCH, STUDY**

SCIENTIST
- Our scientists strive doggedly, working day after day to
- Scientists have recently discovered that
- I'm making this personal appeal asking you to please help our dedicated scientists put an end to the suffering
- No scientists are more dedicated than ours

See also: **SKILL, RESEARCHER, PROFESSIONAL**

SEARCH

- The search must continue
- Together, let's continue to search for
- When a need has been identified, we do the searching
- Supporting the never-ending search for the best in people
- Vowed never to stop searching until the answer is found

Search: investigate, go through, hunt, explore, examine, scrutinize, peruse, inspect, sift through, comb, fish for, probe, peer into, track down, leave no stone unturned

See also: DISCOVER, EXPLORE, LEARN, LOOK, STUDY

SEASON

- To one and all I extend Season's Greetings and best wishes for the New Year
- Capturing the excitement of a new season
- In the spirit of the season, please make a generous donation to
- Looking forward to hearing from you next season
- It's the season to share our own good fortune
- In this season of love and abundance, I'm asking you to give
- So during this season of giving and sharing, I hope you will take the opportunity to make a special contribution to
- The season of giving can get out of control
- Season's greetings to all our donors
- Enchanting us at every season
- Because a lot of people need us most in this season of giving
- All the best of the season
- Compliments of the season
- During this holiday season, let your love flow out
- Magic of the holiday season
- Blessing of the season shine upon you
- May peace, love and laughter fill your holiday season
- This festive season
- Wishes for a joyous season

See also: CHRISTMAS, HOLIDAY, TIME

SECOND

- Standing second to none
- Just can't come out second best in this
- Second their actions by providing
- We must not delay another second
- When seconds count, how can we delay

SECURITY

- The future security of us all may depend upon
- These are concerns underlining the global security we hoped would follow
- Desperately asking for some security in their lives
- A safe, secure home and family is what is really needed
- Security of food and shelter is our first priority

See also: **GUARD, PROTECT, SAFETY**

SEE
- I urge you to come by and see for yourself
- Even if we can't see them, they're there – and they need our help
- If you like what you see, just send us your cheque
- In this case, seeing really is believing
- Enabling you to see, at a glance
- Gives full rein to your personal way of seeing and thinking

SEED
- Your dollars are seeds that become next year's
- Help sow the seeds of change
- From that tiny seed a great enterprise has grown

See also: **BEGINNING, IDEA, START**

SELECT
- We select only the best
- We have selected you to be our partner
- You are invited to join a very select group today

See also: **CHOOSE, CONSIDER, DECIDE**

SELF CONFIDENCE
- That's when I felt the first stirrings of self confidence
- We must first build up their self confidence
- Overjoyed to see them standing tall with new found self confidence

SEND
- Send it to us today
- If you send $ __ , you'll be helping to put
- Perhaps you could even send $ __ to provide
- That's why I'm asking you to send whatever you feel you can manage
- It is critical that you send something immediately
- When you send a donation, you're also sending warming hope and joy
- Whatever you decide to send, please send it today
- Please try to send at least a little

Send: transmit, deliver, convey, direct, mail, remit, post, consign, ship, forward, delegate, assign, address to, pass along, broadcast

See also: **ANSWER, CONTRIBUTE, DONATE, GIVE, MAIL, RESPOND, REPLY**

SENIORS
- You and I can't afford to have seniors without proper care
- Your gift could bring a smile to a lonely senior
- Worked hard for our seniors
- Able to provide additional funding that will allow seniors to stay in their own

homes longer
- Many seniors spend their retirement years in poverty and despair
- Particularly as our senior citizen population grows
- Seniors stuck in tiny apartments with no one to visit them

See also: **ELDERLY, EXPERIENCE, OLD, WISDOM**

SENSE
- It just makes good sense, for you, for us and for the system
- Wouldn't it make more sense to
- Much better in every sense
- You can sense the need before you even speak to them

See also: **REASON**

SENTENCE
- He's not the only one serving a long sentence
- Our indifference sentences them to sickness and neglect
- No one deserves a sentence such as this awful condition imposes

SERVE
- Stand by, ready to serve, 24 hours a day, 365 days a year
- Your willingness to serve has meant so much
- Only by better serving the public at large can we
- Serving you better by serving them
- Choose one of the many ways to serve your community

See also: **AID, ASSIST, BACK, BENEFIT, CARE, ENCOURAGE, CONTRIBUTE, DONATE, FUND, GIVE, HEARTEN, HELP, REACH, SUPPORT, VOLUNTEER**

SERVICE
- She wept with relief when she finally found out about our service
- As a service user, you can understand
- We're sowing seeds of service and watching them grow
- We've expertly serviced thousands of
- Our ability to provide well-rounded service
- The service is available to provide assistance for difficulties occurring at home, at school and in the community
- A confidential and dedicated consultation service
- To continue to provide the service you want and need most
- We're working hard to make sure our service is the best it can be
- Outstanding service and public support of
- Committed to expanding this vital service and providing an even broader range of essential information and
- A wonderful innovation in service
- An even greater reliance is being placed upon community-based service organizations
- More and more organizations are successfully able to provide this type of service

- It is our hope that this wonderful service can continue to grow
- But each year, the need for our service increases
- We pledge the same dedication to service
- Invaluable and irreplaceable service
- Legacy of good work and service
- Do a service for those less fortunate

SERVICES
- These services are costly to provide
- You gave your services and staff top marks
- If we are to continue to provide our present level of services in this community, we need your help
- Now we can offer a wider range of services
- You understood how important it is to protect the services you and your family rely on.
- We expanded services so that more people can get
- Help protect the services that are so important to you
- And the many vital services provided by
- Along with many new and innovative services we are striving to bring to those in need
- Like all other publicly-funded services, we're under the gun
- Your generous donation will be used to provide these vital services
- It's one of the services we've helped to pioneer
- Not if we want to protect services for
- To provide services of genuine value
- Services remain fragmented and woefully inadequate
- So that the services will remain there for you or someone you love
- And when times are hard, as they are now, demand presses services to the limit
- Increased delivery of services will be much assisted by
- Exploding demand for services necessitates
- To simplify complex medical services
- To create a network of services stretching all across

See also: **HELP, PROGRAM, SUPPORT, UNDERTAKING**

SESSION
- In these sessions, people learn the painstaking process
- In session after session, we hammered out agreements
- After a very productive session, we bring these encouraging results

SETBACK
- Unless you help, this setback threatens everything we've achieved
- So hard to recover after a setback like this
- With no way to foresee a setback so devastating
- A major setback only you can help overcome

See also: **BLOW, CRISIS, CUT, CUTBACK, DOWNSIZE, SHORTFALL, SLASH**

SHAME
- Shame on them
- Far too often, victims are silent and ashamed about their misery
- Ashamed and scared
- Shame and wasted potential
- The shame of waste
- It's a crying shame that
- To stop this embarrassing shame
- Silenced by fear and shame
- No caring society should all this shameful situation to continue

Shame: disgrace, dishonor, scandal, blot, degradation, stigma

SHARE
- So we'll all share in the glory
- I simply had to share my feelings about
- Surely, they've already paid more than their share
- I'd very much like to share this with you
- Now it's doubly easy for you to share your own good fortune
- We should share with other people
- Sharing a little love with the rest of the world
- I'd like to share a story with you
- Caring and sharing is what life is all about
- Pay their fair share
- I just wanted to share a small part of why I'm so committed to
- Uniting to share resources to empower people living in poverty
- Meeting with them, sharing ways they can work with us to help stop
- The only true satisfaction is in sharing
- Sharing is our motto
- Feel the sheer happiness of sharing
- Only by sharing freely and generously can we

Share: partake, take part in, allotment, grant, portion, part, inheritance, dividend, piece of the pie, ration, handout, lot, division, divide, assign, parcel out, share and share alike, partake, participate, have a stake in
See also: **AID, GIVE, HELP, PARTICIPATE, PARTNER**

SHELTER
- They pay for a well-managed shelter whose doors are always open
- We were able to provide safe shelter, warm clothing, hot food and, over the long term, counselling and support
- Shelter and assistance to the homeless
- All they ask is shelter from the storm
- Love, warmth and caring, even in the humblest of shelters

See also: **DEFEND, HOME, HOMELESS, PROTECT**

SHIPMENT
- Because of you, one shipment after another is leaving port even now

- Made sure emergency shipments of food reached those most in need
- So that urgently needed shipments aren't left sitting on the docks

SHOCK
- It may come as quite a shock to you to find out that
- For those who survive the initial shock
- You may be shocked to learn that
- I glanced out into the street and saw something that shocked me
- Many people would be shocked to learn that
- Though it's frightening and shocking even to contemplate
- After the shock wears off, the real work begins

See also: **AMBUSH, HIT, SURPRISE, TRAUMA**

SHORTAGE
- Struggling to cope with a nationwide shortage of
- With huge shortages looking us in the face
- These shortages mean death for many
- Help cut the shortage of shelter space and food
- Must act now to prevent shortages that will almost certainly be fatal

SHORTFALL
- What will happen if this shortfall catches up with us
- Urgently need funds to cover the shortfall
- An unexpected shortfall we must make up in a hurry
- Tragic shortfalls could leave many without help of any kind
- Grave revenue shortfalls have driven that figure to
- The shortfall can claim other victims too

See also: **CUTBACK, DOWNSIZE, NEED, REDUCTION**

SHOT
- Shot down in cold blood because
- More than just a shot in the dark
- Come on, have a shot at helping
- Taking a shot at solving this problem

See also: **BET, EFFORT, TRY**

SHOULDER
- You'll stand shoulder to shoulder with
- Our shoulders are strong enough to bear this load
- So that this burden will not fall upon their shoulders
- To help those who would otherwise be shouldered aside
- Providing a shoulder to lean against when life overwhelms

See also: **CAREGIVER, JOIN, PARTNER, RESPONSIBILITY**

SHOUT
- The sight of such unexpected help made them shout for joy

- The shouting has become louder in recent days
- Still wonder what all the shouting was about
- Show them what the shouting means

See also: CELEBRATE, VOICE

SHOW
- Show them they're wrong by joining this effort
- Please show how much you believe in this vital work
- A way of showing how much you care
- Show your concern by sending in a generous cheque

SHOWCASE
- Showcasing the very best we have to offer
- A wonderful showcase for these new services
- To proudly preserve these showcase buildings

SHUDDER
- I still shudder every time
- The very sight would make you shudder
- We shudder at the very thought of what these innocents must endure every day

SICK
- This vigorous person shrank to a very sick patient struggling to cope
- Sick at heart because so much has been already lost
- Sickened by the very idea
- Growing sick of so much misery
- Discovered that this was not a sick joke, but something very real

See also: DISEASE, ILL, ILLNESS, MEDICINE, PAIN

SIGHT
- Even dear friends could no longer bear the sight of her suffering
- Take care not to lose sight of our objectives
- The improvement is a sight to fill the heart with joy

SIGNIFICANCE
- Understand the tremendous significance of
- My own personal commitment during the past six years springs from moving first hand experience of the significance of
- We have never gone through a more significant twelve months
- Their real significance is anything but reassuring

See also: IMPORTANT DISTINGUISHED, NECESSITY, URGENT, WEIGHT

SILENCE
- The silence must be broken
- Most of those afflicted suffer in silence
- We've learned that remaining silent means death

- Today, you can help break the silence for life
- We can no longer remain silent in the face of this outrage
- It's not enough to sit in silence
- Your silence could kill someone
- Silence is the coward's way

SIMPLE

- It really is as simple as that
- Simple, effective and very do-able
- A very simple but effective way
- The simplest way is often the best
- It's so simple to help
- It's as simple as taking action now
- It's just that simple
- What I have to say is very simple

See also: COMFORT, EASY

SINCERE

- Now we can say a sincere, "Well done!"
- With the sincerest of intentions in our hearts
- I know you are sincere in your desire to relieve this suffering
- This appeal is short, sincere and direct

SIT

- Well, I expect that, like me, you don't intend to sit back quietly acquiescing while
- How can anyone sit by when such suffering is going on
- I know you won't sit this one out

SITUATION

- The present situation is urgent and critical
- The current situation demands immediate attention
- Bravely making the best of an almost impossible situation
- Determined to cope with a very difficult situation
- Hardly the best of situations
- We've already improved this situation dramatically
- Because of this urgent situation, your gift is needed right now
- People who shared our situation gave us comfort
- What are the best ways to handle these situations

SKILL

- Acquire these valuable skills for life
- Our work can give children and adults alike the skills they need to unlock the door to a brighter future
- Help provide a family with the skills to cope with
- They bring their special skills and talents
- Our goal is to enhance knowledge, skills, attitudes and experiences

- Designed to provide the entry-level skills necessary
- Learning critical thinking skills enhances the ability of the individual
- To refresh slightly rusty skills
- Your support lets us apply our own hard-won skills
- Important to develop skills in critical analysis
- Bringing together many skills

See also: ABILITY, EXPERTISE, GUIDANCE, LEADERSHIP, PROFESSIONAL, TALENT, TECHNIQUE

SLASH
- They just can't wait to slash budgets
- We mean to slash the incidences of this disease
- A devastating policy of slash and burn
- Our basic funding has been severely slashed

See also: CUT, DOWNSIZE, SETBACK, SHORTFALL

SLEEP
- Don't wait to sleep on it, act now
- They'll think we're asleep at the switch
- The almost unimaginable luxury of sleeping safe and secure in bed
- I can't sleep for worrying about these defenceless people

SMALL
- No sum is too small
- The smallest gesture means so much
- Tremendous results from a such a small and modest start
- Even a small amount would help so very much

SMILE
- See your generosity reflected in a joyful smile, a grateful heart
- What a smile that will put on her face
- Their smiles tell the story
- You will be repaid with smiles and singing
- Smiles appear right before your eyes
- You leave with a smile
- All it costs is a smile
- Caring smiles, kindness, compassion and encouragement

See also: DELIGHT, CHEER, HAPPINESS, JOY, PLEASURE

SOCIAL
- Ruthless cuts to social programs
- You know what this kind of ruthless social policy will do to the poor
- Imagine how much worse things will be without our social safety net
- Now is the time to prove that human beings are social animals
- The social consequences are unthinkable

SOCIETY
- A task that this society is best fitted to perform
- Every one of us has a solemn duty to our society
- Better able to succeed in a modern, complex society
- Still want to make a contribution to society
- Society as a whole is as only as good as each individual
- Is success truly derived from achieving society's goals

See also: ASSOCIATION, COMMUNITY, GROUP, FAMILY, NATION, PEOPLE, POPULATION

SOLUTION
- This might be the solution we've all been looking for
- Seeking new solutions and new understanding of age-old questions
- You can be part of these creative, long lasting solutions by supporting
- But to seek global solutions that work for the world's poor
- Help find realistic solutions
- Working to find better, safer solutions to our problems
- Despite what some people would have us believe, there are no simple solutions
- A versatile and creative solution
- The most economical solution to
- A solution-oriented program that is the answer to a prayer
- Solutions for a small planet
- Not an instant solution
- There are no simple, easy solutions
- Help us work for a solution to this tragic problem
- To create a workable solution
- Help us work toward a fast solution

Solution: answer, explanation, key, discovery, clarification, definition, clue, reason, justification
See also: ANSWER, KEY, RESPONSE, PUZZLE, RESULT

SOLVE
- This situation is not easily solved
- You can help solve a very difficult problem
- Working day and night to solve

See also: DEFEAT, DISCOVER, FIND, OVERCOME, PUZZLE

SOMEONE
- Please make sure they can be there for you or someone you know
- Help someone who really needs it
- Just to know that someone cares
- The someone I'm talking about is you

SOMETHING
- There's something you should know
- I'm sure you, too, have felt that something must be done

- Please give even a little something to help out
- There is something for everyone regardless of age or interest

SORROW
- Still an occasion of great sorrow in that family
- The sorrow of it all is that this problem can be so easily solved
- A sorrow lodged very deep in their hearts
- A great sorrow to us all

See also: DESPAIR, GRIEF, PAIN, SUFFERING, TEARS

SORRY
- I was truly sorry to learn about
- Better to help right now than to be sorry later
- A very sorry sort of situation
- We can't just say we're sorry – we have to do something to help
- Will only end up becoming a sorry excuse for

See also: APOLOGY, SAD, GRIEF, REGRET, SORROW

SOURCE
- Always working to find new sources of funding for
- These come from a variety of sources such as
- You have always been our primary source of support
- Other sources have been drying up at a shocking rate
- Accessing non-government sources of funding
- Providing an invaluable and almost inexhaustible source of
- Sources, techniques and options for obtaining the non-government funding we require
- Nothing can replace going back to the source

SPARE
- Please spare me five minutes right now
- Please give whatever you can spare
- To help spare them so much pain

See also: EXTRA, REPRIEVE, RESCUE, SAVE

SPARK
- She needed that spark in her life
- Sparking change for the better
- To nurture such trembling, uncertain spark of life into a steady, glowing flame

See also: BEGINNING, IMAGINATION, INITIATIVE, SEED

SPEAK
- With your help, we can be there to speak for them
- If ever there was a time to speak up, it is now
- That's why it's crucial that you speak out immediately
- In addition to speaking out on women's behalf, there was another role to play in

helping
- If you don't speak out, who will
- Speak up for those who cannot speak for themselves
- You spoke up firmly
- If someone had only spoken up before it was to late

See also: COMMUNICATE, INFORM, SPEAK, TELL, VOICE

SPECIAL
- You're very special, because you're a part of our
- Taking such very special care to
- Always remain special in our hearts
- No one is singled out for special treatment
- Earlier this year, you contributed to our special fund, and if you could make another special gift before the end of the month
- After this great gift, we wanted to create something special in return

See also: CHOICE, PRIVILEGE, SELECT

SPECIALISTS
- Specialists take time to analyze specific needs
- For now specialists can only try to make their patients as comfortable as possible
- The work of these specialists costs a great deal of money

SPECTACULAR
- And, thanks to you, it was easier than ever to enjoy this wonderfully unique and spectacular treasure
- Ready to make spectacular improvements
- A truly spectacular response to our last appeal

SPEED
- And always, the speed and attention we devote to
- More donations would speed up good results
- Right now, speed is everything
- Please help us get aid to them with all speed possible

Speed up: expedite, facilitate, accelerate, hasten, quicken, bring life to, intercede, lend wings to

SPHERE
- Can successfully work in that sphere
- Uniting all spheres of action and influence
- To boldly enter and succeed in that challenging sphere

SPIRIT
- Humiliated, degraded or ignored until their small spirits are crushed and broken
- I'm writing to you in this same spirit of mutual caring
- This same spirit of loving cooperation governs everything we do
- We've borrowed her name, and her valiant spirit too

- Now that our fighting spirit is truly roused
- Showing a commendable fineness of spirit
- Your support keeps the creative spirit alive
- Getting into the spirit of the thing
- Nurture the spirit of giving
- Foster team and individual spirit
- Join the spirit
- Partake of the powerful, unquenchable spirit of

See also: **COURAGE, DETERMINATION, ENTHUSIASM, EMOTION, HEART, IMAGINATION**

SPONSOR
- If you can sponsor
- Helping brings a whole lot of joy to the sponsor, too
- Proud sponsors of
- It will take many people like you to sponsor one

Sponsor: advocate, champion, patron, supporter, financier, angel, guarantor, promoter, advertiser, proponent, partisan, well-wisher, speak for, promise, assure, back, aid, recommend, sustain, maintain, subsidize, uphold, further, push for, endorse, stick up for, stand by, go to bat for, vouch for, warrant

See also: **ADVOCATE, BACK, BENEFACTOR, GIVE, HELP, PATRON, SUPPORT, VOLUNTEER**

SPONSORSHIP
- We simply must find these sponsorships soon or
- Your sponsorship is absolutely crucial
- You can help increase the number of sponsorships

SPREAD
- Help us spread the word about the excellent quality of this program
- Unless we act at once, this disaster might spread
- A new spirit of hope and cooperation is spreading over the land

SPRING
- Spring is a lovely time – unless you are alone and hungry
- Springing into action at the first hint of trouble
- A new spring of hope and freedom
- Feel the joy springing up in your heart

SQUEEZE
- Now the squeeze is really on
- Every day we're squeezed a little more
- Squeezing every little bit out of our resources

See also: **CRISIS, CRUNCH, EMERGENCY, PLIGHT, CUTBACK, SHORTFALL**

STAFF

- Need a dedicated, knowledgeable staff to get the message across
- The caring staff provided them with
- Assisted the regular staff to
- I've asked our staff to think more entrepreneurially to become more self-reliant
- Our dedicated, knowledgeable staff
- Over the year, we even had to reduce our core staff by more than
- First class care provided by a dedicated and experienced staff
- Thanking our staff for their endless hours of devotion

See also: **CAREGIVER, HELPER, PROFESSIONAL, WORKER**

STAKE

- In view of what is at stake right now, I sincerely hope you will decide to support us again by giving
- You have a big stake in this too
- Everyone has a stake in improving these lives
- The courage to stake everything upon
- Having a fundamental stake in the success of

See also: **INTEREST, PART, SHARE**

STAND

- Take a stand against
- Stand alongside us in this fight
- If you stand with us, it's a fight we cannot lose
- Let your representative know where you stand immediately
- Stand up for our national voice
- Please take a stand with us in favor of
- We're taking a tough stand on the issues
- Could not just stand by and
- While we continue to stand by those struggling so hard to
- Couldn't just stand by while
- United we stand
- Making sure you know exactly where we stand on this
- Standing on guard for
- When it comes to standing up for our cause, there's no better place to start than by protecting
- Finally allowed to stand on their own
- You don't get anywhere standing still

Stand: position, attitude, policy line, platform, point of view, assertion, plan of action, game plan, strategy, belief, confront, boldly meet, face, defy, challenge, uphold, support, defend, affirm, stick with, stick to one's guns, be steadfast, withstand, resist, weather, hold out, sanction, approve of, permit

See also: **DEFEND, POSITION, UPHOLD, PLAN, SUPPORT**

STANDARD

- In order to continue to meet these high standards, we must

- Our standards have never been more rigorous
- Work to the most exacting standards
- Please help us keep our standards high
- Sets professional standards for
- Sets the gold standard for
- You choose the standard, we deliver the results
- And control the standard of service you receive

See also: **MEASURE, PRINCIPLE**

STAR

- You could put stars in someone's eyes by making a donation to
- We reach for the stars every day
- A shining star of hope and love
- Be a star, give today
- Help our star rise and shine out

START

- After a hesitant and trouble-ridden start
- In fact, you can get started right now by
- To start removing the problems from these
- There's no better place to start than by
- Help them make a positive new start
- Everyone has to start somewhere
- It all started one day when
- Get in at the start of something big
- A fresh start has arrived
- You were with us when we started out many years ago

See also: **BEGINNING, INITIATIVE, RENEW, SEED**

STATISTICS

- Today, the horrible statistics cannot be denied
- Only your help can change these shocking statistics
- Our statistics do not lie
- I know you'll look at the statistics I've enclosed and understand how important your help is

STATURE

- Certainly none of could ever have imagined that our organization would grow to possess the stature and influence it has today
- I know you have real stature in your community
- A true measure of personal stature
- Increase your own stature by giving

STATUS QUO

- Today, government support has been hacked back so badly we're struggling just to maintain and protect the status quo

- Sticking to the status quo just isn't good enough any more
- Imperative to look beyond the status quo

STAVE
- Let's stave it off before it is too late
- Help us stave off a real disaster in the making
- Desperately struggling to stave off hunger and despair

See also: PREVENT, REPRIEVE, STOP

STEP
- It's a small step, but it's an important step on the road to stopping
- This first step allows us to gauge our level of comfort about
- We see this as the logical next step
- With your financial support, we're one step closer to ending the misery
- And we've gone one step further
- There are several steps that can reduce the risk of
- By putting these few steps immediately into practice, you could save a life – maybe even your own
- To take specific action steps to save our environment
- You can take simple steps that will mean a big improvement in
- This represents a major step
- We just took a huge step recently
- Follow these easy steps

See also: ACCOMPLISHMENT, ACTION, ADVANCE, EFFORT, PROGRESS, UNDERTAKING

STIGMA
- Far too many face the horror and the stigma of
- Bravely bearing the stigma of their agonizing illness
- Working to remove this unfair stigma once and for all
- Because of this terrible stigma, driven from their homes

See also: DESPAIR, SHAME, SUICIDE

STIMULATE
- Developed a way to stimulate even more support
- A stimulated mind is a national asset
- Stimulating your interest would be a major coup for us

See also: INSPIRATION, MOVE, MOTIVATE

STOP
- Two simple things you can do to help stop
- Only determined action now can stop further onslaught
- Stop them in their tracks right now
- It won't stop unless you help
- But we don't stop there
- We may be able to stop or mitigate

- Stop them from getting their way
- I'd like to ask you to stop for a minute to consider the plight of thousands who
- Making sure it is stopped for good
- Stop the heartache, the despair
- Despite out best efforts to stop this
- Actively trying to stop
- All this must be stopped
- You can make it stop
- You can speed up this stop-and-go progress
- Let's stop this killer now

Stop: halt arrest, prevent, deny, repel, repulse, avert, thwart, balk, check, hold in check, keep within bounds, keep back, hold back, hold at bay, turn aside, ward off, stave off, stand against, hold out against, bear up against, stem/turn/breast the tide, hinder, stall, slow, slow down, deflect, curb, counteract, countervail, counterbalance, counterpoise, countervene, neutralize, correct, rectify, redress, adjust, fix square, amend, rid, right, set right, put straight
See also: BLOCK, DELAY, PREVENT, OBSTACLE

STORY

- Recently, I was asked to tell my personal story
- It won't be the first time I've told this story but
- Such a story dramatically illustrates the climate in which
- May I share a heart-warming story with you
- So many gripping stories are surging through my mind
- After we pieced the story together, we discovered that
- Get them to tell us the straightforward story
- And that is another exciting story
- A few years down the road their stories may have a different, happier ending
- I have chosen to share my story with you because I know that your support can help save someone else
- Please read this rivetting story
- I want to share a special story with you
- Enclosed is a true story about
- You may find the enclosed story difficult to read
- This is a story about a little girl who ran to her parents with a triumphant discovery
- We're sending you these photos so you can see the real story for yourself
- So many stories reveal horrors
- And that's not the end of the story
- You'll share fascinating stories and read real life experiences
- That's why we've asked some of them to tell their own stories
- When people open up and tell their stories, it is heart-rending

STRANGLE

- Time to stop the slow strangling of
- Ready to strangle the flow of vital funds

- Spoke to us in a rasping, strangled voice

STRATEGY
- Pleased to announce we're launching a new national strategy to reduce
- Begin here to map out a strategy
- Actively involved in the latest strategies
- For more winning strategies
- Helping so many develop new coping strategies
- Strategies for early intervention
- A far better strategy for dealing with this
- Planning strategies making use of

See also: IDEA, PLAN, PROPOSAL

STREAMLINE
- A new and better way to streamline service
- A dozen recommendations for streamlining the structure and operations
- Here is our brand new, streamlined mission plan

STREET
- The streets and rooming houses are nasty places to get healthy
- First, let's get the children off the streets
- Do people have to take to the streets to get noticed
- Please help before the streets claim yet another victim
- The streets are no place for the vulnerable
- Immediately gives us street credibility

STRENGTH
- Our strength is people working together
- Living with their pain has given me the strength to ask you to stand with us now
- Has been a special source of strength
- Get the strength and encouragement they need
- Great satisfaction in discovering their strengths and weaknesses
- Support our demonstrated strengths
- Even in our strengths there can be weaknesses
- Strength in teamwork
- You give us strength by caring and participating
- Compliment our strengths by

Strength: power, force, might, vitality, energy, efficacy, potency, toughness, durability, mainstay, foundation

See also: COURAGE, DETERMINATION, POWER

STRESS
- We cannot stress this point too much
- Years of stress had taken their toll
- Working brilliantly even under enormous stress
- Enough stress can undermine even the very strongest

- Rebalance the stresses of life with a sense of peace, harmony and well-being
- Gaining a greater ability to cope with the stress of

See also: ANXIETY, FEAR, WORRY

STRIDE
- We're making such incredible strides forward
- Help us stride boldly into a better future
- It's a big stride but, with you beside them, they can do it

See also: ADVANCE, BREAKTHROUGH, LEAP, PROGRESS

STRIP
- Will strip away all previous ideas you had about
- A stripped-down, streamlined version
- Even stripped down to its bare essentials, it's very effective

STRIVE
- If you believe in striving for
- Never stop striving for excellence
- Always striving to get better

See also: BATTLE, EFFORT, FIGHT, STRUGGLE

STRONG
- Strong enough to give the love and support they need
- A strong and noble country
- Half a century strong
- You've have helped make us strong
- We work strongest when we work together
- Never stronger than when you're with us
- We need one strong organization for all of us
- Helping us become even stronger

STRUGGLE
- Worn down by the unceasing daily struggle
- Thousands of people struggle bravely with
- They, and every other family struggling with
- Meanwhile, they struggle unrelentingly with
- To develop a better understanding of the struggles of the poor
- A struggle of titanic proportions is shaping up
- Makes each day a trial to struggle through
- Those who struggle against almost insurmountable odds
- No longer struggling against life-threatening diseases
- I hope you are willing to support us in this struggle
- Tens of thousands identify with this struggle
- We struggle with the same things you struggle with

Struggle: grapple, contend, tussle, scuffle, wrestle, combat, skirmish, duel, contest, oppose, challenge, take on, fight, battle

See also: **BATTLE, BEAT, EFFORT, FIGHT, STRIVE, WAR**

STUDENT
- Which student will your gift help this year
- Your donation will help students ensure a bright future for all of us
- Students are the intellectual capital we must develop in order to survive and thrive into the twenty-first century.
- Our students are the real wealth of our nation
- Studenthood for life is a necessity in a knowledge-based society
- Designed for maximum student involvement

STUDY
- Need the funds to really study this problem
- Exciting recent studies have shown that
- So many studies now point out

See also: **EDUCATION, INFORMATION, LEARN, RESEARCH**

SUBSCRIPTION
- We trust your voluntary subscription won't affect your support of other areas
- This could be your subscription to helping others
- When you buy a subscription, you're buying the opportunity to help

SUCCEED
- To succeed in our efforts, we must raise a large sum this year alone
- To succeed over the coming months and years
- With your support, how could we not succeed
- By working together, I know we can succeed
- And we've already succeeded in
- It succeeds through the sweat and commitment of those dedicated volunteers who

Succeed: accomplish, complete, do, work out, turn out, carry through, make good, prosper, thrive, grow, advance, get ahead, succeed with flying colors, triumph over, win, conquer, prevail, luck out, strike it rich, hit the jackpot, be victorious, make the grade

See also: **OVERCOME, SOLVE, WIN**

SUCCESS
- Only you can make this work a success
- It was a real success story
- Please make your gift today and feel a part of this year's success
- Helps ensure the continuation of success stories like this
- We've had considerable success to date
- There are many reasons for our remarkable success
- Another reason for our success is our donors
- Despite these successes, critical work remains
- Last year we enjoyed great success in raising money
- Our approach is a proven success

- With your support, and the latest tools, we can boost our success rate even higher
- Together, we've marked great successes and a few disappointments
- Your donation is crucial to this list of ongoing successes
- What is real success worth to you
- Working to emulate the smashing success
- And what is this formula for success
- In order to greatly increase our success ratio
- Now creating an umbrella of success
- Their success is your reward
- Our success or failure lies solely with people like you
- Providing the maximum opportunity to achieve the success they envision
- Taking a different route to success from the traditional one
- Helping each individual achieve greater success in every area of their lives
- Your loyalty is a big part of our success

See also: ANSWER, FRUITION, OUTCOME, PAYOFF, RESEARCH, RESOLUTION, RESULTS, RETURN, SOLUTION

SUCCESSFUL

- So outstandingly successful that no well-informed person would miss the opportunity of supporting
- We've been partly successful
- You've helped us with our most successful programs
- You've made us wonderfully successful

SUCCOR

- So many look to us for succor
- Reaching out to you, with desperate hands, for succor
- To succor the downtrodden and those in despair

See also: AID, CARE, COMFORT, HELP, SYMPATHY

SUFFER

- So families won't suffer needlessly
- Suffered emotionally and psychologically as well as physically
- Don't let them suffer in silence
- Won't suffer this without strenuous protest

SUFFERER

- I'm one of the many sufferers
- Assisting in the development of support groups for sufferers and their families
- Yet tragically, so many sufferers are still beyond our reach
- Sufferers of all ages can still be helped
- Please don't turn your back on these sufferers

SUFFERING

- People are suffering and losing hope
- We cannot accept the terrible suffering caused by

- Too many people, young and old, are already suffering
- Help stop the suffering
- The suffering is incredible
- Suffering under constant change
- Seeing so much suffering is hard to face day after day
- Severe and debilitating suffering
- Helps prevent an unprecedented increase in global human suffering
- I've heard too many heart-rending stories of suffering
- We cannot accept this terrible suffering
- Daily and unpredictable bouts of suffering
- Please help stop the suffering and agony for hundreds of thousands
- The suffering is often indescribable
- Only increases the suffering of the most vulnerable
- Stop so much needless suffering
- Already, so much of the suffering is unnecessary

See also: **ABUSE, AGONY, PAIN, STRESS, TORTURE**

SUGGESTION

- Suggestions on how you can best help
- We welcome any suggestions you might have about
- At the very first suggestion of trouble, we are there
- I welcome your suggestions for further activities
- Please let me know if you have any suggestions

See also: **CONCEPT, CONCERN, IDEA, MODEL, PRESENTATION, PROPOSAL SEED, START, THOUGHT**

SUICIDE

- Turn to the only release they know – suicide
- Otherwise, this will amount to a suicide mission
- At this point, it would be suicide right now to
- Suicide and despair stalk them every day

See also: **DESPAIR, HOPELESS, SAD, STIGMA**

SUM

- Manages consistently to be more than the sum of its parts
- Each small sum adds up to enough money to help
- Even the smallest sum is deeply appreciated
- Little bits of help can add up to an enormous sum

SUPPLY

- Everything but misery is in short supply
- In order to keep supplies up to the necessary level
- Enabling us to keep supplies continually on hand
- You supply the love and support, we supply the practical assistance

See also: **FUND, GIVE, HELP, NOURISH, PROVIDE, NURTURE**

SUPPORT

- Your support matters
- Decide to support us again by making a donation of
- That's why we so urgently need your support
- Please offer your support as we work toward a society free of poverty and misery and crime
- Powered by vigorous support from people like you
- The kind of support that made them believe it was all possible
- To provide these services we need the support of people who care
- You can see why support from our members is critically important
- Thousands have already committed to supporting our high quality programs
- But we still need more support
- The kind of support I'm asking from you today
- We're doing all we can to maintain our support to their work
- I'll be asking for your support in the next few months
- More than ever, we need the support of people like you or we just can't exist
- I'm writing today to ask for your support
- One of the best ways to support
- We can't do it without your involvement and financial support
- We've been there for you
- If you're thinking of not supporting us this year, please think again
- I ask for your support so that I can continue to work for you
- Able to attend a very special support group
- I just know that with your support it can help more people both here and abroad
- Won't you support this valuable program with your personal donation
- Your support can make headlines across the country
- Your support will make good news headlines like these happen again and again
- In appreciation of your support of our ideals and worthwhile efforts
- We need your support to maintain and expand our programs to help
- However, with continuing support from our members, we can continue to meet our mandate to provide
- Thankfully, we can turn directly to you and ask for your support
- Your support will make it possible to provide care and services to
- That's why your support is so vital
- Filling out the enclosed reply card and returning it, you'll support
- Your generous support has maintained us for many years
- Please consider the amount of support you can offer and send it today in the enclosed envelope
- Your gracious support of our work leads me to ask you to help again
- Specifically, I support
- I hope I've conveyed how important your support is in carrying out our work
- Our need for your support is terribly urgent because, even as I write this letter to you, somewhere in the world, victims are being
- If you would like to support our work, please complete the following section and send your donation in the envelope provided
- Unflagging support for over a century

- Appreciate your vigorous and generous support of
- With very gracious support from you
- Give wholehearted support
- Our support is deep and wide
- Each year, we rely on your continuing kind and loyal support
- We need your continued support for this all-out effort
- You see why your support now is more critical than ever
- With your kind support and greater awareness
- Your support would be greatly appreciated
- I ask that you use the enclosed labels to show your support
- Only with your support can we keep up with growing demand
- We urge you to support
- Thank you for your generous support
- Your support is critical to continuing the progress
- This is why your support will make such a difference
- Most grateful for any support you can give us
- In just minutes you can ensure support for
- Support lasting even beyond your lifetime

Support: uphold, brace, prop up, elevate, bolster, enhance, tide over, shore up, buttress, shoulder, keep up, relieve, comfort, succor, cheer, inspire, condole, comfort, sympathize, assure, hold up, hang in, maintain, sustain, cherish, nurture, nourish, foster, provide for, take care of, look after, watch over, tend, mind, finance, subsidize, pay for, fund, sponsor, underwrite, capitalize, put the money for, set up, meet the expense, encourage, further, abet, accommodate, hearten, advocate, promote, vouch for, endorse, make good, adopt, aid, defend, back
See also: ABET, ACTION, ADVOCACY, AID, ASSIST, BACK, BENEFIT, CARE, COMMIT, COMMITMENT, CONTRIBUTE, CONTRIBUTION, DECISION, DONATION, EMBRACE, FRIENDSHIP, GIFT, HELP, INPUT, INVESTMENT, INVOLVEMENT, MEMBERSHIP, PARTNERSHIP, REACH OUT, RELIEF, ROLE, SPONSORSHIP, SUBSCRIPTION, VOICE

SUPPORTER

- As a valued supporter, I'm sure you're as concerned as I am about
- All through the support of our financial supporters and loyal volunteers
- You've been a loyal supporter for years
- Our solid supporters
- Many of our supporters have been with us steadily year after year
- We've come to think of each our supporters as a dear friend
- You and other supporters make it all possible
- Be one of our supporters and benefactors
- We're only as strong as our supporters
- I'd like you to join our supporters today
- By joining our supporters, you
- Slowly building a solid core of committed supporters
- Become an active supporter of
- We are proud to have been one of the first supporters of

- I like to get back to our supporters regularly

Supporter: advocate, advisor, patron, sympathizer, patronizer, backer, champion, endorser, upholder, sanctioner, approver, follower, partisan adherent, disciple, agent, promoter, furtherer, advancer, favorer, subsidizer, underwriter, maintainer, sustainer, benefactor, benefactress, benefiter, fairy godmother, friend in need/deed, comforter, succorer, good Samaritan, ministering angel, sponsor

See also: BENEFACTOR, CAREGIVER, FRIEND, HELPER, PARTNER, SPONSOR, VOLUNTEER, WORKER

SUPPORTIVE
- Professional individuals who are extremely supportive
- But we can't do it without supportive members like you.
- Doing your very best to be supportive to

SURE
- We'll make sure that promises are kept
- She has made sure that her children survive
- It's by no means a sure thing yet
- A program you can be really sure about

SURFACE
- But look just below the surface and you will see
- Everything may look fine on the surface
- Surface cosmetics will not do the job

SURPRISE
- Does that surprise you
- Would you still be surprised if we told you
- You'll be pleasantly surprised at how much your donation can help
- Don't be surprised if you find yourself feeling happy and humming to yourself unexpectedly
- There are still a lot of surprises to come
- Constantly surprised by new situations

See also: AMAZE, AMBUSH, MYSTERY, SHOCK, WONDER

SURROUND
- Want to surround them with love and security
- Surrounded by thriving tourism, residential, recreational, and wildlife areas
- Feeling backed into a corner and surrounded

SURVIVE
- Trying so hard to survive on the streets
- If we are to survive in the twenty-first century
- Ordinary people face tremendous obstacles just to survive
- Survive modern pressures
- Many do not survive

- Those who survive are scarred for life
- Rushing faster and faster merely to survive
- For yourself or someone you love to have a better chance at surviving

See also: **ENDURE, LIVE, OVERCOME**

SURVIVAL

- Increasing the chances of survival
- Depends on you for their very survival
- Comes right down to a stark question of survival

SURVIVOR

- A torture survivor from
- Because of you there are more survivors than ever
- Speaking as a survivor, I can tell you that this work is absolutely vital
- You can help directly to increase the number of survivors

SUSCEPTIBLE

- One of the reasons your health is so susceptible to
- Still so susceptible to damage
- To protect the ones which are most susceptible to

SUSTAIN

- Help us sustain our efforts to
- People like you sustain us year after year
- Doing our best to sustain the villagers
- In critical need of your generosity to sustain the important work we've begun

Sustain: uphold, maintain, sustain, continue, keep up

See also: **HELP, SUPPORT**

SUSTAINING DONOR

- Get the greatest impact from your donation by becoming a sustaining donor
- Our sustaining donor program, the most effective way of giving
- Feel the pride of becoming a sustaining donor

See also: **SECTION FIVE – MONTHLY OR SUSTAINED GIVING**

SWEEPSTAKES

- Our special sweepstakes
- Just like winning the sweepstakes to them
- Turn them into winners in the sweepstakes of life

See also: **SECTION TWO**

SYMBOL

- Symbols of our unwavering commitment to the environment
- Has become both a symbol and a martyr
- A symbol of light and hope
- A symbol of past achievements and enormous future possibilities

- Keep the vibrant, living symbols we all so deeply treasure

SYMPATHY
- Once again calling upon your sympathy
- Springing from the deepest well of sympathy
- Turn your sympathy into direct action
- Our heartfelt sympathy goes out
- Calls and expressions of sympathy from all over the country

See also: CARING

SYMPTOM
- Just another symptom of a system that isn't working correctly
- Coping techniques to alleviate the worst symptoms
- To set them free from the devastating symptoms of this disease
- So many people have no idea of the symptoms that precede
- These are the symptoms, all too real, of
- The symptoms are agonizing
- Must deal with the root cause, not just the symptoms

See also: DISEASE, ILLNESS, SICK

SYSTEM
- Formed clear convictions on how the system should work
- It's unlikely that this system will ever be completed without your help
- A way to beat a slow, corrupt system
- Protect the support system on which we all depend
- Creating a reformed, non-partisan system of awarding
- This includes developing systems that are responsive to the needs of people with

See also: PLAN, PROGRAM, STRATEGY

TABOO
- Struggling with society's last, greatest taboo
- Determined to smash the taboo against
- This taboo is completely senseless

TALE
- Drew out a wrenching tale of
- All they want to do is live to tell the tale
- These woeful tales cannot fail to move

Tale: story, narration, account, recital, yarn, saga, history, epic
See also: INFORMATION, STORY

TALENT
- The belief that such excellent talent should be nurtured
- The waste of brilliant talent is appalling
- Without funds, these wonderful talents will slip away
- I know you have a real talent for helping

- Developing an appreciation for talents, skills and contributions
- A rare, unprecedented collection of talent in one place

See also: **ABILITY, SKILL**

TALK

- It's not easy for me to talk about what happened to me
- Come and talk to us about
- See what all the talk is about
- It's time for some straight talk about
- Not the sort of thing you talk about at parties
- Let me talk to you directly about this need
- It's time to talk about how we really feel
- We don't want to be all talk and no action
- Feel free to talk to our staff about
- Look who's talking about
- I've just had the most incredible talk with
- You should be talking to us
- And I want to know why we aren't talking about this suffering

See also: **COMMUNICATE, INFORM, TELL, VOICE**

TANGIBLE

- Making love a tangible thing
- Your donation quickly produces tangible results
- Give them something tangible to hang onto
- Tangible benefits from even the smallest donation

TARGET

- Help us target the neediest
- You'll be targeting those who
- Target your gift to
- Because of you, we'll reach our target soon
- Not only to hit the target, but hit a bull's-eye
- You can help us achieve the target by donating

See also: **AIM, GOAL, MISSION, PURPOSE**

TASK

- Task of meeting the urgent medical needs of these people
- I need your help to accomplish this historic task
- With your help, no task is beyond our scope
- Help with the enormous task of finding
- Giving isn't just a task, it is a joy and apleasure
- Your invaluable aid in carrying out these tasks
- There to assist in the completion of daily tasks
- A once relatively simple task has turned complex

See also: **CHALLENGE, JOB, UNDERTAKING**

TASTE
- Once you get a taste for helping others
- Just a little taste of what is possible
- Of course it's all in the very best of taste
- Victory so near we can almost taste it

TAX
- Make your tax-creditable gift
- All donations are tax-creditable
- The government should insist on a fair corporate tax system to help cover the debt and fund social programs
- I'll make sure you receive your income tax receipt promptly
- Since we're a charitable nonprofit organization, your contribution will be fully receipted for tax purposes
- All it takes is a tax-creditable donation of
- To provide tax relief to donors
- All the financial contributions qualify for a tax credit
- As a way of saying thank you, we will send you a tax receipt for the full amount of your gift
- Your contribution will be fully receipted for tax purposes
- Of course your donation is tax deductible
- The best way to support the cause is to take advantage of tax credits

TEACH
- Teaching countless caring people like you how to
- It is reputed worldwide as among the finest post-secondary institutions of teaching and research anywhere
- But there was nothing to teach us how to help
- Their job is trying to teach what they think is important for young people to learn
- Every day our staff and volunteers teach
- Creative use of a variety of teaching procedures
- The older they get, the more difficult it is to teach them

Teach: instruct, tutor, enlighten, educate, inform, educate, edify
See also: EDUCATE, INFORM, LEARN, TRAIN

TEACHER
- The right kind of teacher can provide lifelong inspiration
- With your gift of $ __, we would be able to get better teachers
- Think of the difference a single teacher could make
- Each teacher you support means more children will have a chance at education

TEAM
- Please join our team now
- We urgently need you to become part of our team
- Multi-disciplinary health care team is instantly on hand to
- Our highly specialized teams move quickly to

- This devoted volunteer has assembled a team of helpers and leads them by her quiet example
- Feel you are a member of our team
- We want you on our team
- It all depends upon our ability to build effective teams
- Your help to create a productive team
- Frankly, we urgently need you as a part of our team
- Our caring team helped her learn to
- Team up with a winner
- Join a winning team today
- We would be honored and grateful if you would join our team of
- Developing a distinctive group of programs to teach team building
- Now we really feel like a team
- Working hard to add you to our team
- Join our supportive, enthusiastic team
- We are a team – a dream team
- Be a real team player
- The essential elements of team building
- Especially designed to teach goal-setting and team work

Team: crew, squad, company, gang, band, corps, party
See also: GROUP, PARTNER, PARTNERSHIP

TEAMWORK
- Look at the past, present and future of teamwork
- Recognizing and honoring the importance of teamwork
- Real teamwork is the secret of all our accomplishments

TEARS
- Help dry the tears and bring joy to the faces of
- I can't tell you how many bitter tears have been shed
- Tears won't help, action will
- I couldn't help shedding a tear when I saw
- So many bitter tears have already been shed
- Tears of joy and thanksgiving poured down her face
- She stood at the door with tears streaming down her cheek
- Can hardly hold the tears back
- A life that has been bathed in tears
- Her halting voice was full of tears
- To see them just standing there, tears in their eyes

See also: ANXIETY, GRIEF, SORROW, STRESS

TECHNIQUE
- Teaching a simple but powerful self help technique
- Techniques needed for successful work with exceptional children and adults
- The best techniques have been developed through long and careful experience
- Huge advances in treatment and technique are now severely threatened by

funding cuts
See also: **PLAN, SKILL, STRATEGY, WAY**

TELEPHONE
- Helping others is as near as your telephone
- Now that high costs have made us discontinue our telephone campaign, this letter is our only way to reach you
- The telephone is a vital lifeline
- Pick up the phone right now and make a pledge

See also: **SECTION FOUR**

TELL
- First, let me tell you about a little bit about
- Let me tell you more about it
- Tell you a bit more about ourselves
- People like you telling others about us
- Just tell us what you're interested in
- I'll tell you about just one little story
- Of course, after I tell you all this good stuff
- What is it they are trying so hard to tell us
- You can always tell by the look of fear and despair
- There is so much I want to tell you about
- I can't possibly tell you everything in one letter
- I'm going to tell you everything you need to know
- That's why I want to take a moment of your time to tell you about

See also: **INFORM, RECOUNT, SPEAK, STORY, VOICE**

TENSION
- Tension is increasing every day
- Tensions turn quickly into life and death matters
- Releasing the physical, mental and emotional tensions we hold inside
- Resolving the tensions between the need for help and the need to encourage independence

See also: **ANXIETY, FEAR, STRESS, WORRY**

TERRIBLE
- It's a terrible thing to say
- The more terrible things are, the more we must help
- I know you don't want this terrible state of affairs continue any more than I do

TERROR
- I still remember the terror I felt when
- Terrifying roller coaster of worry and fear
- Isolated from others, exploited and terrorized
- The very prospect is enough to terrorize

See also: **FEAR, HORROR, PANIC, STREET**

TERRORISM
- The campaign of terrorism and harassment
- It all amounts to psychological terrorism
- Rescuing the innocent victims of terrorism
- Never give in to the threat of terrorism

THANK
THANK YOU
THANKFUL
THANKS
See SECTION FIVE – SAYING THANKS

THEME
- Our theme for the year end is
- Our constant theme is helping others
- I know this theme is all too familiar to you too

THEORY
- An opportunity to apply the theory through case studies and group work
- Now it's time to turn theory into hard reality
- In theory, it really sounds terrific
- These theories apply to all subject matter
See also: CONCEPT, CONCERN, IDEA, OPINION, PHILOSOPHY, THOUGHT

THINK
- When it comes to helping, you won't have to think twice about
- Think about it
- Take a moment to think about the important things in your life
- I know exactly what you're thinking right now
- Surely now is the time for some cool, hard thinking
- Just think of it
- In order to stimulate thinking, we want to
- Thinking, like breathing, is a natural part of daily life
- People all too rarely stop to think about
- Please tell us what you think
See also: CONSIDER

THOUGHT
- Rather disturbing food for thought
- It's such a good thought that I'm stealing this idea and passing it along
- They are always in our thoughts
- It's the thought that counts – and the action that goes along with it
- Lead to personal growth through clarification of thoughts and feelings
- Have you thought about
- Can't bear even the thought of such suffering

- Please give this some careful thought

THOUGHTFULNESS
- Your thoughtfulness is the most important part
- Because of your thoughtfulness, someone is happy today
- A moment of thoughtfulness helps so many
- The thoughtfulness of strangers has filled their lives with hope

THREAT
- A frightening threat looms on the horizon
- Few realize how great the threat really is
- When I say threat, that's exactly what I mean
- Eliminate the threat of disease and starvation in the future
- Any threat is a cause for terror
- Even worse, many will face a second threat to
- To learn when the threat of self-destruction is serious
- Increasingly seen as the single biggest threat to

Threat: warning, caution, caveat, alarm, intimidation, menace, peril, risk, hazard, jeopardy, menace, scourge, terror, danger
See also: DANGER, ENDANGER, FRIGHTEN, JEOPARDY, RISK

THREATEN
- Threatening lives and threatening security for everyone
- Threaten our children, our legacy, our future
- Must refuse to let this danger threaten all we've worked for
- Now facing a situation that threatens us all

THRILL
- In sharing the thrill of seeing broken lives rebuilt
- Never tire of the thrill of helping
- Nothing can replace the thrill of real achievement
- Thrilled to receive your contribution

See also: DELIGHT, ENTHUSIASM, JOY, RAPTURE, SATISFACTION

THROAT
- It was hard to speak over the lump in his throat
- My throat closed up with emotion at the sight
- Help us grab this menace by the throat

THROW
- Please don't throw this letter away
- If you throw this letter away, you'll be throwing away the hopes and dreams of those who so desperately need your help
- These are not throw-away people

Throw: toss, fling, hurl, pitch, jettison

TIDE

- Prevent them being washed under by a tide of
- A veritable tide of caring
- Just a little bit will tide them over to better times

TIME

- There's no time to lose
- Time could be all the medical community needs to save a life
- As always, time is of the essence
- If only enough caring people like you will respond in time
- Time is the single most effective way of improving the chances
- But even if you're thinking you don't have time to
- Our office can tell you about ways in which your time can help us
- There never seems to be enough time to tell you everything that
- Time out to do some serious thinking
- Save a tremendous amount of time and effort by
- Here's how we can slash the waiting time in half
- A tragic, unnecessary waste of time
- We don't have time to worry about the fine tuning
- It up to us to make time for
- Please, make just a little time for this very worthwhile
- Time is something we can never get back so please help now before it's too late
- Think for just a moment how much time you spend in the course of a single day
- Such a slim victory has only bought a little more time for
- But with each passing day, precious time is lost forever
- There's still time, if you send in your contribution as soon as you can
- It's time well spent when you
- All I ask is one small minute of your valuable time
- At this busy time of year, please pause to
- Time passes with agonizing slowness when you're hungry, sick or scared
- I invite you to take the time to
- This is an extremely short period of time
- Helping to develop time mastery
- Taking a step back in time
- The timing has never been better to take control of
- A way to help without taking precious time out of your day
- Time is running out
- The time has never been better for
- What perfect timing
- A very trying time
- Special help during this difficult time
- Especially in times of difficulty
- These are exciting times
- But these are very challenging times for us to
- Good times, bad times, everybody still has to live through them
- In these hard times, I'm reaching out ask your help

Time: juncture, point, instant, period, span, spell, term, interval, interlude, pause, duration, hour, day, moment, epoch, era, age, high time
See also: **CHANCE, MOMENT, OPPORTUNITY**

TODAY
- Focus on today, for a better tomorrow
- It's today that counts, not some vague, rosy promise that things might improve tomorrow
- Giving today, no matter how small, can make a huge impact on tomorrow
- Today is the best time to take the action you've been thinking about

TODDLER
- Every day, toddlers scream with pain
- Death looms over them while they are still toddlers
- We're still in the toddler stage with this

See also: **CHILDREN, KIDS, LITTLE ONES**

TOGETHER
- Together, we can change the world for the better
- Together, we say we care too much to let our program suffer such a savaging
- Working together we can beat the odds
- Pulling together we can deal with it
- Bringing people together to share ideas
- Everything comes together with your support
- Together, we can make sure no one is left, ever again, alone and lost in their struggle with
- Let's work together today to wipe out the pain of
- Working together we can make a world of difference
- Let's get together on
- Bringing together some of the world's most respected teachers, mentors, coaches and thinkers
- By working together we can succeed
- Together we can take a stand
- Only by working together can we make a difference
- Face it, we're all in this together
- Take time to think this through
- If we all pull together, this calamity need not happen
- Through our donations we can all work together as equals
- Together we can see it through

Together: in unison, in concert, all together, en masse, as a group, collectively, in cooperation, shoulder to shoulder, side by side, arm in arm, hand in hand
See also: **COMMUNITY, FRIEND, MUTUAL, PARTNERSHIP**

TOIL
- The heat, sweat, toil and fatigue are very real
- Toiling selflessly for the good of others

- So that someday, this endless toil will be done

See also: **EFFORT, LABOR, STRIVE, STRUGGLE, WORK**

TOMORROW
- Tomorrow is too late
- For tomorrow, next year and many years to come
- Their tomorrows are counting on you
- The foundations upon which tomorrow can be built

TOOL
- A tool to enhance our ability to think critically about
- All they ask are the tools to do the job
- Give them the right tools and they'll build a whole new world
- A wonderful new tool to add to our
- So important to use the right tool to
- By giving people the tools they need to look after themselves and their families

See also: **IMPLEMENT, MEANS, OPPORTUNITY, WAY**

TOPIC
- A leading-edge topic
- We'll cover every topic you want to know about
- Practical immersion in a wide range of topics
- Covering a very broad range of topics
- Covering every topic imaginable

Topic: subject matter, concept, matter under discussion, theme, idea, field of inquiry, argument, central idea, theory, assertion, hypothesis, premise, assumption, keynote

TORCH
- To keep holding the torch high for all to see
- It's our turn to take up the torch
- Now this shining torch is being passed to us
- Help carry the torch of freedom
- A torch bringing light to the darkest, coldest corners

TORCHBEARER
- A torchbearer suddenly cresting a hill in the darkness
- Remains a torchbearer for this shining belief
- Become a torchbearer for this cause
- Recruiting more torchbearers every day

See also: **ADVOCATE, BENEFACTOR, CHAMPION, SPONSOR**

TORMENT
- Help stop the torment for so many families
- The torment is very real
- For thousands tormented by

See also: **ABUSE, DESPAIR, HURT, PAIN, SUFFERING**

TORTURE
- The terrible agony of torture
- The slow, horrible torture of seeing your only child sicken and die
- Torture is terrible and disgusting

See also: ABUSE, HURT, PAIN, SUFFER

TOUCH
- From time to time, we'll be in touch, making sure you're up to date on our activities and the situation with
- Just keeping in touch
- I like to keep in touch with our most loyal supporters just to let you know how much we appreciate you
- Please consider this opportunity to keep in touch with
- Deeply touched by the personal notes from many of you
- Help us help you keep in touch with
- Comes to your home regularly to keep you in touch with
- Multiplied by the number of lives you touch
- Wanted to get in touch with you and let you know what's new

See also: CALL, CONTACT, INFORM, REACH

TOUGH
- We helped each other through the tough times
- Going through a particularly tough time
- Sometimes a tough approach is the best approach
- The times in our city are getting tougher and the streets meaner
- It's time to get tough with this problem

TRADITION
- Now I'm proud to carry on the tradition
- Maintaining this proud tradition
- Carved out a rich tradition in
- Our tradition is very strong
- Have made a commitment to restore a number of traditions that still have a central and important role in people's lives
- Is to diminish an important tradition which embodies our past and shapes our present
- A proud tradition is celebrated
- Updating our members about more recent traditions associated with
- But that cherished tradition could end quickly
- Keeping a time-honored tradition alive
- In the grand old tradition of
- Firmly rooted in the compassionate traditions of the past
- Standing firmly on the traditions of our forebears
- Building a more traditional value system
- Help us continue this priceless tradition

See also: BIRTHRIGHT, HERITAGE, LEGACY

TRAGEDY
- When tragedy strikes, we are there
- You know as well as I do that any of us at any time could be involved in a similar tragedy
- Facing this personal tragedy, they were able to draw on the strength of their
- Without concerted action, it is a tragedy waiting to descend
- This tragedy has not only affected the family
- A tragedy that has found common resonance with millions of people
- A tragedy that all of us can understand

See also: **CATASTROPHE, CRISIS, DISASTER, GRIEF, LOSS, OUTRAGE, PAIN. SUICIDE, SORROW**

TRAIN
- Train the people who might one day be in charge of
- Each member of the staff is highly trained to
- To avert the train wreck fast approaching
- Disaster approaching with the speed of a highballing train

TRAINING
- Pay for top-notch training for
- Training certainly is not cheap
- Training so they'll be able to keep their children healthy
- We'd like to be able to offer primary health care training and services in many more communities
- Helping to deliver targeted training information
- Lifelong education and training for our community and yours
- Develop a full range of training materials

See also: **EDUCATE, INFORM, TEACH**

TRANSFORM
- Transformed overnight
- Helping others brings an unexpected personal transformation
- The joy of seeing suffering people utterly transformed
- Using the transforming power of love

See also: **CHANGE, CURE, MIRACLE, WONDER**

TRAUMA
- Help prevent the effects of lifelong trauma
- Both immediate and long term trauma
- Recent trauma victims can be helped in very specific ways
- So that trauma victims do not deal with the same horror over and over again in the future
- Trauma response skills are absolutely vital here
- To bring help at last for a traumatized people

See also: **CATASTROPHE, DISASTER, HURT, PAIN, SHOCK**

TREADMILL
- Many of our well-intentioned pursuits become relentless and never-ending treadmills
- The courage to step off life's treadmills
- Maybe you're looking for a way to step off that same old treadmill

TREASURE
- We deeply treasure your participation
- Our national treasures are now under direct threat
- Supporters like you are our most precious treasure
- Help maintain the programs we all treasure so much

TREATMENT
- Great leaps have been made in the treatment of
- Without treatment, they would surely die
- New drugs and treatments free thousands from the constant miseries this condition brings
- For developing more effective treatments, and eventually, cures
- New discoveries are promising truly miraculous treatment options
- Without financial support, the miraculous potential of these treatments will not be realized
- With such effective new treatments for
- Advancing the treatment and finding cures for
- The most innovative treatment design yet
- A science, art and philosophy of treatment second to none

See also: **CURE, DISCOVER, DISEASE, MEDICINE, REMEDY, RESEARCH**

TREND
- The trend continues
- If this disturbing trend continues, we will have to take immediate steps
- A wide range of leading edge trends
- To keep up with the latest trends, ideas and developments
- Current trends indicate that the future may not be any better
- A careful analysis of trends leads us to believe
- Keeping you up-to-date on trends and issues affecting this sector

TRIBUTE
- Our tribute gift program is a beautiful way to honor
- Your contributions are a fitting tribute to these brave adventurers
- Exacting an endless and terrible tribute from
- A tribute anyone would treasure
- Your special tribute gift will help every one

See also: **GIFT, HONOR, MEMORIAL**

TRIUMPH
- A triumph that symbolized the determination of

- Their triumph is also your triumph
- Prove we can triumph over the worst of conditions
- You share this overwhelming triumph with us
- Your support puts us on the road to triumph

See also: JOY, SUCCESS, VICTORY

TROUBLE

- Won't tell us they're in trouble until they're at the end of their rope
- Fear mongers who want to provoke further trouble
- When they stumble into serious trouble, it's sometimes too late
- Signals a far deeper trouble than
- The troubles are receding
- Here comes trouble
- To recognize trouble when we see it

Trouble: adversity, misfortune, worry, concern, nuisance, headache, difficulty, inconvenience, disadvantage, handicap, trial, tribulation, affliction, ordeal, blight, burden, trauma

TROUGH

- Attempting to belly up to the trough
- Watching in alarm as our donations drop into a trough
- Lest we be accused of dipping from this trough

TRUST

- How do you win the trust of people so exploited and abused
- People have trusted us for over one hundred years
- Generous people trust us with their donations
- Trust with their lives
- A unique opportunity to establish a trust fund for
- Funds donated to the trust will be administered through the
- Among so many who have trusted
- Shatters their ability to trust people
- Now loving hands work to restore shattered trust

Trust: faith, confidence, certainty, conviction, assurance, certitude, credit, credibility, security, surety, positiveness, rely on, depend on, count on, put hope in, hope, expect, anticipate, accept, entrust, commit to, believe, confide in

TRUTH

- Nothing could be further from the truth
- It's so true, isn't it
- Look straight into the radiant face of truth
- To help you get straight at the truth
- Truth can transform an individual or a whole society
- The truth is still being painfully uncovered
- We have learned that the truth must be told so that

Truth: naked and unvarnished truth, reality, straight goods, low down, fact,

certainty, actuality
See also: **CREDIBILITY, PROOF, RIGHT**

TRY
- Helping – try it, you'll like it
- Help us try even harder to
- Giving the desire and confidence to try, and the strength to continue
- If we don't try, we'll never know
- Helping all those who are trying so hard to improve

Try: attempt, endeavor, undertake, take a shot/crack at, make an effort, strive, essay
See also: **EFFORT, LABOR, STRIVE, TOIL, WORK**

TURMOIL
- The inner turmoil we must deal with
- To impose some order upon this turmoil
- In the midst of turmoil there is always hope

See also: **CHAOS, DISASTER, DISORDER, MESS, STRUGGLE**

TURN
- There's no one else for us to turn to
- Today, we're turning to you for help
- Helping to turn things around
- Taking a very unexpected turn
- One good turn pays wonderful human dividends for years

UNBELIEVABLE
- As unbelievable as this all seems, we must remember that
- Unbelievable gains have been made and we cannot stop now
- While all this may seem unbelievable to you, let me assure that this story is perfectly true

Unbelievable: incredible, unimaginable, unthinkable, fantastic, fabulous, remarkable, inconceivable, extraordinary

UNCOMFORTABLE
- Do you feel uncomfortable at the sight of a homeless person sleeping in the gutter
- To a thinking person, these are very uncomfortable assumptions
- Poverty and sickness are the most uncomfortable of conditions in which to live
- Does the sight of this misery make you uncomfortable

UNDECIDED
- If you're still undecided about helping those in need, read on
- Few can remain undecided after seeing the situation first hand
- Undecided minds will change quickly at the sight of such suffering
- It's the undecided people who will swing the decision

UNDERSTAND

- We now better understand the range, population and habits of
- It's easy to understand why this has caught on so quickly
- We don't understand why it's caused or how to start the progression
- They don't even try to understand
- Please take the time to understand
- Please understand I'm not saying that
- To objectively understand what steps we must take
- I'm sure you can understand the gravity of this situation
- I know you will understand our precarious position
- Making sure the right people understand

Understand: comprehend, fathom, penetrate, figure out, grasp, recognize, see through, perceive, discern, make out
See also: KNOW, LEARN, SEE, RECOGNIZE, THINK

UNDERSTANDING

- Promote understanding among people
- Knowing more about this issue is vital to understanding how we can ensure the
- It takes a very deep understanding to
- Our biggest asset is the love and understanding in your heart
- Designed to develop a conceptual understanding of
- For those who want a clearer understanding of
- You, too, can foster increased understanding and peace
- Unlocking the door to understanding
- Ask for your understanding and continued support

Understanding: comprehension, consciousness, cognizance, knowledge, realization, awareness, conception
See also: AWARENESS, EDUCATION, KNOWLEDGE, INFORMATION

UNDERTAKING

- Will you join me in what I believe is the most important undertaking of my life
- It's a huge undertaking and we certainly need your help
- All these undertakings, and many more, are made possible by your generous support of
- Cannot allow ourselves to be daunted by the sheer size of the undertaking
- Together we will venture forth on a glorious undertaking
- Only now realizing the full scope of this undertaking

See also: JOB, GOAL, MANDATE, MISSION, PURPOSE, RESPONSIBILITY, WORK

UNEMPLOYED

- Job retraining to the unemployed
- Goal of getting every unemployed person a job or some schooling
- With the percentage of people unemployed or underemployed shooting up by a staggering number

UNFAIR
- It's terribly unfair to everyone
- But it all seems so unfair
- Again, how very unfair
- When life has been horribly unfair, you can help

UNITE
- United we stand
- United, there is nothing we can't accomplish
- Please help keep us strongly united

See also: COMMUNITY, JOIN, TOGETHER, PARTNER

UNIVERSITY
- Have their eye on the universities for more major deficit reduction
- Our universities can't stand any more cuts without serious damage to our future
- Universities have more than paid their share and now they look to us all for relief

- We who have benefited so very much from universities now owe it to them to defend them

See also: EDUCATE, LEARN, SCHOOL, TEACH

UNJUST
- What could be more unjust than punishing those who need protection most
- Now face that same unjust system and that same outcome
- How unjust to leave anyone in such circumstances

See also: ABUSE, INJUSTICE, OPPRESSION, UNFAIR

UNPREDICTABLE
- Tormented by unpredictable pain and sickness
- While so many live with the unpredictability of these diseases
- We are trying to cut down the unpredictability of our funding
- Help put an end to the fiendishly unpredictable torments of

UNREALISTIC
- They said it was unrealistic, but with your help, we did it
- We need to bring unrealistic expectations into line
- Such an unrealistic plan is bound to crash

UNTHINKABLE
- Because it is unthinkable that
- It''s unthinkable that you should turn away
- Just a little while ago a problem such as this would have been unthinkable
- Too many previously unthinkable things have begun to happen
- If you supposed such a thing was unthinkable, think again
- Help stop the unthinkable – act now
- Should the unthinkable happen, we want to be ready

- Subjected to unthinkable cruelty even as I write

See also: **UNBELIEVABLE**

UPDATE
- Let me give you a brief update on some of the major events of the year
- The latest update was very necessary – and very costly
- We have to keep updating regularly
- A quick update on some of our priorities in the last few months
- You help us update our program continually

UPHOLD
- I want uphold the same fine principles that you do
- To uphold truth and justice in all circumstances
- Sometimes upholding a principle means digging deep into our pockets
- Support those determined to uphold the law in all its aspects
- If enough of us uphold this ideal, we cannot help but prevail
- In order to keep on upholding these ideals, we need

See also: **SUPPORT**

UPWARD
- Costs are always climbing upward
- In order to keep up with the upward trends, we need your help
- Our gaze is always fixed upward, on the very highest of ideals
- Each step is another step upward, toward a shining goal
- We've had to adjust out funding goals upward, I'm afraid

URGE
- I urge you to move with us into our next decade as a generous supporter of
- Listen when those inner feelings urge you on
- Let your heart urge you to act now
- We urge you to please use
- I cannot urge you strongly enough
- I urge you to consider purchasing one for yourself or for an attractive holiday gift
- On behalf of us all here, I urge you to make your gift as soon as possible
- That's why I'm writing – to urge you to look at the pamphlet I've enclosed
- That's why I urge you to take a moment right now, while you have my letter in front of you, to complete the enclosed form and

See also: **ASK, DEMAND, REQUEST**

URGENT
- These courageous people urgently need your help
- The situation is urgent
- As urgent as a house swiftly catching fire
- So urgent that it's literally a life and death matter
- Far too urgent to put off for one more minute
- This is our most urgent appeal yet

- Thank you for giving this urgent matter your immediate attention
- The need is urgent
- One look in their eyes tells you how urgent it is to
- Urgent needs require urgent remedies
- So many groups in need are urgently pounding on our door
- As urgent as a frantically beating heart
- This is our most urgent appeal yet
- Please help with this urgent need
- The need is urgent, the task immense
- That's why I'm including this urgent note

Urgent: critical, vital, essential, crucial, desperate, fundamental, important, frantic, imperative, compelling, exigent, grave, severe, high-priority, necessary, primary, indispensable, requisite, compulsory, pressing, clamoring
See also:: CRISIS, DESPERATE, HURRY, PRESSURE, SPEED

URGENCY

- This pressing urgency will not go away
- I only hope my letter can convey the urgency of our work to you
- Please respond to the urgency
- You can actually feel the urgency in your very bones
- The urgency is on their faces and in their voices
- From every side, coming at us with a terrible urgency
- In order to respond to the urgency of these demands
- The urgency is frightening
- With urgency piling upon urgency, they are quickly becoming overwhelmed
- I can't overemphasize the urgency here
- The urgency cries out all around us
- I cannot tell you the urgency with which we need

Urgency: dire necessity, exigency, matter of life and death, extremity, importance, needfulness
See also: EMERGENCY, NEED, RUSH, THREAT

US

- It's up to us, you and me, to free these
- So many more are coming to us for help
- Putting us at the very center of this raging controversy
- It's not an us-and-them scenario
- When you help one person in need, you help us all

See also: TOGETHER, PARTNER, UNITE, YOU

USE

- What better use for your money than to let it help
- There are so many uses for your input
- Sometimes people just sit down and say it's no use
- Every dollar you give has a vitally important use
- Now is the time to make use of your outrage about this issue

- With your help, we can make even better use of
- Everywhere, popular use of our sites is increasing
- Use would skyrocket if

USEFUL
- Mutually useful
- Everybody wants to be a useful and valued member of society
- At last, they feel useful again and they're so happy and grateful
- This has always been a very useful and effective argument in favor of extending their mandate
- The most useful arrangement has always been
- The most useful thing you could do is send an immediate donation

See also: PRACTICAL, VIABLE

UTILITY
- The utility of the items we provide is invaluable
- First and foremost, we look for utility
- You'll be impressed with the utility and versatility of all our newly revamped programs

UTMOST
- Always striving to do our utmost
- Let them do their utmost, we will not retreat
- There is no escape, even at the utmost ends of the earth
- Even our utmost efforts need your backing
- Tested to the utmost and still proved steadfast

VACANCY
- We plan to fill this vacancy quickly
- Such a vacancy can't be tolerated
- The team's departure has created a very noticeable vacancy on the scene
- Waiting for you to step into the vacancy
- We're counting on you to make sure this vacancy is rapidly filled
- We always have vacancies for people to help out regularly

VALUE
- Destroying the most basic and most universal human value
- To add extra value to your gift, you can
- A value you and I really care about
- If there's anything we need to value, it's this
- A value that you want to preserve
- Working to give young people a bedrock of positive values upon which to build better lives
- If you value human decency, please give your support to
- A smile is the best value for your dollar
- To teach the value of generosity

- It is impossible to calculate a comparable value
- Bring value beyond measure to their lives
- Focused on the rediscovery of such basic values as self-reliance and individual responsibility
- I'm more convinced than ever of the value of this program
- These values, which have always been the stable bedrock upon which our society was built, are now threatened by
- When I think back to the values my leader instilled in me
- The core values haven't changed over the years
- These values have always been at the heart of
- Still embodies the traditional values of

Value: worth, merit, utility, advantage, benefit, usefulness, gain, profit, avail, good, importance, consequence, significance, moment, weight, esteem
See also: BENEFIT, IMPORTANT, WORTH

VENTURE
- Venture boldly into this new field
- Join with us in this glorious new venture
- Getting up the courage to venture beyond the old accepted boundaries
- Venture with us into a region of yet undiscovered possibilities
- A very promising joint venture with
- Enthusiastically describing this latest venture
- To help fund collaborative ventures
- Committing funds to this exciting new venture over the next few years

VERSATILE
- Even the most versatile of programs would be challenged by such unexpected and unplanned for events
- An easy way to demonstrate our versatility is
- A choice so versatile it will cover every possible eventuality
- Taking full advantage of its versatility, we want to recommend

VIABLE
- It's more viable than you think
- The most viable way to do it is through your support
- Because of modern advances, we now have perfectly viable methods to ease the suffering
- In order to make this viable, we need your help
- I know you will want to endorse the most viable of these plans

VICTIM
- We can't rest while a single victim remains to be rescued from
- Victims of inhuman treatment
- No one expects to become a victim of such a disaster
- No two victims are alike
- The very innocence of these young victims would break your heart

- We are all potential victims of the unforseen
- Offering aid and comfort to the victims

See also: **PAIN, POVERTY, REFUGEE, SUFFER, TORMENT**

VICTORY
- Fight together to ensure our victory over
- This victory, though partial, is still significant
- Because of your gift you, too, share in this wonderful victory
- Victory is so close we can almost taste it
- Just imagine how satisfying this victory could be
- Holding victory in our very hands
- The opportunity to celebrate their personal victory
- Join now and help bring victories within our grasp
- Determined that victory shall be ours

See also: **OVERCOME, SOLUTION, SUCCEED, TRIUMPH, WIN**

VIGILANCE
- Endless vigilance means we can never afford to lose our focus
- The most vigilant people are those most deeply involved and closest to the events we are describing
- The best vigilance is the kind we all contribute to
- It takes a lot more than just vigilance to prevent
- Constant vigilance is the price we have to pay

VIEW
- A view endorsed enthusiastically by
- A donation is the best way to make your views known
- May we suggest a different point of view
- Your views must be heard loud and clear
- We want to show the views of people very close to the action
- And not just the view from the top of the mountain, remote from what is really going on

See also: **OUTLOOK, PERSPECTIVE, SEE, UNDERSTANDING**

VINDICATE
- The results certainly vindicate our long-term faith
- Your support has vindicated our firm belief in the rightness of this project
- Help those who have been waiting for years to vindicate themselves
- The best vindication is the happy, smiling faces of all those your gift has helped

VIOLATION
- More work must be done to fight violations
- Members could not stay silent about violations
- Which will address violations of
- So that, together, we can turn our attention to the terrible violations happening right now in

- In violation of everything civilized, these monsters are trying to bring about a total collapse of
- The worst violation is the violation of a person's very right to live
- Frighteningly, there is a growing trend toward open, blatant violations
- Helping people recover from this cruel violation of their deepest personal self
- Violation of human rights and contempt for the sanctity of human life is unacceptable and will not be tolerated

Violation: infringement, breach, infraction, offence, transgression, trespass, contravention, illegality, delinquency, misbehavior
See also: ABUSE, BREACH, INJUSTICE, OPPRESSION

VIOLENCE
- A stand against the violence that is eroding our rights
- Violence against women must be stopped immediately
- Weary people who only want an end to all the violence
- You want to do your bit to end the violence as soon as possible
- Help call a halt to a dizzying downward spiral of violence and grinding poverty
- They see violence daily
- Immersion in violence takes away its shock value, replacing it with a high degree of tolerance
- Help stop the soaring incidence of family violence
- Your input helps us get at the hidden causes underlying the hair-raising violence invading our streets

See also: ABUSE, ATTACK, BATTLE, HIT, HURT, TORTURE

VIRTUAL
- This isn't some ephemeral aspect of virtual reality
- The virtual truth is a good deal harsher
- Virtually speaking, we stand a very good chance of success

VISCERAL
- Respond on the most immediate and visceral level
- This issue cannot help but have a deep, visceral appeal
- The very sight of it gives a powerful visceral shock
- Visceral emotions provide the driving force
- Something with real visceral punch
- Wanting to solve this difficult visceral conflict
- Caught up in a tumult of visceral feeling

VISION
- By joining with us, you become part of this bright new vision
- Please help those with true vision to step forward
- Only through a totally new vision of the future will we find hope
- This new proposal embodies a clear vision and a strong purpose
- Bound to win the struggle between opposing visions
- Just as everyone has their own vision of how things should be, we know you have

yours
- Please share your vision of the future with us by
- Just a few cents can save the vision of a child or adult
- Imagine your own life without the vision we take for granted every day
- Developing a strong vision of where we're going
- The support of someone who will realize the vision with you
- To give something back for the great vision we have received
- A vision so compelling you can't help but want to know more
- Attention is focused on creating the vision
- A glorious vision of progress and success

See also: **DREAM, FUTURE, IMAGINATION, INSPIRATION, MISSION, PLAN, STRATEGY**

VISIONARY
- She is good-humored yet decisive, practical yet a visionary
- You too can be a visionary when you support this cause
- It is the visionaries who make the real changes for the better in society
- It's so exciting to be part of this pioneering, visionary process

VOCAL
- Show that more than a "vocal few" oppose this scheme
- Those who are most vocal get the most attention
- You and I can be very vocal too
- It's time to get vocal about this abuse
- Unfortunately, the most vocal elements draw the most attention

VOICE
- Raise your voice
- Provided a voice for considered loyal opinion to be heard
- And spread, with clarion voice, the case for
- Please add your voice to their defence
- Because of you, their voices are heard more and more
- Now a major voice of low-income people
- We can make our voices heard
- Our unique national voice
- Once clear strong voice rising above the babble
- It's time for a new voice on the national scene – your voice
- You can voice your concerns by supporting our organization
- Only by joining our voices together can we
- Voices are swelling louder every day
- Speak out in a strong voice for those too lost or ill to speak for themselves

VOLUNTARY
- Support us with a voluntary subscription gift
- The amount of voluntary support has been truly overwhelming
- All the help is voluntary and freely given

- We need voluntary funding this year to top up public funding
- Our voluntary income comes from a wide variety of sources

VOLUNTEER

- An outstanding volunteer of a different kind
- If you can spare just a few hours a week, consider becoming a volunteer
- And what a difference vigorous volunteer support can make
- Ask us for the address of the volunteer association nearest you
- Your gift, added to the thousands of volunteer hours, multiplies the impact tenfold
- Gratified that so many volunteered their time and talents to
- Seeing such tragedies turned me into a volunteer for
- We are an underfunded volunteer organization and desperately need money and volunteers
- As one of our most involved donors, I hope you will become a volunteer
- Brings a solid background of practical experience both professional and volunteer
- Once the need is known it is amazing how many people will volunteer
- If you would like the opportunity to work in any of these volunteer capacities, please call
- Offered by suitably qualified and experienced volunteers
- Our volunteer record is equally impressive
- Volunteering to help a housebound senior or helping with a community meal are just some of the ways to give.

Volunteer: put oneself at the disposal of, give, present, grant, bestow, need no invitation, step forward, offer, confer, unpaid worker, shoulder, by choice

VOLUNTEERS

- Seeing the amazing difference dedicated supporters and volunteers like you have already made
- I want to share with you some of the splendid work brave volunteers do each day
- Without our steadfast volunteers our program would collapse
- Volunteers have done all they can
- Loyal volunteers and honed professionals presenting a strong, united front in the effort to
- Courageous, highly-skilled volunteers stand ready to
- Volunteers with special skills are carefully nurtured
- The key to success is its network of volunteers or "cooperants"
- Skilled volunteers have devoted years of their lives to help families and communities solve urgent problems and grow stronger
- These caring volunteers are the backbone of our organization
- We started with a few willing volunteers
- All through the dedication of our financial supporters and our loyal volunteers.
- Springs from seeing the amazing difference dedicated volunteers and supporters like you have already made
- These unselfish, caring volunteers are the backbone of our organization

- We are always in need of volunteers to help with fundraising
- Volunteers provide vital support in the running of
- Volunteers participate in every aspect of our work
- Committed to the training and support of our volunteers
- We always need new volunteers to work as
- A list of volunteer positions has been posted
- We are issuing an urgent request for volunteers
- Thank you for so graciously volunteering
- Thanks for generously volunteering your time
- Volunteers will be on hand to

See also: **BENEFACTOR, CAREGIVER, FRIEND, PARTNER, SUPPORTER, WORKER**

VOLUNTEERISM
- Doing everything we can to promote volunteerism
- Volunteerism is the lifeblood of our network
- Volunteerism makes a community work

VULTURE
- Poverty and despair roosting like vultures in a tree
- They descend like vultures to exploit the poorest and weakest
- Vultures were already circling, ready to drop, as we drove into the first of the overcrowded refugee camps
- Sometimes it takes time to sort out those truly trying to help from the vultures there only to prey upon most vulnerable

See also: **ATTACK, EXPLOITATION, OPPRESSION, ROB**

WAIT
- Wait a minute
- Why wait
- Don't wait, join now
- We just can't wait any longer
- The waiting is the hardest part
- If we wait any longer, it will be too late
- Together, we can wait it out
- Waiting for you to help
- When waiting is nothing but a slow, endless agony
- When so many wait so eagerly, how can we possibly disappoint them
- They've been waiting for help all of their short lives
- Every morning they gather to wait for food and medicine that will get them through another day
- The waiting is the worst
- When you need help desperately, the wait can seem interminable
- But the average person still has to wait to get urgently needed care
- Let's not wait for the worst to happen
- But there are so many more still waiting for our help

- I can't wait to tell you about
- Why wait any longer to help out
- What are you waiting for
- Don't wait one moment longer
- Desperate people just can't wait on whims
- You've waited long enough

WAKE

- Wake up before it's too late
- We've got to wake up right now
- Naturally, we all want to wake up to a better world
- I'm afraid we've just received a very rude wake up call
- The sooner we wake up to this new reality, the better for us all
- The world has to wake up immediately
- Waking or sleeping, this problem is all I can think about
- We'll all have to wake up with a jolt

WALK

- First, we have to understand just what we are walking into
- Please take a little walk with me, so I can show you everything we've already accomplished
- Find the courage to walk straight ahead and never deviate from our purpose
- Now is the time walk our talk
- Like everyone else, they have to walk before they can run
- Sometimes they have been walking for days, just to get to our clinic

WALL

- We hope you'll help dismantle the wall of ignorance by continuing to help
- Demands are coming from every direction and our backs are really up against the wall
- Will no longer tolerate these walls between us
- We must do our best to tear this wall down
- Breaking down the wall between you and me
- Stop butting our heads against a stone wall and
- Frankly, we're up against a wall and we need your help

WANT

- To rescue those deeply sunk in want and misery
- I know you really want to get involved
- Everyone deserves freedom from want
- Not everyone can have what they want when they want it
- What they want and what they need do not always coincide
- No one wants to improve their lives more than these people
- Spirits being slowly ground down by want and loneliness

See also: **NEED, POVERTY**

WANTED

- Wanted: caring donors
- You are on our most wanted list
- Helping everyone we wanted to help

WAR

- War and armed conflicts that have destroyed their countries
- Get ready for the war to heat up between
- Make peace between the warring parties immediately
- Our war is upon poverty, disease and ignorance
- Now we must march together, as to a noble war
- There's more than one war going on
- There's a war going on here
- Sufficient to put an end to this deadly and invisible war

See also: ATTACK, BATTLE, FIGHT, STRUGGLE

WARNING

- We've had fair warning of the rough times ahead
- Storm warnings are going up everywhere
- It is a warning we must heed
- We've been sending up warning signals as fast as we can
- The quickest way to send up warning flags
- Sending out a clear warning about
- It is not difficult to understand this warning signal
- Warning – something wild is happening
- These are the warning signs of
- We ignore these warnings at our peril
- Warning signs that should send us immediately to
- Warning signs that may save your life or the life of someone you love
- Please familiarize yourself with the warning signs listed

See also: ALARM, FRIGHTEN, THREAT

WASTE

- The most appalling waste
- Caring is never a waste of time
- Stop the waste now
- This mustn't be a wasted opportunity
- Nothing is sadder than a precious life needlessly wasted
- We can't let them lay waste to such good plans

WATCH

- At home, we also keep watch
- Watch out for hugs and kisses
- I know you couldn't just stand by and watch this happen
- Keeping anxious watch by the side of a sick loved one
- We don't want things to fall apart on our watch

- Please help us watch over them lovingly
- We're watching very closely

WATER
- Already been to three water holes and all are dry
- Remembered her children's voices pleading for a drink of water
- The nearest water is twenty miles on foot
- All they dream of is cool, sweet water to drink
- A simple drink of water can become far more precious than gold
- A great idea can still be watered down and gutted
- Safe clean water is the most precious gift you can give
- Even the water contains a deadly mixture of disease
- Enough clean water to meet the needs of many families
- Imagine what safe clean water means to this community

WAY
- In order to do this in any meaningful way, we must
- You helped her in a way no one ever has before
- Could achieve so much, if only someone would show them the way
- We still have such a long way to go
- If you would like to help us in this way
- It's a long way back after such severe illness
- And it's a terrific way for people like you to keep making all the difference
- But we can point the way
- Choose the way of peach and cooperation
- They keep telling us it's the only way to
- We need your help to keep them that way
- We've come a long way, but there's much, much more to do
- Another small way to help even more
- We must not let them get their way
- I can think of no more enjoyable way to
- Other ways you can help
- Dozens of ways to strengthen your
- This is one of the most helpful ways for us to build support

Way: method, manner, mode, fashion, process, procedure, system, wise, technique, means, rule, direction, route, path, road, channel, access
See also: DIRECTION, MEANS, METHOD, PLAN, STRATEGY, TECHNIQUE

WAYSIDE
- They were almost left by the wayside
- Standing by the wayside, offering the kindest of help
- To function as a sort of wayside help station

WEIGH
- These thoughts weigh upon us so heavily

- Seriously weigh the alternatives
- With your donation, you weigh in on our side

WEIGHT
- Weighted down with such cumbersome concerns
- Hardly able to bear up under the weight of so many worries
- The sheer weight of this argument must soon swing opinion around to our side
- A letter from you carries a lot of weight

WELCOME
- I want to welcome you to
- Every contribution is warmly welcome
- A great way to put out the welcome mat
- Your gift will be so very welcome
- So please make a special effort to welcome these new members
- A place where everyone is welcomed no matter what their
- I look forward to saying, "Welcome aboard!"

WELFARE
- The welfare of everyone must be our first concern
- The quickest way to get people off welfare is to provide them with help of a much more substantial kind
- Help us look out for the welfare of
- Utterly devoted to the welfare of our community
- The welfare of the weakest is an ongoing worry
- Always putting the welfare of others first

WHIRLWIND
- If we don't act now, we'll reap a whirlwind later
- In a whirlwind of activity
- Innocents caught up in a terrible whirlwind of war and famine
- All the old known patterns just carried away by the whirlwind

WHISPER
- The merest whisper of change can cause a great deal of anxiety here
- A way to whisper their needs into your ear
- Whispers and rumors stir up an already agitated population
- There's never even been a whisper of corruption associated with

WHO
- Who do you know who needs this kind of help
- No matter who you are or where you live, there's always time for
- Here's who we are
- This is when you find out who your friends are
- You find out who you really are inside
- Who would have guessed that helping others could be so much fun

- Now is the time to stand up and take a measure of who we really are

WHY
- We don't know why
- That's why I'm writing to you today
- There really is no answer to why some people must suffer so much
- They don't ask why, they just pitch in and help
- In case you're wondering why I'm asking this way
- It soon became apparent why
- What do you say when a suffering child asks why
- But I can't tell you why we keep going back

WILL
- Consider leaving a gift to our organization in your will
- Remember us in your will with a bequest
- Please send me information about including you in my will
- Together, we have the will to win
- The saddest thing is when people lose their will to go on
- The best will in the world is no good without money to help

WILLING
- Now, more than ever, we need people willing to help
- It all comes down to whether people like you and me are willing to dig into our pocketbooks
- Be a willing donor
- More willing than ever to give
- Our willing helpers work long hours just for the satisfaction of

WIN
- There would be no win for either side without
- Everybody wins big
- Never have I seen anyone so determined to win against such odds
- The more you give, the more you win
- Make it a win-win proposition
- The odds against winning are great
- What does it take to win you over
- Determined to win here too
- Able to deal everyone a winning hand

Win: persuade, convert, conquer, gain, achieve, sweep, triumph, vanquish, overcome, overpower, take by storm, earn, prevail upon, mastery, success, reclaim, recover, advance, gain, gain ground, make headway

WIND
- There's plenty of changes in the wind already
- The winds of change are sweeping violently through
- Cold, lonely and hunched against the wind

- When the winter winds are howling, think of the homeless
- The winds of revolution can sweep everything away

WING
- Watch great ideas hatch and take wing
- You can almost see the happiness mounting up on shining wings
- All they want to do is spread their wings
- Without you, they could never spread their wings, never discover what they could really do

WINNER
- We're all winners when we help
- Back a winner every time
- Join the winners
- Help make every one a winner
- Walk straight into the winner's circle
- I knew you were a winner all along
- With dignity, everyone is a winner
- And you become a winner too
- Help turn a forgotten child into a real winner

WINTER
- Without our center, it will be a cold, dark winter for many people
- A heart locked in eternal winter
- You have warm winter clothes and plenty to eat while many others have none of these things
- With winter fast approaching we need extra money to prepare
- The icy clutch of winter grips hungry children the hardest
- The hardships of winter can freeze the very soul
- Winter so often brings only bitter want to our city's poor
- The winter is the hardest, with hungry, shivering people at our doors

WISDOM
- I know you will see the wisdom of this immediately
- Centuries of accumulated wisdom and experience are crumbling away
- Historically, when anyone wanted to share the wisdom of any of these individuals, it was necessary to
- Real wisdom resides in the heart of a people
- No one would question the wisdom of this action
- A case of too many facts and not enough wisdom
- The kind of wisdom that wells, unasked, from the heart

See also: **ADVICE, INFORMATION, KNOWLEDGE, SENIOR**

WISE
- If we are wise, we will start solving this problem at once
- Giving is a always a very wise thing to do

- A word to the wise – I mean you
- Sometimes the wisest of decisions doesn't produce the results we so confidently expect
- You are certainly wise enough to see
- A wise society takes care of its needy and its sick
- You always strive to be wiser and better informed

WISH
- If I had a single wish, it would be to help
- But we know wishing isn't enough
- It's heart-rending to see them wishing so very hard for what all the rest of us take for granted
- Wishing harder won't make it happen
- All our good wishes go with you
- If only you could see how hard they wish for a normal life
- Their wishes are so simple and so modest
- I know you wish for this just as much as I do
- Feel the joy of making this heartfelt wish come true
- Here's what's at the very top of our wish list
- Good wishes don't pay our bills
- Best wishes for happiness, heath and prosperity
- Warmest wishes for a bountiful, joy-filled season
- Wishing you peace, prosperity and good health
- Wishing you a world of peace
- Wishing you and your family a joyous holiday season
- Wishing you an abundance of love and joy

See also: BLESSING, BENEFIT, WANT

WITNESS
- Our workers are the ones who witness what it is really like
- Strongly bearing witness to the truth of the matter
- No one could witness such a thing without deep effect
- We shudder at the very thought of what these people must have witnessed

WITHOUT
- Without your help, I don't know what we would have done
- So that no one will have to go without
- We can't sit by while people go without the barest necessities
- It goes without saying that we really need your support
- Without you, we won't get very far
- Cannot do this without you

WOMEN
- A woman who has won more than a few struggles herself
- Every woman should be able to live her life safe and protected
- Help win for women a new respect and power in the world

- Battered women flee to us for refuge
- Help growing up into an independent, confident young woman
- Providing women with the resources and education to fight for equality
- If we get help to the women, the rest takes care of itself
- Our program focuses on women since women are most often denied education
- Working to help women gain access to land, credit and training
- Women in developing countries deserve the right to choose
- Poverty and overpopulation are directly related to the status of women in a society
- The risk is greatest for older women who live alone – almost half of them live in poverty
- As always, it is the hard work of the women that makes progress happen
- The women fight like lions for the well-being of their children
- We will launch an action on the human rights of women
- The central role of women in development is recognized
- Women make decisions and create positive change
- Recognizing that women's economic status is central to healthy local development
- First and foremost we must support the women for they are the very heart and life-source of any society
- So many women who commit murder do so in self defense
- Domestic violence against women exists in all countries and cultures around the world
- All it took was the women's determined effort to solve problems together
- The central role of women in development is recognized
- Women make decisions and create positive change
- Recognizing that women's economic status is central to healthy local development
- See what women can accomplish when you give them the tools

WONDER
- Did you ever wonder what we do with your gift
- You may be wondering whether
- It's really a wonder what can be accomplished in a hurry
- I wonder what would have happened to them without our help
- You're probably wondering why
- Perhaps you've always wondered about
- You are probably wondering how we get
- Working together can work wonders

See also: AMAZE, MIRACLE, QUESTION, SURPRISE

WORD
- Have been energetically spreading the word about
- To many, the printed word is simply inaccessible
- Perhaps there is no one to whom these words have more meaning than to someone who is

- Helping us to get the word out in a hurry
- As you read these words, please try to understand how deeply heartfelt they are
- Words are all I have to tell you how great the need is
- She was so overcome with emotion that she could not get words out to thank us
- These were the words that kept going through my mind last night as I wrestled with the problem
- I'm groping for the words to tell you this tragic story
- As conveyed by most remarkable words and images
- We hope you'll be moved by these words of compassion
- Words can't express how much it means to me
- Words cannot do justice in this case
- Her few halting words clutched at my heart
- No words can express how much your help means to everyone here
- What a wealth of meaning there in those few simple words
- To me, those words will never grow old or trite
- Word of mouth referrals
- At a loss for words to describe

See also: ADVERTISE, INFORMATION, MESSAGE

WORK

- The satisfaction of continuing the good work
- Necessary front line work
- Working so tirelessly to fix that which is broken
- I hope you will be as generous as you can because we have a lot of work to do
- To help people work through their difficulties one by one
- More of your dollars go into doing the work for which you support us
- But our life-saving work can only continue if caring, unselfish people are willing to play just a small, yet important, role in stopping
- Done all our work in a moderate, sensible way
- We work to secure their
- Your help today ensures we can continue our work at current levels tomorrow
- But all this work costs money
- Yet hard work and popularity alone cannot pay for
- Such worthwhile work
- However, our work goes well beyond this
- To continue our work, I'm asking you now for your help
- As you can see, hard work by all concerned has restored the
- The good and loyal work which you do on our behalf
- This makes it easy for you to see and appreciate the value of this work which is funded by many generous supporters
- We need you to work on committees, programs and special events
- The work is done by the people of the country receiving assistance
- Front line work is desperately important right now
- Behind-the-scenes work
- After twenty years of working here, we need your help more than ever
- We want to continue our work

- Worked hard for our success
- Continue our unique work
- Work with hundreds of groups and thousands of individuals on a regular basis
- Direct the work of our staff and volunteers
- Works for today so that fewer children, single mothers, and others will be forced to lead a life of poverty
- We depend upon your support to continue the work we share
- Yet hard work alone won't pay for the rich variety of
- It's not unusual to receive hearty bravos for our work
- You may not know about all the good work we do
- Doing the work of three
- Will it work
- Of course it will work
- Work hand-in-hand with these courageous people
- You should see how they give themselves to the work wholeheartedly
- They're not afraid of hard work, only that there won't be enough money to carry through
- We want to share the work and share the burden
- Help us get on with this crucial work
- The work is very fulfilling.
- I know how hard you've worked in your own local
- I'm inviting you to help us continue this crucial work
- We need your help for this important work
- Without donors like you we could not carry out our important human rights work around the world
- Confirms that our work is necessary and worthwhile
- Help us continue this important work
- In brief, your help is vital to our work
- Work brutal hours following up each hopeful lead
- When others have done all they can, work here is just beginning
- Future work must address the people's issues
- We work hard on your behalf
- If you could only see the back-breaking work loads our people carry
- It really works
- They finally see there is a way to make their lives work
- Well done and keep up the good work
- Nothing worked out until
- Please fill in the enclosed form and join us in our work
- But with even hard work
- Please don't leave this important work up to someone else
- Time to roll up our sleeves and begin the actual work
- To continue our work, we need your help – urgently
- You need the benefits of this pivotal work
- Believe me, no one has worked harder to make this dream come true

Work: labor, toil, exertion, effort, endeavor, sweat, deed, performance, function, act, enterprise, undertaking, occupation, industry, business, trouble, pains, spare no effort,

bring about, effect, attain, exercise, cultivate
See also: **EFFORT, ENTERPRISE, JOB, LABOR, STRUGGLE**

WORKERS
- The people the front line workers turn to
- Our workers in the field depend on us for ongoing support
- It takes a lot of courage to do some of the things our workers must do
- If only our workers had as much money as they have dedication

See also: **SUPPORTERS**

WORKHORSE
- Has turned out to be a workhorse that never quits
- This reliable workhorse of a program is responsible for
- More than just a plodding, dependable workhorse

WORKING
- You're working beside us
- We're working beside you every step of the way
- It means so much to know you're working beside us
- With your help, we're working hard to find out
- Working with you to get the best possible results
- Clear evidence that our plan is really working
- Working shoulder to shoulder, we can accomplish miracles
- A cause worth working for
- We're working as hard as we can to get donations
- Already working hard to ensure as many children as possible are given the opportunity of
- How we've developed better working knowledge of this situation than anyone
- Doing what seems to be working best for
- Working day in and day out to
- Working effectively at all levels within the organization
- Mothers and fathers working alongside us

WORLD
- In the neediest regions of the world
- Unless the world says, "No"
- In an ever-changing world
- That was when their whole world shattered around them
- They're the envy of the world, a source of pride to all
- Then the world you and I live in would be a lot different, wouldn't it
- We once led the world in the field of
- We don't have to be worlds apart
- Every day the world is getting smaller
- Stop the world, I want to get off
- Here is one way to change the world into a better place
- With us, you'll explore the fascinating world of the

- You can make their world a much less painful place
- Opening a new and vitally important world of
- It was like entering a whole new world
- Like to tell how the world kids are going to inherit is being destroyed
- More than ever before, our world needs us
- To provide all the people of the world with a decent life
- A rare peek into the world of
- Like holding a whole new world in your hands
- Offering the world as it could be, fresh and reborn
- A world away, we go about our business with quiet determination
- Don't take their whole world away
- Trying to cling to a world that no longer exists
- Whose world is it anyway
- A common worldwide phenomenon
- If you are really concerned about the way the world is going
- Step into an extraordinary world of living and learning and serving
- Making sure the world doesn't change faster than we do
- Give a gift that will make a difference round the world
- Constantly being set loose upon the world
- It's a wicked world, you are thinking
- A world gone crazy
- A world changing before our very eyes
- Success in making a brighter, kinder world
- A world transformed by you
- People like you make the world a better place to live
- It's a world apart

See also: EARTH, GLOBAL, INTERNATIONAL, PLANET

WORRY

- I know you're worried about what's happening to
- Worried about how to
- Faces furrowed with constant worry, backs bent from care
- Was at the end of her rope from worrying
- So very worried about
- When you look into the faces of mothers worried about their little ones
- I want to share some very big worries with you
- I know that you're worried about what's happening to
- The worry about how they'll be taken care of never ends until you die
- The last thing they need to worry about is basic necessities
- Hours in hospital waiting rooms, racked with worry

See also: ANXIETY, FEAR, STRESS

WORSE

- Conditions just couldn't be any worse
- And there's worse
- I've never seen anything worse than this

- The wrong choices could make the situation much worse
- Things quickly go from bad to worse
- And even worse scenario is
- For better or worse, we're all in this together
- Things are now worse than ever
- Without your help now things are just going to get worse

WORSEN

- Conditions began to worsen immediately
- The more prospects worsen, the more I'm asking you to help
- Without immediate aid, things could worsen very fast

Worsen: deteriorate, degenerate, decline, sink, turn for the worse, slip, slide, go downhill, go to pieces/pot/seed, go to the dogs, hit the skids, crumble, disintegrate, break up, fall apart, erode, exacerbate, aggravate

WORST

- And this isn't even the worst of it
- Nor have we seen the worst, I'm afraid
- And we're truly afraid that the worst is yet to come
- The worst abuses must be cleaned up first
- With your help, we can improve even the worst of circumstances
- We are faced with the worst case scenario right now
- Just when we expected the worst, you came to our rescue

WORTHWHILE

- Seeing him open up again makes it all worthwhile
- One of the most worthwhile things you'll ever do
- Supporting a truly worthwhile pursuit
- In order to make all these efforts truly worthwhile
- The most worthwhile thing you can do is help
- Raising critical funds to support out worthwhile work
- You've done something very worthwhile

See also: USEFUL, VALUE

WORTH

- What would it be worth to help them improve
- The long struggle is more than worth it
- Your participation adds worth
- Only time will give us the true worth of what we've accomplished together here
- These children are really worth the effort

WORTHY

- What matters most is that you feel we are worthy of your generous support
- You won't find people worthier than this
- We hope you add us to your list of worthy causes
- A time when worthy citizens band together to support others

- No one is more worthy of your help and support than these hardworking people

WOUND
- Never to have their wounds cared for before it is too late
- An invisible but never-healing wound
- I'm asking you to understand what a crippling wound poverty creates
- Here's how you can help heal these cruel wounds
- A failure here will deeply wound a significant part of society
- About stopping behavior that opens up old wounds

See also: **ABUSE, CUT, HURT, PAIN**

WRINKLE
- And we're getting ready to add a new wrinkle
- We've worked very hard at getting the wrinkles out
- Now we have to deal with a nasty new wrinkle
- It always takes a while to get the wrinkles out of a new program

WRITE
- That's why I'm writing you today
- As I sat down to write to you
- How difficult it is to put such thoughts into writing
- Today, I am writing on behalf of
- Please understand I'm not asking you for something frivolous
- That's why I'm writing to ask you to support
- Please write soon
- Asking you to write and tell them you want a change

Write: correspond, communicate, jot a line/note, draft, draw up, scribble, jot down, pen, dash off, let know, compose, drop a line

WRONG
- Very soon, we noticed that something was wrong
- We can't get it wrong again
- It is very wrong to look away when there is so much suffering
- Correcting a wrong-headed decision immediately
- These people have been deeply, cruelly wronged
- To right an ancient wrong is very satisfying
- They've been involved in just about everything you can do wrong in this world
- To help when everything seems to be going wrong
- Doing nothing is absolutely the wrong thing to do
- Wrong in principle, devastating in practice

See also: **CONFUSED, MISCONCEPTION, MISGUIDED, MISUNDERSTAND**

YEAR
- This has been such a momentous year for
- Remember, this is a very crucial year for

- In less than one year, we have been able to
- But first, let me tell you a little bit about last year and the year ahead
- Last year was an unusually difficult year for us
- Last year alone
- Year after year, hope has been dwindling
- Many more years ago than I care to admit
- Finally earned some calm for her sunset years
- During her incredible years of working with
- Thousands who are not looking forward to a happy year
- Now entering its fiftieth successful year
- We've been helping people for years
- Seeing life differently as each year evolves
- We have not seen its like in years
- May this be the best year yet
- Wishing you all the best this coming year

YEARNING
- Underneath it all, there's a powerful yearning for
- The strongest yearning of all is for
- Just to see the yearning in their eyes would move the hardest heart
- The yearning for love and security is only natural

YES
- The simple answer is yes
- Please say yes
- Say yes to caring, yes to love
- Yes, I'm asking you to help out once again
- Yes, the problem is big; yes, the solution lies in your hands
- Yes, I want to help
- We need you more than ever to say yes, it's about time I did something

See also: **AFFIRMATIVE, AGREE, POSITIVE**

YESTERDAY
- We can't use yesterday's solutions for today's problems
- We needed it done and we needed it done yesterday
- Yesterday's mistakes are haunting us now
- Don't let them become yesterday's news
- Constantly learning from yesterday's mistakes and today's successes
- So urgent, we needed to start this project yesterday
- As close as yesterday, the situation was desperate

YIELD
- There's no way we're going to yield on this crucial point
- Yields of joy and satisfaction have multiplied far beyond what any of us put in
- Must not yield to the temptation to give up
- We must find out why harvest yields are dropping so drastically

- Only relentless research will yield up an answer

YOU
- We need you
- You are very special to us
- You are very special to those you help
- You're different, though
- You're one in a million
- You really do make a difference
- So now it's up to you
- That's how you can help
- That's for you to choose
- You keep everything going
- Like you, I too
- What we can do depends on you
- That's where our organization and you come in
- So now it's all up to you
- We're counting on you
- There is only so much we can do; the rest is up to you
- I know you will do what you can to help
- You're there when there's no one else
- If it weren't for people like you
- The collective message is, "If I can do this, so can you"
- It's all up to you now
- Where would we be without you
- You are a vital part of this organization
- You'll love to be what we've become
- We know you will judge for yourself
- If not you, who
- All you have to do is

YOUNG
- Those young people should fill our hearts with gladness
- Benefits thousands of young people every year
- Precious young people whose lives are being destroyed by drugs and gangs
- Let's not forget what it's like to be young
- While our organization is still very young, it's growing at a tremendous rate
- It's not much fun to be young if you have to live in such frightening conditions
- Reach young people out of control
- Help young people in those areas where they need support so much
- Young people today, perhaps even more than when I was young, need such values to succeed
- You know as well as anybody the problems our young people face
- Burdens far too great for a young person to carry
- It is to the young we owe the most
- Young people drawn into lives of petty crime or prostitution

- There are thousands of young people like him waiting for the right treatment
- Watching over and guiding young people as they approach maturity
- It's the young who will inherit our mistakes if we don't soon act
- Makes you feel young again
- You and I know it's tough to be young today
- Big problems overwhelm young minds
- Why do young people come from far and near to
- Like the idea of living, working and making friends with other young people of their own age
- Several services to help young people with
- So that we can save even more young lives
- Help for troubled and abused young people

Young: adolescent, teenaged, pubescent, underage, minor, juvenile, unfledged, callow, childish, puerile, inexperienced, green, wet behind the ears, unsophisticated, naive, innocent, immature

YOUNGSTER

- Reach out to the youngest, poorest, most threatened youngsters
- Maybe you can send $ __ or more to help even more youngsters grow up to be responsible adults
- Enormous satisfaction in seeing the youngsters grow
- Because we teach youngsters responsibility and to be good citizens

See also: CHILDREN, KIDS, LITTLE ONES, FAMILY

YOUTH

- In the very blossom of youth
- The most vulnerable of our youth in danger of going astray
- The first priority is to put more money into youth programs
- To train youth up in the straight and virtuous path
- A youth-oriented program is absolutely essential
- Youth is such a fearful, joyful time of life
- If we catch them in their youth, before it's too late, we can really change lives
- When youth gets into trouble we must all take some of the responsibility
- Help put joy and hope back into the faces of our youth

Section Two

Contests
and
Sweepstakes

ACTION

- Get in on the action
- Do it for the action
- It's all action here
- The most action for the least money
- Maybe more action than you can handle
- Nothing but action, action, action

ADVANTAGE

- Take advantage of unbeatable odds
- The advantage is all yours
- Treat yourself to a winning advantage

ADVENTURE

- Join in the adventure
- Try out the adventure of winning
- Every ticket is an adventure in the making

BIG

- You could be the next one to hit it big
- The bigger the numbers, the bigger your chances
- This could be the start of something big
- Get ready to be one of the big winners

BINGO

- Bingo, you've won
- The small weekly bingo games have been the backbone of our funding
- Through humble bingo nights we've accomplished all this

BUBBLE

- Someday this easy-money bubble might burst
- Hope of the big win continually bubbling
- Always chasing the elusive bubble of hope

BUY

- When you buy a ticket, you're doing much more than just indulging yourself
- Buying a ticket is one of the simplest ways you can provide support
- Find out why millions of people are buying tickets
- You know why you buy our tickets
- You're not just buying a lottery ticket, you're investing in very precious young life
- Here's who you're helping when you buy a ticket
- You're really buying a chance for people in need
- The more chances you buy, the more people you're helping
- Avoid disappointment, buy your ticket now
- The more tickets you buy, the better your odds

- Every time you buy a ticket, you're helping
- Buy your ticket today
- Buy a ticket and buy some time for someone at risk
- With every ticket you buy, the odds get lower
- When you buy a ticket, everybody wins

CALL
- You must call now to order your ticket in time
- Hear the call of the action
- Calling everyone to join in the fun

CARNIVAL
- A carnival of chance and fun
- Ticket-selling is turning into a regular carnival
- Join in the joyous carnival atmosphere

CASH
- The cash doesn't end here
- More cash prizes to be won
- Of course, the cash keeps on going
- Largest ever cash prizes
- Mountains of cash to spend any way you like
- You'll be awash in cash
- All this lovely cash can be yours
- More than a thousand cash prizes to be won

CASINO
- Casino competition for the gaming dollar
- Come to the casino, help the less fortunate
- Our biggest casino ever

CAUSE
- It's a good thing for a good cause
- Buy a ticket for a truly worthy cause
- A really fun way to help the cause
- Take a chance for a wonderful cause

CHANCE
- Your chances of winning are excellent
- Take a chance, help someone
- Chances are pretty good
- Every time you take a chance, the children's chances get better
- Take a chance on a scrapper
- Take a chance to give someone a chance
- Take a chance, give a chance to a kid who's a fighter
- Nobody gives you a better chance to
- Have you ever seen chances like these

- Now, your best chance ever
- There nothing chancy about the help you'll be giving to
- Getting and giving a fair chance at
- Yet another way to increase your chances
- Your best chance to win because we can't leave helping others to chance
- Take a chance on a real winner
- Take a chance now – and offer others a second chance at life
- We're asking you to take a big chance for us
- This could be the biggest chance you'll ever take
- Not only will you be getting a great chance to win, you'll also be supporting

CHOICE
- The most comprehensive choice of tickets
- Choose the number one choice of millions
- Your choice, benefits all round
- Your best choice in lottery tickets
- You could be making the winning choice right now

COMPASSION
- This lottery is motivated by compassion and a desire to change things for the better
- A game with compassion at its heart
- Buy a ticket because compassion moves you

COMPETITIVE
- There has always been a strong competitive element here
- A productive way to gratify your competitive urges
- We offer by far the most competitive odds

CONGRATULATIONS
- Congratulations, you may have just won
- Congratulations in advance
- Big, big congratulations could be in order
- Congratulations on reaching the top prize level
- Congratulations will come flooding in from every direction

DAY
- This could be your lucky day
- Don't let another day past without playing
- This could be the day you win big
- Don't let another day pass without getting your ticket

DELIVER
- Delivering more fun, more action, more help value for your dollar
- We deliver more bang for your buck
- Deliver help to the needy through your lottery ticket

DOLLAR

- Imagine winning all those tax-free dollars
- You could be awash in dollars
- The best dollar you ever spent
- Just look what one dollar can do

DRAW

- Richest draw ever
- Spectacular daily and weekly draws
- Every winning entry goes right back into the draw
- Draw gives you a chance to win again and again
- All valid tickets are eligible for all draws
- The draw order will be
- Our biggest draw yet
- So very easy to enter the whole family in this draw
- Every draw is our biggest
- Don't miss this draw
- Make sure you are entered in the draw
- Drawing more and more participants every day
- Feel the excitement mount as the draw date approaches
- And that's just one of the fabulous draws we are able to offer during this campaign

DREAM

- You could make your dreams become reality
- Fulfil a dream
- Now – all you've ever wanted or dreamed of
- Do you dream of making it big
- Back up your dreams by buying a ticket
- Fulfil a dream today
- Take a chance on a really big dream
- We could make your dreams become a reality
- An unforgettable dream coming true
- Ways to make your dream of winning come true

DRIVE

- Our biggest ticket drive ever is about to start
- You have a drive to win
- Let your wish to help drive your ticket choice
- Participate in our latest drive by playing the game to win

DRUM

- The entry is then returned to the drum
- That's your ticket, your chance to win spinning round in the drum
- As the drum spins, feel that rush of excitement
- Wait until your heart starts drumming with excitement

EASY

- It's so easy to help this way
- The easy way to participate
- Let's not take the easy way out this time
- It's easy, it's fun, it's delightful
- We've made it very easy to buy a ticket

EDGE

- The thrill of living on the edge
- Give yourself that winning edge
- You're always right on the edge of winning

ELIGIBLE

- Here is your eligibility confirmation
- You may be eligible to win big
- You ticket makes you eligible for the grand prize

ENJOY

- Something the whole family can enjoy
- Something that can be enjoyed by everyone
- Enjoy the thrill of winning and the thrill of helping

ENTER

- Enter today to win your choice of prizes
- We can't urge you enough to enter soon
- Make sure you enter in time
- Do not hesitate to enter

ENTRY

- Every winning entry goes right back into the draw for a chance to win again
- As soon as your entry is selected as a winner
- Act now, make your entry a winner
- Your entry is automatically activated when
- Yours could be the winning entry

EXCITEMENT

- Taste the excitement
- Do it for the excitement and the people you'll help
- Come alive to the excitement
- Everyone is getting involved in the excitement

EXPERIENCE

- Once you experience the thrill you'll be back for more
- Treat yourself to a new experience
- The best experience ever
- We want you to experience the excitement directly

FANTASY
- Fulfil a personal fantasy
- Create your wildest fantasy
- A fantasy that could actually come true for you

FEVER
- Catch the fever
- Feeling the fever to buy and to win
- Lottery fever is sweeping the country

FIRST
- Now you can get there first
- Now you can be first when it comes to winning chances
- Be first in line to win
- If it's your first time playing, you are in for a great surprise

FORTUNE
- Worth a fortune to you, worth a fortune to those you help
- A way to make your fortune – instantly
- A fortune in winnings is waiting just for you

FUN
- Join in the fun
- This game is the most fun of all
- How much fun can a person stand
- The most fun way to help the cause

FUNDRAISING
- Is gaming true fundraising
- Working to expand the philanthropic side of fundraising through the proceeds from our lottery
- Buy a ticket to support our fundraising drive

GAMBLE
- Does gambling give people the hope of being rich
- Gambling can be very exciting
- For those who think gambling is a waste of money
- Dealing with the possibility of gambling being addictive
- What are the positive aspects of gambling

GAME
- It's so much more than a game to us
- Play the game for fun, give serious help to
- The trend is to increasingly interactive games
- Games requiring a greater reliance on technology are inevitable
- Game modifications must be carefully researched
- The hottest game in town

- The game's the thing
- Join in a game that helps so many
- Get in on the best game in town
- A friendly game for a very serious purpose
- Now everyone can join the game
- No better way to play the game

GAMING

- Join in a variety of gaming activities
- The growth in gaming has been phenomenal
- Spending an increasing percentage of income on gaming
- Predicting that legal gaming will grow
- Gaming now provides a significant amount of money to our charity
- The problem of illegal gaming must be addressed
- Gaming activities have little to do with real philanthropy
- Must accept that legalized gaming is here to stay
- Ensure that the gaming always contributes to the public good

GENERATE

- Generating millions to fund programs
- Your ticket helps generate the funds we so desperately need
- A wonderfully fun way to generate much-needed money

GOAL

- If your goal is winning big, come see us
- Achieve your goals and our goals all at once
- The prize is big enough to fulfil all your goals at once

HEARD

- It's time you heard about the action
- Have you heard
- The best way to help you've heard about

HIGH

- You too could be riding high
- The jackpot just mounts higher and higher
- Set your sights on a really high prize

IDEA

- Try out an entirely new idea
- A whole new idea in lottery advances
- A fresh idea, a fresh way of winning

IMAGINE

- Imagine what you could do with a prize this big
- Imagine receiving such a fabulous sum
- Imagine the fun of deciding on your choice

- Imagine the look on their faces when you win
- No limits to what you can imagine doing with the prize

INDULGE
- Indulge in luxuries you never thought possible before
- Indulge yourself, buy a chance to win
- You're not just indulging yourself, you're helping a very good cause

INTEREST
- Something for everyone and every interest
- I bet we've got you interested now
- If you're interested in helping everyone win big
- Just to pique your interest, take a look at this prize

INVOLVE
- A really fun way to get involved
- Buy your ticket and get involved in helping
- Now you can really enjoy getting involved in bettering
- We want you to be involved

JACKPOT
- Hit the jackpot today
- Just look at the jackpot waiting for you
- You have a chance at more than one jackpot
- The biggest, best jackpot yet
- We've been pumping up the jackpot
- Is the jackpot bigger than your dreams yet

LIBERATE
- Liberate yourself
- Just the thought of winning can be very liberating
- With just one ticket, you could liberate all this money for yourself

LIFE
- You could be set for life
- Your whole life could be changed in an instant
- Are you ready for the good life
- Imagine living a totally different life

LOSE
- You just can't lose
- Take us up on this can't-lose offering
- Please don't risk losing out
- If you don't participate, the children lose out

LOTTERY
- A mega lottery to raise mega funds

- A truly big-ticket lottery
- Lotteries are a hot new trend
- Odds in this lottery are phenomenal
- Vast numbers of people bought lottery tickets last year
- Develop a lottery that enjoys superior participation rates
- Lotteries are not a lifeline
- The first in town to try this kind of lottery
- Largest lottery ever
- No other lottery does so much for so many in need
- Biggest lottery ever of its kind
- This lottery is one of the ways we hope to meet our funding needs
- Proud to announce the biggest ever cash lottery

LUCK

- Let this be your lucky day
- Try your luck
- Help your luck, let your luck help others
- Luck will be a lady for you
- Your luck gets better every time you participate
- Luck is booming everywhere
- Your good luck is their good luck too

LUCKY

- Be one of the lucky few who
- Do you feel lucky today
- I know you're feeling lucky right now
- Today could be your lucky day
- Lucky you spotted our offer
- The lucky ones are the children your ticket purchase helps

LUXURY

- Indulge in luxuries you never imagined possible
- You could be living life in the lap of luxury
- This ticket is not just a luxury

MILLIONAIRE

- As a potential millionaire
- Designed to make you feel like a millionaire
- This could make you a millionaire
- Imagine would it would feel like to suddenly become a millionaire

NEED

- Tailored to everybody's needs
- Your need to take a chance on luck
- Fill your need for fun, their need for help
- We need to sell a lot of tickets just to raise enough funds

NEW

- An entirely new line of lottery tickets
- All new, all terrific
- Are you ready for a new level of excitement
- New prizes every day

NOTICE

- No wonder so many are sitting up and taking notice
- This is one lottery you're going to notice
- Notice how owning a ticket makes people smile

NUMBER

- Is your lucky number coming up
- Play your lucky numbers
- No need to check your numbers
- Just imagine hearing your numbers called
- Your number could be the big winner
- The really big numbers could be yours

ODDS

- You're an odds-on favorite to win
- Buck the odds
- Incredible odds
- Great odds on every ticket
- You're smart to take advantage of our unbeatable odds
- Improving the odds for a cure
- You won't find better odds anywhere
- What better way to improve the odds for people at risk
- The odds of winning will depend on the number of tickets sold
- Where all the odds are in your favor
- With odds like these
- Fairest odds you can find
- The odds are dropping every day
- You've never seen odds this small on a prize this big
- Providing remarkably handsome odds
- Have you ever seen better odds than these
- Where the odds are all in your favor
- With great odds on every ticket
- With odds like these, how can you lose
- Our best odds yet

OPPORTUNITY

- Take advantage of this great opportunity
- An opportunity you must not miss
- The opportunity to win is right before you
- An opportunity that comes once a lifetime

- I urge you to take part in this exciting new opportunity

PARTICIPANTS
- Remember, all participants have an equal chance to win big
- If you hurry, you, too, could be one of the participants
- We've been overwhelmed with participants

PARTICIPATE
- When you participate by buying a ticket, you're also helping
- Now is the time to participate
- Please participate by purchasing a ticket
- You get more than one chance to participate

PARTNERSHIP
- The real prize is in increased partnership
- Your ticket is your pledge of partnership
- Partnership with you is not just a game

PICK
- Just make your pick
- You know you can pick them
- Even if you don't win, you know you've picked a winner

PLAY
- Designed to keep you playing
- Why not play
- Play just for the fun of it
- Now is the time to make your play
- You get to play and help at the same time
- Go for the really big play
- The more you play, the better your chance of winning

PLAYER
- Existing player bases can be easily eroded
- Pursuing a new player market
- You can be a player in something big
- A way to really feel an important player

POSSIBILITIES
- Swept away by the possibilities
- Think of the possibilities
- Just look at the possibilities
- More possibilities than ever before
- Join in the possibilities
- Treat yourself to some truly stupendous possibilities

PRIZE

- An incredible variety of prizes
- Still more grand prizes
- Proud to announce the largest cash prize ever
- Hundreds of prizes to win this month
- Buy more chances at an early bird prize
- Total grand prize package valued at
- Prizes must be accepted as awarded and redeemed by
- Don't just enter for the prizes
- I can almost see you holding that big prize check
- Even prizes for the hard to please
- A chance at the most exclusive prizes
- The real prize is help for others
- The prize you win is only a small part of money raised to help
- The prize grows bigger and bigger every day
- Spot prizes, door prizes, you could win so many ways
- Prizes that work
- Be on the list for our next big prize delivery
- Prizes that work hard for those they are helping
- Offering guaranteed jackpot prizes of
- Your chances of winning a major prize are
- Do market research to determine the most attractive kind of prize
- The prize you win is only a small part of the money raised to help
- An incredible variety of prizes

PROFIT

- A way for everyone to profit
- You win, those in need profit greatly
- The profit isn't just money

PROGRAM

- Using the lottery as an addition to our existing program
- Time to get with the program and buy a ticket
- Our brand new lottery program has already extended our capacity to help those most in need

PROJECT

- Ticket profits result in the emergence of new joint projects
- Though the lottery, you can participate in this vitally important project
- Projected lottery revenues could put us through the roof

PURCHASE

- Purchase your ticket early for a chance at
- Tickets must be purchased before this date
- Just one ticket purchase can help bring radical change

RAFFLE
- Have you got your raffle ticket yet
- We're about to raffle off some splendid dreams
- Raffling off everything but the kitchen sink
- Just look what we're raffling off

RESIST
- So hard to resist the allure
- Resist no more
- Why resist any longer
- Don't be the last one to resist temptation

REVENUE
- Lottery revenues are soaring
- Revenues from gaming and lotteries will climb to
- Have become almost totally dependent upon charitable gaming for revenues
- Lotteries can become a very effective revenue source
- The more you participate the more revenue goes to help

REWARD
- Just for buying your ticket early, you could be rewarded
- Reward yourself today
- A small purchase with a big reward
- Winning big could be your reward for helping

RICH
- You could be rich tomorrow
- Do you think you would live the life of a rich person
- It's easy to be rich
- Buy a ticket, you'll be richer for the experience
- Riches for everyone
- Riches come in many forms
- All these riches could be yours for the taking

RISK
- Risky business
- Don't risk forfeiting a prize this big
- It's good for you to take a little risk now and then
- Where risk is kept to a minimum
- Experience the thrill of the risk

SCRATCH
- Scratch and match
- Scratch up a real challenge
- Start from scratch
- Are you up to scratch

- Scratch yourself up a fortune
- One scratch and you could be rich

SELL
- Sure to sell out quickly
- The tickets are selling like hot cakes
- We want to sell you the winning ticket
- Selling you a chance at all your dreams
- Get yours before they're all sold out

SKILL
- Try your skill
- With the right combination of luck and skill, you could win
- Where your skill really counts for something
- No skill required

SOCIALIZE
- Gaming provides the opportunity for some friendly socializing
- People love to socialize around the gaming tables
- A lot of fun, a little socializing, a chance a winning big

SPIN
- Watch us put a different spin on things
- Spin the wheel to help the children
- Where the wheel stops spinning, nobody knows
- A way to put the very best spin on

STAKE
- Look what's really at stake
- The stakes are very high
- When you buy a ticket, you have a stake in our organization
- The need for support has raised the stakes in this game
- In order to win the stakes

STOP
- There'll be no stopping you
- Stop look, buy a ticket, take a chance
- You just can't stop coming back

STRATEGY
- Your strategy for winning
- We'll help you plan your ticket strategy
- In this game, strategy is everything

SUCCESS
- The probability of success is terrific

- The success of winning is contagious
- You're helping to make this game a real success
- Success can be yours in so many different ways

SURE
- No such thing as a sure thing
- Participate enough times and you're sure to win
- It's the surest way to support the cause
- It's a sure thing that you'll be helping a lot of people with your entry

SURPRISE
- Surprise yourself
- You could be one of our early bird surprise winners
- Won't you be surprised when your number is drawn

SWEEPSTAKES
- Just look at some of our past sweepstakes winners
- You're helping them come out ahead in the sweepstakes of life
- Enter the sweepstakes right now

SYSTEM
- Beat the system
- Try out your system for winning
- We set the system up in your favor
- Our system benefits everybody

TEMPTATION
- How can you resist such a temptation
- Admit it, the temptation is just too strong
- Give in to temptation, play the game now

TICKET
- The ticket that just keeps on winning
- Buy a ticket – and feel good all over
- If you haven't purchased a ticket in the last month, it's time
- When you buy a ticket, you are buying hope for a child in pain
- Your ticket to helping others
- A ticket out of misery for those you're trying to help
- The more tickets you buy, the bigger the prize becomes
- Don't wait another moment to buy your ticket
- Your ticket to fun and profit
- Get your lucky ticket today
- Just a ticket to a really good time
- To guarantee your ticket, please order by
- Ticket sales are booming

TRICK
- Teaching some old dogs a new trick or two
- There's no trick to it
- Pull off the trick of winning the grand prize
- Learn some new tricks today

TRUST
- Trust your lottery money to us
- Buy from a trusted name
- Trust us to come up with something truly grand

URGE
- Give in to the urge to win
- I urge you to buy a ticket right away
- Nobody can resist the urge for long

VENTURE
- Join in a brave new venture
- It's a terrific venture with great goals in sight
- Venture into uncharted territory, buy a ticket
- Nothing ventured, nothing gained

VOLUNTEER
- A significant membership and volunteer participation in selling the tickets
- All our games and lotteries are run by caring volunteers
- Only because of our loyal volunteers could we run such a major lottery

WEALTH
- You could become independently wealthy in a jiffy
- Guess your way to wealth
- All this wealth could be yours by tomorrow
- Imagine yourself this wealthy
- Take the easy road to wealth

WIN
- The best way of winning
- You could win today
- Win often, win big
- More ways to win every day
- You could win in every possible way
- A major win will change your life completely
- Every ticket has a great chance to win
- When you win, we'll call and tell you
- Your chances to win get better when
- Now you have a chance to win even more
- You could win the entire cash prize

- Here's how much your ticket purchase helps
- Win big, win often, win for those you are helping
- When you play, everybody wins
- Please help us all win
- Going boldly against the odds to win
- Because of you, people in need win too
- Win right away
- The easy way to win
- Guess who really wins
- Your next big win is right around the corner
- Last chance to win
- Every ticket has a chance to win
- A chance to win something every week

WINNER

- As a potential winner you have the option of receiving your prize money in several ways
- So many ways to be a winner
- To obtain the most recent list of winners, just call
- Put yourself in the winner's circle
- Beat out the previous top winners
- Just imagine how good it feels to be a winner
- Join the ranks of our many winners
- Everyone's a winner, whichever way you look at it

WINNING

- Here's how you keep on winning
- You'll love winning
- The joy of winning can be yours
- Odds of winning depend on the number of entries received
- We follow through with real winnings
- Winning can work for you
- Your best chance of winning
- Take a chance on winning
- Get used to winning
- Get serious about winning
- Could you get used to winning this often
- Hooked on the thrill of winning
- Just imagine how good winning will feel
- Everyone has a shot at winning
- Try your hand at winning

WONDER

- It's much more than a small wonder
- The wonder of winning
- If you're wondering about your chances, rest easy

- You'll wonder why you never bought a ticket before

WORD
- The word is out
- Pass the word – big winnings are here
- The last word in lotteries
- Through word-of-mouth, the news about this great lottery has been spreading across the country

WORTH
- Worth much more than the price of your ticket
- Can't calculate the worth of the help you give
- Judged not by its cost, but by its worth
- A chance worth taking
- What do you think a human life is worth
- Worth every penny you invest

Section Three

Internet and Technology

ABILITY
- A very useful addition to our present abilities
- The ability to reach thousands, even millions, of people
- Extending our ability by incredible dimensions

ACCESS
- A far cry from real live Internet access and capability
- Now providing easy access to every area
- Now you can have instant, twenty-four hour access to
- Let us help you improve your access to
- To find out whether the much-trumpeted electronic access really means anything
- Such easy access could prove very attractive to many small and medium-sized organizations
- If you need to have quick access to a broad source of information
- For direct access to the Internet and thousands of other services
- One-stop access to the Internet

ACCUSTOM
- Unless you're accustomed to using computers
- We'll simply have to get accustomed to this new world
- Until we accustom ourselves to the Internet, we'll have to go carefully

ACHIEVE
- Energized toward achieving and sustaining
- Achieve a sound working knowledge of this new technology
- Achieving even more electronically
- Computers will help us achieve far more toward helping others than anyone ever dreamed possible

ADDRESS
- Ever more innovative ways to publish our electronic address
- Our Web address gives thousands more instant access to our organization
- The address of our Web site is your ticket to the best information

ADVANTAGE
- Experience the advantage of the Internet
- Now the electronic advantage is immeasurable
- As our organization grows, we need the advantage of digital

ALTERNATIVE
- Now a highly-affordable alternative to old-fashioned direct mail campaigns
- An alternative communication exceeding all expectation
- It's time we tried this brand new alternative

ANSWERS
- Searching out the answer for you

- Find the answers faster
- Now all the answers are right at your fingertips
- The Internet is an answer we've waited for, for years

ANXIETY

- Overcome with anxiety at the sight of a computer
- Dealing with the anxiety of learning a new medium
- All our anxieties about the Internet have proven unfounded

APPEAL

- On the Internet, only the briefest, simplest of appeals catch the eye
- An Internet appeal along the basis of a direct mail package
- Effective appeals can also be made via email

APPLICATION

- Setting up applications so you can find and work with them easier
- The Internet is a continually evolving set of applications which we must keep up with
- Changing applications are now being driven by users and supporters
- The hottest emerging applications
- Making sure all these applications can run simultaneously

ARTICLES

- Easy-to-read articles enhanced with audio explanations, video clips, slide shows and animations
- Search our valuable archives and articles on the Internet
- Now everyone interested can have access to these informative articles

ASK

- Ask us in your own words
- Now you can ask us your questions directly by email
- We don't yet know yet how much we can ask of our new Web site

ASPECT

- The most practical aspect of all is the most useful
- Every day there's another new aspect we haven't thought of before
- Just one more exciting and unexpected aspect

BACKGROUND

- Without a technological background, it's hard to make informed judgements
- None of us really have the backgrounds for this
- No matter what your donor background, you should be able to relate

BARRIERS

- Breaking down the barriers to entering cyberspace
- Breaking down communications barriers

- So that there are no more barriers to widespread use

BASIC
- The unavoidable basics of utilizing the Internet
- Recommend expert help to show you the basics
- Some basics about fundraising on the Internet

BONUS
- Bring an digital bonus for everyone
- Visitors to our new Web site are a gratifying bonus
- The Internet is a bonus we have to start taking very seriously

BROWSE
- Why not pop by and browse
- Be sure to browse the bookshelf for
- While you're at it, please take a moment to browse
- Just point your browser to

BUBBLE
- The Internet isn't just some bubble that will someday burst
- A swelling bubble of interest in
- The bubble is getting bigger and bigger

CAMPAIGN
- We're now taking our campaign onto the Internet
- We've had to invent a whole new type of campaign
- Even our campaign veterans are shaking their heads

CATCH UP
- Here we are playing digital catch-up
- Don't get caught playing the game of catch-up
- We must catch up or be left in the dust
- So we're able to catch up with leading edge technology

CHALLENGE
- Using the Internet effectively can be a challenging process
- We also provide help for the Internet challenged
- There's never been a better time to challenge old ideas of communication

CHANGE
- Leading the current phenomenon of accelerated change
- Important to keep updated on changes throughout the Internet that affect our organization
- The reasons for the changes are clearly given
- Clearly and usably explains the coming changes
- It's downright scary how fast things are changing

- Putting the Internet to work for you changes everything
- These massive changes will be mapped into society as a whole
- Your support drives the changes
- Changing ingrained assumptions about how we work and raise money

CHILDREN
- Children can now access a way to learn about this important cause
- Children and computers take to each other naturally
- Computers helping children to make good decisions about

CHOICE
- Working to develop a full range of choice
- The choices we offer will be critical in determining response
- It's today's best choice to reach supporters

CHOOSE
- A fair amount to choose from
- An overwhelming mass to choose from
- Now you get to help us choose online

COMMENTARY
- Because of your computer, you no longer have to miss insightful commentary on
- You, as a caring donor, can now add your commentary
- Join the continuous running commentary on our Web page

COMMUNICATE
- Giving us the power to communicate with potential donors we could never reach before
- To even more effectively communicate with our existing constituents
- Now we can communicate daily
- New ways for us to communicate in a shrinking world
- Designed to communicate just this kind of information

COMMUNICATION
- The principles of effective communication always remain the same whatever the technology
- The Web is also an excellent means of communication within our organization
- Developing a new relationship with this unique form of communication
- Speed of communication is creating an unusual situation
- Turning into a communication evangelist for
- The focus of communication is shifting radically
- A whole new way to handle communications
- Cherishing direct, commercial-free communication
- Must factor in the future of personal communication technology
- It's still all about communication between people
- Becoming one of our greatest communication strengths

- The place where stronger communication efforts must start
- Increasing our ability to quickly and effectively communicate
- But the emphasis remains on genuine communication

COMMUNITY
- Eager to join the rapidly growing world wide community connected to the Internet
- Please become part of our online community
- The sense of community has been enormously expanded
- Taking the online community by storm

COMPUTE
- Non-stop computing is becoming more and more common
- Taking joyfully to full throttle computing
- Working with top-of-the-line computing capacities
- Now make everything compute

COMPUTER
- Dealing with all the different kinds of incompatible computers we need to reach
- Computers can really help kids
- Calling all computer lovers
- Help for all those intimidated and confused by computers
- Acquiring a whole new power and meaning when attached to millions of other computers on the Internet
- Computers are everywhere
- The use of computers is a great way to explore the issues that affect
- Using the computer soon becomes second nature
- Our humble office computer has been transformed into a personal broadcasting station for our cause
- Modern management simply must include the computer and the Internet
- First building skill in basic computer characteristics and components
- Now computer-based training programs are allowing us to expand the benefits to
- As long as you are familiar with your computer you can do it
- You don't have to be a computer genius

CONCEPT
- First we need to learn about a few concepts
- Explaining the background and concepts
- Eager to embrace radical new concepts
- A concept that barely existed a short time ago
- Familiarizing our staff with fundamental computer concepts
- Reaching a level of comfort with concepts, jargon and most-used applications

CONFERENCE
- With the use of excellent conference software, we can
- By conferencing over the Web, we can get together sooner

- Can now run a continual, online conference including all supporters

CONFIGURE
- Getting the system configured correctly was a true pain in the neck
- Took careful planning on how to configure
- Our initial configuration will be all important
- Initial configuration might determine the future history of
- Concentrate on understanding configuration problems

CONNECT
- No one can connect like us
- Now a fast, friendly way to connect with your favorite charity
- Lets you connect to almost anything from just about anywhere
- Everyone's getting connected
- Take advantage of our new Internet connectivity

CONNECTION
- Thus making the connection utterly seamless
- Forging connections in cyberspace
- We're all racing to expand our connection to the world

CONSTRUCTION
- We're especially sorry that this page is still under construction
- Please be patient while we're under construction and visit us soon
- Please come back, construction will be finished soon

CRISIS
- Helping us figure out what to do about the crisis
- Flung into the midst of a numbering crisis
- A much quicker way to deal with a crisis situation
- One click of the mouse and your crisis is over

CULTURE
- Becoming part of the new electronic culture
- Joining in the digitalization of our culture
- Already we have a new culture that grows and changes daily

CYBERSPACE
- Our appeal may be in cyberspace but our feet are firmly planted on the ground
- Be a buddy from cyberspace
- Daring to take a ground-breaking leap into cyberspace
- In cyberspace, the only boundary is your imagination
- Women are forging cyberspace
- Taking the fight against poverty into cyberspace
- Visit us in cyberspace
- Welcome to cyberspace

- Joining the cyberspace act in order to
- Now we're expanding into cyberspace
- Developing our own niche in cyberspace

DATA
- Now handling data with such ease
- Allowing us to update our data more quickly and ensure the best possible service
- Now using these machines to analyze data in a very different way
- Can compare vast amounts of data in a single millisecond
- Everything needed to safeguard valuable data
- Handles data with enormous ease
- Helping you understand the underlying data relations
- Allowing us to customize, manipulate and query our data

DATABASE
- The importance and use of database systems must be addressed immediately
- Now you can search our databases for
- Accessing the immense usefulness of a truly customized database

DETAIL
- Making sure we know all the grisly details of the system
- Sooner or later, we have get down to the gruesome technical details
- Using the Internet, we can now explain our policies in detail
- A place where the details really count

DIFFERENCE
- To see who is making a difference and who is on the move
- Making a huge difference in cost and efficiency
- Finding ways to measure the difference the Web is bringing

HYPE
- Are you wondering what the hype is all about
- So important to separate the hype from reality
- Not to get carried away by the hype

DISCUSSION
- Now able to keep up a running discussion to topics of concern to us and our supporters
- The discussion inevitably swings round to the Internet
- The discussion has broadened dramatically since we created an online discussion forum

DISTANCE
- Working well over the longest distance
- Distance becomes nothing
- When distance suddenly becomes insignificant

- Distance is now completely irrelevant

DISTRIBUTE
- The Web is proving to be an extremely effective way to distribute information
- Please distribute this message digitally to your friends, colleagues and other interested parties
- So much easier to distribute the facts and figures

DIVERSITY
- Learning about the incredible diversity now available
- Now we can appeal to a huge diversity of folks
- Diversity become one of our very best tools

DO
- When you can't figure out what to do next
- Showing our donors what to do and how to do it
- Able to do it in a whole new way
- Tons of exciting things to do

DONATION
- Click here for donation form
- Make your donation instantly effective by filling out the Web form
- It's the easy way to make a much-needed donation

DONOR
- Happily increasing our donor base through the Internet
- A value-added service to our donors
- Generating a large donor base via the Internet
- Using email as part of our campaign to reach potential donors

DOWNLOAD
- Download your future
- Once connected to the Internet, you can download valuable ideas
- Now able to download the latest from
- Download some joy

EMAIL
- Without doubt, email is the most widely used Internet service
- Email is making real inroads into
- Constantly expanding our email contacts
- Without email, friends and contacts seem further and further away
- Grasping the fact that email is more than just information
- Email us for the paperwork
- Email messages turning from to trickle to a stream to a raging flood
- Our email technique is changing and being refined

EGALITARIAN

- Putting us all into a truly egalitarian mode
- Egalitarian and socially unstratified
- One of the most egalitarian mediums yet

ENCRYPT

- Our new secure server means your credit card details will now be encrypted when they are sent to us
- If your browser does not support encryption, you can still make a donation online
- You may feel perfectly confident about our method of encryption

EVENT

- Visit our media event center online
- The Coming Events section updates continually
- Expansion on the Internet has been a really big event for our organization and those we are trying to help

EXPERIENCE

- Nothing can replace hands-on experience
- Computer experience is not necessary
- A whole new experience for our staff

EXPERT

- Without having to become the world's greatest Internet expert
- When we know it's time for expert help
- Highly recommend expert assistance with planning
- Beware off the self-styled experts saying you would be a fool to try anything else
- Able to get expert attention when things get fouled up and confusing

EXPERTISE

- Necessary technology and expertise to assist our organization in developing an ongoing Internet presence and strategy
- Pleased with our rapidly developing expertise in this area
- Expertise on the Net is crucial to our success in the future

EXPLAIN

- Explaining the necessary commands and syntax to get you started
- Lucidly explains concepts, uses and low-level details
- Must, above all, be very easy to explain to neophytes

EXPLORE

- You can choose to explore the Internet
- Exploring more and better ways to compliment our
- Now you can explore a lot more possibilities
- With a bit of patience and exploration, you can find out so very much

FAMILIAR
- As Internet possibilities become increasing familiar to you
- The Internet is now familiar to millions of potential donors
- The Internet is as familiar as a telephone

FAST
- Wickedly fast connections
- Now faster than ever
- A fast, effective and convenient way to
- Offering blazingly fast connecting ability
- Helping you finish faster

FEATURE
- One of the most engaging features of the program is
- Please check out our feature of the month
- Discover the many new features of this exciting new operating environment

FEEDBACK
- Received such a lot of positive feedback when our site was launched
- Please keep the feedback coming
- Regular reports on the activity at our Web site will provide continuous and vital feedback

FINGERTIPS
- We've had the Internet under our fingertips and not known until now
- The Internet puts most of the world at our fingertips
- Thousands more donors now at our fingertips

FIRST
- There is a first time for everything
- To be first onto the Web is to become a pathfinder
- This really is a major first for us

FORMAT
- Translating everything into this new format
- Placed in a very easy-to-use format
- Requiring a fresh and innovative format to get the message across electronically

FREE
- Providing vast numbers of services free for the taking
- The world at your fingertips, all free of charge
- Though it appears to be free, there are costs involved

FRONTIER
- Come with us into the next frontier
- As with any frontier, there are obstacles and difficulties

- A new frontier to conquer

FUNCTION
- Targeted toward those performing the day-to-day functions
- Preparing to function with increased competence
- Increasing and combining functions for better efficiency
- Functioning together, a new kind of consciousness can emerge

FUNDAMENTAL
- Fundamental to understanding and getting the most out of your system
- Have to learn the fundamentals of operating our system quickly
- Getting the fundamentals down pat in a hurry

FUNDRAISER
- A way to create world wide fundraisers
- The Internet has proved a real boon to fundraisers
- Fundraisers are flocking to use this amazing method

FUNDRAISING
- After careful examination of many online fundraising examples, we must conclude that
- Add the Internet to your fundraising strategy
- Internet based fundraising appeals have increased very substantially
- The biggest foundation block of today's fundraising world
- Working to develop a fundraising survival guide to the Internet
- For more information on any aspect of fundraising, please email us at
- Working to develop a powerful fundraising presence on the Internet
- Our Web site and Internet presence compliment our existing fundraising effort
- Marrying fundraising to the Internet in a happy union
- Conquering the right way to integrate fundraising and the Internet
- A growing number of nonprofits are now transferring aspects of a whole range of fundraising activities to the Internet
- Putting corporate fundraising online
- About to radically alter our fundraising practices
- State-of-the-art, Internet-integrated fundraising is here
- Taking our fundraising efforts even more onto the Internet

FUTURE
- So that our record of success can continue into the future
- Show we have what it takes to take hold of the future
- Step directly into a brand new future
- Many future thinkers are of the opinion that
- Preparing for the demands of a technologically advanced future
- Gaining the knowledge and skill to face the future
- I'm afraid the future has arrived dizzyingly fast
- Get the jump on planning for a technological future few of us could have

foreseen
- Prepare for the future now
- Making the Internet part of comprehensive planning for the future
- Powerfully challenging our view of the future

GIVING
- The hottest, coolest way of giving this side of virtual reality
- Are you up for some online giving
- Generating a brand new kind of excitement and a lot more giving

GO
- Then poof, it's gone
- Old methods going the way of the dodo bird
- Go modern, go world wide, go for more on the Web

GRAPHICS
- Considering the ease with which graphics can vividly show our point
- With graphics to spice up presentations
- Good graphics have become vital

GROWTH
- The growth has been explosive
- A new way to promote continued growth and success
- Taking advantage of a wild growth period

GUIDE
- Let us be your guide
- Need a guide – click here
- Have to be our own guides in the uncharted new region
- For a guided tour of our organization, click here

GURU
- Our rapid progress is thanks to our resident online guru
- Having to continually ask our resident guru for advice
- Without our trusty computer guru, we'd be finished
- If you're looking for a technical guru you can trust

HELP
- There's lots of online help
- Now you can help the charity of your choice on the Net
- The fastest, friendliest way to help you when you need it
- You can get help faster by asking for it on the Internet

HIGHWAY
- We are speeding faster and faster along the digital highway
- Making sure the information highway leads right to our door

- Take a ride to the future on the information highway

ICON
- This icon points to places of wonder
- You may visit related home pages on the World Wide Web by clicking on one of these icons
- Click on this icon for additional information

IDEA
- Click for the latest fundraising ideas, employment opportunities, funding sources, upcoming
- Conferences, seminars, book reviews, legislation, ideas and much more
- Visit our research section for hundreds of ideas in a huge array of subject areas
- Open up to new ideas
- Delivering rapid-fire ideas about our evolving techno culture

IDENTITY
- Think of it as a chance to create a whole new identity for
- Helping to maintain and enhance our organizations identity electronically
- Giving us a modern, leading-edge identity
- Moving very quickly to establish our identity on the Net

IMMEDIACY
- The need for immediacy is steadily increasing
- The immediacy and ease of sending email
- Now immediacy has become all important

INFORMATION
- Hundreds of pages of information, tools and discussion to help you get your job done more effectively and efficiently than ever before
- Now you can link to specific information with a single click
- Instant information for the truly fact-hungry
- Sooner or later, we'll all have to convert to this new form of information transfer
- You can be a leading global provider of information about your field
- It's a one-stop information spot
- Get the latest expert information instantly
- The information is processed for you at lightning speed
- Information can now be offered in real time
- Your international online information center
- Now the easiest way to organize your information
- Plug in to a wealth of valuable information now
- Introduced to the most current information about

INTERACT
- The Internet is quickly revolutionizing how we interact with the outside world
- Turning around our interactions with the world at large

- Connecting and interacting with the outside world in a whole new way
- We must learn even more about how people interact in the Internet
- To interact appropriately on the Internet
- Drawing youth into daily interaction with
- Start with learning basic interaction
- Blaze through an interactive program
- And speaking of interactivity
- Interactivity connects people to each other via the machine

INITIATIVE

- Announcing new Internet initiatives
- Learning to grab the initiative in the new digital world
- Now we can get our prospects to take the initiative
- We must take the initiative and do it on the Net

INTERFACE

- Prefer working with a full screen terminal interface
- It's the most natural interface of all
- Keeping the basic interface smooth and sophisticated

INTERNET

- The Internet is giving our whole campaign a facelift
- The Internet is a friendly place
- The Internet provides a wildly entertaining and educational experience
- A weird place called the Internet
- Internet sites abound
- Ideas and resources to help build and improve your organization's Internet presence
- Direct Internet access
- Putting the Internet to work helping others
- The Internet can be a rough and tumble place
- Increasing overall awareness of our presence on the Internet
- Is the power of the Internet working for your organization
- Working directly with organizations interested in developing a presence on the Internet
- The Internet is a huge and happening place
- You'll wonder why you're not doing more on the Internet
- Now offered via the Internet
- Try an adventure on the Internet today
- The Internet itself can offer all kinds of excellent advice about
- Internet produces substantial benefits in all areas of our organization
- The best and brightest are competing on the Internet
- The Internet can be a mixed blessing for many organizations
- Have a demonstrated track record on the Internet
- Here's the real scoop on the Internet
- One of the great joys of the Internet is

- A brief overview of email and the history of the Internet for starters
- Taking a chance on the Internet
- Don't let the Internet leave you feeling helpless
- Gleaning a great harvest of information from the Internet

INTIMIDATE
- Sometimes the Internet can be truly intimidating
- We mustn't become intimidated by the new technologies
- Those of us intimidated and confused will have to get over it
- Please don't be intimidated by our new electronic personality
- To get over being intimidated by overwhelming Internet choices
- The smallest child is no longer intimidated by these great gizmos

INTRODUCTION
- Providing and easy introduction to the Internet
- Making sure our Web site effectively introduces our organization
- What better introduction than a lively Web page

ISSUE
- Already coming to our Web site to learn about the kinds of issues that concern them deeply
- Exploring important ethical issues created by the Internet
- Probing our most worrying contemporary issues

JOB
- The sometimes very daunting job of using the Internet effectively
- The Internet is the fastest way yet to get our job done
- Tap into our Web site to see the job we all have to do

KNOWLEDGE
- Even if you have little or no prior knowledge of how computers work
- Participants should have a working knowledge of
- The purpose is to enhance the knowledge of
- For all those wishing to update their knowledge

LEARN
- It's not too late to learn
- You learn by doing and each mistake is explained
- Everything you need to learn what you need to know about
- Through the Internet, we can do most of our learning at home
- A flexible and accessible way to learn
- Has spurred interest in learning all about digital possibilities
- Hands-on, experiential learning cannot be replaced

LINK
- As simple as putting in a link to your site – but please do something

- Link yourself to hundreds of caring
- Simply your best link to everything necessary
- Hundreds of links to the world's best Web sites
- The biggest change is the online links incorporated directly from
- Walking you through hundreds of cross-links on your fact-finding mission

LIST

- One way to go is to get on mailing lists or create a mailing list
- Our electronic mailing list will become as valuable, or more valuable, than our traditional list
- Another way of making our list very easy to get on
- You should see the way our list is expanding

MAIL

- Sending mail is now so very easy
- No more trudging out to the mailbox
- The Web saves us a fortune in printing and mailing costs
- A stratospheric improvement over old fashioned mail
- New mail, new methods, new world of fundraising

MANAGE

- Helping you manage, innovate and motivate
- Looking for ever better ways to manage the flow
- Manual management provides the great advantage of personal service
- Managing our Web site well becomes a major priority

MESSAGE

- Sometimes it can seem like sending a message out in a bottle
- Listening to our message via new media
- Carrying our message further than ever before
- Our message zapped into thousands of email boxes in mere minutes
- The stunning possibilities inherent in being able to exchanges messages with anyone on the Internet
- On the Internet, our message will have to be more concise, punchy and grabbing than ever before
- Our message can say anything we want
- Making our message stand boldly out amongst the great mass of stuff

METHOD

- Our old method of fundraising has finally outlived its usefulness
- Much easier than any of the other methods
- Learning to use new methods for a new era

MODEM

- Your modem is a good place to start
- Working to see that everyone has a modem as a means to connect

- A simple modem has become a magic carpet to the world

MONEY
- Now raising money even more creatively on the Internet
- The answer might not be more money
- Turning our Web page into a conduit for donor money

MOUSE
- Help is just a mouse click away
- All it takes is a couple of mouse clicks
- Using a mouse and the onscreen tools to succeed

NET
- Click here if you're new to the Net
- Turning into one of the most comprehensive and extensive support areas on the Net
- Visit us on the Net at
- Now you can volunteer on the Net
- It might take some time to get comfortable on the Net
- Make the Net work for your concerns

NETIQUETTE
- Careful to follow the philosophy and netiquette of the Internet
- An offense against netiquette can bring down a royal flaming
- Netiquette codes are becoming much more flexible
- Taking care not to offend against netiquette

NETWORK
- Vastly expand your networking possibilities
- Now we can tap into a world wide grid of networks
- Taking advantage of a world wide network of supporters
- The mother of all networks is the Internet
- Nothing is as simple as it should be as we set out to take advantage of the world's largest computer network
- The larger the network, the more appeals we can make
- Really a network of networks
- Networking technologies are revolutionizing nonprofit communications
- Networks are fast becoming critical to the daily operation of many charitable organizations
- Quickly learn what is involved in creating a successful communications network
- A network that is very large and useful

NEW
- Some relatively new technologies are included and used
- Something new every day at our Web site
- Something new is going on in your computer

- Taking care to always provide something new to see

NEWS
- It's your free online source of news, information and resources for the nonprofit community
- Delivering the latest news about
- Now good news travels on the Internet
- Bringing personalized news about our programs to you
- Now you can get red hot news immediately

ONLINE
- Bringing our organization to online, real-time, day-to-day transactions
- If you've been considering getting online
- Check us out online
- Our top professionals are now online
- Take advantage of this online world
- Follow us online
- Able to professionally represent our organization in the online world
- Your online exchange for gifts-in-kind
- Putting kids in contact with heroes online
- An online way to support our organization's future needs

OPPORTUNE
- Not the most opportune way to find out
- Discovering the opportune moment takes skill and patience
- Is there a more opportune time than now to move onto the Web

OPPORTUNITY
- The Web is providing many more opportunities than we could possibly have imagined
- I get dizzy just thinking about the opportunities
- A great opportunity for you to keep instantly up-to-date
- Opportunities are appearing in such different guises that we're even having trouble recognizing them

OPTION
- Now your options are no longer limited
- Now the world has another option
- Displays a list of available help options for your convenience
- Generating more options than ever before imagined

ORGANIZE
- The easiest way to organize your giving
- The first necessity is to be well organized
- We have to organize ourselves much more efficiently on the Web

PAGE
- A simple Web page housing so much information
- Impressing everyone with an appealing Web page for the use and benefit of your organization
- Please visit our Web page as soon as you can

PEOPLE
- Cyberspace people are often friendly and welcoming to newcomers
- The Internet is composed of the people who use it and the vast information residing in it
- An electronic means of putting us in touch with real people

PERFORMANCE
- Determined to get a high performance result
- Enhancing daily performance
- Now we can measure our daily performance
- Steadily improving our communication performance
- A whole new way to enhance the performance of
- Optimum performance is our top priority

PLAN
- The excitement of learning to plan and create Web pages
- The Internet has become central to all our plans
- Preparing various sections of our plan as we progress

PLUG
- Plug in to us and away you go
- Plug into practical ways to upgrade your organizations
- Now you're plugged into the entire globe
- A way to plug ourselves into the whole world
- A Web site becomes a vehicle to show just how plugged in we are

POST
- Post your needs for willing hands
- We'll keep you posted
- Posted to various user groups, mailing lists and bulletin boards
- Please do not post in places where this message would be inappropriate

POWER
- Giving them power, hope and knowledge through the Internet
- Gaining a truly awesome power to
- Now the power of the Internet is working for those in need
- Using the full power of the Internet to

PRACTICE
- A system also working pretty well in practice

- In practice it works far better than expected
- It just takes a little practice to get used to

PREPARE
- Designed to prepare us for a new age of
- Become prepared for a global explosion of
- Working hard to prepare ourselves for this medium
- The Internet caught up with us before we were quite prepared for it

PRESENCE
- In order to monitor the effectiveness of our Internet presence
- Establishing a strong Internet presence is one of the most important steps an organization can take
- Working together to build the best possible Internet presence
- Web site shows we have a presence on this new mass medium

PRESENT
- Now able to present our information with interest and pizzazz
- A totally new way to present our ideas to others
- The future has suddenly become our present

PROBLEM
- Proven effective problem solvers
- Hoping fervently that this doesn't turn out to be a problem
- Overcoming brand new problems, one by one

PROCESS
- Every step of the process must be made transparent to those who really need to know
- First, we must understand the process
- The process of learning this can seem painfully slow

PROGRAM
- A huge program with even more capabilities
- A program that meets your needs
- The main concrete progress in this new medium has been because of

PROMOTE
- Already promoting improvements in a broader, more innovative and more effective context
- Increasingly promoting our organization on the Web
- Promoting our site is crucial to its success
- Since we've been promoting ourselves on the Web, results have shot up bigtime

PROSPECT
- Targeting exact Internet locations where our prospects would meet

- Plenty of prospects are to be found on the Internet
- The trick is to get prospects flocking to the Web site

RESEARCH
- Enabling thorough research and insightful analysis
- A new way to strongly encourage independent research skills
- The Web has vastly expanded our research capability

RESOURCE
- The Internet itself provides you with so many resources
- Downloaded software will provide the resources for
- Discovering more resources at our fingertips than we ever would have dreamed possible
- Is being quickly adopted by other enterprising resource centers
- Now providing access to resources around the clock
- A first aid kit for your sinking resources

RESPONSE
- To dramatically increase our rates of response
- To avoid getting a mechanical response from
- The excitement of beginning to get responses within a few minutes of sending out our message
- Taking advantage of the newest kind of response devices

RESULT
- Wondering why this has been causing some extremely peculiar results
- Terrific results from only a small amount of conversion effort
- Once on the Web, our results increased dramatically

REVOLUTIONIZE
- The way we work has already been revolutionized by
- Revolutionizing the way we connect with you
- Revolutionizing everyone's thinking about personal communications
- Revolutionizing the way we raise money

RULE
- Contrary to the usual rule of thumb
- An area so new the rules haven't formed yet
- The rules are changing all the time

SAVVY
- Becoming much more tech-savvy
- So that your colleagues and donors will know that you are Internet savvy
- Applying your Net-savvy to helping others
- The new and savvy way to reach one's prospects

SEARCH
- Just put our name into your favorite search engine
- A way to widen our search for donors
- Search for us on the Net – we're easy to find

SECURITY
- Creating some really embarrassing security holes
- Though security issues may not be our primary concern
- Need to know about a few security concepts

SERVICE
- Special services instantly for nonprofit managers and fundraising pros
- Now offering a full range of electronic services
- Now able to offer instant service over the Internet

SHARE
- Getting a bigger share of supporters' attention through the Internet
- Solving the need for better ways to share information
- Increasing our donor share via the Internet

SIGNATURE
- This facility cannot be provided online because it requires a signature
- Electronic signatures can then be attached to
- Our signature logo on every Web page

SITE
- A site purposefully designed with lots of attractive features to keep people coming back
- Visit our site, find out more about our work
- The site is suffering from underfunding
- More depth, more information, more ease at our site

SKILLS
- Developing the skills essential to successful Internet use
- Quickly building the skills that we require
- Internet skills are now in the highest demand

SOCIETY
- How is society affected by the Internet
- Raising new issues that have a new impact upon society
- Now bringing diverse sections of society together on the Web

SOLUTION
- The perfect solution where space and budget are limited
- Designed to offer time-saving solutions to
- A traditional solution for the conscientious

- An accessible, easy-to-use solution for creating Web sites
- Integrated telecommunications solution to
- Become a leading solutions provider

SPEED
- Full speed ahead
- All the speed you need to
- You finally get all the speed you want to

STANDARD
- A standard already being widely adopted
- The obvious thing to do is adapt and improve existing standards
- Thus ending up in complete violation of standards
- Getting us to stop squabbling about standards

START
- All we need to know to get started
- The start-up costs are surprisingly minimal
- Shows you how to get started using them

STEP
- Taking that first shaky step onto the Internet
- In order to have as few extra steps as possible
- Eliminating an extra forwarding step
- Very simple steps required to install the software

STRETCH
- Really stretching it to
- This will be a real stretch for our organization
- Stretching our capabilities in a new, exciting way
- Stretching a helping hand deep into cyberspace

SUPPORT
- A clear leader in Internet support
- Does your organization suffer from lack of computer support
- Pulling a great deal of support through digital means

SURF
- Get your feet wet and start surfing more effectively
- Our supporters are steadily surfing the Internet
- We're able to get more and more Web surfers to drop in
- Now you can surf right into the world of caring
- Take a break from surfing for a moment to open your heart to
- Joining all the others blithely surfing the Internet without drowning
- Surf's up; let's go ride the wave to prosperity

SWAMP
- Suddenly, we were swamped by calls
- We've been swamped by your responses
- The information swamped our system in no time

SYSTEM
- Aimed at getting best results without putting a huge load on our system
- Realistically taking the best system we can get
- We've configured a really hot system here
- The heart of the system is
- Unique within the bounds of our system
- The fabulous thing is that it's a two-way communications system
- Must understand the system networks use to communicate
- So as not to end up engaged in hand-to-hand combat with the system
- Getting around easily within the system
- Perhaps getting boxed into a system that's not quite right
- Locking into a unique system that combines
- All systems go

TECHNICAL
- This part is unavoidably quite technical
- Not dazzled by technical brilliance
- Keeping up with the technical advances is crucial
- Able to start without any requirement for a technical background

TECHNOLOGY
- This technology just keeps on ticking
- A widespread adoption of this new technology
- Learn how these new technologies affect the way we live and work
- Technologies for communications, creativity and problem solving
- Taking us straight to the cutting edge of this technology
- Keeping up with changing technology
- Making first use of a pioneering technology
- Technology is making it easier to do just that
- Leading edge technology offering far faster service to you
- Technology is changing every aspect of our lives
- Testing the limits of wireless technology
- How well we use this new technology is up to us
- Helping you get savvy to current technologies
- Encouraged to explore cutting-edge technology
- Providing the fruits of a working relationship with the technology
- By this time next year we'll be discussing yet another exciting technology
- Converging technologies are increasing our pull
- Sophisticated technology has laid the groundwork for
- With technology moving faster than ever before, we need to keep on the ball
- Learn how to use the latest technologies from the experts in the field

- Must examine the effect these new technologies have upon

TECHNOPHOBES
- To accurately identify the technophobes in your organization
- Ferreting out and retraining hardened technophobes
- Even a hopeless technophobe can deal with this

TECHSPEAK
- Not to fall into the trap of techspeak
- Guarding against creeping techspeak
- Techspeak and gobbledegook are not far apart
- Techspeak will turn our prospects off quicker than anything

TERRITORY
- Those who venture forth into this uncharted territory tend to be adventurous
- Charting new territory
- Laying claim to our bit of territory on the Web

TIME
- We're getting completely onto the Web in a nick of time
- Just click on the time line to find out when
- Isn't it time you moved up in the new digital reality
- Giving us the freedom to set our own timetable

TOOL
- Tools to help us make sense of the mountain of information available
- Now giving you the straight tools to
- Now, the tools you need to really help
- Has quickly become a fundamental tool
- Tools to manage your information burden
- Now a powerful generative and analytical tool
- A powerful tool in facilitating effective learning
- A powerful tool with which to tailor information
- A tool we can use immediately

TRADITION
- Help us continue the tradition in this very untraditional way
- Our tradition of outstanding service is carried on into cyberspace
- Starting a new tradition electronically

TRANSACTION
- Turn ourselves into a charity prepared to accept secure credit card transactions on the Internet
- We've already encountered amazing transactions via the Internet
- Transactions speeding up astronomically

TRIALS
- Gamely facing the trials of getting our organization fully onto the Internet
- We hope the trials and tribulations are finally over
- Running continual trials to gauge the best approach

TRICK
- Learning all the tricks of effective Internet use
- Now we come to the tricky part
- Learn all the tricks to making it work
- Not just another clever trick
- Some people might wonder whether there is some trick to it

TRIP
- You'll find something new and interesting at every trip
- Take a trip into the future right now
- A rather wild trip down the information highway
- Making contact with those taking regular trips on the Internet

TUNE
- Stay tuned for these and other issues
- Tuning in on the whole world
- Now a tune that everyone can hear
- A finely tuned communications plan

TUTORIAL
- Online interactive tutorials must provided
- Able to offer very specific tutorials
- To help you learn, there are pages of tutorials
- The program offers a mini-tutorial on

UNDERSTANDING
- Something quite momentous is happening to our traditional understanding of space and time
- First, our people must develop a conceptual understanding of this new technology
- Striving to increase our understanding every day

UNLOCK
- Now unlocking undreamed-of possibilities
- Unlocking a gate we have only to step through
- Unlocking a vast new universe

UPDATE
- Continuously updated
- Imperative to keep ourselves update to the minute
- Get round-the-clock updates

- We intend to update this site regularly

UPGRADE
- Upgrading ways of giving
- Upgrading to a whole new level of
- Time to upgrade ourselves onto the Web

USE
- Bringing an unmatched ease of use
- Making full use of every new technology
- Something rapidly coming into common use
- We've only begun to figure out its many astonishing uses

USER
- Striving constantly to make it more user friendly and effective
- Turning Internet users into willing donors
- Designed to take new users through the basics

VIEW
- Information designed to be viewed after visiting our home page
- A whole new way to view us
- How you view us is important to us
- Talk about a way to expand our world view
- Our world view changed overnight

VIRTUAL
- Now able to create a virtual classroom
- Turn virtual reality into real reality by giving
- A huge virtual organization that everyone can join

VOLUNTEER
- Volunteers are also creating for us a fundraising appeal online
- An email appeal which we asked all our volunteers to forward
- Volunteers are flocking to us from the Net

WAIT
- You've waited long enough to try this new way
- Now you don't have to wait
- Finally, what your organization has been waiting for
- No more waiting when you want to participate

WATCH
- We're the one to watch
- Keep watch with us
- Now you can watch us get better every day

WAY

- Unlike many of the old-fashioned ways of communicating
- We'll help you find your way
- Leading the way for Internet users
- Introducing a whole new way to
- A way to take greater control of
- The simplest, easiest way to get attention on the Internet is to
- The Internet is becoming the fastest, most reliable way to move information
- Reaching out in ways undreamed of only a few years ago
- Far too many different ways now exist to

WEB

- Time to get on the Web bigtime
- Learning to be Web magicians
- Exploring reasons to care on the Web
- Supplying access for almost as long as the Web has been around
- Women on the Web have felt disenfranchised until very recently
- Top-notch Web development to help charitable organizations
- The Web is building even more credibility for
- The Web sites are good and improving every day
- An uncluttered, easy-to-understand Web site is essential
- Explore the fundamentals of sound Web authoring

WEB PAGE

- Our Web page is enjoying immense popularity among our supporters
- If you are serious about designing documents and Web pages that
- The all-in-one Web page for
- Our Web page is now considered the hub of
- We're hoping our Web portal page will be a big hit
- Taking us rapidly into advanced Web page creation
- Proven enhancements have increased the hits on our Web page

WEB SITE

- A very attention-getting Web site
- Server space for this Web site has been provided free of charge
- A complete Web site service especially for nonprofits
- Web sites are popping up right and left
- Transforming our Web site into a virtual reality visitors can explore
- Never know who we will encounter at our Web site
- Creating and managing our own home Web site
- View our new and critically acclaimed Web site
- This way to our Web site
- The new Web site everyone is rushing to view
- We have launched a new Web site
- The purpose of the Web site is to help
- Just visit our Web site at

- A Web site consistent with our organization's image
- Promoting your Web site could be the key to promoting your cause
- This Web site is provided in support of
- Have you visited our Web site today
- Visit our Web site for weekly updates

WEBMASTER
- Join our webmaster's club
- Resources and ideas for webmasters
- Now we're developing shrewd webmasters
- Now is the time to encourage your office tinkerer to turn into your office webmaster

WORD
- Stumped by an unfamiliar technological word
- No easier way to get word to the masses
- The last word in technological advances
- Now we're getting the word out electronically

WORK
- Allowing us to work even more closely together
- Working hard to make the Web work for you
- A wonderful new way to work with you to help
- Now, a faster, better way to advance your crucial work

WORLD
- What in the world is going on
- Your point of departure for the world of
- Across the country and around the world
- Now you can give your family the world
- Take advantage of the online world with full connectivity
- Now giving you the world right at your desk
- Now you can track the whole world
- Suddenly confronted with people, places, issues and crises from around the world

Section Four

Telephone
Fundraising

BLITZ

- We're conducting this telephone blitz in order to
- Getting it all over with one telephone blitz leaves our workers free to concentrate upon
- We're all geared up for a major telephone blitz
- It's the biggest telephone blitz in our history – to fill the biggest need we've ever had

CALL

- Then call us immediately at
- Yours is a call that really matters
- Your call matters
- Call in now
- Please call in right away
- Reach out and call someone
- That phone call is a chance to interact with precious donors
- Call now to save starving children
- Please help us by calling in now
- We'd like at the very least to match our previous calls
- It all starts with a single phone call
- A single phone call can start so much
- We're waiting anxiously for your call
- Please keep our staff busy with your calls
- Our staff is only too pleased to be busy with your calls
- Surprise us with your call
- Our operators are waiting to take your call
- Please call and let us add your name to our list
- We still have lines open waiting for your call
- Even the government is encouraging you to call in
- Check this out while you make your call
- I can only ask you to make that call
- We need everyone to do their part by calling now
- We need your call if we are to reach our goal tonight
- Your call is vital
- Our research shows that many more of you should be calling
- What we need from you is your phone call
- Whatever your reason, it is urgent that you join with others right now and call
- Use your call to tell the world how important you consider
- Call right away to save a life
- Cast your vote by calling
- Show us your interest is alive and well by calling now
- Your call is the one way you can make a difference tonight
- How can you help – just by calling
- Your call is just another way you can help
- We're on hold waiting for your call
- I know those calls will come in

- I know you'll be calling soon
- Just think of the lives hinging on your phone call
- As time runs out, we won't be able to wait much longer for your call
- Programs you help support when you call
- Call us please
- It's your call now
- Picture all those little faces waiting for your call
- I can see you right now, reaching for that telephone
- One of the few times when you can help immediately
- We're strongly encouraging you to call
- A simple phone call away
- Call now to protect animals and people
- We need your call to make this a real success
- For someone in need, your phone call could mean a lifeline
- How could any caring person not call
- If you believe things can be changed for the better, please call
- Perhaps the most important phone call you'll ever make
- In the next few minutes we need your call because those in need have no one else to turn to
- Please keep those calls coming in

CAMPAIGN
- Solving our fundraising problems through a telephone campaign
- Telephone fundraising is a very important aspect of our campaign
- A simple phone call is the key to our campaign
- We're conducting this campaign over the telephone in order to save
- Please, please respond to this urgent telephone campaign
- We've been campaigning for weeks now over the telephone
- You calls in response have made this the very best campaign ever

CARE
- If you care, you'll call now
- Nobody could care more than our loyal callers
- No one who really cares could turn away
- No easier, faster way to make your caring count
- Your caring will sing to us over the wire
- It's so easy to pick up the phone and make a caring contribution
- An instant way to show how much you care

• CHAIR
- Asking you to get up out of your chair right now
- Don't just keep sitting in your chair
- No chair could be so comfortable that you couldn't get up for this
- Appealing to all you people sitting in your comfortable chairs
- Don't just think about calling – get up out of that chair

CHARITY
- Telemarketers need a thorough knowledge of the charity they represent
- Charity has now moved on to the telephone
- The telephone is one more way to help the charity of your choice

CLOCK
- We're racing against the clock to get enough calls in
- We just can't let the clock beat us in this one
- Every time that clock hand moves, we see time our running out
- We only have so much time to make this appeal – and the clock is ticking

COMMITMENT
- Please make that commitment very quickly
- Make the commitment right now, before you do another thing
- Join the hundreds of others making that all-important commitment tonight
- Put your commitment into action before the hour is up
- Commitments have been flooding in

CONTACT
- Calling is conducted to maintain contact with the alumni while increasing the Annual Fund
- Pick up the phone and make instant contact
- The quickest way to make contact is to just pick up your telephone
- Some people think telephone fundraising is a contact sport
- We can't tell you how pleased we are that you've made contact with us
- We wish to contact every potential donor or supporter by telephone just as soon as possible

CONVENIENCE
- Enjoy the convenience that telemarketing offers
- Nothing can beat the convenience of your telephone
- The most convenient way to give is to just pick up your telephone and call today

COST
- The telephone is very cost-effective for charities
- We're calling you by telephone to keep costs down
- A simple phone call will cost you nothing but a moment of your time

CREDIT CARD
- We encourage you to use your credit card
- Thank you for being nice enough to use your credit card tonight
- You can space the payments on your credit card
- Here's a way to use your credit card for something other than consumer gratification
- A few easy payments on your credit card will do so much good for
- Here's a use for your credit card that perhaps you haven't thought of

- Using the telephone and your credit card, you can get desperately needed help to
- When you use your credit card here, you're using it to spread happiness and comfort
- All you have to do is tell us your credit card number
- One of the best uses you could put your credit card to
- Nonprofits turn to prepaid telephone cards as a fundraising vehicle
- Please get your credit card out now and call
- You can give so easily over the phone by using your credit card
- Telephone giving offers you the convenience of using your credit card

DATA

- Accurate, quality data collection is vital
- Your telephone data will be kept strictly confidential
- The data you provide by calling is absolutely essential

DEDICATE

- The calls show that so many dedicated people really care
- We dedicate this drive to you
- Now a telephone campaign dedicated only to you
- You can dedicate your call to a cause dear to you
- Once again our dedicated callers are rising to the occasion

DEPEND

- You know how much we depend on your call
- More and more, we depend on telephone fundraising
- Everything depends on us getting enough calls to
- We're depending on getting enough support today to

DIAL

- It's urgent that you dial now
- Have you got your dialing finger ready
- All you have to do is dial this number
- Lots of people are dialing in already
- It's so very easy to pick up that phone and dial now
- Nothing could be simpler and dialing us immediately

DO

- If you've always wanted to do something but didn't know quite what
- Now you can finally get around to doing something about
- The time to do something is now, this minute
- Do it right now, while your phone is within reach

DOLLARS

- Millions of dollars were raised nationwide by tireless telephone fundraisers
- The children depend on the dollars raised today over the telephone – your telephone

- Now you can donate these much-needed dollars over the telephone

DONATION

- People much prefer a call requesting a donation to one selling goods and services
- Dial a donation
- Simply pick up the phone and make your donation right now
- We need those donations to pour in over the telephone
- Your donation can go to work instantly
- Get your donation to the people who really need it without a lot of fuss and bother
- Even the most modest donation is welcome today
- The children are waiting eagerly for your donation
- The faster your donation, the faster we get to work solving the problem
- What better way to get a donation to
- Success all built on the willing donations of generous viewers like you

DONOR

- Reaching the hard-to-reach donor by phone
- Turning a casual caller into a donor isn't always easy
- Every donor counts, so please call now
- Your telephone can turn you into a caring donor
- The easy way to become a donor is over your telephone

DRIVE

- Please don't wait until the end of this drive – call now
- Don't hesitate until this drive is over
- Our annual telephone drive powers the rest of the year
- Drive after drive, you've always come through for us

EFFECTIVE

- An effort to spread the word about the effectiveness and professionalism of not-for-profit telemarketing
- A way to make really effective use of your telephone
- Giving by telephone is a very effective way to help

EFFICIENCY

- The telephone enhances our fundraising efficiency enormously
- Telephone fundraising is number one in efficiency and speed
- Your call increased our efficiency at helping that much more
- I know you value efficiency, so pick up that phone right now

EXAMPLE

- The example of letting your children see you make that call
- Here's an example of what your telephone pledge buys
- Your call is one of the best examples you can set

FUND
- With each call, our fund climbs encouragingly higher
- Major funding provided by your call will turn things around
- Desperately needed funding provided by you
- Take a moment now to help put our fund over the top

FUNDRAISING
- Telephone fundraising is becoming very big business
- Keeping up our year-round telephone fundraising effort
- Your call will help our fundraising effort so very much

GIFT
- We have a lot of thank you gifts to give out
- The sound of the telephone ringing is gift enough for us
- A gift you'll be proud to show off – it says you've helped someone
- I know you'll find plenty of uses for this thank you gift
- The best gift is your phone call
- A thank you gift for every pledge level
- When you call, you'll receive this lovely gift
- Your gift will go a long way toward helping

GOAL
- Just ten more calls and we've reached out goal
- Your call could be the one that puts us over the top of our goal
- The need is more intense so our goal is even higher than last year
- We know we can rely on you to help us reach our goal
- Imagine the feeling if your call is the one that lets us hit our goal
- Each call inches us higher toward our goal

GRATEFUL
- We're grateful to those who have already called, but if we're going to continue, we need your donation
- The children are so very grateful for every call
- You should see their grateful faces when they hear the phones ring

HEAR
- We need to hear from you
- The more of you we hear from, the sooner we reach our goal
- We know you're hearing us right now
- Please show you can hear us by calling soon
- Your call right now shows us you hear our message

HELP
- Help is just a simple phone call away
- A quick phone call is all it takes to help
- When you pick up that phone, you're already helping

- It's crucial that we get your help tonight
- So if you want to help, perhaps you'll give us a call

HESITATE
- Please don't hesitate to pick up that phone
- If you're hesitating, just listen to this
- If you hesitate too long, this could all just slip away
- Reaching the last holdouts who are still hesitating to call

HOLIDAY
- Telephone fundraising has become as much a part of the holiday season as street corner Santas
- Make that call now while you're in a holiday mood
- Please make a call to us part of your holiday ritual
- A telephone campaign carefully aimed at the brief holiday season window

HOPE
- Things are going a lot more slowly than we had hoped
- This funding drive is really driven by hope
- We're putting all our hope in your quick and compassionate response
- Look at the hope on the faces of all these people waiting for your call
- Your call right now is really our last hope
- I'm hoping so much you'll pick up that phone now

INPUT
- And while we're talking, we really want your input
- Dial now for instant input
- Your telephone can provide the quickest input of all

LINE
- We're keeping a line open especially for you
- Not all of our lines are busy, so there's still room for you
- Now you can get a line directly right into the heart of the action
- We want those lines humming with calls
- We hear you – all the way down the line
- An easy way to keep a line on us

MEMBER
- When you become a member, you become part of the family
- The more members who join up tonight, the closer we are to our goal
- We want you to be part of our membership drive
- It's so very easy to become a member by phoning

MEMBERSHIP
- We need those membership numbers to go up
- Call in your membership pledge now

- Building up our membership means this organization can continue to
- You can help our membership grow by calling right away
- On drives like this, we can increase the membership we rely upon
- We have to tell you how important your membership is to us
- Each membership is a foundation stone of our organization

METHOD

- The telephone is a key method of giving because it is so convenient
- Phoning in now could be your preferred method of helping
- Choose the easiest method of giving your support by simply picking up your phone

MOMENT

- Could you spare just a moment to talk to us
- A moment is all it takes to help
- Inside of a moment you could be giving help to

NUMBER

- The number to dial if you want to say, " Yes, I support you"
- You've got our number; we want you to use it
- We're simply overwhelmed by the numbers of calls we've received from a very concerned public

OPINION

- A way of finding out our supporters' reactions and opinions right away
- Make your opinion known immediately
- By making this call, you're stating your opinion loud and clear

PEOPLE

- People of all vocations have come together tonight
- All over the country, people are picking up the phone right now to call
- I know you are one of those people who sees a need and calls in at once to take care of it
- People reaching people instantly
- Please join all the other people making that important call right now

PHONATHON

- Our twenty-four hour phonathon is our single biggest fundraising event
- We concentrate everything on this phonathon so that, for the rest of the year, our staff can concentrate on working with people in need
- Everything depends on how many caring people like you respond to this phonathon

PHONE

- Your phone call is so very important
- Please phone just as soon as you can

- We really want to thank all the people who phoned in
- Your phone is a tool with which you can help and support
- If you're heading for your phone, keep on going
- Another minute to give everyone an opportunity to get to that phone
- The phones are suddenly beginning to come to life
- I urge you to pick up the phone and do what your heart is telling you
- Please, please phone in your support
- Don't hesitate another moment – pick up that phone

PLEDGE

- For lack of enough pledges, these children will keep on suffering
- Pledge from the heart and make a dazzling difference
- Thanks to all those who have already called in with your pledge
- Please call us with your pledge
- Please call right now with your pledge of financial support
- Please ring up now with your generous pledge
- This lovely premium is our way of thanking you for your phone pledge
- And that makes it a very affordable pledge for everyone
- Boy, it would be wonderful to take your pledge over the phone
- Your pledge tells us what you approve of and what you like
- Here's the good things your pledge will do
- It will be your pledge that is financing so much good work
- Without your pledge, who knows what horrors await
- Your pledge helps stop the madness

POSSIBLE

- Here's just a few of things your call makes possible
- Without your call, right now, none of this will be possible next year
- Because of the magic of the telephone, all this is now possible
- Through telephone use, we are able to cut fundraising costs way down

PREMIUM

- When you increase your donation, you'll receive this lovely premium
- This splendid premium set is all yours when you go up to the next donation level
- This is the best premium we've ever offered

PROFESSIONAL

- Talented professionals work the phones
- Your call will be received in a very professional manner
- Busy professionals are using the telephone to do their charitable giving
- Telephone giving is a very professional, efficient way to help out

PROJECT

- The telephone ensures that donors thoroughly understand our project and its needs
- You can be part of this crucial project by participating through the telephone

- Just to get this telephone campaign up and running was a major project

PROSPECT
- A telephone survey was tops in prospect generation
- More prospects responded via the telephone than ever before
- Initial telephone response has given us the prospect of a very good year

QUESTION
- The telephone gets questions answered
- We're calling to ask you a very special question
- It's a question of truly desperate need so please call
- My question is why you still haven't called

RECEIVER
- Pick up the receiver now
- Just grip that receiver tight and make your pledge
- I know you're already holding that receiver, now just dial

RELATIONSHIP
- Telephone contact has helped so much in building up our donor relationships
- Building a warm relationship with you over the telephone
- When you call, you're joining with us in a caring relationship that will benefit everyone
- We're calling because we already have a relationship with you

RESOURCE
- Your call will help give us the resources we need to fight
- With your telephone pledge, we'll finally have enough resources to help those who have been waiting so long
- You, at the end of your telephone line, are our best resource
- Your biggest resource, right now, is your telephone

RING
- We're waiting for our telephones to start ringing
- Ring us up now
- Pick up the phone and make our hearts ring with hope
- Help make our campaign a ringing success
- It isn't as if the telephone is ringing constantly
- Oh boy, we like to hear those phones ringing
- When you give us a ring, you're spreading happiness
- It's such a joy to hear all those telephones ringing at once
- As long as the phones are ringing, we know you care
- It's so wonderful to hear our phones start ringing
- Do you hear all the phones ringing in the background
- Give us a ring
- Each telephone ring makes someone's heart leap with hope

- Please keep those phones ringing

SCHEME
- A unique mail/telephone fundraising scheme
- It's a scheme to help others through the telephone
- Participate in this ingenious scheme by dialling now

SCRIPT
- Responsible for successfully scripting so many segments
- Your telephone response is part of the script
- I'm not just reading some script, I'm speaking from the heart

SOLUTION
- Providing telephone-based solutions
- A massive telephone campaign was proposed as the solution
- Your call now is a vital part of the solution
- The solution is as near as your phone

STANDARDS
- Dedicated to establishing ethical standards for telemarketing
- Show your support and appreciation of these high standards by calling
- When you call, you're supporting the best standards yet

SUPPORT
- Call in your support now
- Your pledge of support
- So if you want to support excellence, give us a call

SURVEY
- Fundraising efforts very fruitfully combined with a telephone survey
- Telephone surveys are a highly accurate, cost-effective way of reaching the most desired segment of the population
- Please participate in the survey to help us find out how best to allot the money people like you have so generously donated

TALK
- We're waiting now to talk to you
- We really want to talk to you
- Talk to us
- Call so you can talk to us directly about your concerns
- Unless you call now, this appeal will be just talk

TEAM
- Call now and join our team
- Someone on our team will call you soon
- We need you on our telephone team

- Our team includes every one of you within reach of your telephone
- With each person who calls, our team grows bigger

TECHNOLOGY

- Using the latest telephone and computer technology to help
- It's a simple technology, right at your fingertips
- Through the miracle of technology, you can get your help to those who need it instantly

TELECOMMUNICATOR

- Good telecommunicators are more at a premium than ever
- The true measure of a telecommunicator is how much response is generated within a given time frame
- Helping us all to become better telecommunicators

TELEMARKETING

- Telemarketing has turned out to be a very powerful tool
- Non-for-profit telemarketing can offer twenty-four hour service
- Telemarketing is an efficient way of defraying costs

TELEPHONE

- The telephone is something you use day in and day out
- Through the telephone, you can now give twenty-four hours in the day
- Tonight, your telephone can turn into a magical instrument
- Your telephone is right beside you
- Your telephone is only a reach/heartbeat away
- Your telephone is the easiest way to
- Your telephone call means immediate help for
- Via high-capacity telephone hookups
- You can help so much simply by picking up the telephone
- Enjoying ourselves on the telephone
- Go to your telephone and let us know we've done the right thing

TELETHON

- Our annual telethon is the pivot around which all our fundraising efforts revolve
- Everyone here is getting caught up in the excitement of this telethon
- This telethon is our way of being heard across the country

TELL

- Tell us anything you want
- Your call tells us how well we're doing
- Nothing is more telling than the number of calls received

THANK YOU

- If you've already called, thank you
- Thank you for listening, thank you for calling

- Thank you for caring enough to pick up your telephone and pledge

TIME
- Time is rapidly running out
- Just one more hour, then our time is gone
- Won't you take the time right now to put through that vital call
- Now is the time to make your call
- Now is the time to get up and act
- Only a few calls to go, but my goodness, time is slipping by

TOUCH
- Keeping continually in touch with our vital donor base
- Reach out and touch someone
- Your telephone call will keep you in touch with this campaign
- The quickest way of getting in touch with us

TRAIN
- To hire and train callers to execute an effective solicitation plan
- Our workers are trained to respond to your call immediately and answer all your questions
- A well-trained staff is key to the success of any telephone campaign

TRUST
- With telephone fundraising, trust becomes a bigger issue than ever before
- We're going to trust in you that you're going to your telephone now
- So many people in need are trusting that you'll help today

TRY
- If you haven't been able to get through, please, please try again
- Don't give up trying because of a busy signal
- If you try to reach us now, you'll be sure to get through
- We want to you to keep trying

VERIFY
- Potential donors may call the charity to verify that a telemarketing campaign is on
- Call us whenever you wish to verify
- We'll be glad to verify every fact over the phone

VOLUNTEER
- Our telephone volunteer will explain
- Our telephone volunteers gladly give their time and energy
- We have lots of volunteers waiting to take your call
- Wouldn't it be great to have every last one of our volunteers busy with the phones
- Those who volunteer here have also joined up

- Just the number of people who volunteer indicates how devoted
- Our volunteers will be very, very happy to talk to you
- Our volunteers have given up their weekend to be here
- You will instantly reach one of our eager volunteers
- All these volunteers are just waiting for the phones to ring

WAIT

- Don't wait another minute, please call now
- We can hardly wait for your call
- Rows of volunteers are waiting for your call
- The longer you wait, the more your help is needed

WIRE

- We're really coming right down to the wire here
- Your last chance before we get right to the wire
- If you call right now, you can just get in under the wire

WORK

- Because of your call, the work can continue
- Make your call a working call
- Show you are working with us to stop
- Yes, a telephone donation really works wonders

YOU

- We have to please you
- We need you tonight
- People like you are our mainstay
- Everyone here is waiting to hear from you
- You are the one who makes it all work tonight
- It's all happening because of you
- You are the key to this campaign's success
- Those at risk really need you to make that call now

Section Five

Saying
Thank You

ACCOMPLISH
- You accomplished so much under very difficult circumstances
- You have accomplished the impossible
- I only wish everyone could see what has been accomplished

ACCOMPLISHMENT
- What an accomplishment
- Taking enormous pride in your accomplishment
- Look forward to your accomplishments in the years ahead

ACHIEVE
- I know how hard you've worked to achieve this
- And you achieve even more in the future
- No one imagined you could achieve so much
- Every so often, someone achieves something truly spectacular

ACHIEVEMENT
- Even the preparations were a real achievement
- This level of achievement is rarely reached
- We're proud and happy about your achievement
- Derive great pleasure from your achievements
- You have a good solid record of achievement
- Your achievements quickly came to my attention

ACKNOWLEDGE
- Acknowledging that there is still room for improvement
- We would like to acknowledge the following organizations
- First, I want acknowledge all the effort that went into
- Acknowledge your dedication and commitment in such a special way

ACKNOWLEDGEMENT
- I would like to make the following acknowledgements
- I really appreciate the acknowledgement of such a special occasion
- Really value your acknowledgement of all the contributions

ACTION
- To everyone who cared enough to take individual and collective action
- Thank you for taking such prompt and effective action
- I always find you where the action is
- Your quick, compassionate action saved the day

ADMIRE
- I want to tell you how much I admire you
- Someone who we understand and admire
- I admire your perseverance and commitment
- I respect and admire your work

ADVICE
- You always give such good advice
- Thank you so much for your helpful advice
- Thank you very much for the extremely valuable advice
- A grateful thank you for all your help and advice

AGREEMENT
- Coming to a very quick agreement
- So glad that you and I are both in agreement
- There can be nothing but agreement about

APOLOGY
- Again my thanks and apologies
- Apologies for our absence
- I want to apologize for taking so long

APPLAUD
- I want to applaud your stand
- Now there's something we can really applaud
- Every one of us applauds your decision
- The more we applaud, the more you deserve

APPRECIATE
- To make sure how much we appreciate you
- Your continued support is greatly appreciated
- Appreciate all who have helped and contributed
- I really appreciate the fact that I can call on you at any time
- I appreciate your review of my proposal
- To let you know we appreciate all your hard work
- I deeply appreciate your invitation
- I appreciate your taking on the responsibility
- Always remembered, shared and appreciated
- Each gesture, no matter how large or small, was deeply appreciated
- It's about appreciating the little things in life
- You'll appreciate the value
- For those who appreciate the best
- You are appreciated so much by all of us
- To show how much we appreciate your patronage
- The faster your life moves, the more you'll appreciate
- Few things are more appreciated than
- I appreciate you
- Appreciate your willingness to take risks
- You'll never know how much I appreciate
- Someone who truly appreciates you
- We appreciate how rare it is to find a real gem like you
- You are most heartily appreciated

APPRECIATION
- Expressing my thanks and appreciation
- With warmest appreciation
- Just a little token of our appreciation
- We just can't show our appreciation enough
- A gesture of appreciation
- Every year my appreciation of you becomes stronger
- With warmest appreciation
- I'd like to express our deepest appreciation for
- Thanks and appreciation
- A growing appreciation is developing
- Appreciation changes and increases
- On behalf of our organization, I wish to express our appreciation
- There's never a better time to express our profound appreciation
- In appreciation of our continued association
- Showing a keen appreciation for
- Expressing heartfelt thanks and deep appreciation
- This is the kind of appreciation you get when you come to us for
- Constant appreciation in value is only one benefit of
- I want to show my appreciation for everything you have done
- As guilty as the next person in not expressing my appreciation

ASK
- Thanks for asking
- No matter what we ask, you always come through
- How comforting to know I can always ask this of you
- You helped out without being asked

ASSET
- You have proved an invaluable asset
- Find you such an asset to the organization
- You are our chief human asset

ASSIST
- Thanks so much for assisting us
- You are always so ready assist
- The one person who can always be counted upon to assist

ASSISTANCE
- I sincerely appreciate the assistance and support you provided
- I hope you will let me know if I can be of assistance in the future
- I want to thank you for your prompt assistance in this matter
- Thank you for your consideration and assistance

ATTENTION
- Thank you for calling our attention to this problem
- I appreciated your prompt attention

- Thank you for your attention to my views

ATTITUDE
- Reflected in your positive attitude
- Especially appreciate your cheerful attitude
- Your helpful attitude has made such a difference

AWARD
- Earned every one of your numerous awards
- This award is richly deserved
- So very happy to know you won this award
- Congratulations on winning such a prestigious award

BENEFIT
- You will reap the benefits for many years to come
- The benefits of this achievement are tremendous
- Extending a thank you benefit
- In gratitude for so many unexpected benefits

BEST
- Definitely one of the best
- I wish you all the best
- Best wishes for the coming year
- You are one of the best and brightest
- It's great to work with the very best
- Have the best of everything right here

BUSINESS
- I enjoyed doing business with your from start to finish
- Good luck in your business
- You make it your business to amaze us every day
- Appreciate the generous actions of local businesses during the emergency

CARE
- We know how much you care
- I'll never forget the compassion and professional care
- People who care are thinking of you today
- I was genuinely touched by how much you care
- Thank you for a day full of warmth and caring
- Please know that we care very much
- Thank you for caring so much
- The care and concern of friends like you got us through
- Thank you so much for your expression of caring
- Care for it as much as you
- Want to thank you personally for caring
- Thanks for caring enough to work so hard toward our goal

CELEBRATE
- We truly have something to celebrate
- Thinking of you as you celebrate this wonderful occasion
- Now there really is something to celebrate
- Thanks for helping us celebrate
- Come help us celebrate
- I look forward to celebrating many more such anniversaries

CELEBRATION
- In this time of celebration
- This certainly is a cause for celebration
- We wanted to be part of your celebration
- So grateful you wanted to join our celebration
- We rejoice in celebrating this wonderful occasion together
- The celebration would have been ho-hum without you

CHANCE
- Thanks for taking a chance on us
- Without you, I wouldn't have had a chance to try
- Bless the lucky chance that brought you to us
- Thanks for giving me the chance to show what I can do

CHOOSE
- We're delighted that you've chosen us
- Just one more way of saying thank you for choosing
- Thank you for choosing to help so much

COMMITMENT
- Your personal commitment contributed overwhelmingly to our success
- This is the biggest decision and the biggest commitment we've ever made
- A lasting commitment like yours is very hard to find
- So happy to recognize your commitment

COMMUNITY
- You've never been too busy to give back to the community
- On behalf of the entire community, I want to convey our thanks
- Your relationship to others and your community has always been splendid
- You help with so many worthwhile projects in our community
- Recognize your outstanding contributions to our community
- Aware of your efforts to make our community a better place to live
- You have so many great ideas for our community
- You are a great resource to the community
- Touched by the care our community members demonstrated
- We are fortunate to have such dedicated people in our community
- Thank you for being partners with our community
- Making the community aware of these generous actions

COMPLIMENT
- Thank you for the kind compliment
- My compliments
- So much more than just a simple compliment
- We have received many compliments throughout the community

CONCERN
- Thank you very much for your concern over our recent misunderstanding
- I want to express my concern
- Reflected in your genuine concern for others
- I thought a long time about how to convey my concern
- Thank you for your thoughtful attention to my concerns

CONGRATULATE
- I want to congratulate and thank the committee for
- I congratulate you for passing such a significant milestone
- I look forward to congratulating you in person
- I want to congratulate you on your recent appointment

CONGRATULATIONS
- Congratulations are in order
- Congratulations and many thanks to
- I wanted to send you a personal note of congratulations
- Please accept my love and congratulations
- Congratulations on the wonderful news
- Congratulations and much affection
- Congratulations on reaching such a major turning point
- My congratulations and love are with you
- Thank you for your letter of congratulations
- Congratulations on spreading your wings
- Congratulations on opening your own business

CONTRIBUTION
- I hope you know how much your contribution helped
- You have made a significant contribution to our fundraising effort
- I would like to thank you for your generous contribution
- Your contribution is sure to be remembered for a long, long time
- I want you to know how much I value your contribution
- Wherever you go, you make an important contribution
- To recognize your personal contributions
- Judged on the contribution you have made to our lives
- You've made a genuine contribution
- Enabled us to make a valuable contribution
- Your contributions have been exemplary

COOPERATION
- Thanks so much for your cooperation

- Thank you for your cooperation in this matter
- I would particularly like commend your spirit of cooperation
- Grateful for your cooperation and willingness to assist

COUNT
- I know I can always count on you and I'm so grateful
- I can always count on you to help convince others
- I can count on you to take appropriate action

COURAGE
- I've always admired your courage
- Thank you for facing this challenge with such courage
- You hung in there with courage and determination
- Always admired your inner strength and courage

CREDIT
- You deserve all the credit for
- The credit is all yours
- I wish to credit all the generous individuals who donated their time and talents
- Crediting you with this wonderful success
- So much of the credit belongs to you

DAY
- A day we've marked to celebrate
- Hope you'll be here forever and a day
- You really made my day
- I know this is a really great day
- Congratulations on your special day
- You provided a day I shall never forget
- Today is your special day
- Wonderful to have a special day to honor you
- So happy to share your special day
- Even though I don't see you every day
- An unforgettable day for all of us
- I'm counting the days until we meet
- Wishing you a super day and a wonderful year ahead
- Remember this day as one of the most important in your life
- Thanks for brightening the day
- The most spectacular day we have ever experienced

DEAR
- You are very dear to us all
- Success is sweet when so dearly bought
- Want you to know how dear you are

DECISION
- You had a major influence on our decision

- Applaud your decision to
- Your input really helped us make a critical decision

DECLINE
- As it is too late, we must decline
- At the last moment, I regretfully decline
- So sorry to have to decline your kind invitation

DEDICATION
- Truly inspired by your energy and dedication
- Your dedication and outstanding accomplishments in the field of
- So impressed with your hard work and dedication
- Proud of your dedication and accomplishments
- I truly appreciate your time and dedication
- Your dedication and excellent qualifications
- Expressed dedication to the many causes publically espoused

DEED
- Your kind words and good deeds are precious
- So many caring words and deeds
- Too many splendid good deeds to name

DELIGHT
- Always a delight to be with
- I am delighted that your opinion is similar to mine
- I know how delighted you must be

DESERVE
- You really deserve a really special thank you
- You deserve the best
- You deserve a lot more than
- You deserve a medal
- Congratulations on well-deserved recognition
- I can't think of anyone who deserves this position more
- Well-deserving of this prestigious recognition
- Deserve a resounding thank you

DETAIL
- You made sure every detail was perfect
- No detail was too small for your attention
- Absolutely loved every detail
- Your attention to every detail made the day run smoothly

DETERMINATION
- We are very proud of your determination
- Applaud your determination to stick to your own convictions
- Your strong determination to succeed

- Very few people have your magnificent determination

DONATION
- I want to thank all of you who made a donation or volunteered
- Thank you for your concern and your donation
- We appreciate your donations in support of
- Thanks for your in-kind donations
- We are so very pleased to accept your generous donation
- Thank you for your considerate donation

DREAM
- Never in my wildest dreams did I think you could pull this off
- Now we are seeing so many of those hopes and dreams come true
- You've worked very hard to make your dreams come true
- Now you have made your dream a reality
- Thank you for a dream come true
- The achievement is the fulfilment of a longtime dream

EASY
- You make the hardest tasks look so easy
- It's so easy to say thanks to you
- I know it hasn't been easy

EFFORT
- I know how much time and effort you invested
- Certainly clear that the effort was worth it
- Nobody puts more effort into things than you do
- The many new, exciting innovations made possible by your efforts and generosity
- Appreciate your dedication to team effort
- All the effort and sacrifice takes on new meaning
- Your fine efforts will be recognized soon
- Please continue your efforts on behalf of the cause
- Very much aware of your efforts
- My appreciation for your effort is enormous
- Thanks again for your efforts
- Want you to know we greatly appreciated your efforts
- We appreciate this gift of time and effort more than you can know
- Thanks for making it possible to join this great effort
- Your efforts are always sincerely appreciated
- Very grateful for your outstanding efforts
- Thank you for all your efforts on our behalf
- Thank you for your extraordinary efforts

ENCOURAGEMENT
- I appreciate your encouragement
- Couldn't have done it without your encouragement and determination

- Always there with encouragement when it was needed most
- You probably don't realize how much your encouragement has meant
- Thanks to your support and encouragement
- Thank you for your encouragement, help and advice
- I am particularly grateful for your encouragement

ENJOY
- Everyone enjoyed themselves so much
- I enjoyed every minute
- So enjoy your irrepressible humor
- I so enjoyed being part of this adventure
- I thought you might enjoy this
- Just wanted to you know how very much I enjoyed
- I hope you enjoyed it as much as I did

ENRICH
- You've enriched our lives
- So enriched by your many kindnesses over the years
- Enriched by your strength, patience wisdom and guidance
- Enriched us in so many ways

ENTHUSIASM
- I've never seen so much enthusiasm
- Your enthusiasm will ensure your success
- I just had to write to express my enthusiasm for
- Thank you for your enthusiasm and participation
- We share your enthusiasm
- Look forward with great enthusiasm

EVENT
- It was lovely to see both of you at this event
- You guys really made this event
- Went above and beyond to make this event a success
- So many guests said it was the best event they'd ever been to
- Resulted in the most successful event ever
- One of the most successful events we've ever had
- This is a real landmark event
- The event will be complete if you are there
- No one throws parties or events like you do
- Thanks for helping make the event bigger and better than ever
- Thank you for making this event run so smoothly
- One of those lucky enough to be present at this event
- Your continued interest and participation in this exciting event

EVERYTHING
- Thank you so much for everything
- Many thanks for everything you and your staff did

- I just wanted to thank you again for everything
- Everything was excellent

EXPERIENCE
- It has been a powerful and positive experience
- I thank you personally for such a supportive and educational experience
- The experience wouldn't have been the same without you
- I know we've experienced difficult times and disappointments
- You always generously share what you have learned from your own experience
- Sharing a universally cosmic experience
- So exciting to be part of the experience
- We have shared so many outstanding experiences
- A truly new experience for most of us

EXPERTISE
- You alway lend additional insight and expertise
- An enthusiastic audience and very appreciative of your expertise
- We need your expertise
- The professional expertise needed on this crucial project

FAITH
- You have restored my faith in humanity
- Your faith in me means so very much
- You always had faith in the outcome
- Thanks for reminding me to have faith
- Thanks for keeping the faith when everyone else gave up

FAMILY
- My family and I will never be able to thank you enough
- My family and I would like to thank you
- You made us feel part of the family
- I wish to thank my loving family which has put with so much
- How fortunate to be part of such a warm, caring family
- A family with so much to give
- Looking forward to making you part of our family
- Our thoughts are with you and your family

FEELING
- My feeling is one of sublime happiness
- My feelings about it amount to a state of euphoria
- I don't want to leave a single caring feeling unsaid

FRIEND
- I now consider you a good friend
- All your friends are there for you
- So lucky to have friends like you
- Counting on you as a friend

- Wonderful to be with such dear friends again
- Once again reminds me of what a good friend you are
- Not only as a partner but as a friend
- Have known you as a personal friend for years
- We look forward to meeting a dear friend
- You have become such a dear and valued friend
- We were friends long before this situation occurred
- Thanks for being my friend
- Thank you for telling friends about us
- Thanks for being such a steadfast, loyal friend

FRIENDSHIP

- Our friendship and love are always here for you
- Thinking of our many years of friendship
- Such a comfort to know you are a dear friend
- Thanks for your friendship in bad times and good
- I value your friendship

FUTURE

- I am very excited about the future
- You'll be seeing more of us in the future
- You ensure there's a great future ahead
- Now you can create the kind of future you want for yourself

GENEROSITY

- We're blown away by your generosity
- We can never repay you for such generosity
- Thanks for your generosity
- Your generosity is awesome
- Your generosity springs directly from your heart

GENEROUS

- One of the most generous people in the city
- Thanks again for all your generous help
- Always so generous with your time and your expertise

GESTURE

- A simple gesture of thanks
- Please join us in a gesture of appreciation
- What a kind and wonderful gesture

GIFT

- It's clear you spent a great deal of time and care in choosing our gift
- A great comfort knowing the gift has been put to good use
- Your gift fitted perfectly
- Thanks for your very thoughtful gift
- No gift is really ours until we have thanked the giver

- Your generous gift is greatly appreciated
- I really value your gift
- Your gift will grow more precious every year
- Your gift was a memorable keepsake
- Thank you for the lovely gift
- Your gift will always remind me of you
- Each time I see your gift, I think of you
- As always, you picked out the perfect gift
- We wish to honour you by offering this gift in your name
- Just a small token gift to thank you for
- Thank you for sending me such a perfect gift
- Thank you for the exquisite gift
- Each time I look at your gift, my spirits lift
- I'm so glad you chose the gift you did

GIVE
- If it were up to me, I'd give you everything
- You give richly of your time, talent and resources
- Thank you for giving us such a terrific treat
- A gift that gives over and over
- We thank you for the things you gave us
- If giving makes life happy, you must be very happy indeed

GOAL
- Your participation and cooperation has helped us achieve our goals
- A time to think of your goals for the years ahead
- You've certainly achieved your goals
- Good luck in your pursuit of this very worthwhile goal
- You have made many sacrifices to achieve your goal
- Always a genuine interest in our goals

GOOD
- You make me feel so good
- Had such a good time last night
- Thank you for doing such a good turn
- We never forget a good turn
- Good food and good fellowship
- It feels so good just to know you are there
- It was so good of you to help out
- To recognize all the good you are doing
- I just can't say enough good things about

GRATEFUL
- We're grateful for you every day
- I wanted to tell you right away how grateful we are
- So many good things to be grateful for
- Feeling grateful but with no one to thank

- We are so grateful for everything we receive
- I am very grateful to you for
- I just want to convey to you how very grateful I am
- You were there for me and I'm deeply grateful
- I am eternally grateful for your help
- A few words from a very grateful guest

GRATITUDE
- I would like to express my deepest gratitude for
- To each and every member we would like to express our sincere gratitude and understanding
- How can I pack a lifetime of gratitude into a single letter
- Our attitude is one of gratitude
- Gratitude is one of the most beautiful virtues
- Gratitude is the mother of all other virtues
- Gratitude is the greatest form of courtesy
- I want to say everything in the language of gratitude
- We humbly express our gratitude
- Our gratitude knows no bounds
- The heartfelt gratitude of those in need
- Presenting you with a small but loving token of our gratitude

GREAT
- We think you are great
- The crowds thought you were great
- Great to know we have such dedicated people in time of need
- It was really great to have you there

HAND
- Such a comfort to be in your capable, caring hands
- Hand in hand, we can meet the future
- Always ready to reach out a helping hand

HAPPY
- I'm so happy for you
- We are so happy you arrived safely
- Happy to be so well matched
- You've made me very happy
- How proud and happy you must be

HEART
- You will always have a special place in my heart
- My heart prompts me to add these words
- You are always in our hearts
- The key is in our hearts
- You touched our hearts in a very special way
- May you soon have all your heart's desires

- A helping hand and a willing heart
- Thank you for making our hearts so much lighter
- You always share right from the heart

HELP
- You've been such a big help
- You really helped us through
- Let me know if there's anything more I can do to help
- Want to help you through this difficult time
- Offer whatever help will be of value to you
- If I may help you in some way
- Always willing to help
- Thank you for your help
- We felt you did a splendid job helping out
- Is there anything we can do to help or ease the burden
- You are a very special help to us
- Thank you again for your help and support
- I want to thank you again for all your help
- You help us a lot
- Always more than willing to help us out
- You really went all out to help
- It goes without saying it was great of you to help

HONOR
- I cannot tell you how pleased and honored I am
- I can't think of anyone more deserving of this honor
- I can imagine no better way to honor you
- An honor you richly deserve
- So pleased and honored you could join us

HOPE
- Turned out even better than we could have hoped
- With high hopes and a fresh start
- Just talking to you gives us so much hope
- A time when hopes rise for peace and understanding
- Thank you to everyone who urged me not to give up hope

HOSPITALITY
- Thank you for your gracious hospitality
- You give new meaning to the word, "hospitality"
- Thank you for your hospitality during my visit

HOST
- Thank you for hosting such a marvellous educational experience
- Never met a more thoughtful host than you
- You are the best host ever

HUG

- Consider this a hug
- On days when you really need a hug
- Hearing from you is as good as a hug

IDEA

- I always look forward to hearing your ideas
- Thank you for coming and sharing your ideas
- Your hard work and creative ideas have already helped improve
- Your ideas are always so creative
- Hiring you was the best idea yet

IMPRESS

- I particularly wanted you to know how much I am impressed
- So impressed about how you are able to balance both sides
- Impressed by your clear and reasoned arguments
- All were impressed by your artistry

INFORMATION

- Everyone enjoyed hearing the information you had at your fingertips
- Thanks for the valuable information
- We had such a great time trading information
- Thank you for making such vital information available

INSPIRE

- You are so inspiring
- It's inspiring to see so many new faces this year
- You inspired me deeply
- I felt inspired after we met

INTEREST

- Just thought you'd be interested in this
- You always have our interests at heart
- We appreciate your interest
- Thank you for your interest and response
- Thank you for your continued interest and support
- I have followed your progress with great interest
- Persuade you to continue your interest
- Thank you for your kind interest
- Thank you for your interest in our products
- Thank you for your interest in staying updated
- Excited by your interest in
- I know you are particularly interested in
- I would like to take a moment to confirm my strong interest in

JOB

- Please accept my congratulations on a job well done

- The job you did for us was truly special
- A great pleasure to work with you on this recent job
- Thank you for doing such a wonderful job
- You really do a great job
- You've done an amazing job
- When we want to job done, we always call on you
- Each of you did an outstanding job
- Appreciate the excellent job you are doing
- Your presence makes our job easier
- I think you have done a super job
- My compliments on a job well done
- Dedicated and proficient in your job duties

JOIN

- It was a great pleasure to join you
- Thanks for letting me join in
- You joined us on a real voyage of discovery
- Thank you for joining our team

JOY

- It is a joy to know what a wonderful person you've become
- I wish you joy – and more joy
- You are someone who brings joy into my life
- I remember with joy the time when
- Even though we cannot be present to share in the joy
- Thanks for bringing laughter and joy

KIND

- You are one of a kind
- Always there with a kind word and a helping hand
- Thank you very kindly
- Thank you again for being so kind

KINDNESS

- Thank you very much for your kindness
- Your kindness and good ideas will be sorely missed
- Your many kindnesses will be remembered
- How can anyone forget such kindness
- Sincere thanks for the kindness you have shown
- Thank you for you kindness, gentleness and words of encouragement

KNOW

- Thanks for wanting to know something about this
- I know how much planning went into making this day a success
- Wanted you to know you are always in our thoughts
- Please let me know if you can use some help
- We feel as though we know you personally

- Although I do not know you well
- You will be so pleased to know
- I don't know how you do it

LETTER

- I know how hard it was to write that letter
- This is the easiest letter I've ever had to write
- I wanted to write a letter of appreciation
- This letter of thanks is very important to me
- It's not often I get to write a thank you letter for
- Thank you for your recent letter
- Your letter made all the difference
- My first priority was to write this letter expressing our gratitude

LIFE

- You've changed our lives forever
- I wanted to tell you how much you improved my life
- I know this is a very exciting time in your life
- Knowing you has changed my life
- You've shared some of the happiest moments in my life
- Privileged to mark one of life's most precious moments
- Thank you for letting me be part of your life
- Thank you for bringing new life and hope to us all
- We look forward to hearing all about your new life
- The ability to laugh and keep life in perspective
- Convey my gratitude to a mentor who made such an impact on my life
- Filled with dignity and enjoying life to the fullest
- Life is so much easier because of you
- You help us celebrate life
- You are the best part of my life
- You fill our lives with sunshine

LOOK

- I look forward so much to working with you again
- Look forward to continuing our dialogue
- Look forward to lots of interesting
- Look forward so much to seeing you soon
- I look forward to introducing you
- We are looking forward to a great victory
- Now you can look back and access your accomplishments

LOVE

- I send you my love
- I love you all
- My love and wisdom always follow you
- Making us feel so loved
- You've always had our love and our pride

- You are a testament to the power of love
- You've always been there to love, guide and protect

LUCK
- Good luck with your efforts
- Good luck with your campaign
- Luck has nothing to do with it
- The fabulous good luck of finding you
- Just my luck

LUCKY
- I count myself lucky to know you
- Know how lucky we are to have you on board
- We are very lucky to persuade you to join

MEET
- Very happy to have met and shared with you
- I look forward to meeting with you back home
- We enjoyed meeting with you about
- I can't wait to meet you
- Thank you for meeting with me so soon
- I can't tell you how much I appreciated meeting you
- So glad I finally had the opportunity to meet you
- I've never met anyone like you
- What a pleasure it was to meet you
- Though I have yet to meet you personally
- It seems we met you only yesterday
- Thank you for meeting with us so promptly
- Planning a mutually convenient time to meet
- I am very grateful for our meeting

MEMBER
- Every member is exceptional
- A very responsible member of our community
- All our members were delighted
- Activities would not be possible without the generous support of our members

MEMORABLE
- You put such a memorable event together on short notice
- You help us relive a memorable day
- Your gift was such a memorable keepsake

MEMORY
- Such a nice memory
- A joyful memory shared by all
- So happy to have this for our memories
- Now I have one more fond memory

- Thanks for the memory
- You have honored a precious memory
- You bring back so many fond memories
- Given us memories we will always cherish
- I want to thank you for the treasured memories and those yet to come

MESSAGE

- Your message was so meaningful
- Thank you for your message of appreciation
- Everyone is very interested in your message
- Thank you for taking the time to bring us such an important message

MILESTONE

- Congratulations on reaching such a milestone
- You've passed a very impressive milestone
- A real milestone in your growth

MIND

- You've been on my mind a lot lately
- Thank you for keeping an open mind
- Thanks for keeping me in mind

NOTE

- Thanks again for your note and your interest
- I'm sending you this little note to thank you
- Your personal note made me feel touched and remembered
- Your note really cheered me up
- Your note was a very special reminder of how much you care
- Your note said just what I was feeling
- Just a short note to thank you for
- I really appreciated your note
- A thoughtful note is even better than a gift

OCCASION

- How could we let such a significant occasion pass without acknowledgement
- This is one occasion that really means a lot
- One occasion I truly look forward to
- An occasion I'll always remember with fondness
- Take pleasure in helping you celebrate this special occasion
- Such joyous occasions require substantial planning
- This occasion is very special to me too
- I know this is a solemn and joyous occasion
- Thanks for making the occasion so meaningful
- Enure a memorable occasion for everyone
- Thank you for making the occasion so exceptional
- You made the occasion so much fun

OFFER
- Very gratified by your offer
- Thank you very much for this offer
- I am really excited about this new offering

OPPORTUNITY
- Thanks for talking to me about this wonderful opportunity
- Very glad to have the opportunity to
- I welcome the opportunity of continuing our association
- Now so many new opportunities are opening to you
- A rare opportunity to touch hearts
- Thanks for the opportunity to grow in new ways
- I would appreciate the opportunity to serve
- An excellent opportunity to meet
- Saved us from missing this fabulous opportunity
- How gratified to be offered this opportunity
- Thanks again for the opportunity to
- Thanks for offering this exciting opportunity
- Thank you for the opportunity to serve you
- I would like to take this opportunity to express my thanks for
- Thank you for creating an additional opportunity

PARTICIPATE
- I would like to thank everyone who participated
- We would like to take this opportunity to thank you for participating
- I just wanted to thank you for letting me participate
- We hope you will continue to participate
- I encourage everyone to participate and contribute

PEOPLE
- I extend a very special thank you to people who have gone out of their way to
- It's wonderful to work with such an outstanding group of people
- Strongly committed to serving the people
- You always take care of people first
- If it wasn't for people like you, I don't know what I would have done
- People are still talking about it

PERFECT
- Having you this close makes everything perfect
- You proved yourself the perfect companion
- You came up with the perfect solution

PERFORMANCE
- Your performance has been unfailingly superior
- Performance is consistently first class
- Thank you for the magnificent performance

PERSON

- Simply put, you are the best person
- You are a swell person
- You were the perfect person to ask
- What a remarkable person you are
- You were certainly the right person to handle this difficult assignment
- Persons whose accomplishments earn special recognition
- Knew you were just the person we were looking for

PERSONAL

- I wanted to write to you personally to convey my thanks
- Permit me to extend a personal thanks and welcome
- Thank you for discussing this with me personally
- A very personal thank you
- I so enjoy getting personal mail from you
- How much I personally, and collectively, thank you

PLEASE

- So glad to hear you're pleased
- I hope this gesture of thanks will please you
- I was extremely pleased to learn

PLEASURE

- It was such a pleasure to have spoken with you
- A tremendous pleasure to see you moving up quickly
- Taking much pleasure in your accomplishments
- As always, it is a pleasure dealing with you

POSITION

- I am very excited about this position
- Thank you for considering me for this position
- Look forward to discussing this position with you

POSITIVE

- How wonderful to hear something so positive
- Your involvement has been such a positive
- I'm positive you have what it takes

POSSIBLE

- Without your help, the job would have been impossible
- It wouldn't have been possible without you
- You made it all possible
- I look forward to the possibility of working with you

POTENTIAL

- Justified our trust in your potential
- Gratifying to see so much potential finally realized

- With such a great deal of professional potential

PRESENT
- What a lovely present
- Thank you all again for such a fabulous present
- You dream up the most original presents

PRESENTATION
- Everyone loved the whole presentation
- Your presentation was both entertaining and informative
- A presentation delivered with the confidence of someone thoroughly familiar with this complex subject
- Your presentation was so enjoyable it seemed to end all too soon

PRIDE
- I take great pride in my long association with you
- Your pride in taking such a big, important step
- You can't imagine the pride we feel in you
- You can look back with pride
- With great pride we say thank you to
- Great pride in all that you are and will become
- I was gratified to see the level of personal pride expressed

PRIVILEGE
- I can't tell you how privileged you make me feel
- Such an honor and a privilege to shake your hand
- A privilege like this doesn't come every day
- Such a rare and special privilege
- Privileged to know such a special person

PROGRAM
- I'd like to express my appreciation for the fine program you presented
- I am very impressed with programs currently in place
- Delighted with the facility and the programs you are offering

PROJECT
- Undertaking an important national project
- Thank you for sponsoring such a worthwhile project
- I appreciated the chance to look over this project
- Without you, this project could have been a train wreck

PROMPT
- Thank you for contacting me so promptly
- Your prompt action saved the day
- You are always prompt and considerate
- You never have to be prompted to act

PROUD

- You have right to feel proud
- You must be so proud
- I'm extremely proud of you
- We are so proud of you on this wonderful day
- I know how proud you must be
- Proud to know such a thoughtful, compassionate person
- I know that you are proud of yourself

RAVE

- I just want to rave about you
- There were raves about the
- Your performance produced nothing but raves

RECOMMEND

- I do not hesitate to recommend
- Like to recommend you to all our friends
- I won't hesitate to recommend you
- We will recommend you at every opportunity

RECOMMENDATION

- I would like to thank you for your favourable recommendation
- Pleased to offer this recommendation
- Delighted to give my personal recommendation

REGRET

- It is with particular regret I must decline
- I regret we will be unable to attend
- I'd like to express my sincere regrets

RELATIONSHIP

- I hope we'll always have a close, loving relationship
- Let's make this relationship permanent
- Always deepening your relationship
- Now that we have such a wonderful working relationship

RECOGNITION

- Equal recognition for all involved is well deserved
- It took a lot of time and effort to reach this kind of recognition
- What a perfect recognition of your outstanding contribution

REMEMBER

- Helped make it something we'll remember forever
- We will always remember what you have so kindly done
- Thank you for remembering
- You always remember the important things
- Each time I remember, it brings a smile

- I want to say something that will be remembered long after this occasion is over
- You are gratefully remembered
- How thoughtful of you to remember in such a special way
- It was so good of you to remember
- Thanks for remembering

RESPECT
- To communicate our great respect for
- Deeply respected, professionally and personally
- Respected as a consummate artist at what he did
- I want you to know how much I respect you
- Won the respect of all who work with you

RESPONSE
- I really appreciate your prompt response
- Thank you for your candid response
- Thank you for your compassionate response
- Thanks so much for your quick response
- Want to thank you for your great response
- I was really touched by the enthusiastic response
- Your fast, on-the-scene response was genuinely appreciated
- The depth of response has been remarkable
- Your response has been diligent and conscientious

RESPONSIBILITY
- One of my primary responsibilities is to thank you warmly
- Must salute the large responsibilities you have volunteered to take on
- Taking on new responsibilities for your community
- A time to reflect on our ongoing responsibility
- Demonstrating a strong sense of responsibility

SERVICE
- A free service for you and your family to enjoy
- Savings on service you might need in the future
- Avail yourself of this service
- A low price that still gives you personal service
- We offer services to the general public
- I'm very impressed with the services you offer

SHARE
- That's one memory we will always share
- I can't wait to share this day with you
- I look forward to sharing a very special evening
- It meant a lot to have you share
- Thank you for sharing your wisdom and experience
- Work becomes a joy when shared by you

SHOUT

- You make us want to cheer and shout
- Shout your virtues from the rooftops
- Time to do a little shouting about you

SKILL

- You are making the best use possible of your skills
- Glad you have the opportunity to use your talents and skills in your new position
- Thanks for all your organizational skills

SMILE

- There's always room for a smile
- You make me smile just thinking about you
- We really appreciate your friendly smile
- With sleeves rolled up and smiles all around

SORRY

- You'll never be sorry
- Sorry! We'll be right back
- We're sorry
- I'm so sorry to have to do this
- Sorry to take so long to congratulate you
- Sorry to learn of your recent troubles
- So sorry you weren't able to share our day

SPEAK

- Thank you for speaking out so powerfully and effectively
- Thank you for having the courage to speak out publically
- Thanks for daring to speak up in support
- You are speaking our language
- Thank you for taking the time to speak to me
- I appreciate the opportunity to speak with you personally

SPECIAL

- So nice to be thought of in such a special way
- Acknowledge a very special relationship
- You are a rare and special person
- You are so special to us
- Let it be known you are special
- You are part of a small, special group
- It really means something special to me
- Love and special strength sustains you
- Reflect on the special times we have spent together

SPIRIT

- How comforting to know you are always with us in spirit
- Your actions spring straight from the spirit

- Always admire your strong and soaring spirit

SPONSOR
- And now a word about our sponsor
- I am very honored to sponsor
- I couldn't have handpicked a better sponsor
- A huge thank you to our loyal sponsors
- Thanks to our conference sponsors
- We'd like to thank our sponsors for their generosity
- Thank you for being our sponsor

STAFF
- I would like to take this opportunity to commend your staff
- I want to compliment your staff for their superb effort
- Please pass on our thanks to all your friendly staff
- Thank you and your staff for working so hard
- The efficiency with which your staff worked was truly memorable
- Your staff was very professional and friendly
- Your cheerful, efficient staff contributed so much
- Comforted by the efforts of your staff
- A terrific addition to our staff
- I would like to express my appreciation for the kindness and consideration of your staff

STAY
- So glad you chose to stay
- Your excellent hospitality made our stay very pleasant
- If you are ever in our area, please feel welcome to stay with us
- Thank you so much for our wonderful stay
- Thanks so much for making our stay such a delightful one
- We thoroughly enjoyed our stay
- Thank you for the kindness extended to me during my recent stay
- One more time I thank you for our lovely stay

STORY
- We have many delightful stories to tell
- Your success is a story in itself
- We would love to hear all your stories
- You gave my story a very happy ending

SUCCESS
- You have made this project such a big success
- You played a big part in making this a success
- Your help ultimately resulted in success
- Thanks to everyone who helped make the weekend such a great success
- You have a secret formula for success
- I'm crowing about your level of success

- I have every confidence in your continued success
- You made the event an outstanding success
- Thanks for everything you did to make this such a resounding success
- Such a great success is always gratifying

SUGGESTION

- Your ideas and suggestions are greatly appreciated
- Thank you for your comments and suggestions
- Thank your for your creative, ingenious suggestions

SUPPORT

- You are always willing to offer support when you can
- Thank you so very much for your continued support
- Any time of the day or night when we need support
- Would like to thank those people and organizations for your support
- Thank you for your advice and support
- You are tremendous source of support and solace
- Our community would like to thank those people and organizations for their support
- Thank for your continuing support of our fundraising activities
- I wish to thank everyone for their support and kind words
- I would like to thank you for all your support and compassion
- The respect and support you share
- So deeply appreciate your continuing support
- In facing such a challenge, your support has been invaluable
- Receiving your support was terrific
- Thank you for your beautiful gesture of support
- Your support means a great deal to me
- Happy to give you our wholehearted support
- Thank you for your comfort and support in my time of trouble
- Thank you to our foundation support
- Thank you for your generous cooperation and support
- Thanks to everyone who helped and supported
- You continually strengthen our support network
- Really appreciate your ongoing support

SURPRISE

- I have been very pleasantly surprised
- What a wonderful surprise greeted me
- Imagine our surprise
- We all conspired to surprise with this well-deserved tribute
- Your success is certainly no surprise to us
- Each day brings new discoveries and surprises
- Surprised and delighted

TALK

- I look forward to talking with you again

- Thank you for talking to me in response to my inquiry
- Thank you for talking to me so kindly

TALENT

- Offering the talent and capabilities that so clearly demonstrate
- You certainly have the talent for finding unique things
- And now your talents shine even more brightly
- Always seeking new talent to enhance
- Your talent and genius produced something magical

TALK

- Thanks so much for talking to me today
- I look forward to talking with you further
- I appreciated the opportunity to talk to you

TEAM

- Can always count on team support
- Delighted that the team accomplished so much
- Your team was very disciplined and professional
- You fit so beautifully as a member of our team
- You are such an asset to our team

THANK

- A difficult task to thank each person individually
- But first, I have to thank so many of you
- Children around the world will thank you
- For your part in making this possible, I thank you most warmly
- How can I ever thank you for all you've done for me
- I want to thank you and stay in touch
- I want to thank some specific people for their help
- I wanted to thank you as soon as possible
- I also want to take this opportunity of thanking you for you support
- I just can't thank you enough
- I wish to publically thank everyone who has contributed
- I thank you from the very bottom of my heart
- I don't know what I can ever do to thank you enough
- I do so want to thank all of you
- I want to thank each and every one of you
- It gives me great pleasure to write and thank you for your support
- Just wanted to take a minute to thank you
- Just wanted to thank everyone who has written in and provided insight
- Most of all, I want to thank
- No one grows tired of being thanked
- On their behalf, I thank you
- Once again, consider yourself heartily thanked
- Our children's children will thank us fervently for
- Thank you for standing up for

- Thank goodness
- Thanking all who have helped and contributed
- The committee thanks you in advance for your support and your interest in our
- The first order of business is to thank
- The children thank you
- To thank you for your support at this time, we want to
- We would like to thank the following people
- Yet again, I have to thank you for
- Your family will thank you

THANK YOU

- A really big thank you is needed here
- A little thank you note to
- A special thank you just for you
- A resounding thank you for
- A big thank you to all
- Extend a heartfelt thank you from all of us
- It's never too late to say thank you
- No matter what you give, thank you for being a friend to
- Oh, thank you
- Once again, thank you for doing your part
- Our way of saying thank you
- Thank you for your consideration
- Thank you for being so generous
- Thank you for your support which is so urgently needed
- Thank you so much for increasing your latest donation which means so very much to all of us who are
- Thank you for so many years of generous support
- Thank you very much for your continued support
- Thank you from kids everywhere
- Thank you for reading my letter; I look forward to hearing from you
- Thank you for your support and confidence in progress
- Thank you for making a difference in their lives
- Thank you for whatever you can do to help
- Thank you for thinking about causes and solutions in the problem
- Thank you very kindly
- Thank you for putting us in a position to benefit all these
- Thank you for your interest and support
- Thank you for serving alongside us
- Thank you for being a friend of
- Thank you for being such a good friend last year
- Thank you again for personally helping to make that possible
- Thank you for your cooperation
- Thank you so much for your help
- Thank you for your donation which helps prevent disease through research and education
- Thank you for standing up for

- Thank you for your patience
- Thank you for this shot of realism
- Thank you for allowing us access
- Thank you for checking us out
- Thank you for coming
- Thank you for answering so soon
- Thank you for applying
- Thank you forever
- Thank you for your business
- Thank you for your patience
- Thank you for your patient response to my questions
- Thank you once again for
- Thank you for your feedback
- Thank you for your correspondence
- Thank you for fanning the flame
- Thank you to everyone who sent a message
- Thank you for making us your first choice
- Thank you for your order
- Thank you for not giving up in the face of overwhelming odds
- Thank you for your support
- Thank you for the pleasant evening
- There are many ways to say thanks you, none of them adequate
- To those of you who can make the extra sacrifice, we say a special thank you
- We have what they'll thank you for
- We send a heartfelt thank you to
- Welcome and thank you so much for
- What a difference a simple thank you makes
- You've done so much, I hardly know how to thank you

THANKFUL

- What do you have to be thankful for today
- Whatever your reasons for being thankful
- Those in need are deeply thankful that caring people like you exist
- I am so thankful for people like you
- Thankful down deep in our hearts
- If there's one thing for which we can be thankful
- Something for which we are abundantly thankful
- Thankful not for what you have in your wallet but what you have in your heart
- There's always something to be thankful for
- Deeply thankful for all the good things we have
- Thankful we are living in a country where

THANKFULNESS

- Thinking of you, I am filled with thankfulness
- Thankfulness knows no bounds
- Overflowing with thankfulness

THANKS
- A very special thanks for helping a
- A shower of thanks
- A special thanks to all our clients
- A big, big thanks
- A cartload of thanks
- A personal thanks
- A truckload of thanks
- A note of thanks
- A world of thanks
- A sincere thanks to all those who have given of their time, effort and pocketbooks
- A proud thanks for making your voice heard
- Add a note of thanks to those who have volunteered
- Again, my heartfelt thanks for your confidence
- And it's all thanks to you
- As you send your donation, please remember these words of thanks
- As a small token of our thanks
- Bags full of thanks
- Bottomless thanks
- Bursting with thanks
- But thanks to all of you
- Extra special thanks
- First, let me send my heartfelt thanks
- Give more than thanks
- Giving thanks for all that we have
- Heaps of thanks
- Heartfelt thanks
- Here's a world of thanks
- I would like to extend my sincere thanks
- I want to express my personal thanks for your faith in our organization
- I'm sending my thanks just for you
- I'm sending my special thanks to those who
- If you have already made a donation early this year, please accept our sincere thanks
- It's thanks to you that
- It's our way of saying thanks for
- Just wanted to say thanks
- Just a quick word of thanks
- Just our way of saying thanks
- Let us give thanks
- Many thanks to you
- Many thanks for many favors
- Many thanks for looking after us so well
- Many thanks for your help
- More thanks than words can ever say
- My first task in writing you is to express thanks for

- My heart goes out to you in thanks
- My sincere, heartfelt thanks to you
- On behalf of all those boys and girls your generosity will reach, you have my heartfelt thanks
- Once again, a proud thanks for making your voice heard
- Once again, thanks for your support and for speaking up when
- Our company thanks you
- Please convey my profound thanks to all
- Saying thanks is very special to me
- So worthy of thanks
- Special thanks go out across the board to
- Special thanks go out to
- Special thanks to
- Thanks for giving your all
- Thank you for your staunch support during these trying times
- Thanks for making so much possible
- Thanks for doing your very best
- Thanks for sinking your teeth into this
- Thanks for stopping by
- Thanks a heap
- Thanks for the idea
- Thanks to all who helped
- Thanks is going out to all those who
- Thanks for the visit
- Thanks for life
- Thanks for a wonderful, enriching experience
- Thanks for the fascinating discussion
- Thanks to all and sundry
- Thanks to all our partners and sponsors
- Thanks for allowing this event
- Thanks, but no thanks
- Thanks and good wishes
- Thanks be to
- Thanks for the smash hit
- Thanks again for a great time
- Thanks for signing up
- Thanks for the ride
- Thanks for being a true friend
- Thanks a lot, man
- Thanks for the magic
- Thanks to all participants
- Thanks for sharing your observations
- Thanks again for choosing us
- Thanks to all those who have been active
- Thanks for the help everyone has given
- Thanks for letting me join in
- Thanks a lot

- Thanks to the person who did the original work
- Thanks a million
- Thanks for being so cool
- Thanks to new technological advances
- Thanks for lending a sympathetic ear
- Thanks for your deeply valued patronage
- Thanks to you
- Thanks for putting a smile on so many faces
- Thanks for the giggle
- Thanks for being one of the good guys
- Thanks for putting me back together
- Thanks to our crew for
- Thanks again for the chance to
- Thanks a million
- Thanks a bunch
- Thanks for being such a big help
- Thanks very much
- Thanks for giving me a hand
- Thanks for sharing
- Thanks so much for taking the time to
- Thanks for helping recapture the magic
- Thanks for making all the pieces fall into place
- Thanks for stopping by
- Thanks for the valuable information
- Thanks for everything
- Thanks to the talent and generosity of
- Thanks for the memory
- Thanks for being so upfront
- Thanks for the lift
- Thanks again for making your voice heard
- Thanks again for doing your part
- Thanks for too much to count
- Thanks for everything
- Thanks for taking the time to
- Thanks for taking a moment to
- Thanks for rescuing us
- Thanks for want to know more
- Thanks for caring
- Thanks for your consideration and support
- Thanks for wanting to know more
- Thanks for renewing your support
- Thanks to our friends who gave so generously
- Thanks to all of you who helped support this worthy cause
- Thanks for making everything possible
- Thanks for speaking up when every voice means so much
- Thanks for caring
- Thanks for keeping up the good work

- Thanks! You really made my day
- Thanks! Come back soon
- The list of thanks is in chronological order
- They'll carry thanks in their hearts for your kindness and generosity
- Very many thanks
- Way cool thanks
- We owe a great big thanks to
- We owe you a big, big vote of thanks
- We extend a very special thanks to
- We can never say thanks often enough
- We've made it big, thanks to you
- With thanks this week to
- You inspire heartfelt thanks
- You deserve so many thanks for
- You have our heartfelt thanks

Thanks: tribute, thanksgiving, cognizance, benediction, owing to, because of, due to, as a result of, through, since

See also: THANK

THINK

- Thank you so very much for thinking of me
- You really made me stop and think
- I want you to know I'm thinking of you
- Always prodding us to think and learn
- When I think of you, I think of laughter
- Thank you for thinking of us
- I think of you a lot
- I think of you especially at this time
- I was thinking of you the other day

THOUGHT

- I so enjoyed hearing your thoughts and ideas
- Thanks for your unique creative thoughts
- I wanted to share these thoughts with you
- With just a little extra thought, you give so much
- Our fondest thoughts are with you
- Thanks and warmest thoughts
- You are never far from our thoughts
- You are so often in our thoughts
- Comments were well thought out and clearly articulated
- Thank you so much to all who sent positive thoughts
- Special thoughts go out to you
- Warm thoughts are with you

THOUGHTFUL

- One of the brightest, thoughtful, most conscientious people I know
- A pleasant and thoughtful person

- Thoughtful people say thanks in a thoughtful way
- Thoughtful enough to carefully evaluate the issues

THOUGHTFULNESS
- Again, our thanks for your thoughtfulness
- I will think of you and remember your thoughtfulness
- Thanks for your thoughtfulness
- I'll always remember your thoughtfulness

THRILL
- I'm thrilled to be able to tell you
- I feel absolutely thrilled that
- I'm so thrilled for you
- We are thrilled that you are here at last

TIME
- I really appreciate that you took the time
- Thanks for taking the time to talk to me
- I thank you most sincerely for your time, energy and enthusiasm
- Thank you for taking time out of your busy day
- Your gift of time and of yourself
- I would like to thank all the people who gave so much of their time
- We had the best time
- I know this is an important time for you
- This must be a tough time for you
- This is a time to cherish
- One more time, thanks
- Cannot recall a time when you haven't been there
- Before too much time has gone by
- A great time was had by all
- This is a good time to look ahead
- Thank you for cheerful support through good times and tough ones
- This is such a meaningful time
- Though times were not always easy
- It's always a treat to spend time with you
- You obviously took a lot of time and trouble to
- Looking forward to spending some time together
- Thank you for your time and consideration
- Thank you for taking time from you busy schedule
- Thank you for your kind attention and the time you gave
- Grateful for your time and careful preparation
- Thank you for taking time out from your busy schedule to
- Thanks for your time

TOGETHER
- Working together, we are unbeatable
- Thanks for pulling it all together

- Together, we did it

TOKEN
- Presented with the following token of our thanks
- I want to give you this small token of our appreciation
- This modest token cannot begin to show our gratitude

TOUCH
- I am so touched and grateful
- Appreciate all the nice touches you added
- Thanks for adding that special touch
- Whatever you touch turns out right
- You seem to have the magic touch
- You added just the right touches
- You touched my life deeply
- I sincerely hope you will keep in touch
- Let's make a mutual effort to stay in touch
- Gratified and deeply touched by all of the help
- Thanks for staying in touch

TRIBUTE
- Pays tribute to
- Paying tribute to fifty years of
- A real tribute to you
- A tribute to the virtues you stand for
- The entire program was a tribute to
- As a tribute to our donors, we're offering
- We want to pay tribute to you with this
- A tribute to honor your loyalty and

UNDERSTANDING
- Thanks for being patient and understanding
- Thanks to you, I came away with a keener understanding
- Your comments gave me a good understanding
- Your understanding and support mean such a lot
- Your excellent approach enhanced our understanding
- I deeply appreciated your understanding
- Thank you for your assistance and understanding
- My sincere thanks for your understanding

VENTURE
- You have devoted a significant portion of your time to this venture
- You gave us the courage to venture out
- You made this venture possible

VISIT
- You are the main reason we think of our visit so fondly

- Thank you very much for visiting us on the Web
- Thanks to all of you who came to visit
- Thank you for visiting our online store
- Your visit was like a shot in the arm
- Thanks for making my visit so memorable
- We so enjoyed your visit
- I always love it when you visit
- Your visit was a most agreeable one
- Thank you for visiting us

VOICE
- I add my voice to the many others who support your position
- Together, our combined voices have a powerful effect
- Thanks for standing up for our right to a voice
- Your voice was always heard on the side of right

VOLUNTEER
- Our volunteers are the best in the world
- A volunteer like you doesn't come along every day
- With volunteers like you, we'll always come through
- You're the star on volunteer appreciation day
- Thank you for so generously volunteering your time and knowledge
- Thanks to everyone who so graciously volunteered
- Always among the first to volunteer
- Thank you for volunteering
- Thank you to our members and volunteers

WAIT
- I can't wait to come back
- Finally, all the waiting is over
- Waiting for someone like you to come along
- Now that you are here, the waiting is over

WAY
- The world's best way to say thank you
- The ideal way to express your thanks and appreciation
- Only one of thousands of ways to say thanks
- Now you are really on your way
- The beauty of your gentle, caring ways
- Always something special about the way you do it
- Thanks for going out of your way to help

WELCOME
- We welcome the opportunity to
- Thank you for making me feel welcome
- Thanks for your very warm welcome

WISH

- Wishing you all the very best
- Warmest wishes are coming your way
- May your fondest wishes come true
- I wish you all the best
- I only wish you could have been there to see
- I wish you all success in your endeavours
- Your good wishes are my reward
- Sending you my best wishes
- I want to express my personal good wishes
- I sincerely wish you well in your future endeavours
- I wish I could have been there to see
- How I wish we could be present

WITHOUT

- What would we do without you
- Without you, we couldn't have done it
- I never want to try it without you

WONDERFUL

- It's wonderful to be spoiled for a while
- Thanks for being truly wonderful
- I know we will have a wonderful visit
- You are truly wonderful
- Such a wonderful feeling to know you care so much
- People still tell me what a wonderful time they had

WORD

- There are no words to express what you have done for us
- Thank you for being absolutely true to your word
- You are never at a loss for words
- In facing such a debt of gratitude, I am lost for words
- Thank you for your always thoughtful and comforting words
- It's easy to find words to
- It's very hard to find the words to express
- Words fail me now
- Sincere words express something significant
- A few sincere words can have so much impact
- Even though I'm not good with words
- Your caring words made all the difference
- Thank you for your encouraging words
- Your kind words helped me cope

WORK

- So that all this hard work will not be in vain
- I know how hard you worked to make this happen
- You have always been so supportive of our work

- Thanks for working under impossible conditions
- I look forward to working with you again
- Keep up the good work
- Your intervention enabled all of us to work together effectively
- Thanks to you, work is proceeding ahead of schedule
- Expressed great interest in working with you
- Look forward to continuing to work with you
- A work of the heart is a work of art
- Working with you makes the day fly by
- Your hard work makes everything so easy for us
- Thank you very much for your excellent work
- Without your hard work we would never have finished in time
- We really count on your excellent work
- I know it was not an easy environment to work in
- You were terrific to work with

WORLD
- Bravely facing a world full of challenges
- You make the world a little better
- I believe you really will change the world

WRITE
- It's about time I wrote to thank you
- The desire to write about this in a personal way
- I wish I could write something clever
- It's hard to write when every word means so much
- Thanks for writing to me out of the blue
- Thank you again for writing
- I know I don't always take the time to write
- Though I've thanked you in person, I just had to write as well

YEAR
- Some of the most exciting and productive years of my life
- I hope each of you has a fantastic year
- What a great year we've had because of you
- I hope the next year brings you even more success
- Here's to another great year
- This is a very special time of year
- It's that time of year again
- Look forward to many more wonderful years together
- The years have passed so quickly
- A thanks that lasts all year
- Finally, the culmination of years of planning
- I can't tell you what the past years have meant to me
- I look forward to sharing another wonderful year with you
- Looking forward to doing it again next year

Section Six

Donor Renewal

Lapsed Donor

Lapsed Member

Monthly or Sustained
Giving

Salutations

Signatures

DONOR RENEWAL

- It's renewal time again
- We go back a long way
- We need you more than ever before
- You have helped start something very beautiful
- Thank you for your continued support
- As a past contributor you helped with this crucial task
- Help us once again
- We've always depended upon the support of people like you. Now is no different. Now your help is more vital than ever.
- I'm appealing to you now as someone who has already demonstrated real commitment
- Welcome to our family
- We need to keep new friends like you
- Old friends are often our best friends
- No matter how long you have been with us, I want to tell you once again that it's supporters like you who make our work such an ongoing success
- Thank you for all your past kindness to us
- I look forward to many more years of association with you as one of our most esteemed members
- Last year it was such a pleasure to welcome you as a member of our organization. This year, we look forward to your renewed support
- Come back, come back

LAPSED DONOR

- Today we need you back
- We haven't heard from you recently
- For years you have been one of our most valued supporters
- That's why I'm very concerned to learn that your name is about to be deleted from our active list of
- I can't be complacent about the loss of even one supporter
- You are about to become the kind of statistic we don't like, a lost friend and supporter
- Regrettably, I'm forced to ask you once again for
- This need not be goodbye
- Is something wrong
- Please don't leave us now
- Each lost donor jeopardizes our work to
- I've been trying to imagine why you haven't been responding recently
- Have you forgotten us
- We really don't want to lose you
- I checked to see whether your renewal had been mislaid – and it hadn't
- Although I've written you a number of letters, I haven't heard from you at all
- Your renewal is something the children have been counting on

- I'm really getting worried about you
- Please stop us from having to cancel your membership
- There's still time to renew
- Please ignore this letter if you've already renewed
- We want you very much to remain with us as friend and supporter
- I'll be grieved to delete your name from our active list
- Don't say goodbye
- We miss you very much
- We're blaming ourselves for not making the urgency clear enough
- Your envelope is missing
- Please don't go away
- We need you more than ever
- I still believe in your willingness to renew
- I'm at a loss to understand what has caused you to abandon
- As a past contributor, you once helped us with this crucial task
- But we've missed your participation since you sent your last gift a number of years ago
- I'm writing at the end of this busy year to remind you that your renewal fell due but apparently was not received
- Open this only if you have decided not to support our campaign
- I'm sorry you've decided not to participate in our campaign
- If you can't send a contribution now, for whatever reason, I hope you'll still sign the enclosed petition to show your concern for protecting
- Only if you've decided not to support our campaign
- Frankly, I'm disappointed by your decision not to participate in our campaign
- I don't just mean sending money, important as it is to our campaign
- We want you back
- We really need you back
- You may have intended to make a gift and never got round to it
- Let us know today whether we can count on your support this year
- Perhaps you've misplaced my earlier requests
- It's easy to renew your good intentions
- If you're not making a contribution, please tell us why
- If you've absolutely decided not to support us this year, please let us know the reason

LAPSED MEMBER

- According to our records, your renewal of affiliation fell due in
- We wrote you in the month when you first joined and solicited your renewal
- We wrote you again several months later with a friendly reminder
- If our computer is in error, or if you have just sent in your renewal, please accept our apologies and ignore this letter
- I have spent a lot of time, and our organization a lot of money, in soliciting your renewal
- And I can't figure out, at this time when our efforts are needed more than ever,

why you, a loyal supporter of this cause, would not wish to renew your affiliation
- I haven't heard from you since I wrote you in
- That's why, in today's challenging times, each membership is crucial
- Your deeply valued membership has expired and we need you
- Suffering families need you to renew your vital support
- Please take a moment and renew now
- Your role as a member is more critical than ever.
- Make your membership something we can count on
- I haven't heard from you since I wrote you in November
- Won't you please renew your membership right away.
- Frankly, I'm worried
- You supported us in ____, but we haven't heard from you since
- Your support is needed again today
- Convince you to remain one of our loyal supporters for another year
- We want you to stay on our members list where caring people like you belong
- Please don't let your membership lapse again
- Your membership has recently expired
- Our records indicate you are not an active member this year
- You may have made your membership gift in the past to support
- More than ever before, we need you as an active member
- Maybe you didn't get round to calling during our membership drive
- You see, we really depend on your membership gift
- Please become an active member once again
- Please respond right away to reactivate your membership

MONTHLY or SUSTAINED GIVING

- To keep our current donors actively supporting our cause
- I urge you to consider making your contribution through our Research Donor Plan so you can help us every month. It's easy to join and more of your support goes directly to research. The reply coupon has all of the details
- Pledge a monthly amount
- So that we can depend on the resources we need, many people have decided to support our organization in a regular basis
- We can count on your gift and plan ahead
- By giving monthly, you save everyone cost and effort
- Join today! Get the greatest possible impact from your donation by becoming a sustaining donor
- The most efficient way of giving
- By giving monthly, you make your donation go even further
- This kind of steady giving is the best way to break the patterns of
- Providing a reliable and predictable monthly income is the most effective way to support our cause.
- You always have the option of joining our monthly giving plan
- Automatic monthly payments via your checking account or credit card

- It's a wonderful way to give
- It means we receive your support all throughout the year
- It's convenient for you because the transactions are automatic
- More of your generous gift can go directly into our work
- We save the extra mailing costs of having to send out reminder letters
- No monthly cards to reply to in order to avoid unwanted
- Save worry about your donation being lost, stolen or delayed in transit
- You can make your donations in small, easy-to-manage amounts
- Monthly giving is so much more convenient
- A way to use your money more efficiently and effectively
- Monthly giving is environmentally friendly
- You save money. No need to buy postage and envelopes
- You save time. The work is done for you.
- No need to write cheques every few months
- Join our monthly giving club
- Members say they usually don't notice the amount withdrawn
- The monthly giving option is an easy, cost-effective way to provide help on an ongoing basis
- Convenient, automatic monthly donations that suit your budget are the way to help the most
- For donors who prefer to receive less mail, and who want to make a meaningful contribution every month, we encourage you to join our monthly giving plan
- Monthly giving has become a very popular way of supporting us among thousands of our donors
- It is one of the strongest statements of commitment you can make to because it allows you to give every month
- You won't even notice the small, pre-authorized monthly deductions from your checking account or credit card
- You'll find that over the course of year you can actually give more than in a single donation
- And you'll save us the cost of postage and paper for reminders
- More of your dollars will go directly into fighting poverty
- And your support will be automatically renewed every year
- By giving monthly, you ensure the greatest possible impact from your donation
- This kind of steady, reliable help is the best way to break the patterns that keep people living in poverty
- Convenient monthly giving enables you to make your donations in small, easy-to-manage amounts
- More efficient and environmentally friendly
- With one decision, you keep on giving all year long
- Because we only contact sustaining donors once a year, you'll receive less mail – and that saves trees
- It also saves printing and mailing costs, so your donation can be put to work on
- Saves you money – no need to buy postage or envelopes
- Saves you time – no need to write cheques every few months. The work is done for you
- When deciding how much to give, please consider joining our monthly giving

program
- By authorizing a monthly debit, you can help every day of the year
- Help all year long with low monthly donations
- It's the easiest, most cost-effective way of giving
- Many caring people have joined our monthly giving program
- By making monthly donations, you help us plan more effectively for the long term and cut mailing costs
- You can make a commitment to help our many programs year-round with monthly donations
- It's the easiest, most cost-effective way of giving
- So that we can depend on the resources we need, many people have decided to support our organization in a regular basis
- We can count on your gift and plan ahead
- By giving monthly, you save everyone cost and effort
- Get the greatest possible impact from your donation by becoming a sustaining donor
- The most effective way of giving is the easiest
- This kind of steady, reliable help is the best way to break the patterns that keep people trapped in poverty and sickness
- Yes, I'll help now and every month
- I want to become a sustaining donor, making my support even more effective
- I authorize this organization to receive the following monthly donations
- You can help best by making a commitment to a monthly gift
- Pre-authorized charges are the best way to support us
- The program allows you to make small monthly contributions
- Here's how much you can save on your income tax
- As little as ten dollars a month can transform the life of
- Or you may choose to join our monthly giving campaign
- You decide on a small amount you wish to come out of your account
- You'll receive a tax receipt for the value of your contributions over the year
- Monthly giving is convenient and affordable
- You won't even notice the small amount deducted each month
- A monthly donation makes your dollars go so much further
- Not to mention a terrific way to maximize your charitable giving
- You can increase or decrease your monthly gift or cancel it altogether
- Cancel at any time by simply calling or writing to our office
- You can spread your gift out over the year in small, easy installments
- This steady, reliable income helps us plan our long-term campaigns
- Allows us to respond to crises when they occur unexpectedly
- For as little as $5 a month you can join our plan
- More of your dollars will go directly towards providing services
- The savings on postage and administration costs really make a difference
- Monthly giving is a convenient way for you to support
- No more searching for stamps and cheques

See: SECTION SEVEN – REPLY DEVICES, MONTHLY OR SUSTAINED GIVING

SALUTATIONS

- Dear Advocate for
- Dear Alert Citizen
- Dear Animal Lover
- Dear Associate
- Dear Brother
- Dear Buddy
- Dear Caring Citizen
- Dear Caring Person
- Dear Champion of
- Dear Child of Nature
- Dear Companion on the Path of Life
- Dear Compassionate Friend
- Dear Comrade
- Dear Concerned Member
- Dear Concerned Member of our Community
- Dear Concerned Citizen
- Dear Donor
- Dear Earth Dweller
- Dear Environmentally Aware Citizen
- Dear Fellow Dreamer
- Dear Fellow Campaigner
- Dear Fellow Music Lover
- Dear Fellow Watchdog
- Dear Fellow Hiking Enthusiast
- Dear Fellow Idealist
- Dear Fellow Enthusiast
- Dear Fellow Earth Creature
- Dear Fellow Fighter
- Dear Fellow Crime Fighter
- Dear Fellow Visionary
- Dear Fellow Warrior
- Dear Fighter for
- Dear Former Schoolmate
- Dear Former Donor
- Dear Former Patient
- Dear Freedom Fighter
- Dear Freedom Supporter
- Dear Friend
- Dear Friend of Culture
- Dear Friend of our Country
- Dear Friend of Planet Earth
- Dear Friend of Human Rights
- Dear Friend in Fellowship
- Dear Friend of a Troubled Land
- Dear Friend and Neighbor
- Dear Friend of Sick Children
- Dear Friend of the Ocean
- Dear Friend of Mountain Grizzlies
- Dear Friend of Children Everywhere
- Dear Friends and Neighbors
- Dear Generous Donor
- Dear Generous Heart
- Dear Grandparent
- Dear Kind of Heart
- Dear Kindred Soul
- Dear Kindred Budgie Fancier
- Dear Kindred
- Dear Kindred Spirit
- Dear Kindred Nature Lover
- Dear Kindred Freedom Fighter
- Dear Kindred Supporter of
- Dear Kindred City Dweller
- Dear Lover of
- Dear Intelligent Reader
- Dear Loving Parent
- Dear Member
- Dear Members and Friends of the Foundation
- Dear Music Devotee
- Dear Nature Lover
- Dear Neighbor
- Dear New Member
- Dear New Family Member
- Dear New Friend
- Dear Pal
- Dear Parent
- Dear Patron
- Dear Peacemaker
- Dear Potential Member
- Dear Potential Illness Victim
- Dear Protector of
- Dear Sister or Brother
- Dear Special Friend
- Dear Supporter
- Dear Supporter of National

Unity
- Dear Supporter of Cultural Freedom
- Dear Supporter of Cultural Independence
- Dear Supporter of Decency
- Dear Supporter of Universal Freedom
- Dear University Graduate
- Dear Valued Member
- Dear Veteran Campaigner
- Dear Vigilant Citizen
- Dear Visionary
- Dear Water Conservationist
- Dear Wise Friend

SIGNATURES

- Best regards
- Best wishes
- Best of the season
- Bless you during this beautiful spring season
- Bless you for your gift of compassion
- Cordially yours
- Faithfully
- For the love of kids
- Forever yours
- Goodbye for now
- Gratefully yours
- In fellowship and love
- In gratitude
- Joy and happiness be yours
- Look forward to seeing you
- Many thanks
- Peace be with you
- Peacefully yours
- Regards
- Sincerely
- Sincerely yours
- Thank you
- Thank you for helping
- Thanks in advance
- Thanks sincerely
- Very truly yours
- Very cordially
- Very sincerely
- Warmly yours
- With deepest sincerity
- With heartfelt gratitude
- Yours
- Yours in the future of health care
- Yours in peace
- Yours in thanksgiving and loyalty
- Yours sincerely
- Yours truly
- Yours in peace
- Yours in loyalty
- Yours for a fairer future
- Yours very truly

Section Seven

Exclamations

Beginnings
and
Transitions

EXCLAMATIONS

- Ah ha!
- Ahoy, there!
- Aim higher!
- And much, much more!
- Away you go!
- Bah, humbug!
- Be proud and enjoy!
- Be alert!
- Believe in yourself!
- Believe!
- But there's more!
- Calling all angels!
- Cheers!
- Congratulations!
- Don't miss out!
- Don't forget!
- Don't wait!
- Don't even think about it!
- Don't be embarrassed!
- Don't count yourself out!
- Enough already!
- Enough is enough!
- Fantastic!
- Far out!
- Figure it out!
- Gadzooks!
- Get involved!
- Going, going, gone!
- Great news!
- Hello there!
- Help!
- Here's a new one!
- Here's the deal!
- Hey there!
- Hey, wait!
- Hold the phone!
- Hurrah!
- I can do it!
- I love your work!
- I can't believe it!
- If course we can!
- It all adds up!
- It's up to you!
- Just think of it!
- Just do it!
- Make no mistake about it!
- Maybe not!
- No Sirree Bob!
- Not enough time!
- Of course you would!
- Oops!
- Ouch!
- Picture this!
- Please hurry!
- Pssst!
- Rats!
- Red alert!
- Stop the Press!
- Stop right there!
- Surprised?
- Take heart!
- That should get your attention!
- That's right!
- Very nice indeed!
- We need you!
- What perfect timing!
- What's happening!
- Yes, yes, yes!
- You won't believe it!

BEGINNINGS and TRANSITIONS

- A universal right to
- A clear indication that
- A step up
- A nice bonus is
- A fundamental mistake
- A minor annoyance is
- A far cry from
- A petition to remind
- A few years ago
- A further analysis shows
- According to the myth
- Added to this
- Admirably
- Advocating a dramatic departure from
- Already identified are
- Also
- An extra step would be
- An apt description of
- And you must remember
- And this, of course, is not to say
- And there's worse
- And in preparation for
- And you know what
- Another way to put it
- Anyway
- Apparently
- Apropos to
- Arguably
- As you know
- As a result
- As you can see
- As you read this letter
- As a matter of fact
- As an example
- As you can plainly see
- As an added bonus
- As this so vividly demonstrates
- As in the previous case
- As you read this crucial message
- As you probably know
- As it stands now
- As a matter of fact
- As often as not
- Assuming that
- Assuredly
- At one point
- At one time or another
- At this time
- At the end of the day
- Bafflegab aside
- Bafflingly
- Behind the scenes
- Believe me
- Best of all
- Better still
- Better known as
- Beyond that, however, is
- Breaching this wall
- But as usual
- But on the other hand
- But you know what
- But on the more mundane side
- But there it is
- By implication
- Candidly speaking
- Categorically
- Certainly
- Chances are
- Consider this
- Contributing to the shift away from
- Cost-effectively
- Covered exclusively by
- Day in and day out
- Debatably
- Despite all obstacles
- Despite these efforts
- Developed in conjunction with
- Did you know that
- Diplomatically
- Disgustingly
- Don't forget that
- Doubtless
- Dramatically re-interpreted to
- Due to the comprehensive nature of
- Each and every
- Either way
- Elsewhere
- Equally important is

- Equally crucial
- Especially when
- Essentially what happens is
- Even now
- Even better yet
- Even as you read this letter
- Every minute, every day
- Examined closely
- Examples include
- Experimentally
- Famous for
- First off the mark
- First and foremost
- Firstly
- Following through
- For some people
- For emphasis
- For starters
- For myself, I think
- For example
- Fortunately
- Frankly
- Frightening as it may be to admit
- From time to time
- From a practical aspect
- Further conceding
- Getting a grip on things
- Give some much-needed impetus to
- Grinchlike
- Happily
- Has always been our calling card
- Here is a perfect example
- Here's the bad news
- How otherwise could we
- However
- However you choose to slice it
- I want you to know
- I wonder if
- I understand that
- Ideally
- If so, what are
- If possible
- Impossibly
- In the tradition of
- In the meantime
- In so many instances
- In the beginning
- In the final analysis
- In many ways
- In any case
- In a different capacity
- In many instances
- In other words
- In conclusion
- In case you're wondering why
- In fact, I've enclosed a note from
- In anticipation of
- In the best case
- In addition to
- In the grand scheme of things
- In the alternative
- In short
- In the long run
- In the first place
- In brief
- In addition
- Inasmuch as
- Indisputably
- Indubitably
- Initially
- Introducing
- Invite you to
- Inviting as it seems
- It is impossible to calculate
- It also explains why
- It is estimated that
- It is impossible to even estimate
- It also explains a lot about
- It all adds up to
- It is my opinion that
- It really comes down to this
- It's not just a plan to
- It's a pain to
- It's even more unthinkable that
- It's a blessing that
- It's not at all unusual to
- It's the key to
- Just one example is
- Just in case
- Last year alone
- Lastly
- Lessons can be drawn from
- Let me assure everyone here
- Let me assure you that

- Let it be known that
- Let me put it this way
- Little consistency exists
- Make no mistake about it
- Marginally
- May I introduce myself
- Maybe it's time to
- Meanwhile, back on the farm
- Mired in complexity
- More recently
- More efficient than ever
- More often than not
- Most sincerely
- Most of all
- Most frequently asked about is
- Naturally
- Needless to say
- Never mind
- Nevertheless
- Nicely put
- Niggardly as it seems
- No one likes to
- No matter what
- No limitations are set
- Not to mention
- Not to be outdone
- Not if we want to
- Nowhere is this more apparent
- Obviously
- Of course it doesn't
- Of course, on the other hand
- Of course
- Off the top of my head
- Often, all it takes is
- On reassessment
- On behalf of
- On an absolute scale
- On a positive note
- On a different level
- On a much more positive note
- On a continued basis
- On the home front
- On the surface
- On a scale of one to ten
- On second thought
- On the other hand
- Once characteristic is
- Once and for all
- One of the strongest pieces of evidence is
- One of life's perplexing questions is
- One minor simplification
- One way or the other
- One good example is
- One morning, in desperation
- Only an old hand could see that
- Overly optimistic projections can
- Overtly
- Partly
- Perplexingly
- Picture this
- Please understand
- Please read on
- Please be sure to
- Please consider this
- Popularly speaking
- Possibly
- Provide access to
- Rationally speaking
- Realistically
- Recognized as the benchmark
- Regretfully
- Regrettably
- Relatively speaking
- Remarkably
- Remember
- Rest assured, however, that
- Revealed by further analysis is
- Right now
- Sadly
- Secondly
- Simpler still
- Simplified
- Simply stated
- Simply put
- Simultaneously
- Since the major vehicle is
- Since our founding back in
- Small wonder that
- So long as there is still one person being
- Sometimes
- Somewhere along the line
- Specifically

- Stand on guard for
- Starting afresh
- Starting with a clean slate
- Starting out with
- Starting from the top
- Stated in practical terms
- Suddenly
- Summed it up most succinctly
- Surely, however
- That distinction is reserved for
- That's a given
- The easiest way is
- The options are
- The prognosis is
- The data are quite clear on
- The next step is
- The other day
- The irony is that
- The most intriguing thing about
- The question is, how are we going to
- The important thing is
- The list goes on
- The situation now
- The question is
- There's no such thing as
- Thirdly
- This formula applies
- This approach has not be lost on
- Thousands, to be exact
- To say the least
- To start with
- To improve matters
- To begin with
- To commemorate
- To put it mildly
- To most people
- Today
- Too numerous to mention
- Traditionally
- Tragically
- Unbeknownst to
- Unbelievable as it seems
- Undeniably
- Understandably
- Underwhelmingly
- Unfortunately
- Unless we see a dramatic shift
- Unlike the former
- Unquestionably
- Up front
- Upon reflection
- We can easily make the assumption that
- We watched in admiration as
- We pride ourselves on
- What's more
- Whether you're currently involved
- Whether you're concerned about
- With this in view
- With any luck
- Without quibbling too much
- Worst case scenario
- Would have loved to see
- You might conclude that
- You see,
- You even have the choice of
- You can call it what you like
- You might want to consider
- You have the option to
- You may not know this, but
- You should also know that

Section Eight

Address Verification

Name Exchange

Package Duplication

Reply Devices

Monthly or Sustained
Giving Reply

Envelope Teasers

ADDRESS VERIFICATION

- Would you be good enough to let us know whether we are addressing you properly. Your name is important. Please make sure we get it right.
- Please note any name and address changes below so we may correct our records
- As soon as we receive your reply and cheque we will send you an official tax receipt which you can use to receive a tax credit for your contribution to our organization
- We want to ensure that we have your name and address to send your receipt to you promptly
- Please remember to include the form on which your name and address appears. Be sure our address shows through the window. Please make name and address corrections should we have made an error or if you have relocated. Thank you.
- Getting your name and address correct is important to us
- If you're planning to move in the near future, please fill in the information below
- If we have made an error in your name or address, please accept our apologies and kindly correct this form and mail us your changes
- May we have your telephone number for our records?
- Please let us know if we've made a mistake above by making any necessary corrections
- Please help us keep our records accurate by correcting any errors in the spelling of your name and address. Thank you.
- You are very important to us. We do not trade, rent or sell your name to any other organization for any reason.
- Please check that your name and address are correct and make any changes/corrections
- Please make any necessary corrections

NAME EXCHANGE

- It is always necessary to find new donors from like-minded organizations to maintain the same level of financial support from one year to the next. Still, we understand that you may not wish to have your name exchanged and we will certainly respect your choice if that is what you prefer. Please write and tell us.
- From time to time, we make the names of our donors available to other not-for-profit organizations. Simply check the box on the front of this coupon if you prefer to receive mail only from our organization.
- Finally, a word about exchanging the names of donors
- On rare occasions we will exchange lists of names and donors with another registered charitable organization to help offset some of its costs. Please contact us if you would like us to exclude your name from these exchanges.
- Occasionally, we make our list available to reputable companies and organizations whose products and/or services may be of interest to you. Just let us know if you prefer not to receive mailings from these companies or organizations

- From time to time we make the names of our donors available to other non-profit organizations. Simply check the box below if you prefer to receive mail only from
- I prefer to receive mail only from
- Please do not trade my name to other organizations
- In order to help with the cost of finding new donors, we sometimes exchange our mailing list with other organizations
- Please let us know if you prefer not to have your name included
- Please do not exchange my name
- We will not rent, exchange or in any way provide your name and address or other information to third parties without your permission
- If you wish to be excluded, please check here
- If you do not wish to participate, please check the box
- We rent or exchange our mailing list with other organizations in order to help support our services
- Please provide your email address and we'll add it to our list of friends
- I wish to remain anonymous
- Help us keep our records current
- If you have moved lately please provide us with your current address

PACKAGE DUPLICATION

- We've done our best to avoid duplicates, but if you receive more than one of our letters, or if you are already a supporter, please pass this to a friend.
- We do our best to avoid duplication and apologize if you have received more than one copy of this letter. If you have, please pass this package on to a friend.
- I've done my best to avoid duplicates, but if you do receive more than one of my letters, or if you are already a supporter, please pass this on to friend.
- If you receive an extra mailing please let us know and help us by passing it to a friend. Thank you.
- If you receive more than one package, we suggest that you pass the extra one on to someone who cares about children
- Sometimes mistakes happen. You may receive more than one copy of the same letter from our organization, or you may already be a donor. We try hard to stop this from happening but sometimes the computer records contain two slightly different variations of your name and address. You can help us. If you receive a package that has an error in your name and/or address, please correct it and send it back to us with your donation
- If you have received an extra mailing, please forgive us and use it to persuade a friend to join

REPLY DEVICES

- All contributions are tax creditable
- Yes, I want to help people feed their own families with dignity and self-reliance

- I am sending $__ to send good food to families
- I support the effort to tackle the root causes of poverty
- Please send me the following free educational materials
- Yes, I want to help stop this killer
- I wish to support the community outreach and public relations program
- Enclosed is my donation of
- I help my neighbors by supporting
- Yes, I want to help my neighbors in need
- Here is my tax-credible contribution to the
- Yes, I want to subscribe to
- A special invitation to you to play a key role in the future of
- Yes, I believe in high quality support for
- Your response is crucial
- Please respond generously
- We hope you'll answer this appeal
- We look forward so much to hearing from you
- I eagerly await your reply
- Here is my annual renewal gift
- I've enclosed a cheque made payable to
- I want to make automatic monthly donations so I can support throughout the year and receive fewer appeals
- I've filled out the application form on the back
- I prefer to give $__
- Please turn over for important donor information
- I want to help turn someone's life around. Here is my gift of
- My cheque enclosed is payable to
- I cannot make a contribution today, but would like to know more about
- Any amount you choose
- Perhaps a dollar for each year you have lived
- I want to help answer the call for help
- Enclosed is my tax-creditable donation of
- Just send in your reply card today
- Return the enclosed reply card for
- Yes, I would like to learn more about
- Please send me
- Yes, I want to help make a world of difference
- Yes, I'll help now and every month
- I want to become a sustaining donor, so my support is more effective
- Yes, I want to help re-elect
- Here's how you can reach us
- Please fill out this reply card
- No postage is necessary
- Printed on recycled paper
- Thank you for your donation
- Your contribution is used carefully to help in the fight against
- Yes, I want to join the team for
- Yes, I have lots to be thankful for and I'd like to help

- Please take a moment to complete and mail this donor form in the enclosed envelope or fax it to
- This year I'd like to give
- If you've already sent your gift, or give through your workplace, please accept our thanks
- To show my support I'm enclosing a tax-deductible gift of
- Please send in your gift of support today
- Yes, I want to help children read and write today
- Here is my gift
- Please return the completed form in order to process membership
- I have enclosed my membership dues of
- I'd like to make an additional donation of
- A tax receipt will be issued for all donations and dues
- Yes, I want to prevent crime
- Your donation is important
- My financial donation is for the amount of
- Independence, Dignity and Community
- Thank you for your annual support
- Yes, please send me
- Please mail this form with payment to
- Thank you for your generous support
- All donations are fully receipted for tax purposes
- Yes, I believe in high-quality programs
- Please fill out the amount of your contribution and preferred method of payment
- The membership department will be happy to correspond with you in the language of your choice
- Thanks for the offer. I prefer not to receive the magazine.
- Yes, send me a copy of your magazine each month
- Seven reasons why you should contribute
- I'm sending a special gift
- I want to become an international partner
- Please send me pamphlets and application forms to distribute
- Yes, I want to help her and others like her share the hope of Christmas
- This Christmas I will give
- Would you like to know more
- If you would like to know more, indicate which of the following you are interested in and we will contact you
- Yes, I want to help keep the doors of the center open to homeless people throughout the winter. I have enclosed my gift of
- Yes, I want to join the fight against
- We are grateful, and will receipt a donation in any amount
- I want to help fund more research to find effective treatments and lasting cures for
- Education and research hold the key
- Count me among the majority who believe our social programs must be preserved and improved, not destroyed
- I want to remind governments that all people have a right to

- I have enclosed a contribution for the amount indicated below
- I'd like to pledge a monthly amount to
- We're fighting this problem with everything you give
- My answer is yes
- I want to help find a cure for
- I'm sold. I want to join the
- I'm enclosing my membership dues in the amount of
- I'd like to get even more involved. Please tell me how I can volunteer
- Together, we can help make
- Yes, you can count on me
- Please consider a gift of this amount. It is urgently needed
- Yes, I would like to add my voice to yours and join the fight for
- To support your intensive efforts to pass laws like
- Yes, I would like to accept your offer of joint membership
- I support the work of
- I look forward to hearing more about your important work
- Yes, I will do my part to
- Our commitment to you
- Yes, I would like to assist as a volunteer
- Please give this, at your earliest convenience, to
- Thank you for supporting
- Please distribute my donation as follows
- I hereby authorize you to
- My matching gift is enclosed
- I have made provisions in my will for
- I would prefer my name not to be included in the listings of donors
- Here is my emergency contribution of
- Yes, please send me more information today
- Yes, I am interested in learning about
- I'll help stop the killings
- I've enclosed an additional
- Please send me a copy of your report
- I'll spread the word by posting the enclosed
- Inside is a message about a serious illness that will affect up to ten million children
- Yes, I agree that love alone can't fix this disease
- That's why I'm supporting your efforts to improve services for
- I want to help increase public awareness of this illness
- I'm unable to give at this time
- Please contact me at a later date
- I've enclosed my special donation to
- The donation you make today will immediately help someone direct the course of their own life
- Here is my contribution that will help provide
- How your contribution helps
- Yes, here is my donation to renew support for
- Here's my message to

- I'd like you to tell the government that
- Keep your tax break and stop the cuts
- Yes, I support the work for lasting change
- Yes, I'll help now and every month
- I want to become a sustaining donor, making my support even more effective
- Please accept our gratitude for your gift and for your saving secretarial and postage expense
- I want to help save the lives of men, women and children
- Please consider a gift of this amount. It is urgently needed
- I want to become more involved in this work
- Yes, I want to make my year-end commitment to this important work
- Here is my year-end gift
- I will match my last donation of
- Please renew my membership subscription in the league
- I've already reserved by telephone
- Please add me to your mailing list
- You can make a world of difference
- Yes, I want to help bring about lasting change where it is most needed
- Enclosed in the envelope provided is this completed form and my tax-deductible cheque/money order payable to
- We will automatically notify you by mail when
- You can also refer to your label for your expiration date
- Makes it easy and convenient to give a gift any time of the year
- We will gladly help you with these or any other questions you may have concerning your
- Yes, here is my gift to help make a difference
- Please send me the following free educational material with my tax receipt
- Please return this form with your gift
- More information on other side
- If you have any suggestions, please drop us a note
- Your input is always welcomed and much appreciated
- Yes, I want to start my own family tradition of giving
- Yes, Jane, you can depend on me
- Please use my donation to
- Yes, I will help children in need
- You bet I'm in
- I'm proud to help out
- To join, simply check the appropriate boxes
- Please accept my donation of
- Yes, I want to make a cure possible
- Just fill out the box below and we'll do the rest
- Complete and mail this coupon in the enclosed postage-paid envelope today
- Donations of under $10 will not be receipted unless specifically requested
- My preferred method of payment is
- Please send me information about making a bequest
- Yes! I want to keep life-saving research programs going
- I'm enclosing my membership contribution in the amount of

- Please clearly print the information below
- Yes! You can count on my support
- Yes! I would like to receive my charitable receipt by email
- Please detach this stub and retain for your records
- Yes, I want to make a difference in the daily lives of men, women and children
- I want to help meet the challenge of funding desperately needed services
- Yes, I received the enclosed labels and will enjoy using them
- If you can add your name as a partner in our research it will improve our chances of providing

MONTHLY or SUSTAINED GIVING REPLY

- My first cheque is enclosed. I understand this amount will be automatically deducted from my bank account each month until stated otherwise. Please begin deducting on the first day of
- I'd like to pledge a monthly amount to help work on this and other crucial campaigns
- I wish to give a monthly donation of
- Yes, I choose to help
- I want to make automatic monthly donations so I can support your work throughout the year and receive fewer appeals
- My gift will be automatically deducted from my bank account and charged to my credit card each month. I can change this arrangement by notifying the organization in writing
- I authorize your organization to deduct the following amount each month
- I can't possibly become a monthly supporter at this time, but here's a single gift
- To donate on a monthly basis
- Please deduct the amount indicated from my account within the first week of each month
- Please process monthly donations on my credit card
- Please begin my automatic donations on
- I want to support you by making a monthly donation
- Now you can plan and manage your donations with automatic monthly deductions
- I wish to join the monthly donor program
- I understand monthly donations are processed on the first of the month
- You can increase or cancel your monthly donation by writing to
- A monthly, pre-authorized donation that is convenient and helps reduce costs
- You can alter or cancel your monthly giving donations at any time, for any reason
- Guarantee: you can stop or change your pledge at any time by notifying our office or your bank
- By making a monthly donation through my credit card or by post-dated cheques, I know I'll help make difference in the lives of millions of women, men and children around the world
- Please check which option you prefer of the following

ENVELOPE TEASERS

- People's lives must be more than just a game of chance
- Improving your odds against the number one killer
- This disease doesn't have to be fatal
- Stop a killer
- Good news
- Really good news inside
- Stand up and be counted
- Enclosed: Good news about
- Open to find out how you can help your neighbors in need
- Help make a difference today
- When help is needed
- You can count on me
- Our drop-in center prepares lunch for homeless people every day.
- We're feeling the heat in our kitchen. Will you help?
- Fight illness
- Inside you'll find a red ribbon. Wear it with pride
- The red ribbon was designed to show support for the fight against this illness and pay homage to those who have died
- As a supporter, you can wear this ribbon with pride
- Free gift inside
- Official documents enclosed
- Petition enclosed – Please return within ten days
- I want to breathe clean air
- For the future of children
- Special gift enclosed
- Fighting for freedom of expression
- Holiday gift tags inside
- Confidential
- Thank you for your kindness
- If a sick child reached out to you, would you reach out to help
- Use a quote from celebrity signing your letter
- A stamp will help us save a little money
- An exceptional offer
- A whole new world has been introduced to me
- Welcome to our second decade
- Your personal membership card
- Coalition for change
- A community coalition at work for you
- Help stamp out disease
- Protect the programs that protect you
- Campaign for fairness
- Project Love
- Joy inside
- Change of life inside
- Absolutely radical news inside

- Open for love
- Open up for love
- Our love reaches round the world
- Please don't throw away this letter
- Please open immediately
- Please show you care
- Your call to battle
- Important, updated information enclosed
- Forty ways to love your lungs
- Fifty ways to help your heart
- Official documents enclosed
- Accepting the special card that's been enclosed in your name can help change the lives of over
- Yes, I will help financially as volunteer supporter of
- I want to help battle against the disease that afflicts so many and give support to those who need help
- Here is my volunteer supporter contribution for
- Urgent communication
- Delivered by hand
- Your help package
- What is it
- Help enclosed
- News you've been waiting for
- Investment opportunity
- Someone is waiting to hear what you see
- Inside - important information about your
- Premium enclosed
- When help is needed
- Urgent
- Urgent news
- Your concerns
- Keeping the candle bright
- The letter that will change your life
- Half a world away, a mother is hopeful
- Important information about your taxes
- This letter may save your life
- Inside: How you can avoid a crippling
- Improve their odds in the lottery of life
- See inside
- A world of thanks

Marketing Phrase Book

For Everyone with a Product, Service or Idea to Promote

Whether you're the local plumber or a huge multinational, your business depends on successful marketing. The *Marketing Phrase Book* puts the language of the marketplace, the language that sells, right at your fingertips.

For

- Sale Packages
- Presentations
- Newsletters
- Web Pages
- Advertising
- Flyers
- Speeches
- Catalogue

And much more

INSIDE YOU'LL FIND:

- Thousands of **dynamic phrases** designed for the marketplace
- All the **"trigger words"** that send customers reaching for their wallets
- Mix and match columns to help you **name that big sale**
- **Exclamations** to make your customers to sit up and take notice
- **Ideas, ideas, ideas!** Getting a great idea is often the hardest part. Mine the book for bright new concepts you can adapt to your own needs
- **Power words!** The priceless core vocabulary of selling

Small Business Owners - increase your sales, get attention faster and never struggle for words again.

New Entrepreneurs – quickly learn the language that attracts customers, and get a head start on success when you need it most.

Salespeople and Executives – give yourself a crucial competitive edge and let others wonder what your secret is.

Marketing Professionals – save valuable time, come out on top when you're under pressure to perform.

"Words matter. Even the most fluent of tongues get tied. Which is why the Marketing Phrase Book is such a useful resource."
–Entrepreneur Magazine

Check this book out at:
www.hamilhouse.com

1001 Ways to Say Thank You

Thousands of Dynamic Phrases to Help You:

Appreciate, Applaud, Celebrate, Cheer on, Congratulate, Encourage, Honor, Inspire, Recognize, Sympathize, and Thank with Warmth, Grace and Ease

Everyone loves to be thanked. And thanking others makes you feel terrific. A sincerely declared thank you is a powerful thing. It brings smiles, binds the heart and sometimes moves to tears.

In personal life, you show family and friends how much you care. In business, politics or charitable endeavor, your gratitude oils the wheels, tells colleagues and contributors they are appreciated and conveys how strongly you recognize the efforts of others.

Now you need never be at a loss for what to say as you express appreciation.

INSIDE YOU'LL FIND:

* Thousands of ways to thank, congratulate, appreciate, cement friendship and express love

* All the "triggers" that set friends, family, associates, customers and others smiling and thinking of you

* Huge choice of dashing signature lines

* Attention-getting exclamations to emphasize your feelings

* Ideas! Ideas! Ideas! The phrases naturally contain hordes of bright ideas which you can easily adapt to your own special needs.

* Sample Letters! Find an example for just about every occasion to make your thank you notes even faster and more effective.

* Special sections to help you with apology and condolence

Check this book out at:
www.hamilhouse.com

www.ingramcontent.com/pod-product-compliance
Lightning Source LLC
Chambersburg PA
CBHW072039020426
42334CB00017B/1334